SKEPTICAL THEISM

Skeptical Theism

New Essays

EDITED BY
TRENT DOUGHERTY
AND JUSTIN P. McBRAYER

OXFORD

UNIVERSITY PRESS

UNIVERSITY PRESS

Great Clarendon Street, Oxford, OX2 6DP,
United Kingdom

Oxford University Press is a department of the University of Oxford.
It furthers the University's objective of excellence in research, scholarship,
and education by publishing worldwide. Oxford is a registered trade mark of
Oxford University Press in the UK and in certain other countries

First published 2014
First published in paperback 2016

Published in the United States of America by Oxford University Press
198 Madison Avenue, New York, NY 10016, United States of America

British Library Cataloguing in Publication Data
Data available

Library of Congress Cataloging in Publication Data
Data available

ISBN 978–0–19–966118–3 (Hbk.)
ISBN 978–0–19–875739–9 (Pbk.)

This volume is dedicated to our respective wives, Sarah Dougherty and Anna McBrayer. Thank you both for your patience with your philosophers. In you, God is revealed.

Preface

The problem of evil is a collection of philosophical problems confronting any worldview that includes the existence of God. The central concern of these various problems is the worry that if the world is governed by a perfectly good, perfectly powerful creator, it seems unlikely at best that it would include the amount, kind, or distribution of evils that we actually see. Sometimes these problems are raised in terms of logical compatibility (i.e. it is impossible that there be such evils if there is a God). Other times these problems are raised in terms of evidence or probability (i.e. even if it is possible for God and evil to coexist, the existence of such evils constitutes evidence against the existence of God). Still other times these problems are raised as considerations for particular theological commitments (e.g. could there really be a hell if God exists?).

Skeptical theism is a collection of responses to problems of evil. If we specify that by 'gratuitous evil' we mean an evil that God would *not* have an all-things-considered sufficient reason to allow, then what brings skeptical theism to bear on the problem of evil is an agnosticism about whether there are such evils. While skeptical theists vary in their defense of this limited skepticism, they are united in thinking that our epistemic limitations are such that no human is justified in believing that any particular evil is gratuitous. Sometimes this agnosticism is defended by appeal to epistemic principles that function like sensitivity constraints (e.g. see Chapters 10 and 11). Sometimes this agnosticism is defended by appeal to limitations on our inductive capacities (e.g. see Chapters 15 and 21).

Notice that commitment to this sort of limited agnosticism about the existence of gratuitous evils is compatible with either theism or naturalism. One could be a skeptical naturalist, for example. However, the literature has focused on skeptical theism in large part because of the alleged inconsistency between being an agnostic about our ability to see that certain evils are gratuitous while yet claiming that belief in God or God's work in the world is reasonable. If our epistemic position is so weak that we cannot tell a particular evil is gratuitous, how can we tell that God exists or that other divine-related facts hold (e.g. see Chapters 14, 15, 17 and 18)? Skeptical theism also appears to threaten our grasp on the moral world: if it's true that we should withhold belief about whether any given evil is all-things-considered justified, does that mean that we should not interfere to prevent a horrific evil that we could easily prevent? Skeptical theism appears to imply moral paralysis (e.g. see Chapters 20, 21 and 22). In fact, perhaps a commitment to skeptical theism bleeds over into a more radical skepticism that infects our everyday life and judgments (e.g. see Chapters 11 and 16).

This collection of essays moves the debate over the viability of skeptical theism forward. Our goal as editors was to produce a volume that was balanced in its treatment of skeptical theism (one of us considers himself a skeptical theist while the other does not). Each chapter is a new contribution from either an established scholar in the field or an up-and-coming philosopher working in philosophy of religion. The chapters are divided into four loose topics: the epistemology of skeptical theism, the viability of the CORNEA defense of skeptical theism, the implications of skeptical theism for theism, and the implications of skeptical theism for morality. We hope that this volume is useful both for professionals working in philosophy of religion and thoughtful non-philosophers who are reflecting on their theistic commitments.

Trent Dougherty and Justin P. McBrayer
October 2013
Durango, Colorado

Acknowledgements

Putting together a volume of new, cutting-edge chapters from a wide range of philosophers is more work than we could have done on our own. In addition to the 21 authors represented in the volume, we would like to thank the many academics who have contributed to this work in the form of recommendations, feedback, commentaries, and criticisms, including Travis Dumsday, Michael Hickson, Nathan King, John Komdat, Trenton Merricks, Tim McGrew, Doug Moore, Caleb Ontiveros, Ric Otte, Dugald Owen, Ross Parker, Allen Plug, Alex Pruss, Jason Rogers, Jeff Snapper, Jonah Stupach, Joshua Thurow, Chris Tweet, Leigh Vicens, and Jakob Wheeler. Anna McBrayer provided her creative talents to design the cover of the book. Nick Colgrove produced the collected bibliography and did a lot of the leg work in preparing the final manuscript. Thank you, Nick! Tom Perridge at Oxford provided thoughtful oversight of the project, and Cathryn Steele, Elizabeth Robottom, Karen Raith, and Alex Johnson at Oxford provided diligent and prompt administration of the details. Thanks to all of them.

Contents

Analytic Table of Contents

Recently there has been a good deal of interest in the relationship between commonsense epistemology and skeptical theism. Much of the debate has focused on phenomenal conservatism and any tension that there might be between it and skeptical theism. In this chapter I show the compatibility of phenomenal conservatism and skeptical theism by coupling these views with an account of defeat. In addition, I argue that this account of defeat can give the skeptical theist what she wants – namely a response to the evidential argument from evil that can leave one of its premises unmotivated. In giving this account I also respond to several objections from Trent Dougherty and Chris Tucker as well as to an additional worry coming from the epistemology of disagreement.

In this chapter, I go through a dynamic modeling process which is perfectly general, and shows that even granting pretty much everything Matheson claims as premises in this volume, phenomenal conservatism can prove lethal for skeptical theism. In presenting these models, an important methodological point emerges. When we look at the present issue through Bayesian eyes, we see that the typically binary and externalist way most skeptical theists think ignores the power both of strong conviction and of partial doubt. What is missing in the standard account of skeptical theism is the agent's own perspective. Bayesianism and phenomenal conservatism are especially well-suited to representing the first-person perspective.

Most contemporary versions of skeptical theism are motivated solely by the idea that the human cognitive situation is such that we are unable to tell if our judgment about the ultimate justifiability of any given evil is accurate. I refer to this view as negative skeptical theism. I propose the framework of positive skeptical theism where one remains skeptical about the human perspective to discern the justification for apparently gratuitous evils, but which positively recognizes second-order justifications that one would expect to find for the appearance of gratuitous evils if God exists. This alternative framework helps the skeptical theist to be skeptical about one's ability to discern any God-permitting reason for a specific seemingly gratuitous evil, while avoiding the undesirable implications of negative skeptical theism.

4. *Why Skeptical Theism Isn't Skeptical Enough*

Chris Tucker, Assistant Professor, College of William and Mary

The most common charge against skeptical theism is that it is too skeptical, i.e. it is committed to some undesirable form of skepticism or another. I contend that Michael Bergmann's skeptical theism (2001, 2009, 2012) isn't skeptical enough. I argue that, if true, his skeptical theses secure a genuine victory: they prevent, for some people, a prominent argument from evil from providing any justification whatsoever to doubt the existence of God. On the other hand, even if true, the skeptical theses fail to prevent even the atheist from justifiably accepting it.

5. *Minimal Skeptical Theism*

Todd R. Long, Associate Professor, California Polytechnic State University

Utilizing an argument from human knowledge of our cognitive limitations relative to the cognitive power of a perfect creator, I argue, first, that minimal skeptical theism is strong enough to cast doubt on a premise in popular evidential arguments from evil yet weak enough to be epistemically rational. Second, I explain why what I take to be the best objection (that a perfect creator's love for the creation would require the creator to disclose to suffering-capable persons the justifying reasons for allowing suffering) to my argument fails. Finally I respond to those who claim that accepting skeptical theism commits a religious theist to moral and religious skepticism by using Earl Conee's and Richard Feldman's 'explanatory coherence view of evidential support' to explain how believing skeptical theism can be consistent with a robust religious form of life.

6. *Replies to Long and Tucker*

E. J. Coffman, Associate Professor of Philosophy, University of Tennessee

This reply piece, which engages the chapters by Todd Long and Chris Tucker, has two main goals. First, it aims to show that what Long calls "minimal skeptical theism" has the weakness that Tucker ascribes to "Bergmann's Skeptical Theism" in §4 of his chapter ("The Skeptical Theses and Non-Inferential Justification"). That is, it aims to show that Long's minimal skeptical theism fails to completely incapacitate a salient version of the argument from evil, and therefore is not (in Tucker's words) a "complete response" to the argument from evil. Second, this piece tries to defend, from the argument Tucker develops in §4 of his chapter, the claim that Bergmann's Skeptical Theism really does completely incapacitate its target argument from evil.

7. *The Paradox of Humility and Dogmatism*

N. N. Trakakis, Senior Lecturer and Research Fellow in Philosophy, Australian Catholic University

Christianity seems bedeviled by a "paradox of humility and dogmatism." On the one hand, one of the greatest virtues in Christian spirituality is humility, a deeply held awareness of our limitations and sinfulness that propels us to seek guidance and forgiveness from others, and especially from God. On the other hand, there is the equally significant strand of dogmatism, understood as the advocacy of particular doctrines as providing the final truth about reality. It seems that this reliance on dogma conflicts with the espousal of humility, given that an awareness of our (intellectual and moral) weaknesses and failures does not seem consistent with claims to have privileged access to absolute truth. I propose a solution to this paradox that draws upon the Eastern Orthodox tradition.

Part II : Debating CORNEA

8. *Some Considerations Concerning CORNEA, Global Skepticism, and Trust*

Kenneth Boyce, Assistant Professor of Philosophy, University of Missouri, Columbia.

Skeptical theists have been charged with being committed to global skepticism. I consider this objection as it applies to a common variety of skeptical theism based on an epistemological principle that Stephen Wykstra labeled "CORNEA." I show how a recent reformulation of CORNEA (provided by Stephen Wykstra and Timothy Perrine) affords us a formal apparatus that allows us to see just where this objection gets a grip on that view, as well as what is needed for an adequate response. I conclude by arguing that, given some plausible, modest, and independently motivated anti-skeptical principles, this objection poses no threat to Wykstra's brand of skeptical theism.

9. *Skeptical Theism and Undercutting Defeat*

M. J. Almeida, Professor of Philosophy and Classics, University of Texas, San Antonio

I consider William Rowe's (later) direct and (earlier) indirect evidential arguments from evil. I show that the direct argument offers no improvement over the indirect argument from evil. The objections to the indirect evidential argument are the very same objections to the direct evidential argument. I remedy the salient problems with these versions of the evidential argument and offer a better indirect argument from evil. I consider next the skeptical theist's argument that there is an undercutting defeater for our evidence against God's existence. I show that even very good reasons for believing that were God to exist we would still observe the evils we do are evidentially irrelevant. The observations might strongly confirm God's nonexistence anyway. I argue, finally, that we have good reason to believe that the goods we know about are representative of the total goods that exist.

Long before skeptical theism was called 'skeptical theism,' Stephen Wykstra defended a version of it based on an epistemological principle he called CORNEA. In this chapter, I use elementary confirmation theory to analyze CORNEA's core. This enables me to show precisely what is right about Wykstra's very influential defense of skeptical theism and precisely what is wrong with it. A key premise of that defense is that, on the assumption that God exists, we wouldn't expect to know what God's reasons for allowing certain evils are. I show that, while that premise together with CORNEA's core shows that our inability to adequately explain the existence of those evils in terms of theism is not strong evidence against theism, it fails to show that the evils themselves are not strong evidence against theism.

What we call "the evidential argument from evil" is not one argument but a family of them, originating (perhaps) in the 1979 formulation of William Rowe. Wykstra's early versions of skeptical theism emerged in response to Rowe's evidential arguments. But what sufficed as a response to Rowe may not suffice against later, more sophisticated, versions of the problem of evil—in particular, those along the lines pioneered by Paul Draper. Our chief aim here is to make an earlier version of skeptical theism more responsive to the type of abductive atheology pioneered by Draper. In particular, we suggest a moderate form of skeptical theism may be able to resist Draper's abductive atheology.

In "Skeptical Theism, Abductive Atheology, and Theory Versioning," Timothy Perrine and Stephen J. Wykstra attempt to retool Wykstra's brand of skeptical theism so that it is effective against abductive or "Humean" arguments from evil like mine. The result is a radically new form of skeptical theism that is not based on CORNEA. Perrine and Wykstra use this new form of skeptical theism to raise several objections to my premise that naturalism has much more "predictive power" than theism does with respect to what we know about pleasure and pain, flourishing and floundering, virtue and vice, and triumph and tragedy. I show that none of these objections succeeds.

13. *Learning Not to be Naïve: A Comment on the Exchange between Perrine/ Wykstra and Draper*

Lara Buchak, Assistant Professor, University of California, Berkeley

Does postulating skeptical theism undermine the claim that evil strongly confirms atheism over theism? According to Perrine and Wykstra, it does undermine the claim, because evil is no more likely on atheism than on skeptical theism. According to Draper, it does not undermine the claim, because evil is much more likely on atheism than on theism in general. I show that the probability facts alone do not resolve their disagreement, which ultimately rests on which updating procedure—conditionalizing or updating on a conditional — fits both the evidence and how we ought to take that evidence into account.

Part III : Skeptical Theism's Implications for Theism

14. *Skeptical Theism and Skeptical Atheism*

J. L. Schellenberg, Professor of Philosophy, Mount Saint Vincent University and Adjunct Professor in the Faculty of Graduate Studies, Dalhousie University

In this chapter I argue that skeptical theism not only lacks the reach claimed for it by theistic philosophers but suggests ways of extending the reach of atheism. Atheistic arguments, as it turns out, are not prevented by skeptical theism from providing justification for the atheist to be an atheist. Moreover, skeptical theism suggests a new way for the atheist to question the theist's support for her own belief—in particular when the latter is experientially based. Finally, we see how an investigative atheism may be embedded in a wider skepticism and, using a form of reasoning similar to that employed by skeptical theists, promote both new doubts about theism for those left unconvinced by atheistic arguments and new investigation into non-theistic understandings of the divine.

15. *Skeptical Theism, Atheism, and Total Evidence Skepticism*

Michael Bergmann, Professor of Philosophy, Purdue University

This chapter is a response to John Schellenberg's chapter, "Skeptical Theism and Skeptical Atheism," in which he raises objections to theistic belief that are supposed to cause special trouble for skeptical theists. In Section I, I provide some clarificatory comments concerning skeptical theism. In Section II, I evaluate an atheistic argument that Schellenberg finds particularly impressive. In Section III, I examine the view Schellenberg calls "total evidence skepticism" and consider its bearing on theistic belief. In the final section I consider whether Schellenberg is right in thinking that skeptical theism commits one to total evidence skepticism and to some of the other skeptical theses he proposes.

16. *Skeptical Demonism: A Failed Response to a Humean Challenge*

Wes Morriston, University of Colorado, Boulder

Drawing on materials in Hume's *Dialogues*, I develop an argument for saying that it is unreasonable to accept either the hypothesis that the universe is ruled by perfect benevolence, or that it is ruled by perfect malice. I then show how skeptical theists would respond to this argument, and how their response might be imitated by an imaginary "skeptical demonist" (a defender of the "perfect malice" hypothesis). Finally, I give reasons for thinking that neither skeptical demonism nor skeptical theism is successful in blunting the force of the Humean challenge.

17. *Divine Deception*

Erik J. Wielenberg, Professor of Philosophy, DePauw University

The dominant view within Christianity has it that God does not deceive, but there is a minority tradition within Christianity according to which God sometimes engages in intentional deception and is morally justified in so doing. I draw on this minority tradition, together with skeptical theism, to raise doubts about the following thesis:

> (T) God's testimony that all who believe in Jesus will have eternal life provides recipients of that testimony with a knowledge-sufficient degree of warrant for the belief that all who believe in Jesus will have eternal life.

I first argue that there are possible situations in which divine deception is morally permissible. Next, I consider four apparent cases of divine deception found in scripture. I then combine the results of those arguments with skeptical theism to develop a prima facie case against (T). Finally, I address an important objection to my argument.

18. *Two New Versions of Skeptical Theism*

Andrew Cullison, Associate Professor of Philosophy, State University of New York, Fredonia

I defend two new versions of skeptical theism that avoid the Reasoning about God Problem. Traditional skeptical theists appeal to an epistemic principle to argue that we cannot infer God would have no justifying reason to permit the horrendous evil we observe, but this threatens to undermine all reasoning about what a God would do. The first version of skeptical theism I defend offers an alternative principle that is more plausible and avoids the Reasoning about God Problem. The second version of skeptical theism targets the premise that maintains that God would not allow horrendous evil without some justifying reason. I argue that there is a kind of axiological skepticism we should accept that undermines this premise. This yields a substantively different kind of skeptical theism, and it also avoids the Reasoning about God Problem.

19. *Trust, Silence, and Liturgical Acts*
Kevin Timpe, Professor of Philosophy, Northwest Nazarene University

Undermining our trust is God is one of the purported unacceptable consequences of the truth of skeptical theism. I argue that a motivation for adopting skeptical theism can be seen as a way of responding not only to the problem of evil, but also what Mike Rea calls "the problem of divine silence". I argue that how silence should be interpreted depends on what other beliefs we have about God. Silence would only justify a lack of trust in God if God did not provide an accessible way of experiencing His presence despite His silence. I argue that liturgical practices can provide a basis of maintaining one's trust in God even if those practices do not result in propositional knowledge regarding His justification for evil.

Part IV: Skeptical Theism's Implications for Morality

20. *Agnosticism, Skeptical Theism, and Moral Obligation*
Stephen Maitzen, W. G. Clark Professor of Philosophy, Acadia University

Skeptical theism combines theism with skepticism about our capacity to discern God's morally sufficient reasons for permitting evil. Proponents have claimed that skeptical theism defeats the evidential argument from evil. Many opponents have objected that it implies untenable moral skepticism, induces appalling moral paralysis, and the like. Recently Daniel Howard-Snyder has tried to rebut this prevalent objection to skeptical theism by rebutting it as an objection to the skeptical part of skeptical theism, which part he labels "Agnosticism" (with an intentionally capital "A"). I argue that his rebuttal fails as a defense of Agnosticism against the objection and even more so as a defense of skeptical theism.

21. *Agnosticism, the Moral Skepticism Objection, and Commonsense Morality*
Daniel Howard-Snyder, Professor of Philosophy, Western Washington University

According to Agnosticism with a capital A, even if we don't see how any reason we know of would justify God in permitting all the evil in the world and even if we lack warrant for theism, we should not infer that there probably is no reason that would justify God. That's because, even under those conditions, we should be in doubt about whether the goods we know of constitute a representative sample of all the goods there are. In my 2009, I defended Agnosticism against the charge that it leaves us in doubt about whether we are obligated to intervene to prevent horrific suffering we can prevent at no risk to ourselves. In "Agnosticism, Skeptical Theism, and Moral Obligation," Stephen Maitzen argues that, in light of my defense, Agnosticism is at odds with commonsense morality's insistence that we have an obligation to intervene in such cases. I argue that the moral principle Maitzen imputes to common sense is false and that a moral principle much more in keeping with common sense is compatible with Agnosticism and my defense of it.

22. *Skeptical Theism within Reason*

Ted Poston, Associate Professor of Philosophy, University of South Alabama

Skeptical theism insists that our inability to scrutinize a God-justifying reason does not provide good evidence that there is no reason. The core motivation for skeptical theism is that the cognitive and moral distance between a perfect being and creatures like us is so great we shouldn't expect that we grasp all the relevant considerations pertaining to a God-justifying reason. My goal in this chapter is to defend skeptical theism within a context that allows for an inverse probability argument for theism. These arguments are crucial for an evidentialist approach to the justification of theism. I aim to show that there is a natural way of motivating a skeptical theist position that does not undermine our knowledge of some values.

Part I

Knowledge and Epistemic Humility

1

Phenomenal Conservatism and Skeptical Theism

Jonathan D. Matheson

1. INTRODUCTION

Recently there has been a good deal of interest in the relationship between commonsense epistemology and skeptical theism.[1] Much of the debate has focused on Phenomenal Conservatism and any tension that there might be between it and skeptical theism. In this chapter I further defend the claim that there is no tension between Phenomenal Conservatism and skeptical theism. I show the compatibility of these two views by coupling them with an account of defeat—one that is friendly to both Phenomenal Conservatism and skeptical theism. In addition, I argue that this account of defeat can give the skeptical theist what she wants—namely a response to the evidential argument from evil that can leave one of its premises unmotivated. In giving this account I also respond to several objections from Trent Dougherty (2011a) and Chris Tucker (this volume) as well as to an additional worry coming from the epistemology of disagreement.

Before moving into the heart of the argument we need to be clear on the players. There is an alleged tension between commonsense epistemology and skeptical theism. But what is commonsense epistemology? And what is skeptical theism?

---

[1] See for instance Dougherty (2008) and (2011a), Bergmann (2009) and (2012), Matheson (2011), and Tucker (this volume).

2. WHAT IS SKEPTICAL THEISM?

Skeptical theism has two separable components: a skeptical component and a theistic component.[2] My focus here will be on the skeptical component of skeptical theism—a component of skeptical theism that can be endorsed by an atheist or agnostic. The skeptical component of skeptical theism centers on human cognitive limitations as well as the vastness and complexity of reality.[3] Paul Draper formulates the claim central to skeptical theism as follows:

> ST: Humans are in no position to judge that an omnipotent and omnis-
>   cient being would be unlikely to have a morally sufficient reason to
>   permit the evils we find in the world.[4]

According to ST, the combination of our limited cognitive capacities with the vast complexity of reality, have it that we are unreliable in our judgments of whether a particular evil in the world is gratuitous. The skeptical component of skeptical theism has it that those judgments are simply above our cognitive pay grade.

Skeptical theists then utilize ST to respond to the evidential argument from evil. The evidential argument from evil roughly goes as follows:

> P1.   There exist instances of intense suffering which an omnipotent,
>   omniscient being could have prevented without thereby losing some
>   greater good or permitting some evil that is equally bad or worse.
>
> P2.   An omnipotent, omniscient, wholly good being would prevent the
>   occurrence of any intense suffering it could, unless it could not do
>   so without thereby losing some greater good or permitting some evil
>   equally bad or worse.
>
> C.   There does not exist an omnipotent, omniscient, wholly good being.[5]

According to skeptical theism, we should be skeptical about P1, and if we should be skeptical about P1, the argument fails.

However, skeptical theists can differ in terms of how they take it that ST prevents P1 from being motivated. *Strong skeptical theism* claims that ST is true, and that the mere truth of ST has it that P1 is unmotivated.[6] So, according to *strong* skeptical theism, it is the truth of ST that prevents the evidential argument from evil from succeeding. *Weak skeptical theism* claims that if an individual is on balance justified in believing ST (whether or not ST is true), then P1 will also be unmotivated for her.[7] So according to *weak* skeptical theism, it is being justified in believing ST that prevents the evidential argument from evil from succeeding.

---

[2] Here I am following Michael Bergmann.   [3] See Alston (1991: 109).
[4] This parallels Paul Draper's formulation of the skeptical theist thesis. See Draper (1996: 176).
[5] This formulation follows Rowe (1979).
[6] I called this view 'Justificatory Skeptical Theism' in Matheson (2011).
[7] I called this view 'Normative Defeater Skeptical Theism' in Matheson (2011).

Notice that according to *weak* skeptical theism, the skeptical theist's project can succeed even if ST is in fact false, since an individual can be justified in believing a false proposition. At the same time, since not everyone is justified in believing the same things, the truth of *weak* skeptical theism does have it that no one can be justified in believing P1 (even if ST is true)—it only offers a way of blocking the motivation for P1.

P1 is often motivated by way of a certain type of inference—the "noseeum" inference.[8] According to the "noseeum" inference, we cannot find any justifying reasons for some actual evils, so there probably aren't any such justifying reasons for those evils. Skeptical theists, however, claim that this application of a "noseeum" inference is no good due (in some way) to our cognitive limitations as human beings.

Skeptical theists differ in terms of how they take it that ST blocks this application of a "noseeum" inference. According to *strong* skeptical theism, the mere truth of ST has it we cannot be justified in believing P1 on the basis of a "noseeum" inference. On this account, the "noseeum" inference is blocked because of the fact that we would not see such justifying reasons even if they were there. According to *weak* skeptical theism, the mere truth of ST would not block such an inference, but the "noseeum" inference is blocked when one has undefeated good reason to believe that she wouldn't see such justifying reasons even if they were there. According to *weak* skeptical theism, if an individual is on balance justified in believing that she is no position to judge whether particular evils are gratuitous, then she is not on balance justified in believing that any particular evil in question is gratuitous (or not gratuitous, for that matter).

3. WHAT IS COMMONSENSE EPISTEMOLOGY?

What then is commonsense epistemology? I am taking commonsense epistemology as the claim that we are prima facie justified in believing that things are the way that they appear.[9] In what follows, I will take Phenomenal Conservatism as an epistemic principle representative of commonsense epistemology, though there may be ways of being a commonsense epistemologist apart from endorsing Phenomenal Conservatism. Phenomenal Conservatism is the following claim:

PC: If it seems to S as if *P*, then S thereby has at least prima facie justification for believing that *P*.[10]

---

[8] See Rowe (1979).

[9] This follows Dougherty (2008), but is a departure from how Bergmann (2012) understands "commonsensism".

[10] For a further explication and defense of Phenomenal Conservatism see Huemer (2001) and (2007), as well as Tucker (2010) and (2011).

According to PC, when a proposition seems true to an individual, that individual has prima facie justification for believing that proposition. According to PC, seeming states suffice to provide prima facie justification for believing what seems to be the case—it is not a prerequisite that such seeming states are in fact reliable indicators of the world, or even that the subject is justified in believing that they are. PC is thus a form of dogmatism.[11] According to PC, the prima facie justification one gets from a seeming state does not depend upon anything but the seeming state itself—it does not depend on one's environment, one's background beliefs, etc. This is not to say that these things cannot *defeat* the justification provided by seeming states, only that no other states need to obtain in order to provide this prima facie justification.

The defender of PC will also want to distinguish the *amount* of prima facie justification various seeming states provide. After all, not all seeming states are created equal. So, let's take it that the stronger the seeming, the more prima facie justification provided by it. According to PC, the justification provided by seeming states is only prima facie, it can be defeated. However, if that prima facie justification for a proposition is not defeated, then the subject will also be on balance justified in believing that proposition.

An individual's prima facie justification for believing P can be defeated in various ways. First, a defeating effect can be either *partial* or *full*. It will be *partial* when P remains on balance justified for the individual, but becomes less on balance justified for her than it was before she acquired the defeater. A defeating effect will be *full* when P is rendered on balance unjustified for her. A defeater can also go about its defeating task in one of two ways. *Rebutting defeaters* defeat one's justification for P by way of supplying evidence against P, whereas *undercutting defeaters* defeat one's justification for P without providing evidence against P. Undercutting defeaters typically accomplish their task by attacking the *connection* between some bit of evidence and the target proposition.

4. THE PROBLEM

The tension between PC and skeptical theism emerges from the fact that, according to PC, there are justificatory routes to P1 that are not explicitly blocked by the skeptical component of skeptical theism.[12] While the skeptical component of skeptical theism has been advanced primarily to block the "noseeum" inference to P1, PC provides alternative justificatory routes to this

---

[11] For more on dogmatism see Pryor (2000).
[12] See Dougherty (2008) and Tucker (this volume) for more on this point.

premise of the evidential argument from evil. According to PC, P1 can be justified *directly* (i.e. non-inferentially) by it seeming to one that P1 is true.[13] So,
given PC, the advocate of the evidential argument from evil need not rely on
a "noseeum" inference to motivate P1; she can motivate this premise *directly*
since, according to PC, P1 will have prima facie justification for those to whom
P1 seems true. Since PC claims that the prima facie justification for believing a
proposition on the basis of a seeming state does not require anything in addition to the seeming state itself, an individual can be prima facie justified in
believing P1 even if ST is true. According to PC, the mere truth of ST could not
prevent an individual from being prima facie justified in believing P1, since a
seeming state suffices to provide prima facie justification for what seems true.
If this prima facie justification for P1 is undefeated, those individuals will also
be on balance justified in believing P1. Since P1 can seem true to individuals, and plausibly does, it might be thought that the skeptical component of
skeptical theism is unable to prevent P1 from being motivated once PC makes
these additional motivational routes available. If so, then skeptical theism is
rendered ineffective by PC.

5. THE COMPATIBILITY CLAIM DEFENDED

It should be clear that *strong* skeptical theism conflicts with PC. Even if ST
is true, PC has it that individuals can be directly justified in believing P1.
According to *strong* skeptical theism, the truth of ST prevents P1 from being
justified, yet according to PC, P1 can be justified even if ST is true. *Strong* skeptical theism and PC are indeed incompatible—If PC is true, the mere truth of
ST cannot prevent an individual from being justified in believing P1.

Weak skeptical theism, however, faces no such tension with PC. According
to *weak* skeptical theism, the motivation for P1 is blocked when one is justified
in believing ST. While PC allows that an individual can be prima facie justified
in believing P1, if that individual is also on balance justified in believing ST, her
justification for believing P1 will be fully defeated. So, *weak* skeptical theism
provides the resources to prevent P1 from being *directly* justified (in addition
to blocking the "noseeum" inference to P1). This isn't to say that according to
weak skeptical theism P1 *couldn't* be directly justified for an individual. Given
PC it can. The claim here is that when an individual is on balance justified in
believing ST, any prima facie justification that she has for P1 (whether direct or

---

[13] In addition, according to PC, an individual can be justified in believing P1 by having a
particular evil seem gratuitous, and then inferring P1 from this fact. I take it that in these latter
cases P1 also seems true to that individual, and so my focus here will be on cases where P1 is
directly justified.

indirect) will be fully defeated—that being on balance justified in believing ST prevents one from being justified in believing P1, and thus provides an escape from the evidential argument from evil.

Consider the following analogy. Suppose that you are considering whether Smith is guilty of a crime. You know that there is a great deal of evidence relevant to this matter and that the evidence is complicated, although at first you aren't aware of what any of the evidence is. I then tell you a few of the relevant items of evidence. I make it clear to you that you have no reason to believe that the evidence I have told you about is either complete or representative of the total evidence relating to Smith and this crime. Suppose that on your evidence it is *just as likely* that the items of evidence you are aware of regarding Smith's guilt are unrepresentative of the total evidence regarding Smith's guilt as it is that they are representative. I then ask you, "Does the total evidence, which I have partially described to you, support that Smith is guilty?" Suppose that upon consideration it strongly seems to you that the total body of evidence does support that Smith is guilty of the crime. Perhaps this is because certain other things seem true to you about what else is in the total evidence, even despite my disclaimers and cautions. Given PC, the mere fact that it seems to you that the total evidence supports Smith's guilt gives you prima facie justification for believing that the total evidence supports Smith's guilt. Further this justification is direct and non-inferential. Are you also *on balance* justified in believing that the total evidence supports that Smith is guilty? No. At least not if you are on balance justified in believing the following analogue to ST:

> SK: You are in no position to judge how likely it is that there are counter-vailing evidential considerations in the total body of evidence.

Being on balance justified in believing SK would block a "noseeum" inference from what you are aware of in the evidence to what the total body of evidence is like. Further, being on balance justified in believing SK would *fully* defeat any prima facie justification enjoyed by your belief that the total evidence supports Smith's guilt on the basis of it seeming to you that it does. After all, you have (undefeated) reason to doubt that your seeming that the total evidence supports Smith's guilt is indicative of reality. Given that you are on balance justified in believing that you are in no position to judge such matters, the connection between your seeming state and the proposition that the total evidence supports Smith's guilt has been completely undermined. Since you are on balance justified in believing SK, you cannot rationally rely on how things appear to you regarding the total body of evidence. According to PC, you don't need reasons to trust your seemings in order for them to provide you with prima facie justification for what seems true. Nevertheless, if you are on balance justified in believing SK, you have reasons to doubt your seeming. In such a situation, even your direct justification for believing that Smith is guilty has been defeated—you have undefeated reason to suspend judgment about the accuracy of your seeming state.[14]

So, the information about our cognitive limitations as well as the vastness and complexity of reality that *weak* skeptical theists utilize to block the "noseeum" inference to P1 can also prevent P1 from being on balance justified *directly* (i.e. via a seeming state). When you are on balance justified in believing that you are in no position to judge what the total body of evidence supports, this fully defeats any prima facie justification you have for believing that it supports Smith's guilt. Similarly, when you are on balance justified in believing that you are in no position to judge that an evil is gratuitous, this fully defeats any prima facie justification you have for believing that it is. So, the skeptical component of skeptical theism extends beyond blocking the "noseeum" inference—it also can defeat direct justification for believing P1.

6. DOUGHERTY'S CHALLENGE (PART 1)

While we have seen good reason to believe that there is no tension between PC and *weak* skeptical theism, not everyone is on board. It has been alleged that there is a tension between PC and skeptical theism since it *powerfully* and *persistently* seems to many that P1 is the case.[15] Coupled with PC, this empirical claim has it that many are very strongly prima facie justified in believing P1. Since the skeptical theist's response to the evidential argument from evil was to block the motivation for P1, the skeptical theist must have a story about how this prima facie justification can be defeated. The tension is thought to come from the fact that the *power* and *persistence* of the seeming that P1 is the case has it that this prima facie justification for P1 will not be defeated by the skeptical component of skeptical theism. It is alleged that the seeming that P1 is the case is stronger than the seeming that ST is the case, and thus given PC, has more prima facie justification going for it than does ST.[16]

---

[14] What I have said above isn't quite right. After all, one of the bits of evidence of which you are aware in the total body of evidence may itself *entail* that Smith is guilty. In that case, even if you are unaware of what else is in this total body of evidence and how all the relations between the bits of evidence work, you will have great reason to believe that the total body of evidence supports Smith's guilt. Of course, if you were aware of some such entailment, you would not be justified in believing SK either. Applied to skeptical theism, we can ignore such a wrinkle since we can acknowledge that none of the evils that we are aware of *entails* that God does not exist. We should all admit that it is at least *possible* that there is always a justifying reason (however unlikely). The evidential argument from evil simply asserts that it is unreasonable to believe that there is in fact always such a justification.

[15] See Dougherty (2008).

[16] What is ultimately at issue is whether ST can defeat one's justification for P1, when one is less justified in believing ST than one is in believing P1. For ease of discussion, I will take it that the justification one has for believing both P1 and ST comes by way of seeming states.

Here the differences between rebutting and undercutting defeaters are crucial. For a rebutting defeater to be a full defeater, it must provide *as much* support against P as the original evidence gave for P.[17] So, if ST acted as a rebutting defeater there would be a problem here for the *weak* skeptical theist. However, an undercutting defeater does not need to be *as justified* as the proposition whose justificatory effect it is defeating in order for it to be a full defeater. An undercutting defeater will be partial when it doesn't make it the case that one is either on balance justified in disbelieving or suspending judgment toward the target proposition. So, one obtains a partial defeater when one is on balance justified in believing that there is an epistemic support relation between one's evidence and the target proposition, though one has been given some reason to believe that this relation is less strong than had been supposed. For instance, one might receive a report that one's vision is reliable, though less reliable than was on balance justified in believing that it was.

However, an undercutting defeater will be full whenever one is on balance justified in believing that the epistemic support relation between one's evidence and the target proposition is lacking altogether or when one is on balance justified in suspending judgment regarding the claim that one's evidence supports the target proposition.[18] In Matheson (2011), I gave the following case to motivate this claim:

> [S]uppose that it seems to Smith that the table in front of him is red. According to PC, this provides Smith with *prima facie* justification for believing that the table in front of him is red. Suppose further that Smith has a memorial seeming that he put on red tinted glasses that make everything look red. On its own, this seeming is not evidence for or against the proposition that the table that Smith is looking at is red. However, this bit of evidence does give Smith a normative defeater that fully undercuts the support that Smith enjoyed for the proposition that the table in front of him is red on the basis of its seeming red. Upon having this memorial

[17] At least this is true if one is on balance justified in believing every proposition which is on balance supported by one's evidence. I will be assuming that this is the case. If one is only on balance justified in believing a proposition that is significantly supported by one's evidence, or supported to degree .6 or higher, etc., then a rebutting defeater could be full even if it did not provide as much support from not-P as the original evidence gave for P. It could do so by knocking down the individual's on balance justification for believing be to a degree above 5 but lower than the threshold for justifiably believing that P.

[18] Cases of peer disagreement give us good reason to accept that justified suspension of judgment toward the claim that one's evidence supports P is a full undercutting defeater for one's justification for P. In cases of peer disagreement one discovers that someone in an equally good epistemic position with respect to P (equally good evidence, equally intelligent, equally intellectually virtuous, etc.) has adopted a competitor doxastic attitude toward P. Given this discovery, it is plausible that the parties to the disagreement should suspend judgment regarding which doxastic attitude their shared evidence supports. If so, it seems that both parties should also suspend judgment regarding the disputed proposition P. For a more thorough defense of this claim see Matheson (2009). See also Bergmann (2005).

seeming Smith is no longer justified in believing that the table in front of him is red (at least not on the basis of it seeming red).

We can summarize this story as follows:

S1:   it seeming to Smith that the table is red.

S2:   it seeming to Smith that he is wearing red-tinted glasses

C1:   the table is red.

S2 gives Smith prima facie justification for believing that he is wearing red-tinted glasses and this gives Smith an undercutting defeater for the support that S1 gave to C1 for Smith. Assuming that the justification Smith has for believing the content of S2 is not itself defeated, and the only justification Smith had for believing C1 came from S1, Smith is no longer justified in believing C1.[19]

The moral from the story is that S1 might well be a more *powerful* seeming state than S2. And S1 may *persist* even after Smith has the seeming state S2. Nevertheless, in virtue of having S2, and by not having the prima facie justification provided by it (S2) defeated, Smith is no longer on balance justified in believing C1. Applying the analogy to skeptical theism we can consider the following:

S1′:   it seeming to S that there are morally unjustified evils in the world.

S2′:   it seeming to S that ST is true.

C1′:   there are morally unjustified evils in the world.

Since ST operates as undercutting defeaters for any direct justification for P1, it can be a *full* undercutting defeater for one's justification for P1 even when P1 *more strongly* seems true to you than ST does, and even when P1 *continues* to seem true even after you consider ST (which seems true to you). What this shows is that there is no tension between PC and *weak* skeptical theism, even when P1 seems true. One can coherently maintain both PC and *weak* skeptical theism. Further, the *weak* skeptical theist can affirm PC while still claiming that P1 of the evidential argument from evil is unmotivated. For individuals to whom ST seems true, and the prima facie justification provided by these seeming states is undefeated, any justification for P1 (whether direct or by way of a "noseeum" inference) will be *fully* undercut or blocked. Coupled with this account of defeat, the apparent tension between PC and *weak* skeptical theism dissolves.

---

[19] Matheson (2011).

7. TUCKER'S CHALLENGE

Chris Tucker (this volume) has recently challenged the claim that the skeptical component of skeptical theism can or will block direct (or non-inferential) justification for P1. Tucker provides the following example to motivate the claim that the skeptical component of skeptical theism is so limited. He asks us to suppose that a mother is looking for her baby. She quickly scans the house and doesn't see the baby. She recognizes that she has failed to look in numerous places and that she should suspend judgment as to whether the places she looked are representative of the places the baby could be in the house. Nevertheless, as she realizes this she looks out the window and sees the baby chasing a dog. Tucker's claim is that despite the fact that she is justified in withholding judgment regarding the representativeness of her sample, she is nonetheless (directly) justified in believing that the baby is not in the house. So, being justified in suspending judgment regarding the representativeness of her sample did not defeat her direct justification for believing that the baby is not in the house.[20]

Tucker's focus is on the skeptical scope of Michael Bergmann's set of skeptical theist skeptical theses, and not on ST. According to Bergmann, the skeptical theist's skepticism is comprised of the following four theses:

ST1:   We have no good reason for thinking that the possible goods we know of are representative of the possible goods there are.

ST2:   We have no good reason for thinking that the possible evils we know of are representative of the possible evils there are.

ST3:   We have no good reason for thinking that the entailment relations we know of between possible goods and the permission of possible evils are representative of the entailment relations there are between possible goods and the permission of possible evils.

ST4:   We have no good reason for thinking that the total moral value or disvalue we perceive in certain complex states of affairs accurately reflects the total moral value or disvalue they really have.[21]

Tucker's focus in on ST1–ST3 in particular since he is not sure how to understand ST4 and Bergmann himself holds that "[ST4] is not needed to make the skeptical theist's point."[22]

It seems that Tucker is correct in claiming that the woman is both justified in suspending judgment regarding the representativeness of her sample as well

---

[20] Tucker (this volume).

[21] Bergmann (2012: 4). It may be helpful to read ST1–ST4 with "we should suspend judgment or disbelieve that" in the place of "we have no good reason for thinking that."

[22] Bergmann (2009: 379).

as (directly) justified in believing that her baby is not in the house. This shows us that a justified suspension of judgment regarding the representativeness of one's sample does not always defeat any direct justification that one might have for believing the conclusion of that inference.[23]

However, we can take that conclusion in one of two ways. It might (as Tucker claims) show us that the skepticism of skeptical theism cannot prevent P1 from being motivated, or it might show us that there is more skepticism in the skeptical theist's skepticism than is evoked in ST1–ST3. I think that the better explanation is the latter. The heart of the skeptical theist's position is that judgments about whether a given evil is gratuitous are simply beyond our cognitive pay grade. More traditionally this has been defended by way of blocking the "noseeum" inference to P1, but not all considerations that block this inference fully capture the skepticism of skeptical theism. So, the full force of the skeptical theist's skepticism is not brought to bear in Tucker's case. While the mother is justifiably skeptical about some things (e.g. the representativeness of her sample), she is not justifiably skeptical about others. For instance, filling out the case in a plausible way, the mother is not justifiably skeptical about her perceptual faculties or her ability to discern perceptions of her child in good light. Put differently, it is not the case that the mother is justified in believing that she is in no position to judge how likely it is that her child is causing her visual perception. If she was justifiably skeptical about her abilities on this front, then it is clear that she would not be justified in believing that her baby was outside of the house, despite the prima facie justification she has for believing this (coming from her perceptual experience). This prima facie justification would be defeated by her higher-order (justified) skepticism about her abilities to discern the location of her child.

Similarly, the *weak* skeptical theist maintains that if we are justifiably skeptical about our abilities to judge whether a given evil is gratuitous, then this defeats any direct justification we have for believing that the evil in question is gratuitous. So, either Tucker is wrong about the consequences of Bergmann's skeptical theses, or there is more to the skeptical component of skeptical theism than Bergmann maintains.[24]

---

[23] That said, it's not clear to me that a justified suspension of judgment concerning the representativeness of some sample cannot ever defeat direct justification for believing the conclusion of such an inference. Suppose that there is a very large mosaic with many tiles, however all of the tiles are initially turned backwards. Suppose then that a small number of tiles are flipped. Not many tiles are flipped, and there is no reason to think that the flipped ones are representative of the whole lot. So, an inference from the flipped tiles to what the whole mosaic looks like appears to be unwarranted. Suppose, however, that it also just appears to you that the mosaic is of a forest. Given PC, this gives you prima facie justification for believing that the mosaic is of a forest. Are you also on balance justified in believing that the mosaic is of a forest given what else you know about the vastness of the mosaic and how few tiles have been flipped?

[24] These considerations seem to be what Bergmann hopes to capture with ST4. So, while my task here is not to defend Bergmann's conception of the skeptical component of skeptical theism, I also am not convinced that there is a problem with it.

8. DOUGHERTY'S CHALLENGE (PART 2)

Dougherty claims there are several flaws with my case for the compatibility of PC and *weak* skeptical theism. He claims that the theory of defeat I deployed is flawed (as is defeat talk in general), and that my account doesn't give the skeptical theist what she wants, or at least enough of it.[25]

First, Dougherty finds my account of defeat implausible and claims that all talk of defeat is utterly misguided. Motivating this conclusion is Dougherty's claim that "if there is defeat, then there is something that is defeated."[26] Since Dougherty finds no viable candidate for something that has been defeated when one gains a defeater, he concludes that defeat talk is misguided and we should opt for simply talking about the probability of a proposition given a total body of evidence.

Here Dougherty is mistaken in taking the meaning of the technical term "defeat" to be too much like the folk sense of "defeat." It is no challenge calling a shot in tennis "a winner," to note that the shot is not a competitor and winners must be competitors. Dougherty is right that when a body of evidence E supports a proposition P, E will *always* support P. Adding a defeater to E will not destroy this timeless relation between E and P. But when one starts with E as a total body of evidence, and adds a defeater for E's justification for P to E, this new total body of evidence, E*, does not support P at least as much as E did (and still does). Defeat language simply reflects this change—a change in what is on balance justified by one's total body of evidence (or to what degree it is on balance justified). It is true that this has only changed by changing what one's total body of evidence is, but this is a noteworthy kind of change—one we note with defeat talk.

Further, the account of defeat on offer is one that is already utilized by defenders of PC. As such, it is fair game to deploy it in showing the compatibility of PC and skeptical theism. For example, Michael Huemer's response to external world skepticism embraces this account of defeat. According to Huemer, the external world skeptic fails to render our beliefs about the external world unjustified since she fails to provide us with any (undefeated) positive reason to think that her skeptical hypothesis is true or that we are in fact mistaken. The external world skeptic offers only the *mere possible truth* of

---

[25] In his reply to my (2011), Dougherty (2011a) moves from PC to RC.

RC: If it seems to S that P, then S thereby has a *pro tanto* reason to believe P.

Dougherty seems to think that the move to RC is important since it makes explicit that seeming states provide *reasons* (not just prima facie justification). The motivation is that reasons stick around even when the justification they provide doesn't (at least in some sense). As I am understanding PC, it entails RC (the prima facie justification provided by the seeming state is provided in virtue of the reason the seeming state provides), so I will maintain my focus on PC.

[26] Dougherty (2011a: 4).

her skeptical hypotheses in an attempt to demonstrate that we lack knowledge about the external world. Huemer explicitly notes that *were* the external world skeptic to produce (undefeated) evidence that we are radically deceived brains-in-vats (or that some other skeptical hypothesis were true), then our prima facie justification for our external world beliefs would be fully undercut.[27] Here Huemer is *not* requiring that the skeptic provide reasons for her skeptical hypothesis that are *as good* as the reasons that her hypothesis would undercut. Simply being on balance justified in believing her hypothesis is true would fully undercut out external world beliefs. Fortunately, the skeptic has failed to produce such reasons.[28]

Since Huemer utilizes such a conception of defeat in applying PC as a response to external world skepticism it is legitimate to utilize this account of defeat (and defeat talk in general) in showing that PC and skeptical theism are not in tension—this account of defeat has been seen by defenders of PC to be an extension of their view.

Dougherty's second complaint is that the red-tinted glasses argument from analogy that I have given to show that there is no tension between PC and skeptical theism involves fallacious reasoning. Central to this argument was the claim that an undercutting defeater can be full even if it is less on balance justified than the proposition whose evidential work it is defeating. For example, D can be a full undercutting defeater for the justification that E provides for P, even if S is .8 on balance justified in believing E and only .7 on balance justified in believing D. Dougherty claims that this model is incoherent and that the degrees of justification for both D and E can make a difference, even if S is on balanced justified in believing each.

In particular, Dougherty claims that my reasoning involves committing the base-rate fallacy. He gives the following example to motivate his claim:

> Suppose a subject S is chosen at random from a population where approximately 10% steal from work. So it is .9 probable that she doesn't steal. However, [when] she is asked during a lie-detector test which is 80% accurate whether she steals, it says she's lying when she says she does not steal. We now have evidence undercutting her testimony. I have a reliable source that says she's lying and the proposition

---

[27] See Huemer (2001: 183).

[28] This response may sound anti-Moorean. It is not. A Moorean response to skepticism needn't (and shouldn't) claim that first-order evidence (i.e. here's one hand) defeats higher-order evidence about the quality of that first-order evidence. The skeptic makes evidence the possibility of skeptical hypotheses, but the mere possibility of these hypotheses is not higher-order evidence that the relevant first-order evidence does not justify the belief that I have hands. The skeptic may take it that her concerns are a higher-order defeater, but the skeptic is simply mistaken on this point. Were the skeptic to produce evidence which made S on balance justified in believing that S's perceptual experiences were not indicative of reality, then S would not be able to appeal to such first-order evidence (i.e. here is a hand) to defeat the skeptic's defeater. So, the response on offer here is wholly compatible with a Moorean response to skepticism.

that she's lying *entails* that her testimony is false, so if I was certain of it, I'd have a full, undercutting defeater.

When asked in tests, many respondents think this means we are no longer justified in believing her testimony. However, this is just a fallacy—the base-rate fallacy—and the odds are still better than 2:1 that S is innocent. This illustrates that direct evidence is not the only evidence, and that it's total evidence that counts. Epistemic justification must take into account one's total perspective.[29]

While Dougherty's case does involve fallacious reasoning, he has misunderstood the central thrust of my argument in two critical ways. First, it is important to note that as Dougherty understands a lie-detector, the lie-detector can give positive reasons for thinking that *the subject's testimony is false*, not simply reasons which undermine any evidence that the subject's testimony is true. As such, the type of defeat relevant to Dougherty's case is rebutting defeat and not undercutting defeat (or at least not *purely* undercutting defeat). Since my response focused on how *undercutting* defeaters worked and these two types of defeaters operate differently, this is a critical difference.

Second, in Dougherty's case the subject has other *independent* evidence, which both supports the claim that the subject does not steal *and* has not been undercut by *any* information given by the lie-detector test. So, even if the lie-detector evidence fully undercuts the testimony, we are still left with other evidence regarding the subject which has not been undercut by anything that the lie-detector has revealed. Even if we eschew all defeat talk, we have learned nothing that would undercut the *original evidence* that the subject doesn't steal (the evidence about theft in the general population). As Dougherty is understanding a lie-detector, the lie-detector presents a *partial* defeater (by way of rebutting) the original population data (since we have gained reason to think that she does steal), yet since we have more reason to trust the original data than the lie-detector results (as Dougherty has set up the case), this rebutting defeater will not be a full defeater for that original evidence even if it is a full defeater for her testimonial evidence.[30]

So, Dougherty's example does not show that defeat does not work in the way that I claimed, it only shows that some full defeaters need not fully defeat *all* of an individual's evidence bearing on p. But this we already knew. This is why in the red-tinted glasses case it was important that S1 was the *only* justificatory route to C1 for Smith. If Smith also had testimonial reasons for believing C1, then the prima facie justification provided by that testimony would not be undercut by S2, and Smith would be on balance justified in believing C1.

Undercutting defeaters need not undercut each and *every* justificatory route to a given proposition. Some undercutting defeaters may fully defeat some

---

[29] Dougherty (2011a: 6).

[30] I take it that we are to presume that the population data is more than 80 percent reliable, and so we have more reason to trust it than we have reason to trust the lie-detector test.

justificatory routes, while leaving others unaffected. Recall that undercutting defeaters attack *connections* between evidence and a proposition, but to attack one connection is not to attack all of them. To show that an undercutting defeater D for the support that E gives P still leaves S on balance justified in believing P does not show that D was not a full undercutting defeater regarding E's support of P. It is consistent with this picture that S has some E-independent justification for P which was unaffected by D (or at least no fully undercut by D). In fact, this is precisely what is going on in Dougherty's lie-detector case. So, Dougherty hasn't shown that the account of defeat on offer here fails, he has only shown that full defeaters needn't eliminate all of one's justification for believing a proposition—they only need to fully defeat a justificatory route to that proposition.

At this point it may appear that this response is in conflict with what I claimed earlier in this chapter. I earlier argued that the defeaters employed by the *weak* skeptical theist are particularly wide ranging—covering both inferential and direct justification for P1. I argued that when an individual is on balance justified in believing ST this will fully undercut any justification for believing P1. That said, this consequence followed from *the content* of ST, what this particular defeater claimed, and not from *the nature* of undercutting defeaters in general. While it is possible for some undercutting defeaters to be full while leaving open other justificatory routes to P, my claim is that this isn't the case with ST and P1. My claim is that when an individual is justified in believing ST, all justificatory routes to P1 will be blocked, but this does not commit me to claim that all undercutting defeaters will have such a drastic effect. Some undercutting defeaters don't defeat (even partially) some justificatory routes to a given proposition. So, the defense on offer is simply not committed to the consequences Dougherty claims.

But does this account give the skeptical theist what she wants? Defeaters can themselves be defeated. So, if an individual was justified in believing that that the type of seemings involved in ST seeming true to her were unreliable, the proposed skeptical theistic defeater could itself be defeated for that individual. If that defeater-defeater was itself undefeated and it continued to seem to S that there are morally unjustified evils in the world, then she would be on balance justified in believing P1. How the account on offer plays out will depend upon what seeming states individuals have—an empirical matter. This account leaves open the possibility that some individuals are on balance justified in believing P1 on the basis of P1 seeming true. So, this account may not give some skeptical theists *all* that they want. That said, it does provide an account whereby the direct *and* indirect motivation for P1 *will* be successfully blocked in its entirety—the motivation for P1 will be blocked when an individual is on balance justified in believing ST. While *weak* skeptical theism does not guarantee that no one will ever be justified in believing P1, it does provide a way out of the evidential argument from evil. While some skeptical theists might want more, having a way to successfully, rationally defend their theistic beliefs from the evidential problem of evil should be enough to make them happy.[31]

One final rejoinder that Dougherty lobbies is that this account of defeat makes it *too easy* to be on balance justified in believing P1. Dougherty offers the following principles which he thinks all seem true:

PWR: An omniscient and omnipotent being isn't going to be stuck in the position to choose between the holocaust and something (approximately) as bad or worse.

Anti-STa: A loving God would *want* us to understand, and an all-powerful God *could* make us understand.

Anti-STb: God's concept of goodness is neither exactly like ours nor shockingly different from ours.

~ST: Humans are in a position to judge that an omnipotent and omniscient being would be unlikely to have a morally sufficient reason to permit the evils we find in the world.[32]

Given PC, if these principles seem true to you, then you have prima facie justification for believing them too. If P1 also seemed true, then there multiple lines of justification for P1 for you (some direct and some indirect, but all rooted in seeming states). These independent lines of support make it more likely in some sense that P1 is on balance justified. However, just as the justification provided by it seeming to you that ST is true can itself be defeated, the justification provided by these seeming states can also be defeated.

These further claims interact with ST in different ways. In some cases, an undefeated seeming (one that is not *fully* defeated) that ST is true would fully undercut the justification provided by the principle (like PWR and Anti-STa), since in these cases being on balance justified in believing ST would fully undermine the connection between it seeming that PWR or Anti-STa were true and PWR or Anti-STa being true. This is because ST is a higher-order claim in comparison with PWR and STa. In other cases its seeming that ST is true would be a rebutting defeater for the prima facie justification for the principle provided by its seeming true. This is because the competitor claims are on the same level (neither is a more higher-order claim than the other). In these latter cases, the strengths of the relevant seemings would matter, given how rebutting defeat works. So, even if ST seemed true to S, if it more strongly seemed to S that the negation of ST was true, then S would be on

---

[31] It also might be thought to give the skeptical theist a project—make ST seem true to people. If they succeed in that task, then those individuals would not be justified in believing P1 (at least so long as those defeaters weren't themselves defeated).

[32] Dougherty (2011a: 9–10).

balance justified in disbelieving ST and justificatory routes to P1 would again be opened up.[33]

How strong and how prevalent are the various relevant seeming states? I don't know. The skeptical theist will no doubt care, but even if the desired seeming states are not very prevalent, the skeptical theist still has an available defense of her own theistic belief—she still has a way out of the evidential argument from evil. So long as ST seems true to her, and the justification provided by this seeming is not defeated for her (i.e. it does not seem to her more strongly that ST is false, or that her seeming that ST is the case is an unreliable seeming state, etc.), then she has no (fully) undefeated reason to believe P1. Further, and more germane to this chapter, the skeptical theist's *skeptical theism* has not required her to give up on PC, and no one's commitments to PC has given them reason to abandon skeptical theism (at least in its entirety)— *weak* skeptical theism and PC are compatible theses.

9. THE CHALLENGE OF DISAGREEMENT

However, at this point one might worry about the justificatory work that its seeming to S that ST is true can do when S is aware that ST seems false (and is disbelieved) by other equally intelligent, informed, and open-minded people. While ST might seem true to the skeptical theist, doesn't her awareness of epistemic peers[34] who disbelieve ST neutralize the prima facie justification this principle had in virtue of it seeming true to her? Prominent views in the epistemology of disagreement have it that the awareness of such disagreements call for a suspension of judgment regarding the disputed proposition.[35]

However, far from hurting the skeptical theist, such a skeptical consequence of these views of disagreement actually *enhances* her project. If such a view of the epistemic significance of disagreement is correct and skepticism regarding the disputed proposition is a consequence of the view, then the awareness of the relevant sort of disagreements concerning ST have it that all the parties involved in the disagreement should suspend judgment regarding ST—that this is the uniquely rational response to the disagreement. However, if an individual considers whether to believe ST and justifiably concludes that suspension of judgment is called for regarding this proposition, then she will also have a full undercutting defeater for the justification provided for P1

---

[33] The story in such a case would parallel Huemer's treatment of the Mueller-Lyer illusion. See Huemer (2001).

[34] Two individuals are epistemic peers when they are in an equally good epistemic position regarding some proposition—they are equally likely to be right about the matter. For more on epistemic peers see Kelly (2005).

[35] See for instance Christensen (2007) and Feldman (2006).

coming from P1 seeming true. If P1 seems true to S, and S also justifiably concludes that suspending judgment regarding ST is called for, then S is not on balance justified in believing P1 on the basis of it seeming true to S. This is because a justified conclusion that suspension of judgment regarding a higher-order claim is called for fully defeats the justification one has for any relevant lower-order claim.[36] So, not only do such views regarding the epistemology of disagreement have it that the disagreement regarding ST has the result that the skeptical theist is not on balance justified in believing P1, they have it that *even the atheist defender* of the argument who is aware of the relevant sorts of disagreement regarding ST is also unjustified in believing this premise. So, far from *hurting* the skeptical theist, the seeming consequences of taking epistemic significance of the disagreements seriously regarding ST actually *advances her cause*, at least given the relevant empirical facts of disagreement regarding them. In fact, they might even have it that no one is justified in believing P1.

10. CONCLUSION

There is no tension between skeptical theism and Phenomenal Conservatism. While the resulting account may not give every skeptical theist what she wants (i.e. it does leave the possibility of individuals being on balance justified in believing P1), it will give her what she was principally after—a defense of her own theistic beliefs.[37] On this account, the atheist fails to make theism unreasonable by giving the evidential argument from evil to certain theists—those to whom ST seems true and for whom this justification is not defeated. Further, considerations of the epistemology of disagreement seem to make the skeptical theist's project more far reaching. So, while there may be reasons to reject skeptical theism and reasons to reject Phenomenal Conservatism, there are no (undefeated) reasons to reject either of these claims on the basis of the other.[38]

---

[36] For a more detailed defense of higher-order defeat and how a justified suspension of judgment regarding a higher-order defeater has full defeating effects, see Bergmann (2005), Matheson (2009), and Feldman (2005).

[37] Further, this appears to be an asset, rather than a detriment. It seems that people *can* be justified in believing P1. We want an account that allows for this.

[38] Special thanks to Michael Bergmann, Brandon Carey, Ted Poston, Jason Rogers, Chris Tucker, and Ed Wierenga for helpful comments on this chapter.

2

Phenomenal Conservatism, Skeptical Theism, and Probabilistic Reasoning

Trent Dougherty

This chapter continues a discussion begun in 2008. In "Epistemological Considerations Concerning Skeptical Theism," I argued that if one accepted a form of commonsense epistemology—such as credulism (Swinburne 2001) or phenomenal conservatism (Huemer 2001)—one faced a "tension" in also accepting skeptical theism. One way to think about that tension is this: skeptical theism cannot retain many of its strongest features if one is a commonsense epistemologist. Matheson (2011) suggested that the distinction between undercutting and rebutting defeat gives the lie to my tension thesis. In my reply (Dougherty 2011a), I argued against the theory of defeat Matheson proposed and gave a probabilistic model to illustrate my thesis. In his reply to that in this volume, he alleges that the particulars of my models keep them from being effective. In this chapter, I go through a dynamic modeling process which is perfectly general, which shows that even granting pretty much everything Matheson claims as premises, phenomenal conservatism can prove lethal for skeptical theism. In presenting these models, an important methodological point emerges. When we look at the present issue through Bayesian eyes, we see that the typically binary and externalist way most skeptical theists think ignores the power both of strong conviction and of partial doubt. What is missing in the standard account of skeptical theism is the agent's own perspective. Bayesianism and phenomenal conservatism are especially well-suited to representing the first-person perspective.

1. PRELIMINARIES

Matheson claims to "show the compatibility of these two views [skeptical theism and phenomenal conservatism] by coupling them with an account of defeat" and further to show that "this account of defeat can give the Skeptical Theist what she wants—namely a response that can leave the evidential argument from evil unmotivated," (3). He does not say whether he intends to defend the thesis that the account of defeat in the presence of which the two views are supposedly compatible is *plausible*. So it is unclear whether, in Plantinga's terminology, he is offering a theodicy for the conjunction or merely a defense. But no matter I never claimed they were incompatible.

Skeptical theism comes in many forms,[1] but all versions entail that absence of evidence is not always evidence of absence—like the needle in the proverbial haystack—and that our inability to see reasons for actual evils is one of these cases. For some skeptical theists this is a consequence of general epistemic principles,[2] for others it is motivated by our ignorance, but the end result is, in general, the same. Thus, the fabled "noseeum" inference from "I don't see a sufficient reason for this" to "there is no reason for this" is no good; nor are inferences that tacitly or subtly depend on relevantly similar theses.[3] Skeptical theism is in the *inference blocking* business. There is a certain class of inferences—the "noseeum" inferences—which skeptical theism says are no good and essential to the evidential argument from evil.

With respect to the notion of commonsense epistemology, Matheson and I are agreed that seeming states provide reasons for an individual to believe the propositions that seem to them to be true. In the end, Bayesians often dispense with the notions of justification and belief, and I have great sympathy with that, but at least for the sake of argument, I can endorse the following:

(*)   If S's reasons to believe P sufficiently outweigh S's reasons not to believe P at T, then S is justified in believing P at T.

Furthermore, one ought to have a degree of certainty in P in exact proportion as the discerned[4] weight of reasons for P. Suppose the notion of full belief is coherent. How much does the weight of reasons for P need to be before it is true that S ought to believe P? This is a very difficult question. Belief might just be a state of taking for granted; a state triggered at different levels for different people, and different levels of tolerance for taking for granted might all fall within the bounds of proper function. Fortunately, any work that can be done with belief and justification can be done more precisely with the notion

---

[1] See McBrayer (2010a) and (2010b), and Dougherty (2011) and (2014).
[2] Wykstra (1984).   [3] Bergmann (2001).
[4] One's ability to discern might leave some fuzziness around the edges. I'll bracket discussion of vagueness concerns here.

of degrees of certainty and evidential fit between degree of certainty and weight of reasons. For this reason—and because Matheson says his PC principle entails it, anyway—I will stick with the following formulation of phenomenal conservatism.

RC   If it seems to S that[5] P, then S thereby has a reason to believe P.

Given RC, it is easy to see how skeptical theism's characteristic inference-blocking move is impotent to block one from having reasons to believe there are unjustified evils: one can acquire reasons in favor of the proposition that there are unjustified evils *directly* by its seeming to them that there are unjustified evils. The individual in question is not just failing to see a reason but apparently *seeing that* there is no reason. I call this the "Commonsense Problem of Evil" (CSPOE).[6] Since there is no inference, and skeptical theism is in the inference-blocking business, there is nothing for skeptical theism to do.[7]

2. SKEPTICAL THEISM AND PHENOMENAL CONSERVATISM

Matheson's main thesis is stated with admirable clarity: "If S is *on balance* justified in believing [the skeptical theist's skeptical theses], then *any* direct evidence S has for [the "premise" of the CSPOE] will also be *fully* defeated," (7, emphasis added). So, according to Matheson, even though the standard skeptical theist *move* can't work on what I call the CSPOE, the skeptic who has justification for skeptical theses can be made immune to the CSPOE. But as a Bayesian, I naturally never intended to rule this out—and thought I had made clear that I accepted it. When I talk about a conflict between skeptic theism and phenomenal conservatism, I only mean to point out that it can possibly go in the *other* direction: one to whom it just seems obvious that there are unjustified evils will be on balance justified in rejecting the skeptical theist's skeptical theses. This cuts across the grain of two common components of skeptical theism, which we will discuss in the next paragraph.[8] Later, we'll see that what makes Matheson's statement false is the combination of "on balance" and "any."

---

[5] Matheson says "seems as if", which is a phrase I retain for mere sensory states. I say "seems that" because the states I take to constitute the evidence have propositional contents that are identical to the propositions they evidence. So, in my terminology, the pencil in the glass can seem *as if* it were bent even if, knowing what we do, it doesn't seem *that* the pencil is bent.

[6] For more on this, see Dougherty (2014).

[7] No skeptical theist that I'm aware of has explicitly claimed that skeptical theism applies to every kind of problem of evil. Some even admit that they are skeptical that it does. Yet those same skeptical theists are clear that skeptical theism is about *inferences*. For both these claims, see Bergmann's chapter in this volume. He also there seems to indicate that his skeptical theses don't apply to the CSPOE, in the passage concerning moral intuition of intrinsic wrong on page 211.

[8] For documentation that they are common concomitants, see Dougherty (2014).

Matheson's possible scenario runs counter to what I call the "no weight view." Skeptical theists have almost universally held that due to the *truth* of the skeptical theist's skeptical theses, no one anywhere has any reason to disbelieve in God on the basis of facts about evil. Skeptical theists have not been appropriately sensitive to a fact that comes naturally to Bayesians: rationality of belief is person-relative. So one cannot make, as skeptical theists are wont to make, broad, sweeping generalizations about what "skeptical theism shows." This is the second common concomitant of skeptical theism, which can be called the "universalism" thesis. Since my RC and Matheson's PC (which he says entails my RC) are both person-relative theories of reasons, they rule out the universality thesis and provide for the possibility that there will be cases (and surely there are actual cases) where the unjustifiability of certain evils strikes one as much more obvious than the conjunction of four theses in metaphysics and moral theory. In Matheson's case the skeptical theses are defeating some prima facie justification acquired via RC. Thus, his picture is inconsistent with two common concomitants of skeptical theism.

This puts the skeptical theist in a very different position than she would prefer. Once it is granted that one can get immediate reasons for the proposition that there are unjustified evils, the skeptical theist now has to *make a case* for her skeptical theses to provide enough reason for them to outweigh the weight of reasons for the CSPOE, at least for those to whom they don't seem obvious (they seem to me obviously false[9]). That is a very different position, and not an enviable one, to be in from the position of declaring that no one could have any reasons to disbelieve in God from a whole class of arguments from evil. Maybe it's really true that the skeptical theist's skeptical theses seem obvious to her. And maybe that is good *defensive* ground. But it doesn't do much for the rest of us. If the skeptical theist wants to address the commonsense problem of evil as it arises for those of us who suffer from it, the typical rearguard stance isn't going to help.

3. THE AGONY OF "FULL" DEFEAT

Matheson makes much of the notion of "full" defeat. I will take a closer look at two claims Matheson makes, one stronger than the other. I begin with the weaker[10] claim.

---

[9] One reason is this: we have *some* good reason to think that we have the broad outlines of a correct moral theory which tells us quite general necessary truths about good, evil, and the entailment relations between them.

[10] There are respects in which it is stronger, too, so let me clarify. It is weaker than the claim to follow, because the latter, and not the former, includes the claim that the thing being defeated can be better justified than the thing it is defeating. The latter claim is a weaker *kind* of claim because

a. The weaker claim

> [A]n undercutting defeater will be full whenever one is on balance jus-
> tified in believing that the epistemic support relation between one's
> evidence and the target proposition is lacking altogether or when one
> is on balance justified in suspending judgment regarding the claim that
> one's evidence supports the target proposition. (10)

3.1 General Problems

First, note that the more convinced you were that your moral intuition about
the intrinsic impermissibility of some particularly horrendous evil was accurate, the more this would call into question the accuracy of your intuition that
the skeptical theses were true, so the CSPOE could serve as an undercutting
defeater for the support the skeptical theses get from the intuition that they are
true. #sauce #goose #gander.

Next, note that the distinction between undercutting and rebutting defeat,
so at the core of Matheson's line of reasoning, is blurry. Here's an illustration.[11]
At T1, Smith, who is generally reliable, testifies to you that P. At T2, Jones, who
is also generally reliable, testifies to you that Smith is unreliable on the matter
at hand. Now on the theory of undercutting defeat, Jones's testimony functions
as an undercutting defeater because it challenges the support relation between
Smith's testifying that P and P. Yet it is still just a "he-said/she-said" situation
(Smith is a dude, Jones is a lady, say, Barnaby Smith and Johnna-Sue Jones). You
just have to decide who you trust more: Smith or Jones? The attempted distinction between rebutting and undercutting defeat is not as clean as Matheson
makes it out. Let's apply this to skeptical theism and the CSPOE. Here is a guide.

> Seeming 1, UNJ: It seems that an evil, E, is unjustifiable (call this property "F").
> Seeming 2, SKEP: It seems that the skeptical theses are true.

Let's say that you have both seemings. UNJ says of E that it is F. SKEP says UNJ
is a liar. So, in the end, you have to just ask yourself who you trust more: UNJ or
SKEP. And it's easy to see why one could consider UNJ more trustworthy than
SKEP. SKEP is, in the end "philosophy crap" whereas the reaction to evil is very
instinctual and deals in the kinds of moral judgments that are the stuff of life.

---

it is an existential claim and the former is universal. The epistemic strength is guiding the order
of exposition, not the logical strength.

[11] Some of what I say in Dougherty (2013) is relevant to this section. This is as good a place
as any, I suppose, to note that Matheson's statement in his section five that disagreement that "a
skeptical consequence of these views of disagreement would actually *enhance* the skeptical theist's project" is a bit misleading. For the skeptical theses are not doing any work here at all, since
one has to suspend judgment on *them* as well. The disagreement is doing all the work on his view.

Finally, note that given the "whenever," there is independent (of skeptical theism) reason for thinking that this principle of higher-order evidence is false. Skepticism looms in such a sentiment. Take the case where a philosophical naïf is presented with the brain-in-a-vat hypothesis and asked the following question: "Does an evidential support relation hold between your total evidence and the proposition that you have hands?" What evidence does he have that it is so or not so? He scarcely understands the question. You might as well have asked him whether he believes P where you haven't told him what "P" stands for! And his reaction should be the same: suspension of judgment. On Matheson's account, the student's belief that he has hands is "fully" defeated. But this is the wrong result, for his philosophical naïvety hardly takes away his reasons for his first-order beliefs, such as that he has hands.

Another kind of case is less clear, but still somewhat suggestive. Take the case where the subject has just a bit more training: a freshman in the first few weeks of his first introduction course, say. Suppose he becomes convinced by sophistical arguments similar to Cartesian worries that his sensory experiences don't support his experiential beliefs. It is far from obvious that this dupe all of a sudden doesn't know he has hands. His first-order evidence clearly supports that he has hands, and he can't stop himself believing this, and the reason is tied to those handy experiences, so it's very plausible he still knows it, even though he is plausibly justified in believing that there is no epistemic support relation which holds between his evidence and the target proposition. For these reasons I doubt that *whenever* one's reasons favor non-positive answers to the higher-order question they lose *all* their reasons for the first-order belief. If there is sense in trickle-down epistemology, I doubt it is as simple as Matheson says.

3.2 Specific Problems

In his defense of the "full defeat" claim, Matheson makes it easy for himself by picking simple cases where things work well for him (in normal circumstances) like the glasses example. One is usually *certain* one has on glasses if one believes one does. That skews the example from the beginning. But what if one is only 51% convinced one has tinted contact lenses in? One could easily believe one did without being certain of it, then a lot of room is left open whether their red-y experiences are evidence-providing, and if so, how and to what degree. Here is a similar example. Jones rolled a seven-sided die to determine whether there was going to be red table with normal lighting or a white table with red lighting: if an ace, then the latter, else the former. Or make it a pill with a one in seven chance of messing up your sight. This fits the model of so-called undercutting defeat, but one should still, on balance, trust one's seeming that the table is red. The chance of undercutting defeat is not strong enough to remove *all* the force of the visual evidence. So "undercutting" defeat can run the gamut in its force.

The big problem with Matheson's claim is not so much that what he says is wrong, for there is a reading upon which it is true, but rather that he says the wrong thing. The truth of this statement would not at all solve the problem that the CSPOE raises for the skeptical theist. I will demonstrate this with probabilistic models below, since the stronger claim has exactly the same problems, but I will introduce the problem here. The problem with the statement is an ambiguity in Matheson's use of "full." Whether the statement is true depends on how one reads "full." If "full" defeat means that *all* the force of the thing "defeated" disappears, then my models show this is clearly false. If "full" just means sufficient to be a belief-defeater, i.e. render belief in unjustified evil unjustified, then it is clearly true, but also unhelpful to the skeptical theist in the endeavor to systematically avoid the CSPOE. As we shall see in the following section, the graded notion is much more important than the binary notion, for the binary notion underdetermines whether one should suspend judgment concerning theism, which would be a success for the advocate of the problem of evil.

Being unjustified in full-blown belief that E is unjustified is consistent with *also* being unjustified in full-blown belief in theism. That is, even if one has a "full" defeater (in the defeating-full-blown-belief sense) for the claim that there is unjustified evil arising from its seeming true to one that the skeptical theses are true to a sufficient degree to make the proposition that E is unjustified unjustified for one, the evidence for the proposition that E is unjustified can still be strong enough to defeat theistic belief (insufficiently supported by further evidence for the theist without a theodicy). I will give specific models of this below.

b. The stronger claim

Matheson puts a lot of emphasis on the following claim:

> [A]n undercutting defeater can be full even if it is less on balance justified than the proposition whose evidential work it is defeating. (15)

This statement inherits the ambiguity of "full" discussed above. With "full undercutting defeat" read as "defeat sufficient to render full-blown belief unjustified" there are of course cases where this is true.

Let's look at an example:

Let:

P = The table is red.

Q = There are red jells on the lights.

E = S's total evidence (at the time she comes to consider the faceoff between P and Q, so neither P nor Q are included in E at this time). We will assume that there is nothing in E that is relevant to P other than that it seems to S that the table is red, so E is functionally equivalent to <The table looks red>.

Assume: 90% is the minimum cut-off for justified belief.

P is the target proposition. Q is the "undercutting defeater." Now we need a set of assignments that makes P (the thing being defeated) more justified than Q (the thing that is doing the defeating). The following assignments will do for illustrative purposes, I don't really believe that introspection is infallible or anything like that.

$Pr(E) = 100\%$

$Pr(P|E) = 90\%$

$Pr(Q|E) = 60\%$

Now, if E doesn't support P at all (which we may assume is a direct consequence of the truth of Q), then P's probability reverts to its prior probability. Red tables are fairly rare, so let's say the prior is, say, .17. The only thing that would drive P's probability higher in our scenario is E, and Q says E provides exactly *no* support for P. So if Q is true, then S has no new support for P. But S is not *sure* Q is true. S is only just beyond counterbalanced with respect to Q. So what we have is a situation where there is a 60% chance that for S the probability of P is .17 (this is the value of $Pr(P|E \& Q)$) and a 40% chance that the probability is .9. That gives us $(.6*.17) + (.4*.9) = .462$, which is well below the threshold for justified full-blown belief. So, *voila*, Matheson's case is possible. But notice that, in this scenario, the probability for the defeater is *also* well below the threshold for full-blown belief. And, what's more, if the probability for one that there are unjustified evils is .462, then unless one has really good evidence from natural theology or religious experience, full-blown theistic belief will be unjustified, in the absence of a theodicy to serve as a defeater-defeater.

Now let's apply this more closely to the skeptical theism case. Here are the

Target proposition (P)	That table is red.	That evil is unjustified.
The evidence (E)	The table looks red.[12]	That evil seems unjustified.
Proposed defeater (Q)	The lights are tinted.	The skeptical theses are true.

parallels.

We will proceed by exact parallel with the previous case. S has an intense experience—S becomes familiar with some horrendous evil that seems to him intrinsically wrong to permit—which confers a strong probability, .95, say, on the proposition that there is an unjustified evil. Then the skeptical theist comes

---

[12] Or, on the experiential model I tend to prefer, the table's looking red.

and tries to kick the legs out from under this support. If the skeptical theist is maximally successful—if she fully convinces S that the skeptical theses are true, then the probability that the evil is unjustified reverts to its prior probability, say, .5 (it won't matter, more on that in just a bit). But S, as it turns out, is unimpressed. The skeptical theses seem extreme and arcane. S gives them a 4% chance of being true. So now there is a 4% chance[13] that that the probability of an unjustified evil is .5, and a 96% chance that the probability is .95. Thus, S's degree of certainty in P ought to be (.04 * .5) + (.96 * .95) = .932. So there are limits on the work partial defeaters can do. In this case, when the seeming is so overwhelming *and* one is not at all convinced of the skeptical theses, they do next to nothing.

It is natural to wonder if the middling value for the prior probability of an unjustified evil is doing most of the work. Let it go from .5 to .1. The probability of P goes from .932 to .916. Let it go from .1 to .01. Then it goes from .916 to .912. It is also natural to think that, if it is not the prior probability of unjustified evil that is doing the work, it is the extremely low value for the skeptical theses. And this will potentially make some difference (we'll see just how much in a moment), but that's just how it goes: some of us are utterly unconvinced. I find the skeptical theses to be without any significant support, and they strongly seem implausible to me. Still, suppose one grants the skeptical theses significant weight without being convinced by them. Suppose S gives them a 1-in-3 chance of being true. That's significant. Then the probability for S of P is almost .64 (holding fixed the prior for unjustified evil at an unreasonably low .01). With the strong force of the seeming that the evil is unjustified, even with a quite low prior on unjustified evil and significant weight given to the skeptical theses, S's evidence still on balance favors that there are unjustified evils (.715). Here is a model like we discussed above: P is "fully" defeated for S in the sense that full-blown belief in P is unjustified. But since the existence of unjustified evils entails the non-existence of God (and entailment transmits probability without loss), the fairly skeptical S would still need evidence from religious experience or natural theology or else a theodicy (probably some combination of all them) to be justified in full-blown belief in theism.

Suppose one just can't make up one's mind about the skeptical theses, suppose S sees as much reason to affirm as to deny them and assigns them a probability of .5. Now there is a 50/50 chance that the probability of P for S is .01 or .95. This effectively halves the support that gets transferred from the seeming to the target proposition leaving the probability of P for S at .48. Here, the balance shifts against P, but the effect is almost exactly the same as above.

---

[13] "Chance" may well have some unwelcomed connotations, but it is never easy to talk about higher-order probabilities. The Bayesian is concerned about the flow of probability across time, and how probabilities are divided up, however it is described, whether it is mud on a board, chocolate bars, or loaves of bread.

So how convinced would one subject to the strong sense of seeming that there is unjustified evil need to be of the skeptical theses in order for the skeptical theses to allow for justified full-blown belief in theism? Well, let's say that .9 is minimally sufficient for justified belief (some tend to think it is lower, most tend to think it is higher). So we need a confidence value for the skeptical theses that drives the value of P down to less than 10%. With the prior set at next to nothing, that value is unsurprisingly just above 90%. It would take some serious argument to get someone skeptical of the skeptical theses or agnostic about the agnosticism it recommends to have that level of confidence in them. But it is also unreasonable to think the prior probability that a world would contain evils that it would be impermissible to allow is so low. If we raise it from 1/100 to just 1/10, one would have to be over 99% sure of the skeptical theses in order for full-blown belief in theism to be justified.

4. CONCLUSION

Bayesian models are good for doing at least three things in the skeptical theism debate. First, they are good at showing how important it is not to neglect prior probabilities. The force of evidence is always measured in a context, not in a vacuum. They are good at showing the resilience of strong irreligious experience. Finally, they are good at exposing the power of significant doubt. Skeptical theists tend to focus on showing that it cannot be *proven* that there is unjustified evil. But proof of the negation of a proposed defeater for P is not necessary for doubt to render belief in P unreasonable. So without sufficiently strong religious experience to balance a strong irreligious experience or sufficiently strong arguments from natural theology, such an individual will not be justified in believing theism without a theodicy.

Matheson surely thinks that justification supervenes on evidence and comes in degrees. The same is true of evidential probability. The most natural account of degree of epistemic justification is as degree of evidential probability. If Matheson wishes to disassociate them, he owes a story about the relationship between justification and probability. And, of course, even if he could divorce them, the probability facts remain, and while the exact relation between belief and probability (if we wish to retain the notion of full-blown belief) is hard to pin down, it is a truism that it is irrational to believe that which has a low probability on your evidence. Without something other than skeptical theism, most theists can't sensibly assign a probability to theism to make it rational to believe.

To return to a point from above, even granting Matheson pretty much everything he wants, one still has to *be* justified in accepting the skeptical theists' skepticism for it to significantly defeat the appearance of unjustifiability of

certain evils. There are two ways that could come about: directly or via inference. As I mentioned above, there is really only one argument given for the
skepticism, and I have argued elsewhere that there are serious flaws in that
argument.[14] So could they be directly justified via their just strongly seeming
true (more strongly enough than the appearance of unjustifiability of evil to
make you justified in fully believing it)? I invite skeptical theists to try to motivate the theses for me. I would welcome that. But until that happens, I am like
a lot of people for whom skeptical theism is cold fish.[15]

[14] Dougherty (2012).
[15] Thanks very much to Paul Draper and Justin P. McBrayer for very helpful comments.

3

On the Epistemological Framework for Skeptical Theism

John M. DePoe

Ever since the deductive argument from evil has been put to rest by the work of Alvin Plantinga,[1] the evidential problem of evil has become the central focus of the debate concerning the compatibility of traditional theism and the existence of evil.[2] The evidential argument is[3]

(1) There are some cases of gratuitous evil in the world.

(2) If God exists, then it is not the case that there is any gratuitous evil in the world.

Therefore,

(3) It is not the case that God exists.

The majority of the debate on the evidential problem of evil has focused on the veracity of the first premise, which is usually cast as a probabilistically justified claim.[4] Perhaps the most influential defense against the evidential problem of evil is known as "skeptical theism," which is founded upon a prima facie non-controversial claim:

(4) Given theism, there are true propositions about the world that God knows and no human is in a position to know.

The viability of skeptical theism depends on what may be inferred from (4) concerning our epistemic perspective on whether God could have morally sufficient reasons for permitting particular evils to exist. Roughly, the idea of

---

[1] Plantinga (1974: chapter IX) and (1977).

[2] Due primarily to the discussion around Rowe (1979).

[3] Cf. Rowe (1996: 263) and Rowe (2006: 80).

[4] There are some theists that reject the second premise while accepting the first, including Hasker (2004), van Inwagen (2006), and MacGregor (2012).

the skeptical theistic position is that (4) provides justification for believing that God has morally sufficient reasons for permitting evil, although we may not ever be in a position to know what those reasons may be. However, (4) is a double-edged sword. A host of recent challenges to skeptical theism argue that (4) not only justifies someone in accepting God may have reasons for allowing evil to exist which we are not in a position to know, but that (4) also supports more severe and untenable skepticisms: God may have reasons for allowing just about *anything*, which we may not be in a position to know. This counter-argument implies that if theism is true, then God may have good reasons (which we cannot know) for instituting widespread, pervasive deception about the world. Even worse, some critics of skeptical theism maintain that (4) implies that we cannot be in position to judge whether any action is actually morally good or evil since for all we know God may have a reason for making what appears to be evil to be actually good (and vice versa).

In this chapter, my intention is to provide the proper epistemological framework for skeptical theism such that it can deflect some of the evidential disconfirmation that seemingly gratuitous evil is believed to bear on theism, while avoiding the negative implications that have been raised against skeptical theism. I'll take for granted the assumption that skeptical theism by itself is not sufficient to defend theism and that the rational defense of theism requires some positive arguments in favor of theism as well as a theodicy. Thus, I will assume that skeptical theism is best used as one part of a multifaceted philosophical response to the problem of evil. But even with these assumptions, there are important questions about the epistemic framework in which skeptical theism is used. In what follows, I will argue that there are two frameworks for employing skeptical theism, and that the version that affirms the positive role of mystery is the better theistic framework in which to deflect some of the disconfirmation of seemingly gratuitous evils.

1. TWO FRAMEWORKS OF SKEPTICAL THEISM

At the risk of being accused of loading the terms to my advantage, I will distinguish positive skeptical theism from negative skeptical theism. Positive skeptical theism provides some positive reasons as to why we should expect there to be seemingly gratuitous evils if God exists. By contrast, negative skeptical theism casts doubt on our ability to understand any reasons God may have for permitting seemingly gratuitous evil, and it does not give any reasons that entail or probabilify the existence of seemingly gratuitous evil given theism. The key difference is that in the case of positive skeptical theism the motivation for the skeptical component of skeptical theism is generated from one's positive knowledge of God's reasons for creating a world where there is seemingly gratuitous evil, whereas in the case of negative skeptical theism it is supported only by one's inability to know God's reasons for anything, including reasons He may or may not have for permitting seemingly gratuitous evil.

2. NEGATIVE SKEPTICAL THEISM

Negative skeptical theism is the dominant version of skeptical theism in contemporary philosophy of religion. Stephen Wykstra's account of Conditions on Reasonable Epistemic Access, or CORNEA, is one of the most prominent accounts of negative skeptical theism.[5] Wykstra maintains that the inference from "one cannot see that p" to "it is not the case that not-p" relies on a "noseeum" inference ("if I no see 'um, then they ain't there"). The strength of a noseeum inference depends crucially on whether one would expect to see 'um, if one were to look for 'um. The CORNEA thesis is that noseeum inferences are justified only when the right conditions obtain—roughly, conditions where looking for p typically provides conclusive evidence whether p is the case. For example, if I look for my car in a standard, relatively clean, illuminated one-car garage, I should be able to see my car if it is there. My inability to see my car under these conditions is a sufficiently good reason to believe my car isn't there. However, if I go in search of one of my wife's earring clasps in the same garage, and I do not see it, the inference that it isn't there is significantly weaker. We typically don't think that the proper conditions obtain such that if my wife's earring clasp were in the garage, I would be likely to see it.

Proponents of the evidential argument from evil justify premise (1) typically on the grounds that no one is able to see any plausible morally sufficient reasons God may have for permitting specific horrendous evils to exist. Since we cannot see these reasons, some have concluded that they must not exist. Wykstra's CORNEA, however, casts doubt on (1) because it is plausible to think that we don't satisfy the right conditions for seeing God's reasons for allowing these seemingly gratuitous evils to exist even if we look for them fastidiously. As Wykstra summarizes, "if we think carefully about the sort of being theism proposes for our belief, it is entirely expectable—given what we know of our cognitive limits—that the goods by virtue of which this Being allows known suffering should very often be beyond our ken."[6] Michael Bergmann has advocated negative skeptical theism by defending three skeptical theses:[7]

---

[5] See Wykstra (1990a) and (1996b).
[6] Wykstra (1984: 159). See Wykstra (1996b: 137) for his "modest" interpretation of the expectation expressed in this statement. His point is not that if God exists, then it is very likely that some evils will be noseeums. Rather, he only means that (psychologically?) it is unsurprising that some evils are noseeums given the human cognitive condition compared to God's.
[7] Bergmann (2001).

(ST1)   We have no good reason for thinking that the possible goods we know of are representative of the possible goods there are.

(ST2)   We have no good reason for thinking that the possible evils we know of are representative of the possible evils there are.

(ST3)   We have no good reason for thinking that the entailment relations we know of between possible goods and the permission of possible evils are representative of the entailment relations there are between possible goods and the permission of possible evils.

Bergmann intends these skeptical theses to be justified by recognizing that any individual set of human experiences is limited and thereby possibly incomplete and unrepresentative of the nature of possible goods, evils, and entailment relations between them. After all, if someone's experiences are not representative of all of reality, then any attempt to reach a conclusion on the assumption that his experiences are representative of reality will be mistaken. For example, suppose someone has only experienced the colors of black, white, and varying shades of gray, and he is incapable of imagining any new color experiences. Next, suppose he concludes that his color experiences are representative of all the colors in the world. Of course, he would be wrong. His limited range of experiences and his inability to conceive of new, alternative experiences misleads him into drawing the wrong conclusion. Likewise, Bergmann believes that for all we know, our knowledge of possible goods, possible evils, and entailment relations between possible goods and evils are like the person who has only experienced black, white, and shades of gray. As he explains, "It is just the honest recognition of the fact that it wouldn't be the least bit surprising if reality far outstripped our understanding of it."[8] Thus, he concludes we aren't able to assume our experiences of goods, evils, and entailment relations between them are representative of all the goods, evils, and entailments relations.

If Bergmann is correct, then it undermines the justification for (1). Since we may not know all the possible goods, evils, and entailment relations between them, our judgment that God does not have any good reasons for permitting the existence of apparently gratuitous evil may be unreliable. For instance, we may not know of some good that outweighs the seemingly gratuitous evil, or some worse evil that was prevented by the seemingly gratuitous evil, or the way in which the seemingly gratuitous evil was necessary to bring about some good. Bergmann is clear that his skeptical theism is fully negative in my sense of the term.[9] He unquestionably intends his skeptical theism to neutralize the atheist's evidential argument from evil without being saddled to defend anything positive about God's reasons for permitting seemingly pointless evils.

---

[8] Bergmann (2001: 284).   [9] See especially, Bergmann (2009: 380).

3. POSITIVE SKEPTICAL THEISM

Positive skeptical theism, by contrast, attempts to give reasons such that we would expect the appearance of gratuitous evils given theism. To my knowledge there aren't many recent accounts of positive skeptical theism. The idea of positive skeptical theism, or perhaps the kernel of such an idea, is present in chapter fifteen, section six of John Hick's *Evil and the God of Love*,[10] and he traces the idea to the seventeenth-century Cambridge Platonist, Ralph Cudworth. The positive skeptical theist will not claim to understand or see God's reasons for permitting some seemingly gratuitous evil (otherwise it would not be a version of skeptical theism). The positive skeptical theist, however, defends the plausibility of some second-order justification or reason that God may have for creating a world with seemingly gratuitous evils. Hick states it this way:

> Our 'solution', then, to this baffling problem of excessive and undeserved suffering is a frank appeal to the positive value of mystery. Such suffering remains unjust and inexplicable, haphazard and cruelly excessive. The mystery of dysteleological suffering is a real mystery, impenetrable to the rationalizing human mind. It challenges Christian faith with its utterly baffling, alien, destructive meaninglessness. And yet at the same time, detached theological reflection can note that this very irrationality and this lack of ethical meaning contributes to the character of the world as a place in which true human goodness can occur and in which loving sympathy and compassionate self-sacrifice can take place.[11]

(I've puzzled over whether Hick's defense is intended to be the kind of positive skeptical theism I have in mind or whether he intends to concede that some evil is genuinely gratuitous and instead reject premise (2) in the evidential argument from evil. Rather than do exegesis on Hick, I'll content myself to use some of Hick's account of purposeless evils to inform the kind of positive skeptical theism that I have in mind where it is used to deny premise (1) in the evidential argument.)

What is the "positive value of mystery" that Hick has in mind? Hick identifies two kinds of goods that are achievable through the existence of seemingly pointless evils. First, it creates epistemic distance between God and creatures that is necessary for creatures to respond to God in genuine faith. By putting epistemic distance between Himself and humans, God makes noetic space for humans to come to know Him and submit to His will without violating their freedom.[12] If God's existence were obvious and incontrovertible, then people would have no real choice in responding to the divine call of salvation. Consequently, any act of faith would be forced, rather than free. Of course,

---

[10] Hick (1978).   [11] Hick (1978: 335–6).
[12] For more on this see especially, Hick (1978: 286–7).

the distance must not be so great as to make holding a justified belief in God impossible. The idea is eloquently captured in Blaise Pascal's phrase, "There is enough light for those who desire only to see, and enough darkness for those of a contrary disposition."[13]

It is worth noting that some of the most ardent evidentialists among Christian apologists have acknowledged some divine purpose in maintaining epistemic distance between God and humans. For instance, Joseph Butler writes in *The Analogy of Religion*, "The evidence of religion not appearing obvious, may constitute one particular part of some men's trial in the religious sense: as it gives scope, for a virtuous exercise, or vicious neglect of their understanding, in examining or not examining into that evidence."[14] In *A View of the Evidences of Christianity*, William Paley acknowledges the importance of epistemic distance when discussing what the probable effects would be if the evidence for God's existence were too plain and obvious:

> One is, that irresistible proof [of the truth of Christianity] would restrain the voluntary powers too much; would not answer the purpose of trial and probation; would call for no exercise of candour, seriousness, humility, inquiry, no submission of passion, interests, and prejudices, to moral evidence and to probable truth; no habits of reflection; none of that previous desire to learn and to obey the will of God, which forms perhaps the test of the virtuous principle, and which induces men to attend, with care and reverence, to every credible intimation of that will, and to resign present advantages and present pleasures to every reasonable expectation of propitiating his favour.[15]

Thus, two of the foremost proponents of evidentialist approaches to natural theology agree that God would have good reason for creating a world with an epistemic distance between Himself and persons.

The significance of epistemic distance has received further treatment in Paul Moser's recent work in religious epistemology where he contends that if there is a God, then we should expect the epistemic situation in which God has placed humans not to be coercive to their volition to acknowledge and worship God.[16] Moser emphasizes that God's purpose in providing evidence of Himself is not merely to provide knowledge that God exists, but that God's purpose is to show His creatures that a Being worthy of worship and to whom they ought to align their wills exists. In other words, Moser maintains that the epistemic situation we should expect God to create for His creatures would be primarily concerned with making possible the free volitional transformation of His creatures. If God's purpose is to bring about the free volitional transformation of His creatures, then some significant divine-human epistemic distance is necessary.

[13] Pascal (1995: 50). [14] Butler (1833: 266, Part II, chapter 6).
[15] Paley (1879: 470, Part III, chapter 6). [16] Moser (2008), (2010), and (2013).

Additionally, Richard Swinburne has argued that if there is God who wants His creatures to acquire certain goods freely, then some epistemic distance between God and His creatures is necessary.[17] One such good is the inquiring and seeking to know whether God exists. A second good is discovering for oneself the answer to the question whether God exists. A third good is for creatures to have the ability to make certain moral choices freely, which would be inhibited by God's existence being obvious. A fourth good that epistemic distance from God makes possible is the choice for theists to help or not help those who are not sure of God's existence. Swinburne's point is that if God's existence were more obvious, then it would deprive humans of the opportunity to acquire a number of significant goods freely. So, if God desires His creatures to obtain these goods freely, then some divine-human epistemic distance is required.

How is this epistemic distance related to the appearance of gratuitous evil? The answer, I believe is that the appearance of gratuitous evil is the most effective way to create this epistemic distance. Notice that Hick claims the problem of evil is part of creating this epistemic distance:

> Thus the hypothesis of a divine purpose in which finite persons are created at an epistemic distance from God, in order that they may gradually become children of God through their own moral and spiritual choices, requires that their environment, instead of being a pain-free and stress-free paradise, be broadly the kind of world of which we find ourselves to be a part. *It requires that it be such as to provoke the theological problem of evil.*[18]

Seemingly gratuitous evils play an important role in preserving the requisite epistemic distance between creature and Creator essential for making possible a genuine, loving response to God in faith. One reason is that the evidential problem of evil is particularly well-suited to bring about the appropriate kind of epistemic distance for virtually all persons irrespective of their upbringing, geographical location, level of education, or period of history in which they live. Seemingly gratuitous evil is a fairly universal and efficient way to create epistemic distance between God and created persons. Secondly, if all evil appeared to be meted out in morally justified ways—in other words, if there were no instances of seemingly gratuitous evil—it would make the epistemic distance between God and creature vanishingly small. Imagine the kind of world where only those known to deserve evil received it in just proportions. In such a world if there were a disease outbreak, for instance, it would only infect those who were known to deserve it, and their suffering would be proportionate to their known wrongdoings. Those who appeared to deserve no ill would never have any haphazard evil affect them. I have a hard time believing

---

[17] Swinburne (1998: 210–11) and (2004: 267–72).
[18] Hick (1981: 48, emphasis added).

that in such a world, reasonable creatures could avoid concluding (on the pain of irrationality) that the hand of divine providence was carefully at work in preserving these fortuitous results. Consequently, the world would lack the kind of epistemic distance that is necessary for genuine faith.

The second positive value of mystery that Hick identifies is its role in provoking some of the greatest human acts of love and compassion. Hick invites his readers to consider a world with no apparently unjustified evil and suffering (as I did in the previous paragraph). He draws the following implications:

> In such a world human misery would not evoke deep personal sympathy or call forth organized relief and sacrificial help and service. For it is presupposed in these compassionate reactions both that the suffering is not deserved and that it is *bad* for the sufferer. We do not acknowledge a moral call to sacrificial measures to save a criminal from receiving his just punishment or a patient from receiving the painful treatment that is to cure him. But men and women often act in true compassion and massive generosity and self-giving in the face of unmerited suffering, especially when it comes in such dramatic forms as an earthquake or a mining disaster. It seems, then, that in a world that is to be the scene of compassionate love and self-giving to others, suffering must fall upon mankind with something of the haphazardness and inequity that we now experience. It must be apparently unmerited, pointless, and incapable of being morally rationalized. For it is precisely this feature of our common human lot that creates sympathy between man and man and evokes the unselfish kindness and goodwill which are among the highest values of personal life. No undeserving need would mean no uncalculating outpouring to meet that need.[19]

Seemingly pointless evil is, therefore, needed to bring about some of the most extraordinary acts of compassion and sympathy freely. In a world where all disasters and diseases only harmed those who appeared to deserve them in proportions appropriate to their just deserts, humans would not have the opportunity to exhibit feats of exceptional love, sympathy, and compassion. In order for God to provoke extraordinary human responses of love and self-giving, it is necessary for some evil to appear as if it is gratuitous. So, if God intends to bring about these kinds of responses through the free actions of his creatures, then the existence of seemingly gratuitous evils is required to achieve that end.

It is important to keep in mind that the positive skeptical theist is not claiming to understand the first-order justification for any allegedly gratuitous evil. The positive skeptical theist must confess that there is no apparent reason or justification that he knows of that justifies any given horrendous evil. What the positive skeptical theist does purport to understand to some degree is a second-order justification for why God may create a world where there are seemingly gratuitous evils. Indeed, the positive skeptical theist will claim that

---

[19] Hick (1978: 334–5).

if there is a God, we should *expect* the world to contain some seemingly gratuitous evils. As such, the two reasons sketched above for the positive value of mystery are supposed to be second-order justifications as to why God may create a world with seemingly gratuitous evils, although they are not intended to provide God's first-order justifications or God's first-order reasons to permit some apparently gratuitous evil. Positive skeptical theists are skeptical theists after all, and will claim not to know of any first-order reasons that justify those evils.

4. COMPARING FRAMEWORKS

At this point, I have sketched two frameworks in which to situate skeptical theism, but I have not argued that one is preferable to the other. To make my case that positive skeptical theism is the better framework, I will contend that the best way to avoid the deleterious consequences of skeptical theism that are pointed out by its critics is to adopt positive skeptical theism. To begin making this case, I will start out with an analogy comparing two meteorological theories. Then, I will present a straightforward comparison of the two using the odds form of Bayes's Theorem.

5. A METEOROLOGICAL ANALOGY

Suppose you are comparing two different theories (let's be boring and call them theory A and theory B) that make specific predictions about the weather. Over time both theory A and theory B accrue a number of anomalous data points. When advocates of theory A are asked about the mounting number of anomalies, they claim that the number of factors that go into predicting the weather are so numerous and our knowledge is so limited and feeble that we shouldn't be surprised to discover that any theory of meteorology will accumulate a large number of outlying data points. Proponents of theory B also admit that they have anomalies that remain unaccounted for by their theory. But they also have a second-order explanation as part of their theory that *predicts* there will be anomalies, because theory B includes some account of a large atmospheric situation that will consequently create conditions such that weather prediction will become unreliable periodically. Most theories can sustain some data that is not consistent with them. But in the long run, as more and more data runs counter to the theory, theories like theory B can remain meaningful theories with anomalous findings longer than theories like theory A can. As the anomalous results are amassed against theory A and the response to its failings is attributed to the frailty of the human cognitive condition, the impression is that the theory ultimately has nothing meaningful to say about the weather (it becomes consistent with all weather conditions). In other words, the accumulations of anomalies with theory A would ultimately confirm that humans cannot know much about weather prediction. Theory B, however, can take on a significant number of anomalies and remain a meaningful meteorological theory (perhaps by confirming the degree and size of the unusual atmospheric situation). Of course there are limits to the number and degree of the anomalies theory B can sustain before it too becomes meaningless. But the point is that theory B can endure more anomalous results than theory A and remain a meaningful statement of meteorology.

Negative skeptical theism, like the case of meteorological theory A, confirms that one's cognitive condition is so poor as to have no reliable grip on what is morally justified. With each case of seemingly gratuitous evil that must be offset by negative skeptical theism, it increases the degree to which one must admit that he must not have an accurate perspective or representative set of beliefs that are relevant to discerning the moral justification of some event. Consequently, the negative skeptical theist can maintain the logical possibility of theism in the face of any amount and degree of horrendous evil, but the cost may require sacrificing one's ability to hold any justified beliefs that are relevant to God's purposes and the moral justification of any event.[20]

Positive skeptical theism, however, can blunt the impact of seemingly gratuitous evils without immediately calling into doubt one's knowledge about the purposes of God or our knowledge that is relevant to making moral judgments and responses. The existence of seemingly gratuitous evils will confirm the positive skeptical theist's second-order purposes. Importantly, when it comes to making moral judgments and responding to apparent tragedy and injustice, the positive skeptical theist has good reason to believe that he should respond to these cases as we ordinarily believe we morally ought to (with actions of compassion, sympathy, and love), since this is one of the second-order purposes God has for creating a world with seemingly gratuitous evils. Rather than resulting in moral skepticism and paralysis, the positive skeptical theist is confirmed in his belief that the proper response to seemingly gratuitous evils is to act compassionately.

Of course there are limits to the extent that even positive skeptical theism can be called upon to defer the negative evidential impact of seemingly gratuitous evils. The degree of evidential impact that positive skeptical theism can deflect from seemingly gratuitous evils will depend on a number of factors. One of the most important ones depends on the justification that the positive

---

[20] For more precise statements of the problems of moral skepticism and paralysis for negative skeptical theism, see Almeida and Oppy (2003), Sehon (2010), Jordan (2006), Schnall (2007), Seigal (2010).

skeptical theist has for the second-order justifications in his skeptical theistic framework. The stronger his case is for these second-order justifications that lead him to expect the appearance of gratuitous evil, the more it can absorb the negative evidential impact of seemingly gratuitous evil. Another important factor is the positive skeptical theist's positive case for the existence of God that is independent of all considerations related to the evidential problem of evil. And, finally, the third factor is the quality and quantity of cases of apparent gratuitous evil. Since I am only discussing the epistemic framework, and not actually making a defense of theism using positive skeptical theism, I only need to add that the success of positive skeptical theism will depend on the values for each of these factors.

6. A BAYESIAN COMPARISON

Rather than leave my analysis at the rough and intuitive level given in the analogy above, I'll try to make my point clearer by using the odds form of Bayes's theorem to highlight the differences I see between positive and negative skeptical theism. The odds form of Bayes's theorem can be a useful tool for comparing the evidential merits of two hypotheses given the same evidence. Let's use "P" to refer to positive skeptical theism, "N" for negative skeptical theism, and "E" for the existence of some seemingly gratuitous evil. The odds form of Bayes's theorem yields the following comparison between the conditional probabilities of positive skeptical theism given some seemingly gratuitous evil and negative skeptical theism given some seemingly gratuitous evil.[21]

$$\frac{P(P\,|\,E)}{P(N\,|\,E)} = \frac{P(P)}{P(N)} \times \frac{P(E\,|\,P)}{P(E\,|\,N)} \tag{5}$$

The first expression after the equal sign in (5) is a fraction that provides a ratio comparison between the prior probability of positive skeptical theism and negative skeptical theism (hereafter, I will refer to this term as the prior probability ratio). The last term in (5) is the comparison of the probability that seemingly gratuitous evil would exist given positive skeptical theism and negative skeptical theism (hereafter, I will refer to this term as the likelihood ratio). Can we say whether the prior probability ratio or the likelihood ratio is equal, top-heavy, bottom-heavy, equal, or inscrutable? The prior probability ratio will be somewhat bottom-heavy, thus favoring negative skeptical theism, because

---

[21] For ease of reading I have omitted the ubiquitous background knowledge, which is usually denoted as "k," from all my probabilistic expressions.

positive skeptical theism is a hypothesis that includes more positive claims about the world. Both hypotheses include the existence of a personal, omnipotent, omniscient, wholly good God whose overall justification for permitting certain evils is beyond the cognitive abilities of human beings. Positive skeptical theism differs from negative skeptical theism by including that humans can discern some positive second-order reasons God may have for creating a world with seemingly gratuitous evils, such as its role in creating divine epistemic distance and eliciting great characteristics from created persons freely.

The likelihood ratio, however, will be extremely top-heavy. Since positive skeptical theism will either entail or highly probabilify the existence of seemingly gratuitous evil, and negative skeptical theism will not, the likelihood ratio is going to favor positive skeptical theism strongly. The top-heaviness of the likelihood ratio is going to exceed the weight of the bottom-heavy prior probability ratio. Thus, the comparison of the probabilities of positive and negative skeptical theism given seemingly gratuitous evil is favorable to positive skeptical theism.[22]

In the meteorology analogy, I have tried to emphasize something more than the results from the prior paragraphs. The real comparative value in positive skeptical theism is the way it manages numerous cases of seemingly gratuitous evil compared to negative skeptical theism. Once again, this is due to the fact that positive skeptical theism either entails or highly probabilifies the existence of seemingly gratuitous evils, whereas negative skeptical theism does not. So, the more accurate comparison between the two will represent the evidential impact of many seemingly gratuitous evils, E_1, E_2, ..., E_n.

$$\frac{P(P \mid E_1 \,\&\, E_2 \,\&\ldots\&\, E_n)}{P(N \mid E_1 \,\&\, E_2 \,\&\ldots\&\, E_n)} = \frac{P(P)}{P(N)} \times \frac{P(E_1 \,\&\, E_2 \,\&\ldots\&\, E_n \mid P)}{P(E_1 \,\&\, E_2 \,\&\ldots\&\, E_n \mid N)} \qquad (6)$$

The prior probability ratio in (6) is unchanged from (5), and so the assessment of that ratio remains the same; the prior probability ratio is bottom-heavy. The likelihood ratio in (6), though, is significantly more top-heavy than its counterpart in (5). Since positive skeptical theism yields the epistemic expectation that a significant number of seemingly gratuitous evils will exist and negative skeptical theism does not, then the existence of many seemingly gratuitous evils will render the likelihood ratio in (6) exceptionally top-heavy. This is the result that I intended to highlight with the analogy from the prior subsection. Thus, by including non-skeptical second-order justifications to support that seemingly gratuitous evil will exist given theism, the positive skeptical theist is in a better epistemic situation than the negative skeptical theist.

---

[22] It is important to notice that this does not take into account any arguments or evidence based on natural theology or revelation for or against positive and negative skeptical theism.

7. CONCLUSION

There are two frameworks in which skeptical theism can be situated. I have argued that the most well known version is negative skeptical theism, and its framework provides only skeptical second-order justifications for seemingly gratuitous evils. Consequently, negative skeptical theism results in confirming that humans may ultimately be ignorant about the nature of God and morality. My recommendation is that skeptical theists consider adopting positive skeptical theism as a corrective. By specifying non-skeptical second-order justifications God would have for creating a world with seemingly gratuitous evil, it weakens the confirmation that humans aren't able to know the nature of God and morality. Rather, positive skeptical theism provides a framework in which we should expect some evil to appear gratuitous, if there is God because there are a number of goods that are best achieved through the existence of seemingly gratuitous evils.

Perhaps to the disappointment of some, I have not provided anything more than a sketch of a couple of the second-order reasons God would have for creating a world with seemingly gratuitous evil. A more rigorous case for the veracity of any such second-order justifications will have to be left as further work in developing this strand of theodicy.

ACKNOWLEDGEMENTS

I would like to thank John Komdat, the editors of this volume, and several of my undergraduate students who have read this chapter and provided helpful feedback that urged me to improve various parts.

4

Why Skeptical Theism Isn't Skeptical Enough

Chris Tucker

The most common charge against skeptical theism is that it is too skeptical, i.e. it is committed to some undesirable form of skepticism or another. I contend that Michael Bergmann's skeptical theism (2001, 2009, 2012) isn't skeptical enough. I argue that, if true, the skeptical theses secure a genuine victory: they prevent, for some people, a prominent argument from evil from providing any justification whatsoever to doubt the existence of God. On the other hand, even if true, the skeptical theses fail to prevent even the atheist from justifiably accepting it.

In Section 1, I introduce the problem of evil and Bergmann's skeptical theses. It's popular to defend the most controversial premise of the argument from evil with a special kind of argument we can call a "negative generalization." In Section 2, I clarify one important feature of negative generalizations. In Section 3, I argue that, if the skeptical theses are true, then the atheist's negative generalization fails and the skeptical theist scores a genuine victory. In Section 4, I argue that Bergmann's skeptical theses do not tell us anything about whether we have some rational, non-inferential means of believing the controversial premise and, consequently, that the argument from evil may justify some in rejecting the existence of God.

1. SKEPTICAL THEISM AND THE PROBLEM OF EVIL

1.1 The Argument from Evil

I restrict my attention in this chapter to what Tooley (2009) calls *direct* arguments from evil. This kind of argument attempts to show that God doesn't exist directly, without comparing theism to any alternative hypothesis other than the mere denial of theism. The indirect approach, championed by Hume and Draper (1989), compares theism with some alternative other than its denial. It then claims that, given the sort of evil in the world, the alternative (often naturalism) is more probable than theism.[1] For the purposes of this chapter, we can focus on this simple version of the direct argument:

E1:   If God exists, God wouldn't permit the holocaust (or insert your pre-ferred evil) unless He had a good reason for doing so.

E2:   There are no good reasons for doing so.

E3:   Therefore, God does not exist.

E1 is fairly uncontroversial, at least if we can agree on an account of good reasons. Following Rowe (1979), something like the following account is usually granted at least for the sake of argument:

> R is a *good reason* for God to allow some evil E only if (i) R is a possible good G which entails E and R is at least as good as E is bad; or (ii) R is a possible evil, E entails ~R, and R is at least as bad as E. (cf., e.g. Alston 1991: 29–30; Bergmann 2009: 376; Hasker 2010: 16–7)

Given this account of good reasons, possible goods and evils can be good reasons to allow some evil E *provided* that they bear relevant entailment relations to E. Although I have a number of concerns about this account of good reasons, I will assume it for the sake of argument.

The most contentious premise is E2. How are we supposed to have justification for this premise? Following Rowe (1979, 1988, 1991) it is sometimes assumed that the argument for E2 should be a special kind of inductive generalization, namely a:

Negative (Universal) Generalization

NG1:   In the sample, no Fs are Gs.

NG2:   Therefore, no Fs are Gs.

Let us say that:

> R is a *potential reason* to allow some evil E just in case (i) R is a possible good G or (ii) R is a possible evil.

Every good reason is a potential reason, but not every potential reason is a good reason. The atheist's negative generalization begins with this notion of potential reasons. We survey all the possible goods and evils—i.e. the potential reasons for allowing the holocaust—that we know of. When we do this, we inevitably find one of two things. We find either that the relevant good

---

[1] I discuss Draper's argument very briefly in Section 5.

(evil) isn't good (bad) enough to outweigh the holocaust or that the good (evil) doesn't bear the requisite entailment relation to the holocaust. More formally, we get the following negative generalization:

NG-Reasons

E2a: In our sample (i.e. the potential reasons we can think of) no potential reasons are good reasons for allowing the holocaust.

E2:   Therefore, no potential reasons are good reasons for allowing the holocaust.

Michael Tooley (2008,[2] 2009) provides an argument for E2 that he takes to be a fundamentally different kind of argument for E2. I focus on NG-Reasons because Bergmann's skeptical theses were designed with NG-Reasons in mind, and I don't think that Tooley's argument enjoys any special advantages that NG-Reasons can't enjoy with some minor modifications.[3]

1.2 Bergmann's Skeptical Theses

Bergmann claims that NG-Reasons fails. To explain why, he directs us to the following skeptical theses:

(ST1)   We have no good reason for thinking that the possible goods we know of are representative of the possible goods there are.

(ST2)   We have no good reason for thinking that the possible evils we know of are representative of the possible evils there are.

(ST3)   We have no good reason for thinking that the entailment relations we know of between the possible goods and the permission of possible evils are representative of the entailment relations there are between possible goods and the permission of possible evils.[4]

---

[2] All references to Tooley (2008) are to Tooley's part of Plantinga and Tooley (2008).

[3] There are two key differences between Tooley's argument and NG-Reasons. First, Tooley's argument concerns right- and wrong-making properties rather than goods and evils. Even Tooley (2008: 132) seems to think that NG-Reasons can be recast in his preferred terminology. The other key difference is that NG-Reasons, and Rowe's argument more generally, focuses on whether there is a (defeasible) good reason for some evil, whether or not that good reason is defeated by further considerations. In contrast, Tooley focuses on whether there is an all-things-considered good reason to allow the relevant evil (e.g. see 2008: 124–6). Rowe's argument and NG-Reasons could be recast with this slightly different focus in mind. Hence, I think what Tooley says in defence of his argument can be applied to a suitably modified version of NG-Reasons.

[4] Bergmann sometimes considers a fourth skeptical thesis (see 2009: 379–80; 2012: 12). I ignore this additional thesis because I'm not sure I understand it and Bergmann holds that "it's not needed to make the skeptical theist's point" (2009: 379).

A key ingredient in each of these theses is the phrase "we have no good reason for thinking." This phrase is, I think, to be interpreted rather loosely. A strict reading would allow the following response: "Fine, we have no reason for thinking that the possible goods we know of are representative of the possible goods there are. But, given your proper functionalist account of justification, justification doesn't require reasons" (Bergman 2006: 63–4). Hence, for all ST1–3 says, "We might have lots of justification that the goods we know of are representative of the goods there are." I don't think Bergmann intended to leave this possibility open.

Taken at face value, the primary intention of the skeptical theses is to *deny* that we have a certain sort of reason, namely a good reason for believing that, e.g. the possible goods we know of are representative of the possible goods there are. I think, however, the intended import of the skeptical theses is to *affirm* that we have a certain sort of reason, namely an undefeated reason to *withhold judgment* about, e.g. whether the possible goods we know of are representative of the possible goods that there are. The connection between the denial and affirmation is not hard to see: our recognition that we don't have a good reason (or anything else that might make it rational) to believe that our sample is representative is itself a reason to withhold judgment about whether our sample is representative. To make this explicit, I suggest that we replace "We have no good reason for thinking that" with "We have undefeated reason to withhold judgment about whether."

Recall that NG-Reasons is essentially this argument: none of the potential reasons in our sample are good reasons, so no potential reason is a good reason for allowing the holocaust. If we combine Bergmann's skeptical theses, modified in the way explained above, we get:

ST1–3:   We have undefeated reason to withhold judgment about whether our sample of potential reasons for allowing the holocaust is representative of the potential reasons there are.

Recall that a good reason is a sufficiently strong possible good or evil that bears a relevant entailment relation to the holocaust. A potential reason is simply some possible good or evil. Each skeptical thesis essentially cites a different reason for what I am calling "ST1–3." We should withhold judgment about whether potential reasons are representative, because we should withhold judgment about whether our sample of goods, evils, and entailment relations is representative of the goods, evils, and entailment relations there are. I will focus on ST1–3 because it will make the sequel smoother. Recall that NG-Reasons secures its conclusion by generalizing from a sample. Ideally, any time we generalize from a sample, we know that our sample is representative. But if ST1–3 is true, we not only fail to know that our sample is representative, but we have justification for *withholding judgment* about it. How serious is this predicament? In the next two sections, I argue it is very serious indeed.

2. INDUCTIVE GENERALIZATIONS AND REPRESENTATIVENESS

2.1 Two Types of Representativeness

In this section, I identify the notion of representativeness that gives ST1–3 the best chance of posing a problem for NG-Reasons, whether or not it is the account of representativeness that is useful to, say, statisticians. In the next section, I argue that, given this account, ST1–3's truth would prevent NG-Reasons from justifying the claim that there are no good reasons to allow the holocaust.

There are at least two different senses in which a sample can be representative. A sample might be:

A-Representative: Some sample of Fs is *A-representative* with respect to G just in case, probably, if n/m Fs in the sample have G, then *approximately* n/m Fs have G.

Something like this sense of "representative" is useful to pollsters. Suppose we are trying to determine whether Obama will be re-elected. We might poll 1,000 voters and 700 of them might say they plan to vote for Obama. We might conclude that *approximately* 70% of voters plan to vote for Obama or, we might make "approximately" more precise by saying something like "70% of the voters plan to vote for Obama *with a 3% margin of error*."

Contrast A-representativeness with:

E-Representative: Some sample of Fs is *E-representative* with respect to G just in case, probably, if n/m Fs in the sample have G, then *exactly* n/m Fs have G.

E-representativeness is the more demanding sort of representativeness. E-representativeness clearly entails A-representativeness: if it is likely that exactly n/m Fs have G, then it is likely that approximately n/m Fs have G. Yet A-representativeness doesn't entail E-representativeness. Suppose that the total population is 1,001. It would be impossible for *exactly* 70% of the population to plan to vote for Obama. Our poll might nonetheless provide excellent reason for thinking that 70% *plus or minus* 3% plan to vote for Obama.

Depending on the type of inductive generalization at issue, both types of representativeness have their place. Consider:

Unqualified Inductive Generalization

(UG1)   n% Fs in the sample are Gs.

(UG2)   Therefore, n% Fs are Gs.

Qualified Inductive Generalization

(QG1)   n% Fs in the sample are Gs.

(QG2)   Therefore, approximately n% Fs are Gs.

With respect to qualified inductive generalizations, what matters, if anything, is that the premise <n/m Fs in the sample are G's> makes it likely that the conclusion <approximately n/m Fs are Gs> is true. A-representativeness seems sufficient for that purpose. But an unqualified generalization may need to be such that its premise makes it likely that *exactly* n/m Fs have G, which would require such arguments to be E-representative.

Qualified inductive generalizations are often sufficient for our purposes, because we only need a rough estimate of how many Fs are Gs. Yet suppose I'm considering whether to believe that there are (exactly) no red ravens. If only 1 red raven exists, it would be true that *approximately* no red ravens exist; however, it still would be false that *exactly* no red ravens exist. If I am to rationally believe that there are no red ravens on the basis of an inductive argument, I presumably need an *un*qualified inductive generalization that relies on an E-representative sample.

When it comes to the problem of evil, it is crucial that there be no good reasons to allow the holocaust. If there is even 1 good reason to allow the holocaust, then God, if He exists, was justified in allowing it. To pose a problem for theism, NG-Reasons presumably needs to make it likely that *exactly* 0 potential reasons are good reasons. Hence, when we consider NG-Reasons, the sort of representativeness at issue is E-representativeness.[5] Henceforth, whenever I use "representative" and its cognates, I will be referring to E-representativeness.

2.2 Representativeness and Reliability

Recall that a sample of Fs is (E-)representative with respect to G just in case, *probably*, if n/m Fs in the sample have G, then exactly n/m Fs have G. Consider again our generic negative generalization:

NG1:   In the sample, no Fs are Gs.

NG2:   Therefore, no Fs are Gs.

---

[5] In claiming that E-representativeness is the relevant notion, I am intentionally deviating from what Bergmann says about representativeness. Bergmann says, "To say a sample of Xs is representative of all Xs relative to a property F is just to say that if n/m of the Xs in the sample have property F, then approximately n/m of all Xs have F" (2009: 376). The main differences between E-Representativeness and Bergmann's notion is that the former has a "probably" qualifier but no "approximately" qualifier. Above I explain why the "approximately" qualifier is inappropriate in this context. The "probably" qualifier is needed for two reasons. First, it is needed to leave open the possibility that representativeness is required for an unqualified generalization to justify its conclusion. It might be required that the samples in our negative generalizations make it *likely* that no Fs are Gs, but it doesn't require that, in fact, no Fs are Gs. The second reason is that the 'probably' qualifier makes what I call 'RepReq3' less controversial. See note 9 on this point.

To say that the sample of this argument is representative is to say that, probably, if the premise is true, then the conclusion is true. But what does this probability operator amount to? I am using the term "probability" very loosely, such that *probably, if NG1, then NG2* is synonymous with each of the following:

(a) The (conditional[6]) probability of NG2/NG1 is >.5.

(b) NG1 (conditionally) reliably indicates NG2.

(c) It is likely that, if NG1 is true, then NG2 is true too.

In other words, I am making no sharp distinctions between probability, reliability, and likelihood. When the concept is used as an operator I tend to use "probably" or "it is likely that." In what follows I tend to use the term "reliably indicates," because it will be convenient to talk about the concept as a relation between the premise and conclusion.

We can say, then, that if a negative generalization's sample is representative, its premise reliably indicates its conclusion. But what type of reliability is at issue? Is it supposed to be bare statistical reliability, some modal reliability, logical probability, or is it just an oblique way of talking about evidential support? For every different conception of reliability, we will get a different notion of representativeness. And it might be that more than one sort of reliability and, consequently, more than one sort of representativeness is relevant to whether an unqualified inductive generalization justifies its conclusion. In what follows, I'm going to leave talk of reliability at an informal and intuitive level. This approach will leave a lot of questions unanswered, but it is the approach that is generally taken in the literature on the problem of evil, and trying to settle the issue would take us too far afield.

3. REPRESENTATIVENESS AND JUSTIFICATION

Recall that, if ST1–3 is true, we should withhold judgment about whether one's sample is reliable. The purpose of this section is to explain why, if ST1–3 is true, it follows that the atheist's negative generalization, NG-Reasons, fails. The short answer is that, if ST1–3 is true, then the atheist's negative generalization fails to satisfy a necessary condition on inferential justification. In Section 3.1, I'll identify the necessary condition that I think Bergmann has in mind, and in Section 3.2, I'll defend this necessary condition. The upshot will be that

---

[6] The "conditional" qualifier indicates that we are talking about the probability of NG2 *on the condition that* NG1 is true. A similar point holds for the qualifier in (b). I suppress the qualifier in all subsequent discussion.

the atheist's negative generalization fails and the atheist doesn't get what she really wants.

3.1 Representativeness Requirements

Although it may not be obvious which requirement Bergmann has in mind, it is clear that it has something to do with representativeness. Consider:

> **RepReq1:** S's negative generalization NG can make its conclusion justified only if NG's sample is representative of G.

NG, recall, is the argument that *in the sample no Fs are Gs therefore no Fs are Gs*. RepReq1 holds that my belief in the conclusion is justified only if NG's sample is in fact representative. As previously mentioned, a negative generalization's sample is representative with respect to G only if its premise reliably indicates its conclusion. Hence, RepReq1 says, in other words, that S's negative generalization justifies its conclusion only if the premise reliably indicates the conclusion. With this gloss, RepReq1 may sound like the sort of requirement that only reliabilists, such as John Greco (1999, 2000), would accept. Keep in mind, though, that we are working with a very generic understanding of reliability, and even internalists will say that one's premise needs to reliably indicate its conclusion in some sense; they will simply say that the relevant sort of reliability is necessary, knowable a priori, and that it doesn't entail statistical reliability in the actual world.

Regardless of whether RepReq1 is true, it's not the requirement that Bergmann thinks will be violated if ST1–3 is true. Bergmann doesn't say that it is *false* that our sample of potential reasons is representative.[7] What he says is that we have *no good reason* to think that our sample is representative, and that "we are seriously in the dark about whether the possible goods, evils, and entailments between them are likely to contain the makings of a potentially God-justifying reason to permit [the holocaust]" (2009: 379). Apparently, then, the problem of evil is supposed to fail because it violates some other requirement related to the representativeness of samples.

Consider:

> **RepReq2:** S's negative generalization NG can make its conclusion justified only if S has a justified belief that NG's sample is representative.

RepReq2 is closer to the relevant sort of requirement, as it concerns, not whether NG is in fact representative, but our epistemic access to whether this fact obtains. In fact, this requirement could certainly motivate skeptical theism

---

[7] Bergmann explicitly denies that this is what he is saying. See, e.g. his (2001: 284).

in the following way: "Given ST1–3, we do not have a justified belief that our sample is representative. But such a belief is required for a negative generalization to make its conclusion justified."

Although RepReq2 can underwrite Bergmann's skeptical theism, it is advisable that he choose a different route. Given the above account of representativeness, RepReq2 is tantamount to the claim that NG provides justification for its conclusion only if one has a justified belief that NG1 reliably indicates NG2. Philosophers will have two sorts of worries about claim. First, they will worry that it is psychologically implausible: "Since we do not ordinarily have beliefs of the relevant sort, given RepReq2, we would not justifiably believe the conclusions of our negative generalizations. Yet we are justified in believing at least some of these conclusions." Second, some philosophers will object that RepReq2 leads to Humean skepticism about induction. This worry will be especially pressing if Bergmann were to demand that one not only have a justified belief that NG's sample is representative, but also that the justified belief be *antecedent* to the conclusion's being justified. If Bergmann wants skeptical theism to be rather uncontroversial, he needs to look elsewhere.

A more uncontroversial requirement that can be used to underwrite Bergmann's skeptical theism is:

RepReq3: S's negative generalization NG can make its conclusion justified only if S doesn't have undefeated reason to withhold judgment or disbelieve that NG's sample is representative.[8]

If we recognize that we have no good reason to believe that our sample of potential reasons is representative, then we have reason to withhold judgment about whether our sample is representative. If RepReq3 is true and the reason isn't defeated, it follows that NG-Reasons cannot provide justification for believing its conclusion. Hence, RepReq3 seems strong enough to do the work Bergmann needs done. But is RepReq3 true?

3.2 Defending RepReq3

RepReq3 certainly seems very plausible. Consider an illustration. Suppose you are trying to determine whether there are any atheists at some particular school. The most pertinent information you know is that (i) in the sample

---

[8] One may argue: "If S doesn't have undefeated good reason to withhold judgment or disbelieve that NG's sample is representative, then S has good reason to hold that NG's sample is representative (cf. Fumerton 2006: 186); therefore, RepReq3 entails that one must have justification for representativeness." I tentatively reject the premise of this argument, but it doesn't matter for the purposes of this chapter. Requiring no reason to withhold is weaker and less controversial than requiring positive reason to believe that the sample is representative. If Bergmann wants his skeptical theism to be as uncontroversial as possible, he should go with RepReq3.

of students polled, no student was an atheist, (ii) the students were polled as they were leaving church on Sunday morning, and (iii) you justifiably withhold judgment as to whether this particular school requires students to sign a statement of faith. In such a case, a negative generalization from (i) would be irrational because (ii) and (iii) together provide you with a reason to withhold judgment about whether the sample is representative. Their conjunction doesn't provide a reason to *disbelieve* that the sample is representative, because given (iii), for all you know, the religious views of a sample of students leaving a church is representative of the students in the school.

RepReq3 also seems grounded in a more fundamental epistemic principle. Recall that, given the account of representativeness at issue, when you have reason to doubt that the sample of your negative generalization is representative, you doubt that your premise reliably indicates your conclusion. Now suppose that you provide what is in fact a sound proof of some mathematical theorem. This proof will not justify its conclusion if you also have undefeated reason to withhold judgment about whether the premises reliably indicate their conclusion. If you are really tired or you just discovered that you were drugged with something known to cause mistakes in reasoning, then you might have undefeated reason to withhold judgment about whether the premise reliably indicates its conclusion. In such circumstances, you would not be rational in accepting the proof, even though the proof is perfectly legitimate.

RepReq3 is, in other words, just a specific application of this more general principle: an argument *P therefore Q* can make its conclusion rational only if S doesn't have undefeated reason to withhold judgment or disbelieve that P reliably indicates Q. But there seems to be an even deeper principle at play. If I have reason to believe that certain experiences are not reliable indicators of their contents (e.g. I seem to see red, but someone tells me the wall is illuminated by red lights, so would look red even if it is not in fact red), then I am not rational in believing the contents of my experience, at least not in virtue of having the experience. Perhaps the deeper principle is something like this: a mental state M can provide justification for holding belief B only if the subject doesn't have undefeated good reason to disbelieve or withhold judgment about whether M reliably indicates B. In any event, the intuitions in favor of RepReq3 are strong, and it seems to be grounded in a more general principle that covers believing something on the basis of any experience or on (believing the premises of) any argument.[9]

[9] In note 5, I claimed that a notion of representativeness which included a probability operator would make RepReq3 less controversial. This sub-section explained why RepReq3 is very plausible when "representativeness" is defined so that it has a probability operator. The basic, widely-acknowledged point is that withholding judgment about whether your premise reliably indicates your conclusion is a defeater. Without the probability operator, E-representativeness would be defined in terms of a mere material conditional that has no tight connection with reliability. On such a notion, if we withhold judgment about whether the sample in our argument is representative, we are in effect withholding judgment about this material conditional: if my

3.3 Why the Skeptical Theist Would Earn a Genuine Victory

Bergmann is correct when he holds that, if ST1–3 is true, then the atheist's NG-Reasons fails. NG-Reasons, recall, is the argument *no potential reasons in the sample are good reasons therefore no potential reasons are good reasons.* Given ST1–3, NG-Reasons violates RepReq3. ST1–3 holds that we have undefeated reason to withhold judgment about whether NG-Reasons' sample is representative, which is equivalent to the claim that we have undefeated reason to withhold judgment about whether NG-Reasons' premise reliably indicates its conclusion. Yet this is precisely the sort of situation that RepReq3 says is incompatible with NG-Reasons' providing justification for its conclusion. Since ReqReq3 seems very plausible, if ST1–3 is true, NG-Reasons fails to provide justification to believe E2.[10]

Recall that, in this, we are focused on this version of the argument from evil:

E1:   If God exists, God wouldn't permit the holocaust unless He had a good reason for doing so.

E2:   There are no good reasons for doing so.

E3:   Therefore, God does not exist.

This argument will provide defeasible justification for the theist to believe that God doesn't exist only if *either* the theist has non-inferential justification for the premises *or* the atheist provides a good argument for any premise for which the theist doesn't have non-inferential justification. Let us suppose that at least some theists lack non-inferential justification for E2, which seems plausible. The atheist, then, needs to provide a good argument that E2 is true or

premise is true, then my conclusion is true too. It's more obvious to me that I have a defeater for an inductive generalization if I withhold judgment about *my premise reliably indicates its conclusion* than if I withhold judgment about the conditional *if my premise is true, my conclusion is too.* And while other epistemologists agree that I have a defeater if I withhold about the reliability proposition, they don't really discuss cases where I withhold solely about the mere material conditional. If I always get a defeater in the latter sort of case, then we could jettison the probability operator in E-representativeness and modify my arguments accordingly.

[10] Hasker complains that ST1–3 have a "strongly *anti-inductive* character" (2010: 20, emphasis original). If I understand Hasker—and I'm not sure I do—his argument is this:

If ST1–3 is true, then S's negative generalization justifies its conclusion only if S has a "fairly complete survey of the reference class in question." But this "fairly complete survey" requirement would lead to a fairly widespread inductive skepticism. So ST1–3 is false.

Hasker never explains why he thinks ST1–3 is committed to such a requirement, and I certainly don't see the connection. In any event, the universal generalizations that Hasker (2010: 21) wants to save plausibly concern regularities that hold in virtue of the laws of nature; the universal generalizations attacked by the skeptical theist don't seem to concern regularities that hold in virtue of the laws of nature. As Tooley (2009, sec. 3.2.3) suggests, it is plausible that our samples need to meet much higher standards in the latter sort of case. Hence, Hasker has failed to show that ST1–3 have some objectionably strong anti-inductive character.

likely true. The atheist puts forward NG-Reasons to secure E2; however, given ST1–3, NG-Reasons fails. It doesn't follow that this argument from evil fails to justify its conclusion for everyone, for perhaps atheists have non-inferential justification for E2 that some theists don't have. It does follow, however, that the skeptical theist achieves a genuine victory if ST1–3 is true, namely that a prominent argument for E2 fails.

4. THE SKEPTICAL THESES AND NON-INFERENTIAL JUSTIFICATION

In the previous section, I explained why the skeptical theses, if true, prevent NG-Reasons from justifying its conclusion. In this section, I explain why these theses do not cast doubt on any non-inferential way of justifiably believing E2, the claim that there are no good reasons to allow the holocaust. In sub-section 4.1, I give a positive argument for this conclusion. In each of sub-sections 4.2 and 4.3, I consider and reject a Bergmannian objection.

4.1 Non-Inferential Justification for E2 is Untouched

Suppose Mommy is looking for Baby. She quickly scans each room from its respective doorway and doesn't see Baby. Of course, she knows that she didn't look behind any big objects, check in any closets, or look under any beds. She then considers the following argument:

P1:   Baby wasn't in any of the places I looked.

C1:   Therefore, Baby isn't in the house.

She quickly realizes, though, that she has good reason to withhold judgment about whether the places she looked are representative of the places there are to hide (this time of day it's quite likely that Baby is hiding from Mommy), so she appropriately withholds judgment about the representativeness of her sample. Nonetheless, Mommy can be well-justified in believing C1 if she sees Baby chasing the cute Westie down the street. Hence, withholding judgment about the representativeness of her sample doesn't prevent her from acquiring justification for C1.

   One may object that this case doesn't get to the point: "What we want to know is whether Mommy can have some *non*-inferential way of acquiring justification for C1, even though she withholds judgment about whether the sample in P1 is representative. In the case at hand, one doesn't have non-inferential justification that Baby isn't in the house; rather, she infers it from her knowledge that he is running down the street." I'm inclined to think that Mommy might really see (non-inferentially) that Baby isn't in the house when she sees Baby running down the street, but assume the objection is correct.

Recall that representativeness of samples really boils down to reliability. To say of a negative generalization that its sample isn't representative is to say that its premise does not indicate its conclusion. But, generally speaking, when we hold that a premise does not indicate its conclusion, it doesn't follow that we can't know that the conclusion is true in some other way. Suppose Mommy sees a blue chair and then considers the following argument:

P2:   There is a blue chair here.

C2:   Therefore, Baby is chasing a cute Westie down the street.

She recognizes that P2 doesn't indicate C2 in the least, but she might have non-inferential justification for C2 because she sees Baby chasing the cute Westie. Generally speaking, then, withholding judgment about whether a premise reliably indicates a conclusion does not prevent one from having some non-inferential way of acquiring justification for the conclusion. So why should it do so in the special case of negative generalizations? I don't see any good answer to this question.

We can, moreover, construct a possible case in which one considers a negative generalization, the subject reasonably withholds judgment about the representativeness of the sample, and the subject nonetheless has a non-inferential justification for her conclusion. To see this, we need only modify the original Mommy/Baby case. Once again, Mommy considers:

P1:   Baby wasn't in any of the places I looked.

C1:   Therefore, Baby isn't in the house.

Can Mommy have non-inferential justification that Baby isn't in the house, when she withholds judgment about whether the sample in P2 is representative? Yes. To help see this, suppose that Mommy is an Alpha Centaurian. Evolution (or God) has given these creatures a remarkable survival-enhancing power. Every member of this species gives off a unique pheromone (or radiation or whatever). Before a child is born, the unique pheromone is encoded in the mother's brain. Although the process is draining and requires great focus, this encoding allows the mother to tell, within a few feet, where her child is, at least provided that the child is within range. We might even suppose that this way of locating Baby—call it "BabyTracker"—is well-understood by the science of the day. Mommy thinks very carefully about the question "Is baby in the house?" BabyTracker then makes it overwhelmingly and non-inferentially obvious that the answer is no.

Surely, it is possible for BabyTracker to provide non-inferential justification for C1, even though Mommy reasonably withholds judgment about whether the sample in P1 is representative. More to the point: justifiably withholding judgment about her sample's representativeness provides no reason at all for her to doubt her non-inferential way of knowing where Baby is. Likewise, suppose an atheist has a non-inferential way of knowing that there are no good reasons for allowing the holocaust. She can justifiably believe that there are no good reasons for allowing the holocaust, and this is so, even if she knows that her sample of potential reasons is unrepresentative of the potential reasons there are.

The analogy with Mommy and Baby suggests that ST1–3 doesn't prevent one from having non-inferential justification for E2, the claim that there are no good reasons for allowing the holocaust. We get further support for this conclusion when we consider that negative generalizations don't seem to be an exception to this general rule: a good reason to withhold judgment about whether one's premise reliably indicates the conclusion does not prevent the subject from having some non-inferential way of rationally believing the conclusion. However powerful these considerations may seem, Bergmann contends precisely the opposite, namely that the truth of ST1–3 would prevent one from having non-inferential justification for E2. He has two argumentative strategies, and we will consider one in each of the next sub-sections.

4.2 Bergmann's First Strategy: The Requisite Psychological States Don't Obtain

Multiple accounts of non-inferential justification can be used to defend the idea that one might have non-inferential justification for E2. Consider:

> **Phenomenal Conservatism (PC):** if it seems to S that P, then, in the absence of defeaters, S thereby has non-inferential justification that P.[11]

A seeming that P is an experience with the propositional content P and a special phenomenal character, called "assertiveness." Seemings, which are also referred to as "appearances", are assertive in that they "have the feel of truth, the feel of state which reveals how things really are" (Tolhurst 1998: 300). A priori intuitions and perceptual experiences are plausible candidates for seemings.[12]

PC holds that (in the absence of defeaters) if we have a certain kind of psychological state, a seeming that E2, we have non-inferential justification for E2, the claim that there are no good reasons for allowing the holocaust. I'm guessing most atheists have very strong and stable seemings to that effect, and even

---

[11] Defenses of PC include Huemer (2001), and my (2010) and (2011).
[12] Others, such as Swinburne (2001: 141), use the term "seemings" to pick out inclinations to believe rather than a special kind of experience or propositional attitude.

some theists report having such seemings (e.g. Dougherty 2008; Swinburne 1998: 20–8). Assuming that these reports are accurate, PC entails that at least some of us have prima facie justification for E2.

I focus on PC because it makes the problem for Bergmann especially clear and decisive, and there is an existing debate about whether a view like PC poses trouble for skeptical theism.[13] Yet reliabilists and proper functionalists also can rely on seemings to defend the idea that one might have non-inferential justification for E2.

Regarding reliabilism, since seemings can figure into reliable processes and can constitute reliable grounds, they can justify beliefs—or at least be integral parts of the processes that justify beliefs. Presumably, most reliabilists think that perceptual seemings play integral roles in justifying perceptual beliefs. In principle, there is nothing preventing the reliabilist from saying that a seeming that E2 plays a similar role in justifying a belief in E2.

Regarding proper functionalism, we know what we are designed to do, in large part, by knowing what we actually do. We all base beliefs on the way things seem, so it is plausible that we are designed to believe things on the basis of the way things seem. For example, most proper functionalists presumably think that perceptual seemings play integral roles in justifying perceptual beliefs. In principle, there is nothing preventing the proper functionalist from saying that a seeming that E2 plays a similar role in justifying a belief in E2. Hence, there are multiple accounts which can be used to defend the idea that a seeming that E2 justifies E2 (or is part of the reliable or properly functioning process that justifies E2).

Bergmann's response to such maneuvers is to deny, not the relevant accounts of non-inferential justification, but that we are ever in the relevant psychological state. He says, "According to [ST1–3], it *doesn't* appear that there is no God-justifying reason for permitting [the holocaust]" (2009: 386). Unless Bergmann means something unusual by "appear," he is simply mistaken. ST1–3 doesn't say anything directly about what experiences or seemings we have. At best, it implies that our seemings concerning potential reasons are not sufficiently plentiful or variegated to ensure that our sample of potential reasons is representative of the potential reasons there are. Yet E2 can seem true, even if our sample of potential reasons is unrepresentative or even if we have reason to withhold judgment about its representativeness.

---

[13] See Swinburne (1998: 20–8) vs Bergmann (2009: 386–9); and Dougherty (2008) vs Matheson (2011), and Bergmann (2011).

4.3 Bergmann's Second Strategy: Deny that
E2 is Common Sense

In a recent paper, Bergmann argues that skeptical theism can be reconciled with:

> *Commonsensism:* the view that (a) it is clear that we know many of the most obvious things we take ourselves to know (this includes the truth of simple perceptual, memory, introspective, mathematical, logical, and moral beliefs) and that (b) we also know (if we consider the question) that we are not in some skeptical scenario in which we are radically deceived in these beliefs. (2012: section I.A.)

At one point in the argument, Bergmann considers a possible objection, according to which, the atheist "can just see directly that a perfectly loving God is *unlikely* to permit the suffering in question and so she knows that God is *unlikely* to have [a good reason] to permit it" (2012: II.A, emphasis original). Bergmann responds that this claim isn't a matter of common sense. I agree. This claim is hardly one of the most obvious things we take ourselves to know. Indeed, some of us, e.g. Bergmann, think it is false. Yet Bergmann then concludes that "A thoughtful person ... will, therefore, refrain from concluding, of any particular instance of horrific suffering we know of, that a perfectly loving God wouldn't permit *that*" (II.B).

The assumption that Bergmann seems to be relying on here is that, if a claim isn't common sense, then one doesn't or can't have a non-inferentially justified belief that it is true. Yet this assumption is mistaken. An expert mathematician might have a non-inferentially justified belief that some argument is valid, even though the argument is too complicated for most of us to understand. Many people find it intuitive that there could be swamppeople or zombies, or that the correct answer in the trolley problem is to pull the switch, or that my nose and keyboard do not jointly compose some third material object. Presumably, their intuitions provide them with some degree of prima facie justification (at least given PC) even if that prima facie justification is ultimately defeated. Perhaps this prima facie justification is defeated by an awareness that many of one's peers disagree with one, but these claims would not be common sense even setting aside such a defeater. Hence, we often have non-inferential justification for a claim without its being common sense.

Although Bergmann is correct that E2 isn't common sense, he is wrong to infer that no one has non-inferential justification for it. It is not unusual for a claim to be non-inferentially justified for someone even though it fails to count as common sense. And, as we saw in the previous sub-section, given some accounts of non-inferential justification, it follows that at least some of us have non-inferential justification for E2. I conclude that ST1–3 tells us nothing about whether we have non-inferential justification for E2. If we take people's reports of their seemings seriously and assume that PC is true, then we also can conclude that some, perhaps many people have non-inferential justification for E2.

4.4 Why the Skeptical Theist's Victory Wouldn't be Complete

Skeptical theism is a complete response to an argument from evil only if it prevents anyone, including the atheist, from justifiably believing that God exists on the basis of that argument. We saw, in Section 3, that if ST1–3 is true, Bergmann scores a genuine victory, namely that a prominent argument for E2 fails. We see, in this section, that the victory isn't complete. The argument from evil may not even defeasibly justify disbelief in God for those who, like Bergmann, have no seeming that E2 is true. Others, however, have strong and stable seemings that E2. Given some respectable accounts of non-inferential justification, these seemings would yield non-inferential justification for E2. Hence, Bergmann's skeptical theses cannot prevent the argument from evil from justifying its conclusion for those people.

Perhaps, though, there is some indirect way that Bergmann's skeptical theses can prevent non-inferential justification. I can report that, after considering Bergmann's skeptical theses and skeptical theism more generally, my seemings in favor of E2 are much weaker and less stable than they used to be. A lot of the time, it seems to me that I can't tell whether E2 is true. In my case, reflection on the skeptical theses has prevented me from having the sort of seemings that would provide strong and stable non-inferential justification for E2. But it doesn't have this effect on everyone—indeed, it may have the opposite effect on some, whereby one gets even stronger seemings that E2 is true.[14] ST1–3 can prevent non-inferential justification for those who lose the relevant seemings upon considering them; however, given respectable accounts of non-inferential justification and that one continues to have the relevant seemings, ST1–3 is powerless to prevent one from having non-inferential justification for E2.

5. CONCLUDING REMARKS

This has been an attempt to determine what follows from Bergmann's skeptical theses. I have argued that the skeptical theses, if true, proffer a skepticism strong enough to gain a partial victory, namely crippling an important argument for a key premise in a popular argument from evil. On the other hand, the skepticism proffered by those skeptical theses doesn't pose a problem for non-inferential ways of acquiring justification for that key premise. Hence,

---

[14] cf. what Plantinga says about the effects of moral disagreement at the end of his (1995).

Bergmann's skeptical theism isn't skeptical enough to prevent everyone from justifiably accepting the relevant argument from evil.

Yet even the partial victory is in doubt. It is conditional on the *truth* of the skeptical theses, and Bergmann has not yet adequately defended his skeptical theses. My concern is that he doesn't rule out a salient way of defending the representativeness of our sample of potential reasons. Bergmann (2009: 385–6) seems to admit that his skeptical theses don't address Draper's indirect argument from evil if Draper relies on the principle of indifference in a certain sort of way. Yet Tooley (2008: 126–31; 2009: section 3.5) defends the representativeness of our sample of potential reasons using a very similar strategy. So Bergmann's defense of the skeptical theses needs to be supplemented by an attack on certain uses of the principle of indifference and other resources that are available to inductive logicians and Bayesians. Hence, more work needs to be done before Bergmann's skeptical theses secure even a partial victory.[15]

[15] Thanks to Michael Bergmann, Nevin Climenhaga, Trent Dougherty, Paul Draper, Matthew Flanagan, Tom Flint, Jon Matheson, Sam Newlands, Joshua Siegal, and the audience at Notre Dame's Center for Philosophy of Religion for their helpful comments on earlier versions of this chapter.

5

Minimal Skeptical Theism

Todd R. Long

1. INTRODUCTION

I will argue that what I call *minimal skeptical theism* is strong enough to cast doubt on a premise in recent evidential arguments from evil and weak enough to be epistemically rational to believe by typical theists, agnostics, and atheists who are familiar with those arguments. I will also respond to the popular complaint that the knife of skeptical theism is sharp enough to excise central features of a robust religious form of life: I will argue that accepting minimal skeptical theism need not undermine the justification that religious theists have for believing religious and moral propositions, and it need not motivate moral paralysis.

Daniel Howard-Snyder (2009) points out that skeptical theism has been used as a strategy for resisting a family of atheistic arguments, which depend on what he calls

> *The Inference*: On sustained reflection, we do not see how any reason we know of would justify God in permitting all the evil in the world; therefore, there is no reason that would justify God (17).

An idea motivating *The Inference* is this: if we do not know of any goods that would justify God in allowing evil, then it is reasonable for us to believe that there are no such goods. Why anyone believes this motivating idea is puzzling. Michael Bergmann (2001) persuasively argues that the success of the relevant atheistic arguments depends on its being reasonable to believe that "the possible goods we know of are representative of the possible goods there are" (279). Consider some implications of that proposition: the possible goods there are would be known by a perfect creator (were there to be one); thus, common to the atheistic arguments at issue is the assumption that the reasons we have for thinking that a perfect creator would be justified in allowing the evil we know about track the reasons (if any) that would justify a perfect creator in allowing that evil; but, obviously we would not track those reasons if God were real and we were to fail to know God's reasons; consequently, the relevant atheistic arguments assume that if God were real, then we would know why God's reasons justify God in allowing the evil we know about. Such thoughts motivate the following atheistic reasoning: [*First Premise*]: if God (an all-powerful, all-knowing, wholly good creator of the universe) were real, then we humans would know why God's purposes justifiably allow the evil that we know about; but, it is assumed, [*Second Premise*] we do not have this knowledge; thus [it is concluded], there is no God.

Although proponents of skeptical theism can coherently engage in theodicy in an attempt to cast doubt on the second premise, their characteristic response is that theodicy is not required to resist the argument, for there is reason to doubt the *First Premise*. The reason becomes salient from an attitude of proper epistemic humility, which aids us in attending to the fact that, due to our cognitive limitations, we are in no position to know what would be all of a perfect creator's purposes; consequently, we are in no position to know that if God were real, then we would know why God's purposes justifiably allow evil.

Howard-Snyder (2009) points out that one need not be a theist to have a good reason to accept the characteristic "skeptical theism" response. In Section 2, I support my agreement with him by means of an argument from incomprehensibility. In Section 3, I consider and reject an objection, which turns on the claim that a *loving* perfect creator would see to it that we know why evil is permitted. In Section 4, I explain how religious theists can accept skeptical theism without being committed to unacceptable epistemic and moral consequences. In Section 5, I encourage a meditation on the propriety of the modest skepticism that minimal skeptical theism can partly motivate.

2. MINIMAL SKEPTICAL THEISM

We are ignorant about many things and we know it. Indeed, each of us is ignorant of *millions of truths* concerning states of affairs within twenty feet of our current locations (not to mention the rest of the universe or multiverse). Even experts are ignorant about much that concerns their areas of expertise.[1] Despite our immeasurable ignorance about the world, our feeble causal control over it, and our severe moral failings, some people have claimed to know many details about the justifying purposes that would be had by an all-powerful, all-knowledgeable,

[1] Examples: cosmologists don't know the size or density of the universe; biologists: how life began; physicists: why there are physical laws; cognitive scientists: how to explain consciousness; seismologists: when earthquakes will occur; politicians: how to achieve a morally upstanding world peace; economists: how to correctly predict future interest rates. Widespread disagreements among philosophers reveal even greater ignorance about philosophical matters.

wholly good creator. But, how could we know that a perfect creator's creating of a world that makes possible the obtaining of the goods that theodicies appeal to (e.g. free choice, agency, autonomy, love, magnanimity, mercy, empathy, compassion, soul building, and the overcoming of evil) fails to justify a perfect creator in permitting horrible evils? Is it that we know that, if our knowledge, power, and goodness were perfect, then there would be no horrors? Surely not, for we do not know what it would be like to be all-powerful, all-knowledgeable, and wholly good. Nevertheless, proponents of the atheistic evidential arguments under consideration assume that we *are* well-justified epistemically in believing that our own thinking about whether God (a perfect creator) would be justified in allowing evil is an accurate indicator of whether God would be justified in allowing evil. But that assumption is incredible.

Here is an argument. We know that we are severely limited in cognitive and other causal powers in comparison to what would be a perfect creator's cognitive and other causal powers; but we do not know what thoughts one would have if one were a perfect creator. Indeed, we are not in a position to be epistemically rational in believing that our minds can comprehend what would be the full purposes of a perfect creator. For all we are in a position to be epistemically rational in believing, what would be a perfect creator's purposes (if any) for allowing horrible evils, are too complex (or simple but otherwise beyond our cognitive power) to understand.[2] But, we would need to be in a position to be epistemically rational in believing that we can comprehend what would be a perfect creator's purposes (if any) for allowing horrible evils in order for us to be epistemically rational in believing *The Inference*, for it assumes that *our failing* to know why God's purposes allow for horrible evil makes it epistemically reasonable for us to believe that *God* has no purposes that justify God in allowing horrible evil.

Likewise, we would need to be in a position to be epistemically rational in believing that we can comprehend what would be a perfect creator's purposes (if any) for allowing horrible evils in order for us to be epistemically reasonable in believing the *First Premise*, for it assumes that *God exists only if we know why God's purposes allow the evils* we know about; but, of course, we would know why God's purposes (if any) allow those evils only if we were in a position to be epistemically rational in believing that we can comprehend what would be a perfect creator's purposes (if any) for allowing horrible evils.[3] The argument may be displayed thus:

3. We know that we are severely limited in cognitive and other causal powers in comparison to what would be a perfect creator's cognitive and other causal powers.

---

[2] My argument is inspired by Alston (1996b).

[3] Analogous to my argument about *The Inference*: my five-year-old son is not in a position to comprehend all my reasons for the family rules I justifiably enforce; so, he doesn't know that any

4. If (3), then we are not epistemically rational in believing that we can comprehend what would be the full purposes of a perfect creator.

5. We are not epistemically rational in believing that we can comprehend what would be the full purposes of a perfect creator. [3, 4]

6. If (5), then we are not epistemically rational in believing that what would be a perfect creator's purposes (if any) for allowing the evil we know about are not too complex (or simple but otherwise beyond our cognitive power) for us to grasp.

7. We are not epistemically rational in believing that what would be a perfect creator's purposes (if any) for allowing the evil we know about are not too complex (or simple but otherwise beyond our cognitive power) for us to grasp. [5, 6]

8. If (7), then we are not epistemically rational in believing that we can comprehend what would be a perfect creator's purposes (if any) for allowing the evil we know about.

9. We are not epistemically rational in believing that we can comprehend what would be a perfect creator's purposes (if any) for allowing the evil we know about. [7, 8]

10. If (9), then we are not epistemically rational in believing that any reasons we can think of include all the justifying reasons (if any) that a perfect creator could have for allowing the evil we know about.

11. We are not epistemically rational in believing that the reasons we can think of include all the justifying reasons (if any) that a perfect creator would have for allowing the evil we know about. [9, 10]

12. If we are epistemically rational in believing either *The Inference* or the *First Premise*, then we are epistemically rational in believing that the reasons we can think of include all the justifying reasons (if any) that a perfect creator would have for allowing all the evil we know about.

13. We are epistemically rational in believing neither *The Inference* nor the *First Premise*. [11, 12]

Assuming neither theism nor atheism, my argument is intended to appeal to theists, agnostics, and atheists alike. The argument from Premise 11 to 13

---

reasons he can think of include all the reasons I have for my rules; thus, he doesn't know that his reasons accurately reflect the reasons that I have for my rules.

Analogous to my argument about the *First Premise*: I have tried but sometimes failed to explain the reason I have for disciplining my son, and these failure-to-comprehend experiences have given him reason to think that there are ideas I have with respect to the family rules I enforce that he doesn't understand. Thus, he doesn't know (because he isn't epistemically rational in believing) that, if I were to exist, then he would know why I justifiably enforce all my family rules.

constitutes what I think of as *minimal skeptical theism*, for it provides good reason to think that the relevant atheistic arguments from evil are failures (even if their conclusions are true). The reasoning from Premise 3 to 11 strikes me as a sound, nonpartisan argument for the key premise (11) in minimal skeptical theism.

3. A NONPARTISAN CHALLENGE TO MINIMAL SKEPTICAL THEISM

There is a line of reasoning worth taking seriously that challenges Premise 6 and, if successful, provides support for the *First Premise* and *The Inference*. This reasoning utilizes an inference about what would be a perfect creator's *perfect love* of all things, including persons like us who are capable of suffering (because we are capable of reflection on evils that befall us). The idea is that, even if we cannot comprehend the full purposes of a perfect creator, no creator would be perfectly loving toward us without giving us knowledge of the reason that the creator allows all the evil which causes our suffering. The idea is put to use in the following three arguments:

14. If God were to exist, then God would be perfectly loving toward all persons who are capable of suffering.

15. If God were perfectly loving toward all persons who are capable of suffering, then we (who are capable of suffering) would know why God's purposes allow all the evils we know about.

16. Thus, the *First Premise* (if God were to exist, then we would know why God's purposes allow all the evils we know about). [14, 15]

17. If we were to know why God's purposes allow all the evils we know about, then our reasons for believing that God is justified in permitting the evils we know about would track the justifying reasons (if any) God has in permitting the evils we know about.

18. If our reasons for believing that God is justified in permitting the evils we know about were to track the justifying reasons (if any) God has in permitting the evils we know about, then *The Inference* would be true.

19. If God were to exist, then *The Inference* would be true. [14, 15, 17, 18]

20. If we were to know why God's purposes allow all the evil we know about, then we would be in a position to know that we are able to comprehend what would be a perfect creator's reasons (if any) for allowing all the evil we know about.

21. If we were to be in a position to know that we are able to comprehend what would be a perfect creator's reasons (if any) for allowing all the evil we know about, then Premise 6 would be false.

22. If God were to exist, then Premise 6 would be false. [14, 15, 20, 21]

In each argument, Premise 15 is the key premise. Its initial plausibility draws from the thought that a perfectly loving creator would not want that creator's suffering-capable creatures to suffer as a result of the creator's creation without explaining to such creatures why the creator created as the creator did.[4] Such a thought may derive from reflection about possible cases of love between humans. It can seem cruel, rather than loving, for me to do something that I know will allow you to suffer, all the while knowing that what I am doing is justified, without informing you of my justification. If I love you, then I care about your welfare for your own sake. Withholding my reasons for allowing you to suffer suggests a lack of care for your welfare. Thinking along these lines can motivate belief in Premise 15.

Despite the plausibility of the general idea when we reflect on typical cases of human love, there are reasons to deny Premise 15. Consider first that there are human cases in which there is no lack of love demonstrated by one's with-holding justifying reasons for doing something that allows a beloved to suffer. There was a time when I allowed my young son to try to walk, knowing that this almost certainly would result in numerous falls, which would sometimes produce in him pain and frustration. Nevertheless, my allowing my son to try to walk was both justified for me and expressive of my love for him. But, when he was learning, he was in no cognitive position to understand anything close to my reasons for allowing him to try to walk; he just couldn't appreciate all the good that my allowing him to try to walk would make possible for his life; neither could he grasp anything close to the depth of my love for him. Thus, I was not guilty of refraining from loving him by withholding my reasons for allowing him to try to walk.

The example is useful as an analogy when combined with the central idea of Section 2. We are in no epistemic position to know that we finite beings can comprehend or appreciate what would be a perfect creator's reasons (includ-ing all the reasons that pertain to a perfect creator's love for us) for allowing us to suffer; and, if we cannot comprehend such reasons, then a perfect creator would not fail to love us by withholding those reasons; thus, we do not know that a perfect creator would fail to love us by withholding the divine reasons for permitting us to suffer. Hence, we have reason to doubt Premise 15.[5]

---

[4] Variations on this reasoning appear in Rowe (1996: 276), and Dougherty (2012).
[5] For a recent criticism of parent-child analogies, see Dougherty (2012).

4. ROBUST RELIGIOUS THEISTS AND MINIMAL SKEPTICAL THEISM

Suppose that a religious theist, say, a Christian, believes minimal skeptical theism on the basis of the reasons I have mentioned. Do such reasons undermine the epistemic justification the Christian has for believing the life-orienting propositions that are part of his or her Christian form of life? Some critics have thought so.[6] The criticism applied to *minimal skeptical theism* (hereafter, "MST"): if one is committed to MST, then one is committed to ignorance about whether one's own reasons track God's reasons; consequently, the Christian may believe life-orienting propositions such as *God is calling me to relinquish trust in my self-will to power*, or *the good news in Christ is the power of God for salvation to everyone who has faith*, but, if the Christian believes MST, then for all the Christian claims to be in a position to know, God has some justifying but humanly inscrutable reason for deceiving the Christian about such matters; thus, the Christian who accepts MST must, on pain of inconsistency, accept religious proposition skepticism.

Critics have said that the same problem applies to moral beliefs,[7] and some have claimed that commitment to skeptical theism motivates moral paralysis or undermines moral decision-making.[8] The reasoning: in any case in which a religious skeptical theist is deliberating about what morally ought to be done, he will have, by way of MST, a reason to be in doubt about what morally ought to be done (perhaps God has some justifying but humanly inscrutable reason to permit the event at issue); but, if so, then one can for one's own reasons be morally paralyzed in situations—such as when one sees a small child beginning to drown—in which it seems obvious to us what one morally ought to do.

Despite these charges, it is plausible that some religious theists can reasonably believe MST without thereby undermining the justification they have for believing various religious and moral propositions and without moral paralysis being justified for them. Some especially plausible cases involve what I call "robust religious theists", by which I mean pious practitioners of a theistic religion who earnestly believe themselves to be in a process of moral transformation by means of their relation to a personal God worthy of unqualified worship, and whose lives display evidence of significant moral transformation.

Consider a robust religious theist who is a Christian. He routinely engages in practices such as worship, the partaking of sacraments, prayer (thanksgiving, adoration, contemplation, petition, etc.) and other spiritual disciplines (such as solitude and fasting), scripture reading, discipleship training, and service to

---

[6] See Beaudoin (2005) and Piper (2008).

[7] See Beaudoin (2005), Hasker (2010), Jordan (2006), and Rancourt (2013).

[8] See Almeida and Oppy (2003), Maitzen (2007), Piper (2007, 2008), Rancourt (2013), and Sehon (2010).

others. Some of his religious experiences involve what strike him obviously as God's calling him to become aware of ways in which his own desires, standing dispositions, and motivational structures produce fear, anger, and contempt that result in selfish, prideful behaviors and which prevent him from expressing the *agape*-love of all creation that the New Testament teaches is the ultimate spiritual goal. Sometimes he responds by what is often described as a giving up, or a surrendering, of his selfish desires to God. Such a giving up requires him to realize that his primary problem is not the social structures he encounters but is rather the evil within himself. This realization he experiences as painful but profoundly liberating. The words of Jesus and the New Testament apostles come to life for him as he understands that his doing good in the world essentially depends on a fundamental moral transformation of his heart (i.e. his motivational center), rather than on making himself follow a set of rules in order to merit praise or reward. As a result of such experiences, he finds himself (often to his amazement) seeing the world in a new way, as it were. He finds himself with an increasingly heightened awareness of others' needs, finds himself thinking of ordinary physical objects as imbued with a value that he had not appreciated before, experiences a new inner peace concerning his place in the world and the meaning of his life, notices a diminishment of his old desires for personal recognition or domination of others, etc., and finds himself with an astounding feeling of gratitude toward God for what he takes to be the gift of his life. As his moral transformation progresses (albeit unevenly, as each new revelation about himself is an occasion for temptation to see himself as righteous and others as unrighteous), he finds himself increasingly performing what strike him as good actions that are much more in tune with the needs of others than he had earlier been capable of discerning. He detects what St. Paul calls "the fruits of the spirit" (Galatians 5:22–3) beginning to grow in him from his own motivational center.

I take it that a story along this line characterizes transformative experiences that many robust Christians have. Similar examples from philosophers are discussed by Thomas R. Kelly (1992), Paul Moser (2008, 2010), and Dallas Willard (1990, 1998). Because the human will plays a role and humans have various genetic and social histories, there is no single way to describe the process involved in a robust Christian's moral transformation from what is artfully depicted in Terrence Malick's *The Tree of Life* as "the way of nature" to "the way of grace." But, the testimony of many others yields reason to think that the phenomena I mention are commonly involved in Christian transformative processes.

Focus on the *humility* that is a necessary condition for such transformation. The characteristic Christian giving up of one's selfishness and pride requires in one a realization that one does not have it all figured out, that one is not doing it right, that one's own ways are the ways of destruction, leading one away from peace, love, and joy. In short, such giving up requires a profound sense of one's need for goods that one lacks. Such a realization resonates in the various affective and cognitive domains of one's conscious experience. But, precisely because one knows that one stands in cognitive, affective, and motivational need, the transformation requires *trust* that God is guiding one in the way of grace; consequently, one who is in the process of this kind of transformation is necessarily in an epistemic position of humility before God. Presuming to know God's full purposes or that one is righteous or that one has achieved spiritual maturity is a sure sign that one is off the good path.[9] Thus, minimal skeptical theism fits well with what I have identified as characteristic Christian transformational experiences.

It does not follow that the robust Christian knows nothing or lacks epistemic justification for many of the religious or moral propositions he believes. The trust in God that is central to the transformational process is neither blind nor is it motivated by mere wishful or hopeful thinking. It is evidentially supported by way of numerous experiences comprising the robust Christian's total evidence.[10] In my view the most promising theory of epistemic justification is some version of what Earl Conee and Richard Feldman (2008) call an "explanatory coherence view of evidential support":

> ... a person has a set of experiences, including perceptual experiences, memorial experiences and so on. What is justified for the person includes propositions that are part of the best explanation of those experiences available to the person....
>
> The best available explanation of one's evidence is a body of propositions about the world and one's place in it that makes the best sense of the existence of one's evidence. This notion of making sense of one's evidence can be equally well described as fitting the presence of the evidence into a coherent view of one's situation.... The coherence that justifies holds among propositions that assert the existence of the non-doxastic states that constitute one's ultimate evidence and the propositions that offer an optimal available explanation of the existence of that evidence. (98)

It seems very plausible to me that the set of experiences of a typical robust Christian evidentially support many of the Christian propositions believed, because those propositions are part of the best explanation of the existence of the robust Christian's total evidence. My brief argument for this claim starts with the insight from David Holley (2010) that we all have "life-orienting beliefs," which are beliefs that help us to get our bearings and formulate courses of action but which transcend the needs of particular situations. They are answers to questions such as "Who am I?," "How does human life fit within

---

[9] This is precisely Jesus's point about the blind man in John 9.

[10] My project here differs from that of Bergmann and Rea (2005): whereas they point out that typical theists (and atheists) have *abundant beliefs* to motivate them to moral action, I explain how robust religious theists can have *epistemic justification* for their religious and moral beliefs, which can rightly motivate them to moral action.

the larger order of things?," "What is important in life?," "How should I treat others?," and "What is the best way to deal with suffering?" These life-orienting beliefs are related to what Holley calls a "life-orienting narrative," which is the cognitive framework within which one's life-orienting beliefs have their role in one's cognitive economy. Examples of life-orienting narratives include naturalism, scientism, and the stories of religious traditions. One's life-orienting narrative is a kind of mental lens through which one makes sense of one's world, one's place in the world, what is good, etc. It has far-reaching consequences for one's cognition; for instance, it helps determine what one will take to be a fact, what actions one will take to be desirable or worthy, and how salient one will take certain experiences to be for belief.[11]

Most robust Christians—even many that are knowledgeable of religious diversity, arguments from evil, etc.—have some Christian life-orienting narrative involving the death and resurrection of Jesus as the means by which humans can be reconciled to God and non-coercively transformed by God to creatures who are in eternal communion with God and all of creation. The combination of the narrative and their various experiences yield for them many Christian life-orienting beliefs (e.g. *Jesus is my lord*, or *God is calling me to repentance through these texts*, or *through this suffering I am being transformed toward having the mind of Christ*, or *I should seek solitude to discern God's will about which career to pursue*, etc.). Surely their total experiences could make many of the Christian propositions they believe the best explanation available to them of their experiences, for those propositions can for them make the best sense of the existence of their total evidence. Robust Christians who have had morally transformative experiences along the lines I have sketched are especially good candidates for having epistemically justified Christian beliefs. After all, their significant moral transformation toward a motivational center characterized by *agape*-love of all creation is exactly what one would expect if the New Testament teaching—involving the depicted career of Jesus and the acts and teaching of the apostles, including the described work of the Holy Spirit—were true. The point is not that such transformational experiences, together with their concomitant charitable actions, prove or demonstrate the truth of the Christian propositions they believe; rather, it is that, for persons who have the relevant experiences, their evidence can make many of the Christian life-orienting propositions they believe part of the best explanation available to them of the existence of their total evidence.

Note that that the assumptions underlying minimal skeptical theism are, for many robust Christians, included in their epistemic package deal; for, their life-orienting narrative is derived in part from a two-part biblical theme according to which (a) the world was created by the almighty God whose ways,

---

[11] See Holley (2010, 2011).

thoughts, and purposes far outstrip those of finite humanity (see Isaiah 55:8–9; 40:28; Job 38:1–7; Job 11:7–8; Romans 11:33; and I Corinthians 2:11); and, (b) although God has not disclosed the divine reasons for permitting evil to test us (Deuteronomy 8; I Peter 1:6–7) or to perfect us (James 1:2–4), God has disclosed the method (*agape*-love) for achieving our good in overcoming evil (Colossians 1:15–20; I Corinthians 13). It is thus part of the robust Christian's life-orienting narrative and beliefs that she is a finite creature who is in no position to understand all of the almighty God's purposes. She knows that neither the Bible nor theologians nor Church teaching has fully explained the mystery of God's permitting evil, but she does not need all her questions answered in order reasonably to maintain the trust in God's leadership for her life that her experiences have confirmed to be trustworthy (any more than a child needs to know all of a parent's purposes in order reasonably to maintain trust in the parent's leadership). I conclude that a robust Christian's epistemically rational religious beliefs do not commit her to believing (a) that her own reasons track the reasons that God has to allow evil, and (b) that if God were to exist, then she would know why God's purposes allow the evils she knows about.

Is a robust Christian committed to sweeping moral skepticism? No. She sometimes finds herself performing acts of service that she has reason to believe are good, in light of her total evidence at the relevant time; thus, she is often epistemically justified in believing that performing some action is the morally right thing to do. Nevertheless, her sensitivity to her own moral weakness yields openness to new moral insight. As her transformation progresses, she finds herself to be increasingly discerning of what the world beyond her needs in light of her own abilities and gifts; consequently, what she reasonably believed last month to be best to do in situation X may differ from what she now reasonably believes best for her to do in situation X.

Suppose that she were to fail to perform an act that she has reason to believe is good. Could God allow that? Yes; and she has good reason to believe that God could allow such an evil because she has reason to believe that God's purposes include freely performed human volitions in the overcoming of evil (such a proposition is part of her life-orienting narrative). It does not follow that she knows what justifies God in permitting evil; neither does it follow that she cannot make mistakes about what is good or bad. She knows that her moral transformation is always in process; thus, humility characterizes her justified attitudes toward right action. Indeed, the litmus test her life-orienting narrative suggests is not whether she is right about moral propositions but rather is whether she is increasing in *agape*-love toward all creation, a test that requires examining the state of her heart as much as her behavior.

Such considerations reveal why moral paralysis need not follow from accepting MST. Although there may be situations in which it is not obvious what a robust Christian ought to do in order to express *agape*-love (e.g. should she give this homeless person $20 or offer to drive him to a shelter?), the robust

Christian's total evidence will often provide moral guidance. When she sees an easily savable child struggling to stay afloat, a typical robust Christian will have—by way of her own evidence—ample reason to think that she ought to try to save the child. Could it be that, if she fails to save the child and the child drowns, God will work to bring a good out of that evil that would not have come about without that evil? Of course: her life-orienting narrative and life-orienting beliefs assure her that God works, within whatever bounds the divine mind has prescribed for divine purposes, to bring about good in the world, no matter what the situation. But, that fact gives her no license not to try to save the child. She rightly judges herself to be in sin whenever she fails to act as her overall evidence gives her reason to believe that she ought.

5. TWO FINAL THOUGHTS

I have observed that some robust Christians have MST as part of their epistemic package deal, but what of atheists and agnostics? Most will not have as part of their epistemic package deal (via their life-orienting beliefs or life-orienting narrative) any commitment to *p: we are finite creatures of God who are in no position to presume to know the almighty God's full purposes pertaining to good and evil*. Does it follow that atheists and agnostics are not epistemically rational in accepting MST? No, and realizing why reveals one dialectical advantage to the proponent of MST. One's not being epistemically rational in believing *p* (a state of affairs that I presume to obtain for many atheists and agnostics) is not nearly sufficient for being epistemically reasonable in believing either the *First Premise* or *The Inference*. Once we appreciate how severely limited with respect to knowledge, power, and goodness we are in relation to *that which would be had by a perfect creator were there to be one*, then we thereby have reason to be in doubt about whether our own thoughts about what would justify a perfect creator in allowing evil track what would be a perfect creator's justifying purposes.

Second, to make my point in Section 4, I have relied on features of a certain kind of Christian theism: the kind of robust Christian I have described is not only reasonably as skeptical as MST requires, but such a Christian also maintains humility about many matters moral and epistemic, a humility that engenders a modest skepticism that is nevertheless broader than many critics are comfortable with.[12] I ask the critics to reflect on the moral status and actions of humanity in general, for I predict that they will thereby gain reason to think that epistemic principles supporting the claim that *humans usually*

---

[12] See, e.g. Hasker (2010).

know the good that ought to be done do not jibe with what we know of human history. A humble, modest skepticism about morality, combined with a strong desire to discover the good and the means to have it characterize our lives, strikes me as direly needed by humanity.

ACKNOWLEDGEMENTS

For helpful comments, I thank Trent Dougherty, Ken Walker, and an anonymous reviewer.

6

Replies to Long and Tucker

E. J. Coffman

I

Many thanks to this collection's editors, Trent Dougherty and Justin P. McBrayer, for the opportunity to reply to the outstanding chapters by Todd Long and Chris Tucker. I have thoroughly enjoyed reading and reflecting on these chapters, and have learned a lot from them, as I know their other readers will as well. Alas, as it typically goes in Philosophy (and as I've been hired to do), I must now repay my friends' fruitful efforts with some critical assessment.

In this reply piece, I have two main goals. First, I aim to show that what Todd calls *minimal skeptical theism* has the weakness that Chris ascribes to Bergmann's *skeptical theism* in §4 of his chapter. That is, I aim to show that Todd's minimal skeptical theism fails to completely incapacitate a salient version of the argument from evil, and therefore is not (in Chris's words) a "complete response" to the argument from evil. Second, I'll try to defend, from the argument Chris develops in §4 of his chapter, the claim that Bergmann's skeptical theism really *does* completely incapacitate its target argument from evil.

Let's distinguish, here at the outset, between two different arguments from evil that we meet in the chapters by Chris and Todd. First, there's what I'll call

Chris's Focal Argument from Evil (p. 46)

E1: If God exists, God wouldn't permit the holocaust unless He had a good reason for doing so.

E2: There are no good reasons for doing so.

E3: Therefore, God does not exist.

Second, there's what I'll call

Todd's Focal Argument from Evil (p. 64)

First Premise: If God were real, then we humans would know why God's purposes justifiably allow all the evil we know about.

Second Premise: We do not have this knowledge.

Conclusion: There is no God.

These arguments differ in some significant ways. Assuming that knowledge is factive, First Premise is logically stronger, and as a result at least somewhat less plausible, than E1. On the other hand, E2 is logically stronger, and accordingly at least somewhat less plausible, than Second Premise. In what follows, I'll be focusing mainly (though not quite exclusively) on *Chris's* Focal Argument from Evil. My reason for this is twofold. First, I think Chris's Focal Argument from Evil looms larger in the literature on the evidential/inductive argument from evil and skeptical theism than does Todd's Focal Argument from Evil (which is reminiscent of argumentation we find in the literature on divine hiddenness). Second, Chris's Focal Argument from Evil seems to me to stand a better chance of success than does Todd's Focal Argument from Evil. The difference in plausibility between (the more plausible) E1 and (the less plausible) First Premise strikes me as greater than the difference in plausibility between (the more plausible) Second Premise and (the less plausible) E2—with the overall result that the conjunction of E1 and E2 strikes me as more plausible than the conjunction of First Premise and Second Premise.

II

Todd's minimal skeptical theism is the following argument (p. 66, my emphasis):[1]

11. We are not epistemically rational in believing that the reasons we can think of include *all* the justifying reasons (if any) that a perfect creator would have for allowing the evil we know about.

12. If we are epistemically rational in believing either *The Inference* or *First Premise*, then we are epistemically rational in believing that the reasons we can think of include *all* the justifying reasons (if any) that a perfect creator would have for allowing all the evil we know about.

13. We are epistemically rational in believing neither *The Inference* nor *First Premise*. [11, 12]

---

[1] Two notes in one. First, I'll simply carry over Todd's labels for the three propositions that constitute (what he calls) minimal skeptical theism. Second, recall what Todd labels *The Inference* (p. 63; cf. Howard-Snyder 2009: 17): "On sustained reflection, we do not see how any reason we know of would justify God in permitting all the evil in the world; therefore, there is no reason that would justify God."

I want to argue two critical points about Todd's minimal skeptical theism. The first critical point is, I think, relatively minor and legalistic: (12) is too strong, in the sense that it implies an implausible skepticism about epistemic justification (rationality).

Following Chris (see section 2.1 of his chapter), let's understand (what Todd calls) The Inference as being an instance of the following inductive argument schema:

Unqualified Inductive Generalization (p. 49)

(UG1)   n% Fs in the sample are Gs.

(UG2)   Therefore, n% Fs are Gs.

Now, once we generalize Todd's (12), it will have the following consequence:

(12-Consequence) A claim of the form UG1 epistemically justifies (rationally supports) a claim of the form UG2 for a thinker, T, *only if* T is justified in believing that T's sample of Fs includes *all* extant Fs.

(12-Consequence) has the following implication: if you're justified in believing that—or even justified in withholding whether—there are Fs lying outside your sample, then no claim of UG1's form epistemically justifies (rationally supports) for you a claim of UG2's form. Another way to put it: (12-Consequence) implies that (what Chris calls) Unqualified Inductive Generalization justifies only if you're justified in believing that the relevant sample is *exhaustive*. Since this implication leads quickly to an implausible skepticism about epistemic justification (rationality)—a kind that, I assume, Todd would want to avoid—, we should reject Todd's (12) on the grounds that it places too strong a condition on having justification to believe *The Inference*. As currently stated, then, Todd's minimal skeptical theism doesn't defeat *either* of our Focal Arguments from Evil.

Of course, Todd could avoid this objection by replacing "... include all ..." with something that would yield a logically weaker, more plausible requirement on having justification to believe *The Inference*. One natural candidate, especially in the present context, is Chris's "... are E-representative of ..." (p. 49). The revised version of (12) would be logically weaker and significantly more plausible. The revised version of (11) would be logically stronger but not, to my mind, significantly less plausible. Such a revision would, I think, make Todd's minimal skeptical theism quite similar to Chris's presentation and development of Bergmann's skeptical theism.

We can set aside this first, rather legalistic objection to Todd's minimal skeptical theism, for there's a second problem that's much harder to solve: minimal skeptical theism really does have the weakness that, according to Chris, plagues Bergmann's skeptical theism.[2] Minimal skeptical theism lacks the resources to

---

[2] I'll clarify what I mean by "Bergmann's skeptical theism" in the next section. For the moment, we can proceed without such clarification.

completely incapacitate Chris's Focal Argument from Evil. As Chris would put it, Todd's minimal skeptical theism isn't a "complete response" to the relevant argument(s) from evil.

To begin to see this, imagine an advocate of Chris's Focal Argument who eschews *The Inference* and instead claims that we can have *non-inferential* justification—arising from relevant exercises of moral/evaluative perception/intuition—to believe E2. Armed only with Todd's minimal skeptical theism, what can we say to such a philosopher?

Not much, so far as I can see. First, the portion of minimal skeptical theism which claims that we lack justification to believe *First Premise* is perfectly consistent with our having justification to believe E1 (recall that the former is considerably logically stronger than the latter). Proponents of Chris's Focal Argument from Evil could therefore coherently concede to Todd that we lack justification to believe (the relatively strong and implausible) *First Premise* but maintain that we *do* have justification to believe (the relatively weak and plausible) E1. So, the portion of skeptical theism which claims that we lack justification to believe *First Premise* doesn't disallow our having justification to believe E1; that portion leaves E1 intact. Moreover, the envisaged advocate of Chris's Focal Argument from Evil doesn't invoke *The Inference*, and therefore can also coherently grant to Todd the remaining portion of skeptical theism—namely, the claim that we lack justification to believe *The Inference*.

So far as I can see, then, while minimal skeptical theism may (as Chris would put it) "score a genuine victory" against *any* advocate of Todd's Focal Argument from Evil, and against *many*—perhaps even *most*—proponents of Chris's Focal Argument from Evil, minimal skeptical theism doesn't rule out the possibility that Chris's Focal Argument justifies atheism for at least some thinkers. Fortunately— and *pace* Chris—, Bergmann's skeptical theism *can* completely incapacitate Chris's Focal Argument from Evil. At least, that's the claim I'll be defending in the balance of this chapter.

III

I'll be focusing on the objection to Bergmann's skeptical theism that Chris develops and defends in §4 of his chapter ("The Skeptical Theses and Non-Inferential Justification"). After reconstructing (and making some necessary repairs to) Chris's objection to Bergmann's skeptical theism, I'll show that phenomenal conservatism[3]—which Chris takes for granted in presenting his argument—actually entails the *denial* of his objection's key claim. Chris's reasoning thus defeats

---

[3] Recall Chris's definition, which I'll adopt as is: "if it seems to S that P, then, *in the absence of defeaters*, S thereby has non-inferential justification that P" (p. 58, my emphasis).

itself, and so fails to establish that Bergmann's skeptical theism isn't a "complete response" to the pertinent argument from evil.

Here's my initial reconstruction of the argument that Chris sets out in §4:

Chris's Objection to Bergmann's Skeptical Theism

(1) Even if ST1–3 is true, a thinker may nevertheless have "very strong and stable seemings" that there are no God-justifying reasons for allowing the holocaust (p. 58).[4]

(2) ∴ If Phenomenal Conservatism is true, then ST1–3 is compatible with a thinker's having non-inferential justification that there are no God-justifying reasons for allowing the holocaust. [1, definition of Phenomenal Conservatism]

(3) If ST1–3 is compatible with a thinker's having non-inferential justification that there are no God-justifying reasons for allowing the holocaust, then ST1–3 is compatible with a thinker's justifiably accepting the conclusion of the argument from evil on the basis of its premises.

(4) ∴ If Phenomenal Conservatism is true, then ST1–3 is compatible with a thinker's justifiably accepting the conclusion of the argument from evil on the basis of its premises. [2, 3]

(5) Bergmann's skeptical theism is a "complete response" to the argument from evil *only if* it rules out a thinker's justifiably accepting the conclusion of the argument from evil on the basis of its premises.

(6) ∴ If Phenomenal Conservatism is true, then Bergmann's skeptical theism is not a "complete response" to the argument from evil. [4, 5]

As it stands, Chris's argument has two problems. First, because Chris sidelines a core element of Bergmann's skeptical theism, (6) doesn't follow from (4) and (5). The element I have in mind is this:

---

[4] Recall that, in Chris's chapter, the term "ST1–3" denotes this proposition: "We have undefeated reason to withhold judgment whether our sample of potential reasons for allowing the holocaust is representative of the potential reasons there are" (p. 48). Chris treats (what he calls) ST1–3 as a concise restatement of the three propositions that Bergmann (2009, 2012) labels "ST1," "ST2," and "ST3". I worry, though, that Chris's ST1–3 doesn't accurately capture Bergmann's propositions. I assume that Chris's ST1–3 implies that we lack undefeated reason to *deny* that our sample of potential reasons for allowing the holocaust is representative of the potential reasons there are. But Bergmann's propositions are consistent with our having undefeated reason to deny that our sample of potential reasons for allowing the holocaust is representative of the potential reasons there are. (Note that a *theist* who concedes that our sample of potential reasons doesn't include any God-justifying ones should *deny* that our sample is [what Chris calls E-] representative of the potential reasons there are.) We can solve this problem by adding the following material to Chris's ST1–3: "… or we have undefeated reason to deny that our sample of potential reasons for allowing the holocaust is representative of the potential reasons there are." Throughout my reply, the term "ST1–3" will denote the disjunctive statement that results from combining *Chris's* ST1–3 with the indicated additional material.

ST4: *At best*, we have undefeated reason to withhold judgment on whether the total moral (dis-)value we perceive in certain complex states of affairs (like the holocaust) accurately reflects the total moral (dis-)value they really have.[5]

As will soon emerge, I think proponents of Bergmann's skeptical theism can defend their view from Chris's objection by leveraging ST4. At this juncture, though, all we need to agree on is this: (6)—which is a claim about Bergmann's overall skeptical theist position, which clearly comprises ST4 (cf. Bergmann 2009, 2012)—follows from prior steps *only if* those steps countenance ST4 along with Bergmann's three other skeptical theses. Letting "Bergmann's skeptical theism" denote the result of conjoining ST1–3 with ST4, we can amend Chris's argument by replacing each occurrence of "ST1–3" with "Bergmann's skeptical theism." Consider it done.

Why does Chris elect to ignore (what I've called) ST4? He writes (p. 47, fn.4): "... I'm not sure I understand [ST4] and Bergmann holds that "it's not needed to make the skeptical theist's point" (2009: 379)." Let's suppose Chris is right to interpret Bergmann as having claimed here that ST4 isn't required for what Chris calls a "complete response" to the relevant argument from evil.[6] Then one upshot of the argument I present below will be that Bergmann has at times underestimated ST4's importance for a "complete response" to the argument from evil.

Even after we make the first recommended repair to Chris's objection, a second problem remains. To see it, consider the substitute for (1) that the first repair will yield:

(1*) Even if Bergmann's skeptical theism is true, a thinker may nevertheless have "very strong and stable seemings" that there are no God-justifying reasons for allowing the holocaust.

Like (1), (1*) fails to make the further normative claim that the thinker's relevant seemings are *undefeated*. So, because (1*) doesn't assert that Phenomenal Conservatism's "no defeaters" clause is indeed satisfied, (2) doesn't follow from (1*) and Phenomenal Conservatism. To establish (2), Chris will need to revise (1*) like this:

[5] More fully: *Either* we have undefeated reason to deny that the total moral (dis-)value we perceive in certain complex states of affairs (like the holocaust) accurately reflects the total moral (dis-)value they really have; *or* we have undefeated reason to withhold judgment on whether the total moral (dis-)value we perceive in such states of affairs accurately reflects the total moral (dis-)value they really have.

[6] For the record, I have doubts about the accuracy of such an interpretation, though I won't stress them here. I'll just say that, as interested readers can easily verify, notwithstanding the bit that Chris quotes from Bergmann, Bergmann continually includes ST4 in the package of skeptical theses he utilizes in his (2009) and (2012).

(1**)   Even if Bergmann's skeptical theism is true, a thinker may never-
        theless have *undefeated* "very strong and stable seemings" that there
        are no God-justifying reasons for allowing the holocaust.

Again, consider it done. So amended, Chris's argument is clearly valid. Its basic
premises are (1**), a duly modified version of (3) (i.e. one that replaces "ST1–
3" with "Bergmann's skeptical theism"), and (5). I'll concede (3) and (5), taking
aim at (1**) instead.

(1**) is not obviously true. What reasons does Chris provide for accepting
(1)? And can they support (1**)?

Here's what Chris says on behalf of (1):

I'm guessing most atheists have very strong and stable seemings to [the effect that
there are no God-justifying reasons for allowing the holocaust], and even some
theists report having such seemings. (pp. 58–59)

I'll grant Chris the following, somewhat stronger claim, and argue that even
it fails to justify (1**):

Seemings: Most non-theists (i.e. atheists and agnostics), as well as many theists, have very strong and stable seemings that there are no God-justifying
reasons for the holocaust.

An initial point about Seemings: We can probably ignore the portion that
refers to *theists*. Since a *theist* arguably couldn't have an *undefeated* seeming
that there's no God-justifying reason to allow the holocaust, the fact that a theist has such a seeming likely provides no significant support to (1**).

To begin to see why a theist couldn't have an undefeated seeming that there's
no God-justifying reason to allow the holocaust, note that the proposition that
there are no such God-justifying reasons is *obviously* incompatible with the
proposition that God exists (i.e. E1 of Chris's Focal Argument from Evil is
obviously true). Plausibly, then, the epistemic situation of the *theist* to whom
it seems that there are no God-justifying reasons for allowing the holocaust is
relevantly similar to Alice's epistemic situation in the following scenario (cf.
Senor 1996: 551–2):

Alice looks across the quad and sees in the distance a person she takes to be her
colleague Ed. However, Alice also believes that Ed is in France and will not return
to the US for another six months.

We can fill in the details of this example so that Alice's belief about Ed's current
whereabouts (namely, that he's in France) keeps her visual experience as of Ed
from (ultima facie, on balance) justifying her in believing that Ed is presently on
campus. Similarly, the *theist's* belief that God exists will keep her experience as
of the absence of God-justifying reasons for allowing the holocaust from (ultima
facie, on balance) justifying her in believing that there are no such reasons at all.

Here's another case that strikes me as relevantly similar to that of the theist who has seemings of the pertinent sort. You're playing that "game of trust" sometimes known as *Fall Back* (players let themselves fall backward to be caught by other players). Throughout your turn to fall, you are extremely confident that your partner will catch you, and so are extremely confident that you are *not* in any danger of hitting the ground. However, notwithstanding your extreme confidence in your partner and thus your physical safety, as you begin to fall backward, it strongly seems to you that you *are* in danger of hitting the ground. This seeming is defeated by your contemporaneous belief that you're *not* in danger—i.e. the belief keeps the seeming from (ultima facie, on balance) justifying you in believing that you *are* in danger. Similarly, the *theist's* belief that God exists will keep her relevant seeming (that there are no God-justifying reasons for allowing the holocaust) from justifying her in believing that there are in fact no such reasons.

In sum, no *theist* can have *undefeated* seemings of the pertinent sort. Accordingly, in asking whether Seemings justifies (1**), we can probably ignore the portion about theists. Nevertheless, to give Chris's objection to Bergmann's skeptical theism the best chance of success, I'll set this worry aside in what follows.[7]

I want to argue two critical points about (1**). First, a rather obvious and legalistic undercutter. (1**) is a claim about *undefeated* seemings that there are no God-justifying reasons for permitting the holocaust. By contrast, Seemings is *not* a claim about undefeated seemings with the relevant content. Rather, Seemings claims only that there are seemings, *period*, that there are no such God-justifying reasons. The relatively weak claim that there are seemings with the pertinent content, *period*, does not by itself constitute a strong reason to believe the considerably stronger claim that there are *undefeated* seemings of the relevant sort. Thus, when basing it solely on Seemings, we're not well justified in asserting (1**).

Second, a not-entirely-obvious (I hope!) rebutter of (1**). Let's suppose, with Chris, that Phenomenal Conservatism is correct. It turns out that, *if* Phenomenal Conservatism is correct, then (1**) is false. To begin to see this, let *Undefeated Seemings* denote this claim:

> Some thinker, T, has undefeated seemings to the effect that there are no God-justifying reasons for the holocaust.

If both Phenomenal Conservatism and Undefeated Seemings are true, then our thinker T has (non-inferential, ultima facie) justification—in virtue of an exercise of moral/evaluative perception/intuition, directed upon the holocaust—to believe that there are no God-justifying reasons for allowing the holocaust.

---

[7] For a fascinating line of reasoning that casts doubt on the possibility of a (suitably reflective) *non-theist's* having undefeated seemings of the relevant sort, see Crisp (2011).

(I'm assuming, uncontroversially I think, that T's having the relevant seemings counts as an exercise of moral/evaluative perception/intuition.)

Now recall ST4. ST4 implies that, *at best*, we have undefeated reason to withhold judgment on the reliability of moral/evaluative perception/intuition, at least when such perception/intuition is directed upon complex states of affairs like the holocaust. But, as Chris himself correctly suggests, a "mental state M can provide justification for holding belief B only if the subject doesn't have undefeated good reason to disbelieve [that] or withhold judgment about whether M reliably indicates B" (p.9). So, if Bergmann's skeptical theism—in particular, if ST4—is true, then our thinker T's relevant moral/evaluative seemings do *not* provide justification to believe that there are no God-justifying reasons for allowing the holocaust—and this consequent, note well, implies the *denial* of what we just drew out (in the last paragraph) from the conjunction of Phenomenal Conservatism and Undefeated Seemings. So, we should conclude that if Bergmann's skeptical theism is true, then either Phenomenal Conservatism is false or Undefeated Seemings is false. It follows that if Phenomenal Conservatism is true, then either Bergmann's skeptical theism is false or Undefeated Seemings is false—and this consequent, note well, implies that (1**) is false.

Thus, if Phenomenal Conservatism is true, then (1**) is false. So, assuming with Chris that Phenomenal Conservatism *is* true, we end up with a rebutter for (1**). A less committal (with respect to the question whether Phenomenal Conservatism is true), somewhat subtler way to put the objection: if I've reasoned rightly, then (the duly modified version of) Chris's criticism of Bergmann's skeptical theism *defeats itself*, since it utilizes both Phenomenal Conservatism *and* (1**), which turn out on deeper reflection to be incompatible. It seems that the argument Chris presents in §4 of his chapter doesn't pose a serious threat to Bergmann's skeptical theism after all.

7

The Paradox of Humility and Dogmatism

N. N. Trakakis

A striking paradox stands at the heart of Christian theology and spirituality. On the one hand, one of the greatest virtues in the Christian spiritual life is taken to be humility, a deeply held awareness of our limitations and sinfulness that propels us to seek guidance and forgiveness from others, and especially from God. While on the other, there is the equally dominant tradition of dogmatism, understood here as the advocacy of particular doctrines as providing the absolute and final truth about reality. That this is a significant part of Christian theology is clearly evidenced by the creeds of the councils of the first millennium accepted as authoritative by most Christian churches. It seems that this reliance on dogma stands in direct conflict with the espousal of humility. In other words, an awareness of our weaknesses and failures, in intellectual as well as moral and spiritual matters, does not seem consistent with claims to have privileged access to absolute truth.[1] This paradox becomes even more pronounced in those strains of the Christian tradition—such as the Eastern Orthodox—which profess an underlying continuity between spirituality and theology.[2]

My aim is to show how this paradox was resolved in the classical Greek patristic tradition, with particular recourse to the life and theology of one of the towering figures of this tradition: the seventh-century Byzantine

---

[1] It is, of course, an important question as to how a knowingly weak (i.e. finite and fallible) creature could ever *know* that it had access to absolute truth, for wouldn't a knowingly weak creature always doubt that he possessed the absolute truth, even if he in fact did possess that truth? This is not, however, the question of the present chapter, which begins from the assumption that a knowingly weak creature does possess some divine knowledge. The aim of the chapter is not to substantiate this claim to divine knowledge, but only to show how it can be rendered compatible with the separate claim to epistemic humility.

[2] On the interdependence between theology and spirituality in the Eastern tradition, see Ware (2000: 13–14).

theologian, Maximus the Confessor. In particular, it will be shown that the paradox was resolved without abandoning either term of the problem—that is, without rejecting (even surreptitiously) the value of humility in theological matters, and also without denying the significance of dogmas and creeds (or reinterpreting them as, say, purely symbolic or metaphorical).

I

But before returning to premodern patristic sources, it will be helpful to consider a recent proposal at resolving the paradox at issue: Merold Westphal's Kantian proposal, which he calls "Theist-Pluralist Creative Anti-realism." Westphal (2001) sees this position as a way of rehabilitating Kantian idealism, and in particular bringing this form of idealism in line with Christian doctrine in such a way as to deflect the criticisms made by Alvin Plantinga against (what Plantinga calls) "Creative Anti-Realism." According to Creative Anti-Realism, "we human beings, in some deep and important way, are ourselves responsible for the structure and nature of the world; it is *we*, fundamentally, who are the architects of the universe" (1990: 14, emphasis in the original). For Plantinga, one of the seminal texts in support of this view is Kant's *Critique of Pure Reason*, where Kant ushers in the "Copernican Revolution" that (in Plantinga's words) "the things in the world owe their basic structure and perhaps their very existence to the noetic activity of our minds" (1990: 15). To render this idea somewhat palatable, Westphal illustrates it by way of the homely example of knowing, even before switching on the TV, that Dan Rather's tie will be grey in color during the Evening News. If such knowledge is not based on induction from past observation, then how could one know such a thing? Westphal's answer: in virtue of knowing that one will be watching the news on a black-and-white TV. From this example, Westphal draws the following Kantian morals: (i) my receiving apparatus (in this case, the television set) may be responsible for some of the features I perceive an object to have (the color of the news presenter's tie); (ii) my receiving apparatus "simultaneously makes it possible for me to see the tie at all (since I'm not in the studio) and makes it impossible for me to see it as it truly is," thus introducing the distinction between "the thing as it is in itself" and "the thing as it appears to us" (2001: 91); and (iii) the "thing in itself" may be understood as "the thing as apprehended by God," in which case a form of realism undergirds Kantian idealism: "For Kant, to be in the studio means, quite simply, to be God" (2001: 93). But as this suggests, Kant's anti-realism does not stand opposed to theism (as Plantinga thinks), but merely reinscribes the time-honored theistic distinction between the infinite knowledge of God and the limited knowledge attainable by the human mind in terms of the distinction between the thing in itself and the thing as it appears to human consciousness (2001: 93–4).

Westphal's view, like Kant's, is therefore anti-realist but also theistic, insofar as the thing in itself is equated with the thing as it is known by God. But Westphal's anti-realism is underwritten not only by Kantian considerations of finitude, but also by Kierkegaardian concerns about sinfulness. In other words, the reason why we do not have access to God's point of view is not only due to our finite nature (e.g. our temporality), but is also due to our fallenness—and specifically "the inveterate human tendency toward idolatry" (2001: 103). As a result of our fallenness, "our sinfully corrupted receiving apparatuses generate gods conveniently suited to our demands" (104). This is precisely what is uncovered by the "hermeneutics of suspicion" practiced by Freud, Marx, and Nietzsche, who sought to unmask the deep-seated motives, and especially the hidden biases and ruses, which underlie claims to "knowledge" and "truth."

But how does this resolve the paradox of humility and dogmatism? Westphal's resolution consists in holding that we can come to know the truth, while also conceding that this knowledge (in light of our finitude and sinfulness) will always be limited and relative, never absolute. For an absolute view of the world can only be had by the Absolute. Elsewhere Westphal puts this in terms of the idea of "hermeneutics as epistemology." This is the idea that human knowledge is embedded in historically particular and contingent vocabularies, and that it is impossible for us to transcend or overcome this embeddedness so as to attain, for example, pure reason or absolute knowledge (2001: 49). As a result, all human claims to knowledge have the status of interpretations, all seeing is a "seeing as," an apprehension of something as something (128–9). In our current predicament, at least, interpretation is inescapable: "Interpretation is what we do east of Eden, after the Fall, prior to the beatific vision" (72). The way we see the world, therefore, will inevitably be partial, relative, fallible, conditioned—in a word, perspectival. This gives rise to a perspectival pluralism, like Nietzsche's, where there are no facts, only interpretations, so that we cannot hope to see things from a God's-eye point of view or *sub specie aeternitatis*, but only have recourse to different perspectives thoroughly mediated by, for example, gender, language, time and culture.[3] This is a theme Westphal finds dominant in much continental philosophy, including Gadamer and Derrida, both of whom "affirm a plurality of perspectives that is beyond our power to totalize and thus unify in any final view from nowhere. For both of them the truth is that we have no Truth. They represent two variations on the theme of perspectival finitism" (137). Westphal contends, however, that

---

[3] In endorsing this pluralism of perspectives, Westphal departs from Kant's universalism, where there is only one "phenomenal world" since the forms and categories that constitute the human "receiving apparatus" are operative in all human cognition, at all times and in all places (Westphal 2001: 103).

the hermeneutics of finitude found in Gadamer and Derrida is insufficient or not sufficiently radical, and so must be supplemented by the hermeneutics of suspicion, which makes sin (in addition to finitude) an epistemological category (138). Westphal's "radical hermeneutics" thus resolves the paradox of humility and dogmatism by allowing for truth-claims and hence the formulation of doctrine, while also highlighting our finitude and fallenness, so that an awareness of the contingent and corrupt nature of our cultural practices will prevent our claims to truth from descending into hubris.

II

The question I now wish to consider is: How consistent is Westphal's hermeneutic epistemology with the theology of the Church Fathers? Unfortunately, the patristic tradition, and in particular the classical patristic period in the Greek-speaking Christian East (running from the fourth to the eighth centuries and encompassing such luminaries as Athanasius, Gregory of Nazianzus, Gregory of Nyssa, and John of Damascus), is rarely brought into the conversation of contemporary philosophy of religion. A redress of this imbalance is long overdue, especially given the philosophical relevance and fruitfulness of the insights of the patristic writers. But the (re)turn to the patristic tradition is also important, if not necessary, due to the crucial role played by the theologians of this period in the formulation and defense of what is now known as "orthodox" or mainstream Christianity. So, if we wish to know whether the kind of epistemology proposed by Westphal is compatible with Christianity, there is perhaps no better way to find out than by consulting the "makers" of Christianity: the Church Fathers. Among the plethora of Church Fathers that could be considered in this respect, I have chosen Maximus the Confessor (AD 580–662), for his life and teachings demonstrate well (indeed, dramatically well) the point I wish to make in response to Westphal's hermeneutics.

Maximus is widely revered in the Christian Church, both East and West, in large part due to the role he played in the Monothelite controversy over the person of Christ.[4] "Monothelitism" (derived from μόνος, "one," and θέλημα, "will") and the closely associated theory of "monoenergism" (from μόνος, "one," and ἐνέργεια, "activity" or "operation") were influential seventh-century

---

[4] The reverence within which he is held is evident in John Meyendorff's remark that Maximus "in many respects, may be regarded as the real Father of Byzantine theology" (1979: 37). A similar assessment, this time from a Protestant source, is given in an article on Maximus published in an encyclopedia of theology in 1903, where Maximus is said to be "one of the... most estimable, one of the greatest, Christian thinkers of all time, known and valued, except from afar, by few, yet nonetheless in the firmament of the Christian Church a star of the first magnitude" (quoted in Nichols 1993: 225).

theological movements, which held that in the person of Christ there is a single will and activity. The background to these views was the earlier Monophysite controversy, with the Monophysites (from μόνος, "one," and φύσις, "nature") holding that Christ has only one nature—a divine nature, or a nature wherein the divinity engulfs the humanity.[5] This view was condemned at the Council of Chalcedon (AD 451), regarded now as the fourth ecumenical council of the Christian Church. In opposition to the Monophysite view, the "Definition" (or Creed) of Chalcedon stated that Christ is to be "recognized in two natures, without confusion, without change, without division, without separation; the distinction in natures being in no way annulled by the union, but rather the characteristics of each nature being preserved and coming together to form one person and subsistence." Despite subsequent attempts to reconcile the proponents of Monophysitism to the Definition of Chalcedon, reconciliation proved elusive, and thus began the first major and lasting schism in Christendom.

Monothelitism was devised as a refinement of Chalcedonian Christology, in the hope of building a bridge to the Monophysites and thus overcoming the schism. The basic idea was that, although in Christ two natures (one divine and one human) had come together, these two natures constituted an indivisible "hypostatic unity," a unity that could be discerned in the single unique activity and will of the Incarnate One. Put differently: although Christ has two natures, he is a single person, and a single person can only have a single activity and will.

Maximus rejected this as a covert reintroduction of Monophysitism. For according to Maximus' "Chalcedonian logic" (to borrow from Louth 1996: 49–51) a single will implies a single nature.[6] But without a distinct human nature and human will, Christ's humanity is compromised and incomplete. What is at stake here, for Maximus, is no mere technical quibble over words, but the very possibility of human redemption.[7] For if Christ was not fully human, then he was unable to save the whole of human nature. Lying behind this view is Gregory of Nazianzus's oft-repeated statement: "The unassumed is the unhealed, but what is united with God is also being saved" (*Epistle* 101, in Gregory of Nazianzus 2002: 158). Our ascent to God presupposes a prior

---

[5] At least that is how the Monophysite view was perceived by its opponents; though today the difference between the "one-nature" and the "two-nature" views is often seen to be more terminological than substantive.

[6] As Louth (1996: 56–7) points out, the underlying "logic" here is that (i) activity and will *qua* processes (acting, willing) belong to the level of "nature" (what we are as human beings), while (ii) activity and will *qua* results (the act done, the deed willed) belong to the level of "person" (what is unique about each one of us, what we have made of the nature that we have). For example, my will to drink and eat is part of my human nature, but how exactly I express my will to drink and eat (sparsely or gluttonously) depends on my personal character. Thus, insofar as will and activity are considered as processes, a single nature entails a single will and activity.

[7] That the Christological controversies of the early Christian period were fundamentally soteriological in nature is generally recognized nowadays (see, e.g., Wiles 1989).

divine descent, where the eternal divine Word "assumes" or "appropriates" created and fallen human nature, making it his very own, and in the process healing and transfiguring it.

Given these high stakes (the reality of salvation), Maximus fought relentlessly against Monothelitism. Therefore, when Emperor Constans II issued his *Typos* (or "Edict Concerning the Faith") in 648, seeking confessional unanimity by forbidding all discussion of the question of Christ's wills and energies, Maximus defied the edict, responding that the truth should never be silenced (Neil and Allen 2003: 149–51). This led to his arrest in Rome in 653, and he was taken to Constantinople to stand trial for his opposition to the emperor and the Church of Constantinople (which supported the *Typos*). An initial trial (in 655) saw him exiled, and by this time—after the death of Pope Martin, who had been arrested in Rome together with Maximus for speaking out against the *Typos*—the opposition to Monothelitism had virtually been reduced to a single and indefensible 75-year-old monk: Maximus.

In 662 Maximus was brought back to Constantinople to face another trial. During the interrogations, Maximus remained steadfast in his defiance of emperor and patriarch alike. As a result, he was stripped of his status as a monk and beaten savagely: they "didn't show any pity for his old age," his biographer reports (Neil and Allen 2003: 175). After a night in prison, his tongue and right hand were amputated the next day, and he was then paraded around the city, exposed to the scorn of the populace (177–9). Afterwards, he was exiled once more, this time by ship to Lazica, on the south-east shore of the Black Sea (modern Georgia). On 13 August 662 he died in the wilderness near the Black Sea, abandoned and forgotten. Within twenty years, however, his teachings were vindicated at the Council of Constantinople, in 680–81, though he did not live to take part in this victory.

My reason for recounting this historical narrative in some detail is that it places the kind of epistemology proposed by Westphal in a new, and somewhat unflattering, light. Consider, to begin with, the following questions:

(i) Was Maximus presuming to be defining and defending nothing more than a limited, relative and perspectival truth regarding the person of Christ, rather than possessing the universal and absolute Truth?

(ii) Was the Church, in its endorsement and canonization of Maximus, claiming to have nothing more than a limited, relative and perspectival truth regarding the person of Christ, rather than possessing the universal and absolute Truth?

I presume it would be safe to respond in both instances with a resounding "No." In both cases, the claims to knowledge and truth are claims to absolute and non-perspectival Truth. This is especially evident in Maximus's biography. He was prepared to suffer terribly and even to die for his beliefs, and it is doubtful that he would have been willing to do this if he did not think of his beliefs as representing the absolute and final truth about Christ. Indeed, the title of "confessor" was conferred on him because he was ready to pay such a high price for his witness to and confession of the truth. Let's suppose, however, that Maximus adopted a radical hermeneutics, taking his duothelite Christology as a valid interpretation of the data of revelation, but not as the final and absolute statement on the matter, not as something that breaks through the limitations of our receiving apparatus to reach the pure and unadulterated truth. Would he have been willing, in that case, to sacrifice his very life for the sake of an "interpretation"? No matter how valid that interpretation may be in his eyes, (*qua* radical hermeneut) he would also recognize its highly contingent and conditioned nature, as something partial and revisable. Given that he recognizes this, could he sensibly commit himself to the truth of his faith in the way that his actual, historical counterpart did? It seems unlikely. Indeed, only a large dose of "bad faith" would enable one to pull off such a feat.

Following Maximus, and (I dare say) the overwhelming witness of the patristic tradition, Westphal's creative anti-realism cannot be reconciled with a commitment to the absolute truth of Christianity. The consistent belief of the Church, through its confessors and theologians, is that God really is a Trinity of three persons, that Christ really is fully divine and fully human, one person with two natures and two wills, etc.—these are not simply how things appear to us, or the way in which we are inevitably given over to perceive (divine) reality due to the vagaries of our historical placement. Rather, this is the way things really are, in and of themselves.

An obvious response is to recall our inescapable embeddedness in history and hence the unavoidability of interpretation. One way to put this is to say that the language we use to describe the divine realities (about the Trinity, the person of Christ, etc.) is mediated, if not distorted, by our finitude and sinfulness. The Chalcedonian Creed, for example, employs the vocabulary of Greek metaphysics ("nature," "hypostasis"), which illustrates how deeply the language of theology (including the language of Maximus' Christology) is embedded in wider social and intellectual currents. But if our theological vocabulary is historically contingent in this way, then it is always open to translation, interpretation, and revision—it can never claim to be the final word.[8] Although there is an element of truth in this objection, what must not be overlooked are the limits to the process of translation, revision, and interpretation. This process cannot be total or wholesale; there must be some limits, otherwise there would be no obstacle to accepting, say, Arianism over Nicene Christianity, or Monophysitism over the Chalcedonian Creed. Indeed, if there are no limits

---

[8] In line with this, there have been calls of late for renewal and reformation within the Orthodox Church, where this would involve the development of a "post-patristic theology," a theology that seeks to translate the categories and formulations of the patristic tradition into a modern or even postmodern idiom. See Kalaitzides (2009).

at all, there seems little to prevent us from adopting an outright religious pluralism, holding (as does John Hick) that the one infinite and ineffable divine
reality can be encountered and interpreted in a multiple number of ways: as
Trinity, but also as Allah, Krishna, Brahman, the Tao, etc.

But if that's the case, where do we draw the line? What is open for revision
or rejection in our interpretations of the divine, and what is non-negotiable
or absolute? Within the patristic tradition at least, the non-negotiable core
is represented by the creeds of the ecumenical councils, as these are aimed at
protecting the divinely revealed truth from distortions and false teachings. The
radical hermeneut, however, is unlikely to be impressed. For aren't the creeds
themselves (or at least the language in which they are couched) contingent and
conditioned, always open to interpretation and revision? Yes, of course they
are. But the truth they disclose is not partial or perspectival, but impartial and
absolute, altogether escaping and transcending the order of the sign, of our
contingent vocabularies and histories.

To get clear on this, it may help to draw a distinction, well known in philosophy of language, between a "sentence" and a "proposition." A sentence may
be understood as "any grammatically correct and complete string of expressions of a natural language" (Haack 1978: 75). A proposition (some prefer to
talk instead of a "statement") is what is expressed by a declarative sentence
(e.g. a sentence in the indicative mood); it is the content or meaning of a
declarative sentence, that which is capable of being assigned a truth-value (a
"truth-bearer") (Haack 1978: 76–7). Although sentences are open to translation and revision, the propositions they express are not—they are immutable
and timeless, their identity and truth (or falsity) remaining forever fixed. This
is because the proposition, on at least one traditional construal of this notion,
is extra-linguistic; it is an abstract or nonphysical entity (a "thought," in Frege's
sense, or as Augustine would have preferred: an idea in the mind of God).
Once the content or meaning that constitutes the proposition is given expression in a (natural) language, it then takes the character of something mediated,
conditioned, and contingent. But, the meaning itself, apart from its linguistic
expression, stands above the fray of historical flux.

Assume, for example, that water is falling from the skies and an Englishman
utters "It is raining," while a Frenchman says "*Il pleut.*" The proposition these
utterances express is not mediated or conditioned (by language, time, culture,
or anything else), and the status of this proposition as a truth (assuming, for
the sake of argument, that it is a true proposition) is "absolute" in the sense that
its truth is not relative to a perspective, language game, conceptual scheme,
etc. This, I am claiming, is a better or more accurate way of thinking about
Christian doctrine, in comparison with Westphal's analogy of perceiving the
anchorman's red tie as grey in virtue of looking at it through a black-and-white
TV. This is not to deny the mediated and conditioned nature of patristic theology. It is clear, for example, that Aristotelian and Neoplatonic metaphysics

heavily colored the creeds of the councils and the writings of the Fathers. But, in the eyes of the Church, such coloring (especially when supplemented by the Scriptures, communal worship, spiritual formation, etc.) does not inevitably result in distortion, of the sort that befalls Westphal's television viewer. Instead, the central doctrines of the Christian faith, confessed in the creeds and (in Maximus's case) before vicious emperors and prelates, give expression (in "sentences") to truths ("true propositions") that transcend the accidents and particularities of history. Our resources are no doubt finite and fallen (language, as well as other media: painting, music, etc.), but properly used and directed these can enable us to hit upon the truth, to rise beyond our embeddedness in time to catch a glimpse of the eternal: the mind of God.[9]

III

But isn't this the height of hubris, building another Babel so as to reach God, and perhaps also dethrone him and take his place? It might seem, then, that far from resolving the paradox of humility and dogmatism, this proposal only intensifies it. Before attempting to directly answer this objection, I want to stay a little longer with the topic of propositions. This has long been a highly controversial area in philosophy, and I cannot enter into the debates here. Merold Westphal, however, has expressed grave concerns about the centrality of the notion of the proposition in contemporary philosophy. In response to Alvin Plantinga's famous "Advice to Christian Philosophers," Westphal decides to dispense some advice of his own: "I think Christian philosophers would do well to forswear the proposition presupposition," this being the presupposition that "at the moment we begin to philosophize, we have already transcended the cave [alluding here, of course, to Plato's cave] and ascended to a realm where our meanings, untouched, as it were by human hands (read traditions, practices) have an unchanging stability and clarity fit for the gods of Pure Reason" (1999: 177).

Westphal offers several significant criticisms of the "proposition presupposition," most of which would take us quickly into the thickets of the philosophy

---

[9] This capacity of religious language to reach the absolute truth is sometimes expressed in Orthodox theology by way of the "iconic" nature and function of religious language. Harrison (1995) explains that, on the Orthodox view, religious language is iconic in the sense that it discloses what escapes conceptual delimitation. But this need not mean that religious language can only make use of metaphors or figurative speech, rather than concepts or definitions. Rather, it means that religious language (at its best) "participates in its divine prototype and genuinely manifests it, yet one can also look through it into the incomprehensible divine presence" (324–5). This preserves the apophatic character of dogmas and creeds, which (as Orthodox writers such as Lossky have emphasized) refuse to comprehend or delimit God, and primarily seek to rule out certain ways of speaking about God.

of language. But one criticism he raises bears directly on the subject of the present chapter. Westphal points out that it is imperative for Christian philosophers to preserve, in their philosophizing, the radical distance or difference between God and humanity. But, in Westphal's view, it is this very difference that is eliminated or minimized by the "proposition presupposition" (1999: 177–8). Westphal's reasoning seems to be that, if we suppose that we can apprehend true propositions (about God, or anything for that matter), then this is to suppose that we can know things as they really are, as they are in themselves, and not merely as they appear to us. And this would be to see or apprehend things as God sees or apprehends things. But then there would be no qualitative difference between God's way of knowing and human ways of knowing. There may be a quantitative difference (given that God, being omniscient, apprehends many more true propositions than we can ever hope to), but qualitatively divine and human knowledge would be on a par: when we know a proposition to be true, we know it in the same way God know this. But, Westphal objects, "God's thoughts are not our thoughts" (cf. Isa. 55:8), and so he encourages Christian philosophers to acknowledge "the infinite qualitative difference between God and ourselves," which means that "God's thought is systematically different from ours" (1999: 178).

Plantinga (1999) went on to reply by emphasizing the distinction between propositions and our grasp or apprehension of propositions. Specifically, he noted (correctly, I think) that "even if propositions themselves are not denizens of the cave, our grasp of them is just what you might expect of cave dwellers," and hence that "it is entirely consistent with the propositional picture that for many or all of the propositions we do grasp, our grasp is imperfect, halting, poor, nasty, and brutish even if not short, infected with error and misconception" (190). On this view, human knowledge is qualitatively (and not simply quantitatively) different from divine knowledge, for (as Plantinga observes) the depth of our grasp of a proposition and the breadth of our knowledge (knowing how one proposition connects with others) inevitably impacts on the quality of our knowledge (191). Since the depth and breadth of our knowledge is vastly, if not infinitely, inferior to God's, the qualitative difference between divine and human ways of knowing is maintained.

Following Plantinga, we may hold that Maximus knows (or claims to know) various true propositions about God that find expression in, for example, the conciliar creeds. But no individual theologian, Maximus included, or even the community of Christian believers that form the Church would presume to have perfect, comprehensive, or complete knowledge about God. (That would be an absurdity, especially given the strong emphasis placed by patristic writers on apophaticism, or negative theology, which insists on the ultimate incomprehensibility and ineffability of God.) Nevertheless, in the light of Maximus's response to teachings (such as Monothelitism), which he found incompatible with the Chalcedonian Creed, it seems reasonable to suppose that he took himself to have knowledge of at least some true propositions about God—that is to say, to have knowledge of truths that are objective, universal, and absolute. And it was in virtue of thinking himself as having such privileged access to the truth (to the real as it truly is) that Maximus was motivated to fiercely oppose the attempts of the State and Church to silence him.

IV

Now we may return to our original question: humility or hubris? Specifically, how is the claim evidently made by Church Fathers such as Maximus to possessing "absolute" knowledge (i.e. knowledge of things as they are in themselves, and not merely as they are relative to some historically contingent perspective) to be reconciled with their claim, made with equal force, to be espousing the value of humility? The charge of hubris seeks to render these two claims mutually incompatible. The idea here, as Westphal and others formulate it, is that to suppose that you have (absolute) knowledge is to suppose that your knowledge is analogous to God's knowledge, and/or that you have special or privileged access to truths which are denied (seemingly arbitrarily) to most others. Westphal (2001: 98–9) dubs this "hubristic theism," a form of theism that pridefully suppresses human finitude and sinfulness, failing to take seriously the apostle Paul's admission that "we know only in part" and even that part "in a mirror dimly" (1 Cor. 13: 9, 12). In a similar spirit, John Caputo has often objected to the exclusivist position that there is only one religion (typically, the exclusivist's religion) which contains the fullness of divinely revealed truth. Caputo writes, with characteristic wit: "The Revelation, 'la' revelation, … commits us to thinking of something that happens to just those of us (and notice it is always *us*, not the other guy) who happen to have the luck (grace, gift) to be standing in the right place at the right time as the divine motorcade goes speeding by so that we could catch a glimpse of the god, while those poor chaps down the street missed it entirely" (2010: 115). Much like Westphal, Caputo takes the assumption of privileged access to truth as betokening a lack of modesty about our capacities as contingent and finite creatures, a lack of modesty which (in Caputo's view) all too often flames the fires of fundamentalist and violent religion.

To counter this charge of hubris—the charge that, in claiming to have knowledge of things as they really are, one is arrogating to oneself (divine) powers one does not have, and is therefore guilty of pride or hubris—I would like to take a brief excursion through the ascetic literature of the Eastern Orthodox tradition, with a focus on the ways in which humility is understood there.

It is quite clear, from even a cursory reading of this literature, that humility is held in very high regard. In the *Sayings of the Desert Fathers*—a compilation of the words and deeds of the desert ascetics of Egypt, Syria, and Palestine, dating from the fifth century—it is not unusual to find humility treasured "above all virtues" (John the Dwarf, in Ward 1984: 90), and an ascetic saying that "neither asceticism, nor vigils nor any kind of suffering are able to save, only true humility can do that" (Theodora, in Ward 1984: 84; cf. Anthony the Great 7, in Ward 1984: 2). This theme is also prominent in *The Philokalia*, another highly influential collection of ascetic writings by Byzantine authors of the 4th to 15th centuries (first published in Venice in 1872 by two Greek theologians, Nikodemos of Mt Athos and Makarios, Bishop of Corinth). There, we find Peter of Damaskos (12th century) writing that humility like that shown by the tax collector in Luke 18:13 "is enough to ensure your salvation" (St. Nikodemos and St. Makarios 1984: 160), and that humility is "the greatest of all the virtues" (Nikodemos and Makarios 1984: 239), a sentiment often repeated elsewhere in the collection.[10]

When turning to the writings of Maximus, we again witness the centrality of humility. Humility is said to be "the highest of all blessings … that conserves other blessings and destroys their opposites" (Nikodemos and Makarios 1981: 282; cf. 117), and when combined with gentleness of heart humility brings about "the perfection of the person created according to Christ" (Nikodemos and Makarios 1981: 297). Interestingly, however, it is this very condition of humility that arises from—rather than being precluded by—knowledge of divinely revealed truth. This becomes apparent in Maximus's *Four Hundred Chapters on Love*, where he opposes "divine knowledge" and "vanity":

> The one who is deemed worthy of divine knowledge and who through love has attained its illumination will never be blown about by the spirit of vainglory. But the one who is not yet deemed worthy of divine knowledge is easily carried to and fro by it. If such a one, then, should look to God in everything that he does, as doing everything for his sake, he will easily escape it with God. (Maximus Confessor 1985: 39–40)

---

[10] Peter of Damaskos also describes humility as the "source of all present and future blessings" (Nikodemos and Makarios 1984: 159), while Theognostos (possibly 14th century) states that "the precious stone of humility is more valuable than them all" (Nikodemos and Makarios 1981: 373). Elsewhere in *The Philokalia* humility is called "a great and highly exalted glory" (attributed to Makarios of Egypt; Nikodemos and Makarios 1984: 346), and "the first of all the virtues" (attributed to Antony the Great; Nikodemos and Makarios 1979: 341). In another major work of Orthodox spirituality, *The Ladder of Divine Ascent* (1982) by John Climacus (AD *c*.579–649), humility is characterized as an "indescribable wealth" (1982: 219) and as making salvation possible (1982: 221, 226). Given the value accorded to humility, it is no surprise that this virtue is unanimously regarded as being very difficult to attain: see, e.g., the comments of Diadochos of Photiki (Nikodemos and Makarios 1979: 292); Hesychios the Priest (Nikodemos and Makarios 1979: 173); and Peter of Damaskos (Nikodemos and Makarios 1984: 239).

In the next "chapter," Maximus again draws a close connection between the lack of divine knowledge and pride:

> The one who has not yet obtained divine knowledge activated by love makes a lot of the religious works he performs. But the one who has been deemed worthy to obtain this says with conviction the words which the patriarch Abraham spoke when he was graced with the divine appearance, "I am but earth and ashes." (Maximus Confessor 1985: 40)

But how can knowledge, and above all knowledge of divine reality, coincide with humility of the sort that compels us to recognize that we are "but earth and ashes"? The answer consistently found in Maximus, as in Orthodox spirituality in general, is that humility is essentially the recognition that all we are and all we have is freely given to us by God—and, moreover, it is given to us by God without our having done anything whatever to deserve or merit this (or, more properly speaking: there is nothing we can do to make ourselves worthy or deserving recipients of such divinely bestowed gifts). The consequence is that we are forever in debt to God for everything, including whatever we know about God. For our knowledge of God is not even in part the product of our labors, of our ascetic or scientific works. Rather, this knowledge is itself a gift from God. And an awareness of the gifted nature of all that we are and have, including our knowledge of God, almost spontaneously brings about in us a profound humility and gratitude. This is a recurrent theme in Orthodox spirituality. Diadochos of Photiki (AD c.400–c.486), for example, notes in his *On Spiritual Knowledge and Discrimination* (a work of great beauty and subtlety) that the sense or awareness of the divine presence ineluctably leads to humility:

> But when the intellect fully and consciously senses the illumination of God's grace, the soul possesses a humility which is, as it were, natural. Wholly filled with divine blessedness, it can no longer be puffed up with its own glory; for even if it carries out God's commandments ceaselessly, it still considers itself more humble than all other souls because it shares His forbearance. (Nikodemos and Makarios 1979: 292)

The reason why humility, and not hubris, results from divine illumination resides in the recognition that this illumination is not something one could achieve or deserve, and so any illumination immediately renders one indebted and humbled. Normally, the greater the debt (whether it be financial or otherwise), the greater the burden and anxiety we carry. But in spiritual matters this is reversed, as John Climacus points out in Step 25 of his Ladder (one of the final steps, dedicated to the cultivation of humility), where he observes the paradoxical way in which the most saintly ascetics become more thankful and humble the more they sink into debt (or, more precisely, a recognition of their debt):

> There are some—and I cannot say if they are to be found nowadays—who humble themselves in proportion to the gifts they receive from God and live with a sense

of their unworthiness to have such wealth bestowed on them, so that each day they think of themselves as sinking further into debt. That is real humility, real beatitude, a real reward! (Climacus 1982: 224)

Maximus makes a similar point when stating that, "A person is humble when he knows that his very being is on loan to him" (Nikodemos and Makarios 1981: 297; cf. 226). This notion, or awareness, of indebtedness is reiterated by many ascetic writers. Peter of Damaskos notes that the "man of understanding"

> . . . looks on himself as in God's debt for everything, finding nothing whatsoever with which to repay his Benefactor, and even thinking that his virtues simply increase his debt. For he receives and has nothing to give. He only asks that he may be allowed to offer thanks to God. Yet even the fact that God accepts his thanks puts him, so he thinks, into still greater debt. (Nikodemos and Makarios 1984: 85; cf. 147)

On this picture, humility consists in recognizing that all we have—even our very humility—is "loaned" to us by God, thus placing us into debt and occasioning even greater humility.[11] Maximus therefore figures humility in terms of the absolute dependence on God, which dispossesses us of our self-centeredness and self-sufficiency:

> Humility is continual prayer with tears and suffering. For this constant calling on God for help does not allow us to trust foolishly in our own strength and wisdom nor to be arrogant toward others. These are the dangerous diseases of the passion of pride. (Maximus Confessor 1985: 73)

If knowledge of God is not so much an achievement or a reward for our efforts, but an unmerited gift from God, then the proper response to being granted access to the divine reality is not hubris, but utter humility: a sense of indebtedness to and dependence on God's love. Peter of Damaskos expresses this well by way of the following episode he recounts from the *Macarian Homilies*:

> One of the brethren ... was praying with several others and ... was suddenly snatched up mentally to heaven and saw the heavenly Jerusalem and the tabernacles of the saints. When he returned to his habitual state, however, he fell from virtue and ended up by being completely destroyed; for he thought he had achieved something and did not realize that, being unworthy and only dust by nature, he was much more in debt for having been privileged to ascend to such a height. (Nikodemos and Makarios 1984: 241)

---

[11] This emphasis on the *gifted* nature of humility raises several significant questions which I cannot deal with here—for example, its coherence with the Orthodox view of salvation as a synergy of grace and merit; and the problem as to why divine knowledge, if it is an unmerited divine grace, is not distributed more widely (this being, of course, a version of the problem of divine hiddenness).

Privileged access, on this view, places us in profound debt, and the awareness of this is a humbling experience, precluding any smug triumphalism.

If we consider, then, the way in which knowledge of divine matters was understood in the ascetic and monastic literature of the East, it is clear that such knowledge does not "puff up" but humbles—at least when it is placed in the context of a broader awareness of our sheer dependency on God, that our very existence and anything that we can claim to have and to know has been freely and undeservedly granted to us by God. This, in brief, is how the paradox of humility and dogmatism can be resolved. However, it is not a matter of making claims to knowledge, or purporting to possess the truth—here is where the language of philosophy may lead astray. It was quite typical of ascetics and theologians in the Byzantine period to be very diffident about their cognitive and moral powers. This was, in part, due to the recognition that truth is not something we can grasp, contain, claim as our own or possess, but is rather something that takes hold of us and possesses us—knowledge of truth is viewed as a pure gift, unearned and unworthily bestowed on us by God. (To be sure, the question remains as to how one knows that one has received the truth, but that is not the question of the present chapter.) It is this conception of divine truth as something that can only be received in humility, and not attained by our own efforts, which made patristic writers suspicious of innovations in theology (without thereby advocating a mechanical repetition of the past). It was not unusual, therefore, for Maximus to respond to his critics that: "I don't have a teaching of my own, but the common core of the catholic church. I mean that I haven't initiated any expression at all that could be called my own teaching" (Neil and Allen 2003: 157).[12] This is why Byzantine theology often strikes us today as "conservative," as lacking originality (in the contemporary sense of the term, as expressing one's individuality)—even though it aspired to originality in a deeper sense, as fidelity to the origins and ultimately to the source of all, God.

V

In conclusion, the reconciliation of humility and dogmatism can be achieved by taking seriously the continuity between theology and spirituality, as was

---

[12] Similarly, during his dispute at Bizya (August 656) with a bishop on the subject of the number of wills and energies in Christ, Maximus is asked for the reason why he is not in communion with the church of Constantinople. His response: because of the *innovations* introduced by the see of Constantinople (Neil and Allen 2003: 89). John of Damascus, likewise, prefaced his major work, *The Fount of Knowledge*, with the admission: "I shall say nothing of my own, but collect together into one the fruits of the labours of the most eminent of teachers and make a compendium" (quoted in Louth 2002: 15). See also Littlewood (1995).

generally done in the monastic and patristic tradition of the East in late antiquity and the Byzantine era. In this tradition, theology was not merely an intellectual discipline, but a spiritual exercise, a way of life (in Pierre Hadot's sense) informing as well as transforming every aspect of one's being. As the fourth-century monastic writer, Evagrius Ponticus, famously put it: "If you are a theologian you truly pray. If you truly pray you are a theologian" (1972: 65). The Cappadocians, similarly, saw theology as involving not simply learning and intellectual subtlety, but as demanding a commitment to the entire Christian way of life, and particularly the purification of heart and mind. This is why Gregory of Nazianzus makes it a cardinal principle of his theological outlook that the knowledge of God is inseparably related to the condition of the human knower.[13] A common refrain in Gregory's work, and in many other patristic writers, is that "purification" (κάθαρσις) is a prerequisite for theologizing, where purification is a radical but costly process of transformation in one's character and way of life.[14] What purification makes possible is *illumination*—knowing God by coming to share in the divine light (though mystics of darkness, such as Gregory of Nyssa and Pseudo-Dionysius, speak of encountering God in the darkness—or a "luminous" or "resplendent" darkness—so as to emphasize the inaccessibility of God in his essential being).

As a spiritual discipline, theology can only produce a form of "knowledge" or "illumination" that will preclude pride, vainglory, or feelings of superiority. This is because the purification process or ascetic struggle that precedes illumination instills in one a profound sense of humility where one comes to see that whatever one has—including one's knowledge of God, and even one's very existence—is not a reward or achievement, but an unmerited gift from God. Therefore, the knowledge of divinely revealed truth, even if it be knowledge free from perspectival prejudices and distortions, both presupposes and produces humility in the knower. On this picture, humility and dogmatism, far from being contraries, perfectly coincide. John Climacus put it well when he stated: "You will know that you have this holy gift [of humility] within you ... when you experience an abundance of unspeakable light" (1982: 223).

---

[13] This may help to explain why Gregory devotes more attention in his writings to ascetical and spiritual themes than he does to Christ or the Trinity.

[14] In Oration 27, for example, Gregory states:

> Discussion of theology is not for everyone, I tell you, not for everyone—it is no such inexpensive or effortless pursuit. Nor, I would add, is it for every occasion, or every audience; neither are all its aspects open to inquiry. It must be reserved for certain occasions, for certain audiences, and certain limits must be observed. *It is not for all people, but only for those who have been tested and have found a sound footing in study, and, more importantly, have undergone, or at the very least are undergoing, purification of body and soul.* For one who is not pure to lay hold of pure things is dangerous, just as it is for weak eyes to look at the sun's brightness. (Gregory of Nazianzus 2002: 26–7, emphasis added)

Part II

Debating CORNEA

8

Some Considerations Concerning CORNEA, Global Skepticism, and Trust

Kenneth Boyce

I OVERVIEW

Proponents of the evidential argument from evil claim that certain facts concerning evil afford us with powerful evidence that there is no such being as God (where "God" functions as an honorific title for any being that is omnipotent, omniscient, and wholly good). Skeptical theists, by contrast, argue that, given our cognitive limitations, we are in no position to judge that our moral insight significantly extends into the sorts of reasons that might justify a being such as God in permitting various evils. This fact, they further argue, significantly undercuts many (if not all) versions of the evidential argument from evil.

This kind of skepticism about the extent of our moral insight may be shared by theists and non-theists alike. But skeptical theists are *not merely skeptics* about the extent of our moral insight; they are *also theists*. And this combination of views, some have claimed, has disastrous epistemological consequences—indeed, that it commits skeptical theists to global skepticism. For all the skeptical theist is entitled to claim she knows (or justifiably believes or even properly judges likely), say the proponents of this objection, God has morally adequate reasons upon which he acts to radically deceive her about such matters as the reality of the external world. And since (proponents of this objection argue) the skeptical theist cannot consistently take herself to be in a position to rule out such a possibility, she cannot consistently take herself to be in a position to know (or justifiably believe) that she is not in fact being radically deceived.[1] As is standard, call this objection to skeptical theism "the global skepticism objection."[2]

I will be concerned with the global skepticism objection as it pertains to a common version of skeptical theism originally articulated by Stephen Wykstra.[3] Wykstra's version takes as its impetus a proposed epistemological principle that he labels "CORNEA." I will argue that a recent reformulation of CORNEA (offered by Stephen Wykstra and Timothy Perrine (2012)) in terms of conditional probabilities furnishes us with a formal apparatus that allows us to see just where the global skepticism objection gets a grip on that view, as well as what is needed for an adequate response. I will conclude by arguing that, given some plausible, modest, and independently motivated anti-skeptical principles, the global skepticism objection poses no threat to Wykstra's brand of skeptical theism.

II CORNEA: A PRIMER

As noted above, Wykstra's variety of skeptical theism (from now on "Wykstranian skeptical theism") takes as its centerpiece an epistemological principle that he refers to as "CORNEA," which he originally stated as follows:

> (CORNEA) On the basis of cognized situation s, human H is entitled to claim "It appears that p" only if it is reasonable for H to believe that, given her cognitive faculties and the use she has made of them, if p were not the case, s would likely be different than it is in some way discernible by her.[4]

The original target of Wykstra's skeptical theism was William Rowe's (1979) evidential argument from evil. Rowe (at least Rowe as understood by Wykstra (1984)) had argued that there are instances of intense suffering for which there *appear* to be no compensating goods that would justify a being such as God's permission of them, and that this fact affords us with prima facie justification for the belief that there are instances of suffering that a being such as God would not permit.[5] Rowe (as Wykstra read him) took himself to be entitled to this appearance claim on the ground that there are instances of suffering for which, try as hard as we might, *we can't see any* compensating goods that

---

[1] I will not consider any response to this objection that consists in denying closure for knowledge (or justified belief) or in taking some sort of contextualist or contrastive view of knowledge (or justified belief). For a response of the latter sort, see McBrayer (2012).

[2] Variants of this objection (or something sufficiently in the neighborhood thereof) have been articulated by Russell (1996: 196–7), Gale (1996: 208–9), and Wilks (2009; 2013: 458–67). For a couple of responses on behalf of skeptical theism, generally construed, see Bergmann (2012) and Rea (2013: 482–506).

[3] It was first laid out in Wykstra (1984).   [4] Wykstra (1984: 85).

[5] See Wykstra (1984: 80–3). In this context, the prevention of an evil that is equally bad or worse (rather than the securing of a positive good) should also be considered "a compensating good."

would justify God's permitting them. Wykstra invoked CORNEA as a means of denying that Rowe is so entitled. Given our cognitive limitations, Wykstra argued, it is not reasonable for us to believe that if there were the relevant compensating goods, we would likely be aware of them. It's plausible that many of God's reasons for permitting various instances of suffering are completely beyond our ken.[6]

Originally, Wykstra took these considerations to show that our failure to see what reasons God might have for permitting various instances of intense suffering cannot properly be taken by us to afford *any evidence* at all for the conclusion that there are evils for which there are no God-justifying reasons.[7] He has subsequently backed off that claim, now claiming only that we may not properly take this failure on our part to provide us with *levering evidence* for that conclusion, where E is levering evidence for a hypothesis H just in case it properly moves one from one "square belief-state to another" (where a "square belief-state" is either a square state of belief, a square state of agnosticism, or a square state of disbelief).[8] Wykstra's considered position is that CORNEA affords us a restriction on which items of evidence for a given claim are properly taken as levering evidence for that claim.

While CORNEA functions as restriction on what is *properly taken as* levering evidence, it is also helpful (as Wykstra and Perrine have recently pointed out) to think of it as having at its core a restriction on what *counts as* levering evidence (a restriction that Wykstra and Perrine label "CORE"):

(CORE)   In cognitive situation S giving new input E, E is levering evidence for Hypothesis H only if it is true that if H were false, E would likely be different.[9]

CORNEA, on this way of thinking about it, says that a subject may properly take a given input as levering evidence for a given hypothesis only if it is reasonable for her to believe that CORE is satisfied with respect to that input and hypothesis.

III COUNTEREXAMPLES TO CORNEA?

Unfortunately, as Justin P. McBrayer has pointed out, there appear to be counterexamples to CORNEA.[10] Here is one of McBrayer's purported counterexamples (one that is representative of the others he provides):

(Lotto)   I am given a lottery ticket in ignorance of how many tickets are sold.... Being rational, I withhold belief concerning the

---

[6] Wykstra (1984: 87–9).   [7] Wykstra (1984: 77–9, 90–1).
[8] Wykstra (1996: 131, 137–9, 145–7).   [9] Wykstra and Perrine (2012: 384).
[10] McBrayer (2009).

> proposition that I will win the lottery. Later I learn that the
> odds of winning are one in a million. . ... My cognitive situ-
> ation in this case warrants a belief revision from non-belief to
> disbelief. The evidence is therefore levering evidence. However,
> it remains irrational for me to believe the required subjunctive
> conditional: I know full well that my cognitive situation would be
> exactly the same in the closest world in which I win the lottery.[11]

As Wykstra and Perrine note, the success of this counterexample depends on
understanding the subjunctive clause that occurs in CORE as expressing a
counterfactual conditional, one that is to be understood in accordance with
the (now) standard Lewis-Stalnaker semantics.[12] Call the CORE principle so
understood "the counterfactual CORE principle" and the version of CORNEA
that corresponds to it "the counterfactual CORNEA principle."

As Wykstra and Perrine also argue, however, subjunctive conditionals
as used in ordinary English are sometimes plausibly understood to express
claims that pertain to conditional probabilities, rather than as counterfactual
conditionals that conform to the Lewis-Stalnaker semantics.[13] This, they conclude, suggests an alternative reading of the CORE requirement; one phrased
in terms of conditional probabilities. Since (for reasons that space does not
permit me to summarize here) they also argue that this formulation can be
given a Bayesian underpinning,[14] I will refer to it as "the Bayesian CORE principle" (and to the resulting version of CORNEA as "the Bayesian CORNEA
principle"):

> (Bayesian CORE)   In cognitive situation S giving new input E, E is lever-
> ing evidence for H only if it is the case that the conditional probability of E
> on not H—viz. $P(E/\sim H\&k)$—is low.[15]

Wykstra and Perrine further argue that, unlike the counterfactual CORNEA
principle, the Bayesian CORNEA principle does not fall prey to McBrayer-style
counterexamples. Their discussion of the issue is summarized below.[16]

Consider a case in which we are evaluating whether some cognitive input
(reported by some proposition) E is properly taken as levering evidence for
some hypothesis H relative to a given body of background knowledge k. We
are also to consider another hypothesis (a skeptical hypothesis) H_s which both
entails that H is false and is such that $P(E/H_s\&\sim H\&k)$ is high. We then note

---

[11] McBrayer (2009: 85).   [12] Wykstra and Perrine (2012: 377).
[13] Wykstra and Perrine (2012: 384–5).   [14] Wykstra and Perrine (2012: 391–5).
[15] Wykstra and Perrine (2012: 392). Instead of "low" here, Wykstra and Perrine say "below .5."
[16] The remainder of this section constitutes my own way of summarizing Wykstra's and
Perrine's (2012: 389–9) discussion of McBrayer's Lotto example. While the substance is theirs,
some of the ways in which things are put are mine, and I make no careful attempt to distinguish
between the two.

(along with Wykstra and Perrine) that (via the theorem of total probability) the following equation holds: [17]

(Schema) $P(E/{\sim}H\&k) = P(H_S/{\sim}H\&k)P(E/H_S\&{\sim}H\&k) + P({\sim}H_S/{\sim}H\&k)$
$P(E/{\sim}H_S\&{\sim}H\&k)$

Keep in mind that (given the kind of Bayesian framework that Wykstra and Perrine employ) the conditional probabilities at issue here are to be regarded as *antecedent* probabilities with respect to E (i.e. as probabilities that are to be assigned independently of the information that E is true).[18]

Now consider McBrayer's Lotto case. Suppose artificially (as Wykstra and Perrine do, for technical reasons that need not be broached here) that one's background knowledge (which is otherwise typical) entails that one's ticket comes from a fair lottery with exactly one winning ticket and that there is a .5 initial probability that the lottery from which it comes is a single ticket lottery and also a .5 initial probability that it is a million ticket lottery. Suppose also that one has received testimony (from a source that one knows to be extremely reliable) that one's ticket comes from a million ticket lottery (and suppose that one's background knowledge renders it extremely probable that one would receive testimony concerning this matter from that source). To get the relevant instantiation of Schema, let 'H' denote the hypothesis that one's lottery ticket is not a winner, 'E' the proposition that one has received testimony from one's source that one's ticket is from a million ticket lottery, and "H_S" the proposition that one's ticket is the sole winning ticket from a million ticket lottery.

Given these stipulations, $P(E/H_S\&{\sim}H\&k)$ is high (one is likely to get the testimony one receives given that one does in fact have the winning ticket from a million ticket lottery). This (as Wykstra and Perrine point out) reflects our intuition that in the nearest worlds in which one holds the winning ticket, one is likely to learn E. $P(H_S/{\sim}H\&k)$, however (as they also note), is quite low, thereby making the first summand of this instantiation of Schema low. It is extremely antecedently unlikely, given one's background knowledge, that one has the sole winning ticket from a million ticket lottery, even on the assumption that one does in fact hold a winning ticket. The second summand is also low, but (as Wykstra and Perrine point out) for precisely the opposite reason. It is low on account of the fact that $P(E/{\sim}H_S\&{\sim}H\&k)$ is low (since ${\sim}H_S\&{\sim}H\&k$ entails that the testimony E reports is false even though one's source is extremely reliable) and in spite of the fact that $P({\sim}H_S/{\sim}H\&k)$ is high.

For these reasons, both summands of this instantiation of Schema are sufficiently low that their sum, $P(E/{\sim}H\&k)$, is also low. So even though it is plausibly true in Lotto that, if one did hold the winning ticket, one's cognitive

---

[17] Put schematically, the theorem of total probability (in one of its forms) is as follows: $P(A/B) = P(C/B)P(A/C\&B) + P({\sim}C/B)P(A/{\sim}C\&B)$, provided that $0 < P(C) < 1$.
[18] See Wykstra and Perrine (2012: 380, n. 19).

situation would likely be just as it is (in the counterfactual sense of this conditional), it is not true that P(E/~H&k) isn't low. Therefore, it is reasonable for the Lotto ticket holder to believe that the Bayesian CORE condition is met.[19] Wykstra and Perrine conclude that the Bayesian CORNEA principle successfully evades McBrayer-style counterexamples.

IV THE GLOBAL SKEPTICISM OBJECTION MEETS CORNEA

Not only does Wykstra's and Perrine's framework help us see how the Bayesian CORNEA principle evades McBrayer-style counterexamples, it also helps us see just where the global skepticism objection gets a grip on Wykstranian skeptical theism.

Let's consider the global skepticism objection in relation to our perceptually based beliefs. Consider the claim that I have hands. There are lots of different cognitive inputs that I take to furnish me with evidence for this claim, but most of these are either perceptual in nature (e.g. its visually appearing to me as though I have hands) or such that I take their evidential status to depend on the evidential status of prior perceptual experiences (e.g. my remembering recently having had visual experiences as of having hands). What bearing does the Bayesian CORNEA principle (from now on just "CORNEA") have on the issue of whether I properly take such experiences as good evidence for the claim that I have hands?

At first glance, it's not obvious that it has any bearing at all. As described above, CORNEA functions as a constraint on what one may properly take as *levering evidence*, evidence that properly moves one from one square belief-state to another. But its perceptually appearing to me that I have hands does not function as levering evidence for me for the proposition that I have hands. I already firmly believe that proposition, and I have done so for as long as I remember. Even so, I do take my belief that I have hands to be primarily *based on* various items of perceptual evidence.[20] And there is a plausible way

---

[19] It's reasonable for him to believe this, at any rate, if he is sufficiently adept at reasoning about the relevant conditional probabilities. If it were up to me, I'd restrict CORNEA to certain kinds of *idealized* cognitive situations (in part, in order to avoid worries like those pressed in Howard-Snyder (1992) to the effect that CORNEA imposes overly demanding accessibility requirements). I'd argue, however, that those situations obtain (or at least approximately obtain) where it matters most to skeptical theists (i.e. in cases of competent philosophical reflection on evidential arguments from evil). I will ignore this issue in what follows, however.

[20] See Wykstra's (2007) discussion of the distinction between a hypothesis being probable *on* a given body of evidence and it's being rendered probable *by* that evidence.

in which CORNEA might be thought to bear on the rationality of my believing that I have hands on that basis. I might reason as follows:

> In order to properly base my belief that I have hands on perceptual experiences as of having hands, it has to be reasonable for me to believe that those experiences (either individually or jointly) constitute *sufficiently good evidence* for the claim that I have hands. And in order for it to be reasonable for me to believe *that*, it also has to be reasonable for me to believe that these experiences are of a sort that the same kind of experiences *could* properly lever me (in conditions not too far removed, epistemically speaking, from those in which I actually find myself) from a state of non-belief that I have hands to one of belief. So, given CORNEA, these experiences are properly taken by me to be sufficiently good items of evidence for my belief that I have hands only if CORNEA is satisfied with respect to the same kinds of experiences in hypothetical situations (not too far removed, epistemically speaking, from those in which I actually find myself) in which I do take those experiences to function as levering evidence for that belief.

While I do find this line of reasoning plausible, I will not spend time defending it. That's because, in the current dialectical context, its soundness can be taken for granted as a concession to the proponent of the global skepticism objection. Without something like this reasoning in the background, it's hard to see how the global skepticism objection even so much as gets a grip on Wykstranian skeptical theism. Keeping the above in mind, then, suppose that I am in following hypothetical scenario:

> (Scenario) Following a terrible accident, I am taken to the hospital with injuries that require surgery. As I drift off off into an anesthetic-induced slumber, I overhear the surgeon say that there's about a fifty percent chance that they will have to amputate both my hands. This causes me to enter into a square state of non-belief that I will have hands upon awakening. Upon awakening I am relieved to find (as I anxiously look down toward the end of my arms) that I have vivid perceptual experiences as of having hands. I take my perceptual experiences, in this situation, to function as levering evidence for the proposition that I have hands.

Do I satisfy CORNEA in this scenario?

Let "H_h" denote the proposition that I have hands, "E_h" the proposition that I have vivid perceptual experiences as of having hands, "H_{Sh}" the proposition that I have vivid perceptual experiences as of having hands in spite of the fact that I do not have hands, and "k" a proposition that encapsulates the background knowledge that I have in Scenario. Now consider the following instantiation of Schema:

(Instantiation) $$P(E_h / \sim H_h \,\&\, k) = P(H_{Sh} / \sim H_h \,\&\, k) P(E_h / H_{Sh} \,\&\, \sim H_h \,\&\, k) +$$
$$P(\sim H_{Sh} / \sim H_h \,\&\, k) P(E_h / \sim H_{Sh} \,\&\, \sim H_h \,\&\, k)$$

Provided that I am aware (in Scenario) of the truth of instantiation, I satisfy CORNEA in this case[21] only if it is reasonable for me to believe that both summands of instantiation are low. There certainly is no difficulty, furthermore, in my believing that the second summand is low. That's because (given the above definitions) $\sim H_{Sh}\&H_h$ entails the denial of E_h. So $P(E_h/\sim H_{Sh}\&\sim H_h\&k) = 0$. When it comes to the first summand, however, the opposite is the case. Since H_{Sh} entails E_h, $P(E_h/H_{Sh}\&\sim H_h\&k) = 1$. So I am entitled to believe that the first summand is low if and only if I am entitled to believe that $P(H_{Sh}/\sim H_h\&k)$ is low.

And here is just where the skeptical theist's skepticism about the extent of our moral insight, combined with her theism, might be thought to get her into trouble. In Scenario, I am entitled to think that $P(H_{Sh}/\sim H_h\&k)$ is low only if I am entitled to think that it is antecedently unlikely (on the assumption that I do not have hands) that God has a morally adequate reason upon which he acts to cause me to have misleading, vivid perceptual experiences as of having hands. That's because (given God's omnipotence) the claim that God has such a reason (one upon which he acts) entails that H_{Sh} is true. So the antecedent probability that H_{Sh} is true (on any jointly consistent set of assumptions) is at least as high as the claim that God has such a reason. So I satisfy CORNEA in this case only if it is reasonable for me to believe that it is antecedently unlikely (on the assumption that I do not have hands) that God does have such a reason. But suppose that (in Scenario) I am a skeptical theist. What grounds can I consistently take myself to have for thinking this unlikely? After all, as a skeptical theist, I concede that, as far as I can tell based on the extent of my moral insight, God might have a fantastically good reason to cause me to have misleading, vivid perceptual experiences as of having hands.

I might try to argue that, in this case, I have good *inductive* grounds for thinking that $P(H_{Sh}/\sim H_h\&k)$ is low. In any realistic scenario like the one that I described, I'll have extensive memory traces of having relied on perception in the past, of my perception's having been veridical, etc. If all of that sort of information is taken as part of my background knowledge, then (given any plausible anti-skeptical view) I'll have good grounds for thinking that it is antecedently unlikely that I would have vivid perceptual experiences as of having hands on the assumption that I do not in fact have hands. But we can remove such items of background knowledge by stipulating that in Scenario my injuries also caused me to have extensive amnesia, causing me to forget nearly all of these grounds. This stipulation is appropriate, furthermore, since part of what is at issue is whether I can consistently take the perceptually based beliefs that would constitute such grounds to be items of knowledge in the first place.

---

[21] See note 19.

Thus, if I am a Wykstranian skeptical theist in Scenario, and all I have to go on is that I can't think of any good reason that God might have to cause me to have misleading, vivid perceptual experiences as of having hands, I do not (by my own lights) satisfy CORNEA. So, assuming that *is* all I have to go on, CORNEA entails that I do not properly take my perceptual experiences in Scenario as levering evidence for the claim that I have hands. But (quite plausibly) if I don't properly take such experiences *as levering evidence* for the claim that I have hands in a hypothetical situation such as Scenario, I also don't properly take such experiences *as good evidence* for that claim in my actual situation.

V CORNEA AND PERCEPTUAL TRUST

Is the Wykstranian skeptical theist committed to global skepticism for the above reason? Before I suggest a reply on her behalf, I'd like to consider a response to this objection that is *not* available to her. According to *dogmatists* about perception, we can reasonably believe that we have hands on the basis of perceptual experiences as of having hands, without its first being reasonable for us to believe that it is antecedently unlikely that our perceptual experiences are misleading.[22] So a skeptical theist who is also a dogmatist about perception might respond to the global skepticism objection by arguing that even though she is not in a position to judge that it is *antecedently* unlikely that her perceptual experiences as of having hands are misleading, once she has such experiences, she is in a position to reasonably believe that she has hands (and therefore also in a position to infer from what she reasonably believes that God does not have a morally adequate reason upon which he acts to cause her to have misleading perceptual experiences as of having hands).[23]

This kind of response (whatever its merits) is not available to an advocate of CORNEA. As we saw in Section III, Schema is to be read in such a way that conditional probabilities like $P(H_{sh}/\sim H_h \& k)$ are to be interpreted as *antecedent* probabilities—as probabilities that are assigned *independently* of the purported items of evidence that one is evaluating. Thus in Scenario, in order to satisfy CORNEA, it has to be reasonable for me to believe that $P(H_{sh}/\sim H_h \& k)$ is low independently of my having vivid perceptual experiences as of having hands.

---

[22] I am loosely basing my characterization of dogmatism about perception on White's (2006) characterization of that view. White, in turn, bases his characterization on that of Pryor (2000). I should also note that someone might (contrary to my somewhat simplified characterization) call herself a "dogmatist" about perception while thinking that the contents that can be rendered reasonable to believe via perception in this manner are not as conceptually thick as *I have hands*.

[23] Bergmann's (2012) response to the global skepticism objection appears very similar to this one (see especially p. 15).

And if this is not reasonable for me to believe, then (according to CORNEA) I am not in a position to properly come to believe that I have hands on the basis of my vivid perceptual experiences as of having hands.

Nevertheless, the dogmatist way of replying to the global skepticism objection does suggest a *general strategy* that the Wykstranian skeptical theist might employ. The *dogmatist* skeptical theist does not argue that she can see *on the basis of her moral insight into God's reasons* that God does not have a morally adequate reason upon which he acts to cause her to have misleading perceptual experiences as of having hands. She argues, rather, that she is able to *infer* this *from other claims* that it is reasonable for her to believe.[24] The *anti-dogmatist* about perception, furthermore, takes herself to be in a position to reasonably believe things on the basis of perception only if she is in a position to reasonably believe that it is antecedently unlikely that her perceptual experiences are misleading. So if the anti-dogmatist about perception is to consistently avoid skepticism about her perceptual beliefs, she must find a way to maintain that she is in such a position. And whatever grounds the anti-dogmatist might take herself to have for maintaining this might also be available to the Wykstranian skeptical theist, and might serve as grounds by which she is able to infer that it is antecedently unlikely that God has a morally adequate reason upon which he acts to cause her to have misleading perceptual experiences.

One way for the anti-dogmatist to attempt to maintain that she is in such a position would be to take up the Cartesian project of trying to infer that it is antecedently unlikely that perception is misleading from other propositions that are self-evident or incorrigible for her. But the history of philosophy suggests that the prospects of success for such a project are not promising. An alternative strategy has been suggested by Roger White and Stewart Cohen.[25] They both suggest that we adopt something in the neighborhood of the following principle:

> (Perceptual Trust):   For any given P (such that P is eligible to be the content of one's perceptual experience) it is reasonable *by default* (i.e. in the absence of any good reasons to believe the contrary) for one to believe that it is antecedently extremely likely that P obtains on the assumption that one has vivid perceptual experiences as of P.[26]

---

[24] The point that this general strategy is available to the skeptical theist is not new. Beaudoin (2005: 44–5) notes that it is available, as does Bergmann (2009: 390–1). Bergmann also deploys it himself in Bergmann (2012).

[25] See White (2006: 552–3) and Cohen (2010: 153–5). My formulation of the principle below is more closely based on White's presentation than it is Cohen's (the "by default" language comes directly from White).

[26] I am here using the locution "one has vivid perceptual experiences as of P" to mean the same thing as "one has vivid perceptual experiences with the content that p". If that doesn't match your own usage, consider this a matter of stipulation on my part.

Allowing "E(P)" to stand for "one has vivid perceptual experiences as of P," we may restate the above principle as follows:

(PT)   For any given P (such that P is eligible to be the content of one's perceptual experience) it is reasonable *by default* for one to believe that P(P/E(P)&k) is extremely high (provided that k, and nothing else of relevance to one's epistemic situation, affords one with good reasons to believe the contrary).

As White points out, a principle like PT, though employed as part of an anti-dogmatist strategy to avoid skepticism, can be motivated by the same sort of modest, anti-skepticism that is used to motivate dogmatism. [27] Modest anti-skeptics typically grant that the Cartesian project of responding to the skeptic is a failure, but deny that the debate is to be conceded to the skeptic on that ground.[28] Rather, they maintain, when it comes to certain basic sources of belief like perception, it is reasonable to place a high degree of trust in those sources in the absence of any good reasons to think them unreliable.[29] There is no obvious reason why the Wykstranian skeptical theist cannot jump on this modest anti-skeptical bandwagon and in so doing endorse PT. And if she does, she has all the resources she needs for responding to the global skepticism objection.

Suppose once again that I am in Scenario. Let "H_h," "E_h," "H_{Sh}," and "k" denote the same items they were previously assigned.[30] It is true that if I am a skeptical theist in Scenario, I cannot consistently take myself to be in a position to judge it antecedently unlikely that God would cause me to have misleading perceptual experiences as of having hands *on the basis of my moral insight into the sort of reasons God might have*. It is also true, however, that my being a skeptical theist does not entail that I have any good, *positive* reasons to believe that God would do this. So my being a skeptical theist in Scenario does not afford any barrier to my consistently taking myself to satisfy the proviso of PT. So (given PT and the stipulation that k, and nothing else of relevance to my epistemic situation in Scenario affords me with any good reason to believe that my perceptual experiences aren't trustworthy), it is reasonable by default for me to believe (in Scenario) that $P(H_h/E_h\&k)$ is extremely high.

---

[27] White (2006: 552–3).   [28] See Pryor (2000: 517–18).

[29] White (2006: 552–3).

[30] I will assume that propositions such as *I have hands* are eligible to be contents of perception. If you disagree, substitute in E_h whatever perceptual contents you take my belief in Scenario that I have hands to be based upon.

A little probabilistic reasoning suffices to show, furthermore, that the claim that $P(H_h/E_h\&k)$ is extremely high entails that $P(\sim H_h/k)P(E_h/\sim H_h\&k) \approx 0$.[31] If we add the stipulation that in Scenario it is reasonable for me to believe that $P(\sim H_h/k) \approx .5$ (which I might do on the basis of my having heard the surgeon's testimony or a judicious application of the principle of indifference or both), it follows from all that it is reasonable for me to believe that $P(E_h/\sim H_h\&k) \approx 0$; i.e. it follows from all that it is reasonable for me to believe that $P(E_h/\sim H_h\&k)$ is low (which is just what is needed for me to satisfy CORNEA!). It *also* follows that $P(H_{Sh}/\sim H_h\&k) \approx 0$ (that's because $P(H_{Sh}/\sim H_h\&k) = P(E_h/\sim H_h\&k)$, since H_{Sh} is equivalent to $E_h\&\sim H_h$). So while it may be true that I am in no position to judge that $P(H_{Sh}/\sim H_h\&k)$ is low on the basis of my moral insight into God's reasons, I am (given PT) able to *infer* that this probability is low from other things that it is reasonable for me to believe. This suffices, I believe, to answer the version of the global skepticism objection pressed against the Wykstranian skeptical theist in the previous section.

Even if PT is not quite right (on account of a need for more Chisholming), furthermore, I take it that *something like PT* is needed by any modestly anti-skeptical, anti-dogmatist. And I take it that whatever the correct principle is, it will serve to provide the Wykstranian skeptical theist with a similar response to the global skepticism objection as the one sketched above. I conclude, therefore, that the global skepticism objection is not a significant threat to Wykstranian skeptical theism. Or, to put the point more cautiously, I conclude that the global skepticism objection is no more of a threat to Wykstranian skeptical theism than the threat of global skepticism is to any modestly anti-skeptical, anti-dogmatist view in epistemology.[32]

---

[31] Assume that $P(H_h/E_h\&k)$ is extremely high. Since, according to Bayes's theorem,

$$P(H_h/E_h\&k)=\frac{P(H_h/k)P(E_h/H_h\&k)}{P(E_h/k)},$$ it follows that $P(H_h/k)P(E_h/H_h\&k) \approx P(E_h/k)$. So it follows, via the theorem of total probability, that $P(H_h/k)P(E_h/H_h\&k) \approx P(H_h/k)P(E_h/H_h\&k) + P(\sim H_h/k)P(E_h/\sim H_h\&k)$. So it follows that $P(\sim H_h/k)P(E_h/\sim H_h\&k) \approx 0$.

[32] For some helpful conversations concerning these issues, I would like to thank Paul Draper, Matthew Lee, Justin P. McBrayer, Timothy Perrine, Philip Swenson, and Stephen Wykstra. I would also like to thank Sarah Boyce and an anonymous referee for some helpful feedback on previous drafts.

9

Skeptical Theism and Undercutting Defeat

M. J. Almeida

1. INTRODUCTION

In defense of the evidential argument from evil, William Rowe proposed that no good that we know of would justify God in permitting some of evils that we know to exist. Rowe observes that no good that we know of would justify God in permitting the terrible suffering and agonizing death of a fawn caught in a forest fire. No good we know of would justify God in permitting the horrible evil of the rape, beating, and strangulation of a five-year-old girl. Not even the great good of the beatific vision, Rowe observes, would justify God in permitting such evils.

Certainly Rowe is right that no good we know of would justify God in permitting the terrible suffering and agonizing death of a fawn caught in a forest fire (E1) or the rape, beating, and strangulation of a five-year-old girl (E2). But many have doubted the inference from the fact that no good we know of justifies God in permitting E1 and E2 to the conclusion that no good at all justifies God in permitting E1 and E2. The inference from (P) to (Q) is widely regarded as no more than a weak inductive inference.

P: No good we know of justifies an omnipotent, omniscient, perfectly good being in permitting E1 and E2.

Q: No good at all justifies an omnipotent, omniscient, perfectly good being in permitting E1 and E2.

In Section 2, I consider the direct and indirect evidential arguments from evil. The indirect argument from evil goes from P to Q and from Q to the proposition that God does not exist ~G. The direct argument goes from P directly to ~G. I show that the direct argument offers no improvement over the indirect argument from evil. The objections to the indirect evidential argument are the very same objections to the direct evidential argument. I remedy the salient problems with these versions of the evidential argument and offer a better indirect argument from evil.

In Section 3, I consider the skeptical theist's argument that there is an undercutting defeater for the evidential value of P for ~G. The undercutting defeater for the evidential value of P for ~G is a reason for denying that P would not be true unless ~G were true. In the simplest case, it is a reason for believing that were G true it would still be the case that P.[1] I show that even very good reasons for believing that were G true it would still be the case that P are irrelevant to the evidential value of P for ~G. P might strongly confirm ~G anyway.

I argue in Section 4 that we have good reason to believe that the goods we know about are representative of the total goods that exist. The epistemic possibility that the actual realm of value is vastly different from the values we know about does not make it rational to believe that the actual realm of value is in fact vastly different. There are in fact good Bayesian reasons to believe that, probably, the actual realm of value does not include values that are vastly different from the goods that we know about.

2. THE DIRECT EVIDENTIAL ARGUMENT FROM EVIL

Rowe abandoned the indirect argument from P to Q to ~G. The latest evidential argument goes directly from P to ~G. But the decision to reformulate the evidential argument is puzzling. The direct version does not avoid the atheistic and theistic objections to the indirect version. But most importantly, since neither argument is well-formulated, they yield artificially high values for $P(P|G \& k)$ and $P(P|\sim Q \& k)$. As a result the evidential value of P against G is unjustifiably weakened and the values for $P(G|P \& k)$ and $P(\sim Q|P \& k)$ are artificially high. These propositions express the conditional probability that God exists, given all of the relevant background information in k and the fact that no good we know of justifies E1 and E2.[2]

The defense of (1) in the direct argument does not escape the objections leveled against the defense of (2) in the indirect argument.

1. $P(\sim G|P \& k) > P(G|P \& k)$

---

[1] The simplest case assumes conditional excluded middle for subjunctive conditionals. See Robert Stalnaker (1981).

[2] The background information in k is all the evidence we possess, other than P, which is relevant to the proposition that God exists. William Rowe restricts k to information that is shared by theists and non-theists who have thought about the problem of evil. But it will make the

$$2. \quad P(Q|P \& k) > P(\sim Q|P \& k)$$

The direct argument for (1) depends on a credible assignment of epistemic probabilities in the following ratios. And Rowe's rationale for the assignment of values is in general plausible.

$$3. \quad \frac{P(G|P \& k) = .33}{P(G| k) = .5} = \frac{P(P|G \& k) = .5}{P(P| k) = .75}$$

Rowe makes the "level playing field" assumption in assigning the equal prior probabilities to God's existence, $P(G|k)$, and God's nonexistence, $P(\sim G|k)$. He assigns a .75 prior probability to the proposition P that no good we know of justifies an omnipotent, omniscient, perfectly good being in permitting E1 and E2. Given the way the direct argument is formulated, the rationale for this assignment is cogent. If God does not exist then, according to Rowe, no good we know of justifies God in permitting E1 and E2. If God does exist, then the probabilities are about even that some good we know of justifies him in permitting E1 and E2. These assumptions seem fair to both theists and non-theists. Since the prior probability that God exists is about even and since we have made the level playing field assumption, the prior probability that some good we know justifies God in permitting E1 and E2 works out to about .75.[3]

If the distribution of values to $P(G|k)$, $P(P|k)$ and $P(P|G \& k)$ are about right, then the probability that God exists, given that no good we know about justifies God in permitting E1 and E2, is about .33. It is therefore reasonable to believe that God does not exist.[4]

The main skeptical objection to the direct evidential argument from evil is that the probability that some good we know of justifies God in permitting E1 and E2, given that God exists, is much lower than .5.[5] This is because, we are told, the goods that in fact justify God in permitting E1 and E2 are probably not within our ken. The objection continues that the value of $P(\sim P|G \& k)$ is much lower than .5 only if the value of $P(G|P \& k)$ is much greater than .33.[6]

conclusion more interesting if k includes the evidence from all of the arguments for and against God's existence except the current argument from evil. We will then have in k all of the background evidence relevant to the issue of God's existence. And it is not unreasonable to suggest that the evidence in k does not favor theism any more than non-theism.

[3] The argument assumes the rule of elimination which states that $P(P|k) = [(P(G|k) \times P(P|G \& k)] + [P(\sim G|k) \times P(P|\sim G \& k)]$. Under Rowe's assignments we have $[.5 \times .5] + [.5 \times 1] = .75$.

[4] Stephen Wykstra comes to a different conclusion. Given that $P(G|P)$ is about .33, he concludes that we have evidence that tilts us toward atheism, but we do not have evidence that justifies us in abandoning agnosticism for atheism. See his (1996b: 138ff).

[5] Here's a sample of the authors worth noting here: Wykstra (1990a: 155–6) and (1996b: 135), Russell and Wykstra (1988), Alston (1996b), and Bergmann (2001).

[6] If we keep the level playing field assumption, then $P(\sim P|G \& k)$ is anywhere from .2 to .1 only if $P(P|G \& k)$ is anywhere from .8 to .9. It follows that $P(G|P \& k)$ is anywhere from .44 to .47. The value of $P(G|P \& k)$ clearly varies inversely with the value of $P(P|G \& k)$. If the skeptical objection is right, it follows that P does not disconfirm G very much.

That is, if the value of P(~P|G & k) is low, then the fact that no good we know of justifies God in permitting E1 and E2 does not disconfirm the existence of God very much.

2.1 The Indirect Evidential Argument

The skeptical objection advanced against the direct evidential argument is also directed to the inference from P to Q above. P does not disconfirm ~Q much, the objection proceeds, since the probability that some good we know of justifies God in permitting E1 and E2, given that there is some good that justifies God in permitting E1 and E2, is much lower than .5. The goods that justify God in permitting E1 and E2, given that God exists, are probably vastly different and much more valuable than any goods we know about. The distribution of values in the indirect version of the evidential argument are pretty much the same.[7]

$$4. \quad \frac{P(\sim Q|P \& k) = .33}{P(\sim Q|k) = .5} = \frac{P(P|\sim Q \& k) = .5}{P(P|k) = .75}$$

The objection continues that the value of P(~P|~Q & k) is much lower than .5 only if the value of P(~Q|P & k) is much greater than .33.[8] So, if the value of P(~P|~Q & k) is low, then the fact that no good we know of justifies God in permitting E1 and E2 does not disconfirm the existence of some good that justifies God in permitting E1 and E2.

2.2 A Better Evidential Argument

In the direct evidential argument from evil the proposition P(P|G & k) provides the probability that no good we know about justifies God in permitting E1 and E2 given that God exists. In the indirect evidential argument

[7] Rowe complains above that his initial argument from P to Q involves an inference from no known goods justify God in permitting E1 and E2 to no goods justify God in permitting E1 and E2. That inference is at best weak because of considerations having to do with our cognitive limitations. These are considerations underscored in Alston (1996b). But the same objection is advanced against the claim in the new evidential argument from evil that P(G|P & k)!< P(G|k), the claim that no good we know of justifies God in permitting E1 and E2 is strong disconfirmation for the proposition that God exists. That's true, the objection goes, only if the value of P(~P|G & k) is high; that is, we get strong disconfirmation only if we should expect goods that justify God's permitting E1 and E2 to be known, given that God exists. But, again, given our cognitive limitations such goods are likely to be beyond our ken. So, the objection continues, the value of P(~P|G & k) is not high.

[8] Again, if we keep the level playing field assumption that P(Q|k) = P(~Q|k), then P(~P|~Q & k) is in the range of .2 to .1 only if P(P|~Q& k) is in the range of .8 to .9. It follows that P(~Q|P & k) is anywhere from .44 to .47. The value of P(~Q|P & k) clearly varies inversely with the value of P(P|~Q & k). If the skeptical objection is right, it follows that P does not disconfirm ~Q very much.

from evil the proposition $P(P|{\sim}Q \ \& \ k)$ provides the probability that no good we know of justifies God in permitting E1 and E2 given that some good justifies God in permitting E1 and E2. But neither of these propositions provides us with the conditional probability that some goods we know about justify E1 and E2. These propositions only provide us with the conditional probability that some *God-purposed* goods we know about justify E1 and E2.

What we want to know in the evidential argument from evil is the probability that an outweighing good we know about entails E1 and E2, given that an outweighing good entails E1 and E2. If an outweighing good entails E1 and E2 and it turns out that God exists, then God is justified in permitting E1 and E2. In this case we learn that the outweighing good is in fact a God-purposed good. God cannot permit the outweighing good without permitting the outweighed evils E1 and E2.

The outweighing good that entails E1 and E2 *might be* a God-purposed good. But, of course, it might not be. The outweighing good might depend for its existence on the existence of God. And again, it might not. The problem in both the direct and the indirect evidential argument from evil is that the propositions $P(P|G \ \& \ k)$ and $P(P|{\sim}Q \ \& \ k)$ only provide the conditional probability that we know about God-purposed goods that justify E1 and E2, since G and ${\sim}Q$ each entail that God exists. Those propositions do not provide the conditional probability that some good or other that we know about justifies E1 and E2. The result is an artificial increase in the value of $P(P|G \ \& \ k)$ and $P(P|{\sim}Q \ \& \ k)$ and (correspondingly) an artificial increase in the values of $P(G|P \ \& \ k)$ and $P({\sim}Q|P \ \& \ k)$.

We can reformulate P and Q to avoid any artificial increase in the value of $P(P|G \ \& \ k)$ and $P(P|{\sim}Q \ \& \ k)$. Let P' and Q' be the following propositions where neither ${\sim}P'$ nor ${\sim}Q'$ entail that God exists.

P': No outweighing good that we know about entails E1 and E2.

Q': No outweighing good at all entails E1 and E2.

If an outweighing good entails E1 and E2, then not even an omnipotent being can prevent E1 and E2 without preventing the outweighing good. It is metaphysically impossible to secure the outweighing good while preventing E1 and E2. The reformulated evidential argument aims to show that Q' is more probable than not given P'. The argument depends on a credible assignment of values to the ratios (5).

$$5. \ \frac{P({\sim}Q'|P' \ \& \ k)}{P({\sim}Q'|k)} = \frac{P(P'|{\sim}Q' \ \& \ k)}{P(P'|k)}$$

The value of $P(P'|Q' \ \& \ k)$ is surely one, just like the value of $P(P|Q \ \& \ k)$, since it is certain that no outweighing good we know of entails E1 and E2, given that no outweighing good at all entails E1 and E2.

But consider the assignment to $P(P'|{\sim}Q'$ & k). There *might* be a reason to assign a high value to $P(P|{\sim}Q$ & k), since there might be reason to believe that the goods that justify God in permitting E1 and E2 are likely to be beyond our ken. But the fact alone that some outweighing good entails E1 and E2 gives us no reason to believe that the good is beyond our ken. We might have some reason to believe that God-purposed goods are unknowable goods or "deep" goods, but we have no reason to believe that any outweighing good that entails E1 and E2 is an unknowable or deep good. This is in part because we have no reason to believe that any outweighing good that entails E1 and E2 is a God-purposed good. Indeed, in the absence of some credible skeptical argument to the contrary, we have good reason to believe that the value of $P(P'|{\sim}Q'$ & k) is less than the value of $P(P|{\sim}Q$ & k) and $P(P|G$ & k).

Suppose the value of $P(P'|{\sim}Q'$ & k) is slightly less than the value of $P(P|{\sim}Q$ & k). We might reasonably put the value at .3, since we have no reason to doubt our cognitive capacities with regard to outweighing goods *simpliciter* that entail E1 and E2. If the prior probability of ${\sim}Q'$ is about .5, then the prior probability of P' is about .65. And the valueof $P({\sim}Q'|P'$ & k) is about .23. Since the proposition that God exists entails ${\sim}Q$, we conclude that the value of $P(G|P'$ & k) cannot be greater than .23.[9]

3. UNDERCUTTING DEFEAT AND EVIDENTIAL ARGUMENTS

Stephen Wykstra takes a position on epistemic defeat that is similar in many ways to the position of John Pollock. There are several kinds of special epistemic defeaters, according to Pollock, but the primary kinds include undercutting defeaters.

> … An undercutting defeater for P as a prima facie reason for believing Q is a reason for denying that P would not be true unless Q were true. To illustrate, knowing about the peculiar illumination gives me reason for denying that x would not look red to me unless it were red. 'P would not be true unless Q were true' can be written as a conditional $(P > Q)$ …

According to Pollock, the perception that an item x is red is evidence that x is red only if x would not look red unless x were red. The perception is evidence, that is, only if were x not red then x would not look red. The undercutting

---

[9] This follows from the principle that $\Box(A \supset B) \supset (P(B|C) > P(A|C))$. Since $\Box(G \supset {\sim}Q)$ it follows that $(P({\sim}Q|P$ & k) $> P(G|P$ & k)). Since $P({\sim}Q|P$ & k) is about .23, we know that $P(G|P$ & k)) is not greater than .23.

defeater is the knowledge (or belief) that either x might look red anyway were x not red or that x would look red, were x not red.

Stephen Wykstra advances a more specific principle of undercutting defeat that is analogous to Pollock's general principle. Wykstra calls his principle CORNEA, the *Condition of Reasonable Epistemic Access*, and it specifies conditions under which evidence is undercut in evidential arguments from evil.

> CORNEA says an inductive inference from (P) 'We see no good with J' to (Q) 'There is no good with J' works only if it is reasonable to believe the proposition that *if Q were false then likely P would be false too*….[10]

But exactly how does Rowe's inference to $P(G|P \& k) = .33$ in the direct evidential argument suffer undercutting defeat? Wykstra urges the following.

> Hence the Adjunct Principle: If Rowe is made aware of good reasons for thinking that God-justifying goods would lack seeability, then conditionally (i.e., unless Rowe defeats these with other considerations) it is not reasonable for Rowe to believe that these goods would be seeable.[11]

Wykstra offers here a principle of undercutting defeat for inductive evidence. The fact that no good we know of justifies God in permitting E1 and E2 constitutes defeated evidence for the proposition that God does not exist if it is not probable that were God to exist, it would be true that some good we know of justifies him in permitting E1 and E2. The general principle of undercutting defeat is formulated in P0 where p and q are propositional variables.

$$\text{P0.} \quad [P(p|q)!> P(p)] \supset [P(\sim p \; \Box\!\!\to \sim q) > .5]$$

According to P0, q strongly confirms p only if it is probable that, were ~p true, then it would be the case that ~q.

P1 instantiates P0 where G stands for God exists and P stands for some good we know about justifies God in permitting E1 and E2.

$$\text{P1.} \quad [P(\sim G|P)!> P(\sim G)] \supset [P(G \; \Box\!\!\to \sim P) > .5]$$

---

[10] See Wykstra (1996b: 135). Wykstra adds:

> … This proposition is virtually equivalent to the proposition that if P is true, Q is likely true. So all CORNEA really says is that premise P justifies our believing conclusion Q only if it is reasonable for us to believe that if P is true then Q is likely true.

But of course these conditionals are not even close to equivalent. This is part of the problem we are addressing. Further on, (p.148, n.11), Wykstra notes,". . . the relation between these [conditionals] is not straightforward in S5. Both the location of the operator 'likely' and the import of the subjunctive character would need to be reckoned with in sustaining the claim that these are 'equivalent'". I believe that this claim, or a close approximation to it, can be sustained; the term "virtually" is meant to cover the finesses this will take. It's unclear to me what this means, since S5 does not entail anything at all about conditional probability or about subjunctive conditionals. Furthermore, there is simply no reasonable sense in which a subjunctive conditional might be equivalent to a conditional probability statement.

[11] Wykstra (1996b: 136).

According to P1, the fact that no good we know of justifies God in permitting E1 and E2 strongly confirms the fact that God does not exist only if, probably, were God to exist, it would be true that some good we know about justifies God in permitting E1 and E2.[12]

There is another principle similar to P1 that is true, given Rowe's level playing field assumption that $P(G) = P(\sim G)$.

P2. $[P(\sim G|P)! > P(\sim G)] \supset [P(\sim P|G) > .5]$

According to P2, the fact that no good we know of justifies God in permitting E1 and E2 strongly confirms the proposition that God does not exist only if, probably, some good we know of justifies God in permitting E1 and E2, given that God exists.

Under suitable conditions P2 is true. But the principle of undercutting defeat in P1 is false. And perhaps more importantly, P1 does not entail P2. The evidence adduced for the claim that the value of $P(G \;\square\!\!\rightarrow \sim P)$ is low, and therefore that the value of $P(G \;\square\!\!\rightarrow P)$ is high, does not in general constitute any evidence that the value of the conditional probability statement $P(\sim P|G)$ is low and the value of $P(P|G)$ is high. That is, evidence which shows that, probably, were God to exist, it would be true that no good we know of justifies God in permitting E1 and E2, is not in general evidence which shows that, probably, no good we know of justifies God in permitting E1 and E2 given that God exists.

3.1 Reconsidering Defeat: Pollock's Red Objects

Reconsider the well-known red items on the conveyor belt in Pollock's example of undercutting defeat. Instead of assuming that the items are illuminated, suppose that the items are in fact red and look red to us. These particular items, let's suppose, are red if and only if they look red. Now suppose we are informed further that had items of another color been on the conveyor, a red light would have illuminated them.

Given the new information, we should conclude that, very probably, were the items on the conveyor non-red it would be true that they look red anyway. But surely the fact that the particular items on the conveyor look red is evidence that they are red. The items that are actually on the conveyor are such that they are red if and only if they look red. Had there been non-red items on the conveyor, they would not be identical to the items that are actually on the conveyor. The alleged undercutting defeater that non-red items would look

---

[12] For convenience we assume the principle of conditional excluded middle is valid for counterfactuals.

red were they on the conveyor does not undercut the evidence derived from the fact that the actual red items look red. Consider the conjunction in (6).

6. $[P(R|L)!> P(R)] \& [P(\sim R \;\square\!\!\rightarrow \sim L) < .5]$

According to (5), an item's being red is strongly confirmed by its looking red and it is improbable that, were the items on the conveyor non-red, then they would not look red.

In the revised version of Pollock's example, learning that, probably, were the items non-red, it would be true that they look red, gives me no reason at all to be skeptical of the evidential value of their looking red. I have no reason to be skeptical of the evidence adduced from their looking red since I have no reason to believe that the second conjunct in (7) is true.

7. $[P(R|L)!> P(R)] \& [P(\sim L|\sim R) < .5]$

It is true of all of the items actually on the conveyor that they are red if and only if they look red. But then the value of $P(\sim L|\sim R)$ is high and, of course, the value of $P(L|\sim R)$ is low.

Despite the second conjunct in (5), we may conclude that L disconfirms $\sim$R. Indeed, it is perfectly possible that the distribution of values in the following ratios is similar to the one in (4) and (3) above. If the prior probability of there being a red item on the conveyor $P(R)$ is .5 and the probability of a non-red item looking red $P(L|\sim R)$ is .1, then the prior probability of seeing a red item $P(L)$ is .5. But then L strongly disconfirms $\sim$R. And that is true despite the fact that the value of $P(\sim R \;\square\!\!\rightarrow \sim L)$ is low.

8. $P(\sim R|L) = .1 = P(L|\sim R) = .1 P(R) = .5 \; P(L) = .5$

We are informed that were the items on the conveyor non-red, they would look red anyway. But that information gives us no reason to doubt the evidential value of our perceptions concerning the actual red items on the conveyor. It gives us no reason to doubt that those items look red if and only if they are red. Learning that were the items on the conveyor non-red then they would look red anyway gives us no reason to believe that the actual items on the conveyor probably have the modal property of being such that were those particular items non-red then they would look red anyway.[13] And so that information gives us no reason to doubt our perceptual evidence concerning the items on the conveyor.

Suppose we were not informed that had there been items of another color on the conveyor, a red light would have caused them to look red. Imagine instead that the skeptical hypothesis simply occurred to us that had the items

---

[13] Note that what we learn in Pollock's original example is that, almost certainly, the items on the conveyor do have the relevant modal property. We observe the red light illuminating the objects.

on the conveyor been *non-red-but-illuminated-red* items, then they would still have looked red. The hypothesis makes the value of $P(\sim R \;\square\!\!\rightarrow \sim L)$ low. And it also makes the value of $P(\sim L|\sim R)$ low. That is, it is improbable that the items on the conveyor look non-red, given that they are non-red-but-illuminated-red items. But this again gives us no reason to doubt the evidential value of our perceptions of the items that are actually on the conveyor, since it gives us no reason to believe that, probably, the items on the conveyor are in fact non-red-but-illuminated-red items.

3.2 Reconsidering Defeat: Poisonous Candy

Suppose there is a bowl of candy from which we choose a piece at random. Let C be the proposition the chosen piece of candy is poisonous. Now, suppose I use a device that has been 95% accurate to detect poisonous candy in the bowl. Of course, since the device has been 95% accurate, it has made mistakes in the detection of poisonous candy about 5% of the time. Let P be the proposition that the device has detected that all of the candy in the bowl is poisonous. So we believe that 95/100 pieces of candy in the bowl are poisonous or that there is a 95% epistemic probability that the piece of candy selected is poisonous. Now, certainly, P strongly confirms C. It is also true that the probability that the device does not detect that the entire bowl of candy is poisonous, given that the piece of candy selected is not poisonous, is high.

9. $[P(C|P)!> P(C)]$ & $P(\sim P|\sim C)$ is high

It is almost never the case that any candy is poisonous, if your experience is anything like mine, and so it is almost never true that an accurate poison-detecting device detects that an entire bowl of candy is poisonous.

But notice that (9) is also true. It is improbable that, had the piece of candy selected from the bowl not been poisonous, the device would not have detected that all of the candy is poisonous.

10. $P(\sim C \;\square\!\!\rightarrow \sim P)$ is low

Had the piece of candy selected not been poisonous, it would still have been true that the device detected that the entire bowl is poisonous. The device simply would have made an error, as we know it sometimes does.[14] Indeed, everything would have been detected in the same way had the selected candy not been poisonous.

---

[14] The alternative is to imagine that the device detects that the entire bowl of candy is poisonous. But if were then to choose a piece of candy from the bowl and discover that it is non-poisonous it would be true, backtracking, that the device in fact detected that the entire bowl is poisonous. But that backtracker is false.

But that gives me no reason at all to become skeptical of the device's accuracy. Given (10) we can infer that, probably, had the piece of candy not been poisonous, it would still have been true that the device detected that the entire bowl of candy is poisonous. But notice that it is not true of any piece of candy x in the bowl that x has the modal property of being such that, probably, were x non-poisonous, the device would have detected that x was poisonous. For any piece of candy x selected from the bowl the epistemic probability that x would be detected as poisonous were it poisonous is very high.

Compare *Pollock's Red Objects*. Suppose we know that 95% of the time red items on the conveyor are not illuminated red. The fact that items on the conveyor look red to us is good evidence that they are red. For each item x on the conveyor, it is highly probable that x does not have the modal property of being such that were x non-red x would look red anyway. This is consistent with the fact that, probably, had an item on the conveyor been non-red, then it would have looked red anyway.[15]

In the *Poisonous Candy* case, I have no reason to revise down my estimation of the device's accuracy, though (8) holds for any arbitrarily chosen piece of non-poisonous candy in the bowl. It is probable that had an arbitrarily chosen piece of candy been non-poisonous, the device would have detected that the entire bowl was poisonous anyway. Indeed, I have no reason to revise my estimation of the device's accuracy on the assumption that had every piece of candy in the bowl been non-poisonous, the device would still have detected that the entire bowl of candy is poisonous. The counterfactual conditional is very probable, since in the closest worlds where every piece of candy in the bowl is non-poisonous the device still detects that every piece of candy is poisonous. *In those worlds* we have reason to revise our estimate of the device's accuracy. But the truth of that counterfactual is not relevant to our *actual estimate* of the accuracy of the device.

What is relevant to the accuracy of the device is the value of the conditional probability $P(P|\sim C)$. If we discover that in fact $\sim C$, the selected piece of candy is not poisonous, then we have reason to revise our actual estimate of the accuracy of the device. Updating the probability of P on the discovery that $\sim C$ we will find that $P^*(P) = P(P|\sim C) < P(P)$. It's not probable that a particularly accurate device detects that the entire bowl of candy is poisonous given that an arbitrarily selected piece of candy from the bowl is not poisonous. If we discover that none of the candy in the bowl is poisonous, then a fortiori our estimate of the device's accuracy must be revised downward.

So we have another counterexample to epistemic principle in P0. The first conjunct states that P strongly confirms C.

$$11. \quad [P(C|P)! > P(C)] \;\&\; [P(\sim C \;\square\!\!\rightarrow\; \sim P) < .5]$$

---

[15] Had a non-red item been on the conveyor there is a 95% probability that it was not one of the actual items on the conveyor, but rather an illuminated red item.

But the second conjunct informs us that it's improbable that, were it the case that ~C it would be the case that ~P. We have an instantiation of P0 where the antecedent is true and the consequent is false.

3.3 Reconsidering Defeat: God-Purposed Goods

Wykstra urged that Rowe's inference from P, that no good we know of justifies an omnipotent, omniscient, perfectly good being in permitting E1 and E2, to ~G, that God does not exist, is defeated if the critic can give good reasons to believe that God-purposed goods would be "nonseeable."[16]

In *Pollock's Red Objects* we are given very good reason to believe it's false that were there non-red items on the conveyor belt then those items would not look red. But the fact that this conditional is probably false is not relevant to the evidential value of the fact that the items on the conveyor look red. An item's looking red is still good evidence for its being red.

In the case of *Poisonous Candy*, we are given very good reason to believe it's false that were the selected piece of candy non-poisonous, then it would be true that the device doesn't detect that all of the candy is poisonous. But the fact that this conditional is probably false is not relevant to the evidential value of the device's detecting that all of the candy is poisonous. The device's detecting that all of the candy is poisonous is still good evidence that all of the candy is poisonous.

Stephen Wykstra gives us some reason to believe it's false that were there goods justifying God in permitting E1 and E2, then it would be true that some goods we know of justify God in permitting E1 and E2. It's the well-known parent analogy.[17] But if the parent analogy were fully successful, it would be difficult to see how we could know anything at all about God. Infants haven't the slightest idea that their parents are rational, mammalian, or conscious. They haven't the slightest idea that their parents are not zombies, or reptilian, or automatons. But we would like to credit ourselves with knowing that God is at least conscious, rational, and good. So our cognitive limitations relative to God are obviously not analogous to the cognitive limitations of infants relative to their parents.[18]

---

[16] Wykstra (1996b: 136).

[17] Wykstra (1996b: 139). See also Wykstra (1990: 155–6).

[18] Obviously, there are ways to attempt to preserve the analogy. One might argue that the analogy is with the relative extent of the knowledge, not with the specific items of knowledge. But the point of the analogy is to urge that there is some specific knowledge we would not have, namely, knowledge of the goods for certain evils. What would the relative extent of our knowledge bear at all on our specific knowledge about goods for evils?

But Wykstra advances other reasons to deny that were there goods justifying God in permitting E1 and E2, then it would be true that some good we know of justifies God in permitting E1 and E2.

> ...I distinguish "shallow" from "deep" universes.... The Parent Analogy, construed along these lines, holds that the disparity between our cognitive limits and the vision needed to create a universe gives us reason to think that if our universe is created by God it is expectable that it would be deep; this is of course reason to think that if there are God-purposed goods, they would often be beyond our ken.[19]

In shallow universes, according to Wykstra, the events we observe are rooted in goods that are close to the surface. So we almost always see the goods for which events occur. But in deep universes observable events often serve goods that are deep and so beyond our ken.

In this case the device that detects whether there are any goods that justify God in permitting E1 and E2 is just our cognitive apparatus. The skeptic urges that our cognitive apparatus is not acute enough to detect God-purposed goods in the axiological foundations of the universe. If the skeptic is right then, probably, we would not know about God-purposed goods that justify God in permitting E1 and E2, if there were such God-purposed goods.

The skeptical argument seems to go as follows. It is true that, probably, were God to exist, then it would be true that God-purposed goods justify him in permitting E1 and E2.

$$12. \quad P(G \,\square\!\!\rightarrow Gp)$$

The next premise is that, probably, if there were God-purposed goods justifying God in permitting E1 and E2, then it would be true that no good we know of justifies God in permitting E1 and E2.

$$13. \quad P(Gp \,\square\!\!\rightarrow \sim\!P)$$

And from (11) and (12) it is concluded that, probably, were God to exist, it would be true that no good we know of justifies God in permitting E1 and E2.

$$14. \quad P(G \,\square\!\!\rightarrow \sim\!P)$$

According to Wykstra, the fact that no good we know of justifies God in permitting E1 and E2 constitutes *defeated evidence* against God's existence if it is not probable that were God to exist, it would be true that some good we know of justifies God in permitting E1 and E2. Recall the principle formulated in P1.

$$P1. \quad [P(\sim\!G|P)! > P(\sim\!G)] \supset [P(G \,\square\!\!\rightarrow \sim\!P) > .5]$$

---

[19] Wykstra (1996b: 140). See also Russell and Wykstra (1988).

According to P1, God's nonexistence is strongly confirmed by the fact that no good we know of justifies him in permitting E1 and E2 only if, probably, were God to exist, it would be that some good we know of justifies him in permitting E1 and E2.

But, as we noted in *Pollock's Red Objects* and *Poisonous Candy* above, the fact that $P(G \mathbin{\square\!\!\rightarrow} {\sim}P)$ is low does not entail that $P({\sim}P|G)$ is low. The fact that $P(G \mathbin{\square\!\!\rightarrow} {\sim}P)$ is low gives us no reason to believe that any actual good x probably has the modal property of being such that were God to exist, then x would be among the goods we do not know about. So, though we may concede that, probably, were God to exist, it would be the case that no good we know about justifies him in permitting E1 and E2, that concession gives us no reason to believe that any actual good x has the modal property of being such that were God to exist, it would be the case that x is a good we do not know about justifying God in permitting E1 and E2.

The right response is to agree with the skeptic that, in the closest worlds in which God exists, there are goods we do not know about justifying him in permitting E1 and E2. But to disagree with the skeptic that, the truth of that counterfactual, gives us reason to doubt our evidence about the existence of God-justifying goods. We have been given no reason to reject the non-skeptical view that the value of $P({\sim}P|G)$ is high, despite the fact that the value of $P(G \mathbin{\square\!\!\rightarrow} {\sim}P)$ is low.

We have underscored that the fact that $P(G \mathbin{\square\!\!\rightarrow} {\sim}P)$ is low gives us no reason to doubt our cognitive capacities with respect to actual goods. The fact that $P(G \mathbin{\square\!\!\rightarrow} {\sim}P)$ is low gives us no reason at all to believe that any of actual goods are beyond our ken. We rightly conclude that $P(G \mathbin{\square\!\!\rightarrow} {\sim}P)$ is low and also that, probably, some good we know about justifies God permitting E1 and E2, given that he exists. The values of the two conditionals in (14) and (15) are perfectly consistent.

15. $P(G \mathbin{\square\!\!\rightarrow} {\sim}P) < .5$

16. $P({\sim}P|G) > .5$

4. ARE THERE ACTUAL GOODS BEYOND OUR KEN?

According to the better evidential argument from evil P′ and Q′ represent the following propositions where neither ~P′ nor ~Q′ entail that God exists.

P′:   No outweighing good we know about entails E1 and E2.

Q′:   No outweighing good at all entails E1 and E2.

The cogency of the better evidential argument depends on a credible assignment of values to the ratios in (16). We urged that a credible assignment would make the probability that no outweighing good at all entails E1 and E2, given that no outweighing good that we know about entails E1 and E2, about .23.

17. $\dfrac{P(\sim Q'|P' \ \& \ k) = .23}{P(\sim Q'|k) = .5} = \dfrac{P(P'|\sim Q' \ \& \ k) = .3}{P(P'|k) = .65}$

The argument that $P(\sim Q'|P' \ \& \ k)$ is about .23 assumed that the value of $P(P'|Q' \ \& \ k)$ is certain. The assumption is reasonable since it is certain that no outweighing good we know of entails E1 and E2, given that no outweighing good at all entails E1 and E2.

The most important assumption in the argument is that the value of $P(P'|\sim Q' \ \& \ k)$ is low. As we noted, there might be some reason to assign a low value to $P(P|\sim Q \ \& \ k)$, since there might be reason to believe that the goods that justify God in permitting E1 and E2 are beyond our ken. And even that argument came in for harsh treatment in Section 3 above. But there are some who defend a skeptical thesis on value that does not assume theism is true. Consider Bergmann's defense of ST1.

ST1:   We have no good reason for thinking that the possible goods we know of are representative of the possible goods there are.[20]

If it were true that God exists, then we might argue that there are God-purposed goods beyond our ken. But if we are not assuming that there is some source of all value that is vastly superior to us in every way imaginable, then we seem to have no reason to deny that our commonsense views about value are reasonably accurate. Compare Bergmann.

> The claim here isn't that we have good reason for thinking that the goods we know of *aren't* representative of the goods there are. Rather, the claim is that we have no good reason to oppose the suggestion that the goods we know of are representative of only a minor portion of the goods there are and that many (or even most) of the goods beyond our ken are far greater than and significantly different from any of the goods with which we are familiar. [21]

That is, concerning the actual goods x, we know about, we do not have good reason to believe that x is not representative of the goods there are. We have no good reason not to place any credence in the claim that the actual goods are not representative. But, according to Bergmann, we also have no good reason to reject the idea that most of the goods beyond our ken are far greater than and different from the goods we know about.

But the fact of the matter is that we *do* have good reason to reject the idea that most of the goods beyond our ken (if there are any) are far greater than

---

[20] See Bergmann (2001).   [21] Bergmann (2001: 284).

and different from the goods we know about. We have very good reason to believe that ST1 is false.

Suppose we concede the epistemic possibility that the goods we know about are not at all representative of the goods there are. We nonetheless have good reason to believe that it's improbable that the goods we know about are non-representative. Suppose, for simplicity, that we have two possible sets of values S1 and S2. Assume that the values we know about might be from set S1 and might be from set S2, but cannot be from both. It is not difficult to show that the values we know about $\{v_0, v_1, v_2, \ldots v_n\}$ are probably from S1, if the items in S1 are in general more similar to the values we know about $\{v_0, v_1, v_2, \ldots v_n\}$. It is possible that the values we know about are from S2, but we have good reason not to believe it. It's in fact probable that the goods we know about are representative of the goods there are.

Let's consider a small model that concerns two possible realms of value, S1 and S2, from which three items in $V = \{v_0, v_1, v_2\}$ might have been chosen. Suppose all of the items in V have the property F or have some property in $P = \{F_0, F_1, F_2, \ldots, F_n\}$. On the intended interpretation, the set P contains the properties of the kinds of values we know about. Suppose that the items in V are representative of the items in S1. For specificity, let 80% of the items in S1 have property F or some property in P. Suppose the items in V are not representative of the items in S2. For specificity, let 5% of the items in S2 have property F or some property in P. It is not difficult to determine the posterior probability that S1 is the *actual realm of value*. Similarly we can determine the posterior probability that S2 is the actual realm of value. What we need, in brief, are the values of the conditional probabilities $P(S1|V)$ and $P(S2|V)$, where h is all of the background information we possess relevant to the truth or falsity of S1 and S2.

According to Bayes's Theorem the value of $P(S1|V)$ is determined by the equation in (17).

18. $P(S1|V) = P(S1). P(V|S1)/[P(S1). P(V|S1)] + [P(\sim S). P(V|\sim S1)]$

We might suppose without losing generality that the prior probability that the realm of value is S1 equals the prior probability that the realm of value is S2. It does not matter to the central point of the argument that we assume S1 and S2 exhaust the possible realms of value, though of course any number of other realms of value are epistemically possible. We have stipulated that $P(V|S1) = .8$ and that $P(V|\sim S1) = .05$. S2 $(= \sim S1)$ has a much richer and varied set of values than the values we actually know about. Only 5% of the values contained in S2 are the familiar values we know about. But then the value of $P(S1|V) = .5 \times .8/[.5 \times .8] + [.5 \times .05] = .4/.425 = .94$. Of course the value of $P(S2|V)$ must be .06.

So given the values that we actually know to exist, the small model illustrates why the epistemic probability is extremely low that the actual realm of value is the vastly different collection of values in S2. It is extremely improbable that, as Bergmann notes,

> . . . the goods we know of are representative of only a minor portion of the goods there are and that many (or even most) of the goods beyond our ken are far greater than and significantly different from any of the goods with which we are familiar.[22]

So Bergmann's skeptical suggestion gives us no reason to believe that the value of $P(P'|{\sim}Q'$ & k) is low. It is of course epistemically possible that the actual realm of value includes values that are vastly different from those we know about. But we have a rational method of determining how probable it is that the realm of value is so vastly different from the part of that realm we are familiar with. And it is extremely improbable that the goods we know about do not represent the kinds of values in the broader realm of value.

Of course we agree that we might come to learn about the existence of other, vastly different, sorts of values. In the distant future we might have vastly more experience and knowledge of the realm of value than we have now. And we might learn that the realm of value that we know about is extremely limited. But then again we might not. All we can rationally do is determine, given what we do know about value, the probability that the actual realm of value is vastly different from the part we know about. And the rational conclusion to draw is that it is probably false that the actual realm of value is wildly different from the part we know about.

---

[22] Bergmann (2001: 284).

10

Confirmation Theory and the Core of CORNEA

Paul Draper

Long before skeptical theism was called "skeptical theism," Stephen Wykstra (1984) defended a version of it based on an epistemological principle he called CORNEA. In this chapter, I use elementary confirmation theory to analyze CORNEA's core. This enables me to show precisely what is right about Wykstra's very influential defense of skeptical theism and, perhaps more importantly, precisely what is wrong with it. A key premise of that defense is that, on the assumption that God exists, we wouldn't expect to know what God's reasons for allowing certain evils are. I show that, while that premise together with CORNEA's core shows that our inability to adequately explain the existence of those evils in terms of theism is not strong evidence against theism, it fails to show that the evils themselves are not strong evidence against theism.

1. CORNEA'S CORE

Wykstra has over the years modified his formulation of CORNEA. He and coauthor Timothy Perrine (2012) now take CORNEA to be an internalist principle that has an externalist core. Thus, while CORNEA imposes a "constraint on when *one is entitled to regard* [a datum] E as strong evidence for [a hypothesis] H," CORNEA's core is concerned with whether "E *actually is* strong evidence for H" (377). The crux of the latter principle can be formulated as follows:

SUBJUNCTIVE CORE: E is strong evidence for H only if E would likely be different if H were false.

One worry about this formulation of CORNEA's core is that there appear to be counterexamples to it (McBrayer 2009). As Wykstra and Perrine (2012) show, however, these counterexamples can be avoided if the subjunctive conditional in SUBJUNCTIVE CORE is replaced with a conditional probability:

> PROBABILITY CORE: In cognitive situation S, E is strong evidence for H only if, relative to S, $Pr(E/{\sim}H) < ½$.[1]

Is this principle true? That depends on the precise meaning of "strong evidence." Wykstra and Perrine use that vague term when they introduce CORE, but they replace it with "levering evidence," which they define stipulatively, in their official formulations of CORE. I examine their notion of levering evidence in Section 4, where I also distinguish three versions of PROBABILITY CORE and show that two of them, one of which is Wykstra and Perrine's, are unquestionably true. Then, in the last two sections of this chapter, I explain the implications of all this for various evidential arguments from evil. Before I do any of that, however, it is crucial to specify the notion of supporting evidence that I employ in my analysis of CORNEA's core.

2. THE POSITIVE RELEVANCE CRITERION[2]

The basic idea behind the so-called "positive relevance criterion of confirmation" is that supporting or "confirming" evidence for a hypothesis raises (or its discovery would raise) the probability of that hypothesis being true. Let's define "hypothesis" broadly, so that it refers to any statement that is neither certainly true nor certainly false. Also, let's use the term "confirms" as short for "is evidence for." One way of trying to make this basic idea more precise is to narrow one's focus to propositional evidence and to employ the notion of "conditional probability" as follows:

> PRC: a statement E confirms a hypothesis H if and only if $Pr(H/E) > Pr(H)$.

In something closer to English, PRC says that a statement is evidence for a hypothesis just in case the probability of that hypothesis given or "conditional on" the truth of that statement is greater than the (unconditional) probability of that hypothesis.

---

[1] "$Pr(E/{\sim}H)$" can be read as "the epistemic probability that E is true on the assumption that H is false" or, more concisely, "the probability of E given not-H." I will say more about this in Section 2.

[2] I take this criterion to be an explication—not an analysis—of one ordinary concept of evidence. For this reason, apparent counterexamples to the theory are of dubious relevance. For more on the distinction between explication and analysis, see Carnap (1962: chapter 1) and Maher (2007).

Though I will have to qualify this later, the probabilities in PRC should be understood as all things considered epistemic probabilities.[3] Thus, "Pr(H/E)" does not denote some binary logical relation that holds between H and E regardless of anyone's cognitive situation, and "Pr(H)" does not refer to the intrinsic or a priori probability of H. Instead, the probabilities here are relative to cognitive situations and so are affected by such things as background information, conceptual frameworks, and even occurrent conscious experiences. Hence, PRC implies—correctly—that judgments of supporting evidence, like judgments of epistemic probability, are relative to cognitive situations.

Using "~H" to refer to the denial of H and assuming the truth of Bayes's theorem, we can derive the following important corollary from PRC:

> COROLLARY: a statement E confirms a hypothesis H if and only if $Pr(E/H) > Pr(E/\sim H)$.

One alleged flaw with both COROLLARY and PRC as formulated above is that they imply that a false statement could confirm a hypothesis. This flaw, if it really is a flaw, is easy enough to correct. Either add the condition that E be true or restrict the criterion and its corollary to evidence we "possess"—i.e. to evidence statements that are known to be true.

A second more worrisome flaw, however, concerns precisely that sort of evidence: PRC and COROLLARY both imply, absurdly, that no statement that is known with certainty to be true can confirm any hypothesis. This is because, if E is certain (i.e. $Pr(E) = 1$), then it is certain whether or not H is true (for any H) and so $Pr(E/H)$ must equal $Pr(E/\sim H)$. Likewise, if E is certain, then assuming its truth (i.e. conditionalizing on it) can't make any difference to H's probability and so $Pr(H/E)$ must equal $Pr(H)$. To claim in response that no evidence statement has a probability of one does not ultimately help because, even if this claim is true, the theory still needs revision so that the degree to which a hypothesis is confirmed by a piece of evidence doesn't depend on whether that evidence happens to have been discovered yet.

To solve this problem, an appropriate abstraction must be made from the cognitive situation to which the probabilities in PRC and COROLLARY are relative. For example, if E is known (whether with certainty or with near certainty) solely on the basis of observation and testimony, then the effect of that observation and testimony on the relevant cognitive situation and so on H's probability must be eliminated. This suggests the following:

> PRC*: a statement E that is known by us to be true solely on the basis of observation or testimony confirms a hypothesis H if and only if, independent of that observation or testimony, $Pr(H/E) > Pr(H)$.

---

[3] Even though I am not a subjective Bayesian, I take unconditional probabilities to be basic.

COROLLARY*:   a statement E that is known by us to be true solely on the basis of observation or testimony confirms a hypothesis H if and only if, independent of that observation or testimony, $Pr(E/H) > Pr(E/{\sim}H)$.

From here on, I will assume that we mean to be talking only about evidence statements that are known to be true (which is of course the sort of evidence statements to which arguments from evil at least try to appeal). I will also assume that an appropriate abstraction from the relevant cognitive situation is built into the meaning of the symbol "Pr." Those two assumptions make it possible to return to the simpler formulation, PRC, and combine it with its most important corollary as follows:

POSITIVE RELEVANCE CRITERION: a statement E is evidence for a hypothesis H if and only if $Pr(H/E) > Pr(H)$—i.e. if and only if $Pr(E/H) > Pr(E/{\sim}H)$.

3. DEGREES OF CONFIRMATION

Of course, no theory of confirming evidence is complete unless it says something about degree of confirmation, about how to measure the degree of support that some piece of evidence provides for a hypothesis. Unfortunately, excessive concern for making philosophical theories fit our intuitions about ordinary concepts has led to much unnecessary debate about what the correct way to measure degree of confirmation is. The debate is unnecessary because there are multiple perfectly legitimate measures of degree of confirmation. Which of two statements confirms a hypothesis to a higher degree may depend on which measure is used, but that should hardly be surprising. As long as one is clear about what *exactly* one is measuring, there are no important deeper issues about which measure is "the" right one, especially if the goal is *explicating* instead of *analyzing* our ordinary concepts of evidence (see note 2). Here I will distinguish two very useful and natural measures. The first I call "evidential strength" and the second "evidential significance."

One thing one might want to know about a piece of confirming evidence is how many times greater it makes the odds in favor of a hypothesis—that is, how many times greater it makes the ratio of the probability of a hypothesis to the probability of its denial. It is very natural to call this measure of degree of confirmation "evidential strength," partly because we intuitively want to allow for the possibility of something being strong evidence for a hypothesis that is already highly probable, and this measure, unlike other standard measures, allows for that. If E increases the ratio of the probability of H to the probability of H's denial manyfold, then I will say that it is "strong" evidence. Using the "greater than" sign with an exclamation point after it (>!) to mean "is many times greater than," we can state a criterion for strong evidence symbolically as follows:

STRONG EVIDENCE: E is strong evidence for H if and only if Pr(E/H) >! Pr(E/~H).

A second thing one might want to know about a piece of supporting evidence is how much difference (in the literal mathematical sense of "difference") it makes to the probability of a hypothesis. For example, if a hypothesis that would otherwise be improbable is highly probable because of some evidence, then that evidence makes a very large difference to the probability of that hypothesis. It is very natural to call this notion of degree of confirmation "evidential significance," partly because evidence, no matter how strong, that makes little difference to the probability of a hypothesis is typically of little practical importance. Notice that this is true even if the evidence in question makes the hypothesis many times more probable, e.g. raising its probability (by a factor of 1000) from one in a billion to one in a million. Such an increase to the probability of a hypothesis is typically of little significance because the probability of that hypothesis remains very low. If we use a double "greater than" sign (>>) to indicate a large difference, then a criterion for "significant" evidence can be stated symbolically as follows:

SIGNIFICANT EVIDENCE: E is significant evidence for H if and only if Pr(H/E) >> Pr(H).

Obviously, yet interestingly, strong evidence won't always be significant, because the significance of a piece of confirming evidence for a hypothesis depends both on the strength of that evidence and on the probability of the hypothesis independent of that evidence. For example, if one's current cognitive situation already makes the probability of some hypothesis H very high, then no new evidence for H can be significant, no matter how strong that evidence is. And if the prior probability of H is currently low enough, then new evidence for H won't be significant unless it is extremely strong. Switching to the trickier question of whether significant evidence is always strong, the answer to that question depends on one's precise standards of strength and significance. If one's standards of what counts as a "large" difference are not too high, and of what counts as "many times" greater are not too low, then significant evidence won't always be strong.

4. THREE INTERPRETATIONS OF CORNEA'S CORE

These two notions—strong evidence and significant evidence—suggest two versions of CORNEA's core (neither of which is Wykstra and Perrine's):

STRONG CORE: In cognitive situation S, E is *strong* evidence for H only if, relative to S, $Pr(E/{\sim}H) < 1/2$.

SIGNIFICANT CORE: In cognitive situation S, E is *significant* evidence for H only if, relative to S, $Pr(E/{\sim}H) < 1/2$.

Although STRONG CORE is worded identically to what I earlier labeled PROBABILITY CORE, it uses the term "strong evidence" in the technical sense explained in the previous section, which is not what Wykstra and Perrine mean by "strong evidence." STRONG CORE is unquestionably true. If $Pr(E/{\sim}H) \geq \frac{1}{2}$, then (since E can't be more probable than 1) E can't be more than twice as likely given H as it is given ~H and so can at most double the ratio of the probability of H to the probability of ~H. And obviously anything no more than twice as great cannot count as many times greater! SIGNIFICANT CORE, however, is more controversial. For even if $Pr(E/{\sim}H) > \frac{1}{2}$, it is still possible for E to make a difference to H's probability that is in the neighborhood of 1/6 or even slightly greater than ⅙. Of course, this is possible only when H's prior probability isn't too far from ½ and preferably a little less than ½ —the optimal level is actually very close to .42. But it is possible. For example, if H's prior probability is exactly ½ and $Pr(E/{\sim}H)$ equals ½ while $Pr(E/H)$ equals one, then E might fail to meet CORE's condition and yet still raise the probability of H from ½ to ⅔. Should that count as a *significant* increase to the probability of H? I think it should, because such a change in probability could easily (i.e. even when the stakes are modest) make an important *practical* difference—it could easily alter what a reasonable person would do in a relatively wide range of realistic circumstances. So SIGNIFICANT CORE is false unless one's standards of significance are unreasonably high.

Wykstra's notion of levering evidence is distinct from both strong evidence and significant evidence. He equates it with evidence that would "lever" a rational person all the way from what he calls "square non-belief"—that is, a credence of around .5—to what he calls "square belief"—that is, a credence fairly close to 1 (say, .99 or higher). In other words, levering evidence is evidence that would make a (positive) difference of close to .5 to the probability of a hypothesis if the probability of that hypothesis independent of that evidence were close to .5. Thus, Wykstra and Perrine's version of CORNEA's core is distinct from both STRONG CORE and SIGNIFICANT CORE:

LEVERING CORE: In cognitive situation S, E is *levering* evidence for H only if, relative to S, $Pr(E/{\sim}H) < 1/2$.

Like STRONG CORE, LEVERING CORE is unquestionably true, though it is worth noting that it cannot be used to dismiss arguments from evil that do not satisfy its condition as *complete* failures, since evidence can be significant without being levering.

5. CORNEA'S ACCOMPLISHMENTS

Once CORNEA's core is formulated in terms of conditional probabilities and in terms either of strong or levering evidence, its implications for Rowe's two arguments from evil (and Michael Martin's argument from evil (1978)) are clear. Let's use the term "atheism" to refer to the hypothesis that theism is false. In both the final version of his first argument from evil (1988) and in his second argument from evil (1996), Rowe employs the evidence statement that no good we know of justifies God's (producing or) permitting E1 and E2, where E1 and E2 report two instances of horrendous evil, one involving human immorality and one involving animal suffering that is not the result of human choices. In these arguments, the fact that E1 and E2 are true (i.e. that the evils they report have actually occurred) is part of our background knowledge instead of a part of the new evidence upon which Rowe's arguments are based. Thus, Rowe's arguments are not arguments *from* E1 and E2, but instead are arguments from the fact that

> FAILURE: attempts to conceive of good theistic explanations for evils like E1 and E2 have all failed.

In that sense, Rowe's arguments are arguments from the failure of theodicy instead of arguments from evil in the strict sense.[4]

More importantly, this is exactly what makes Rowe's arguments vulnerable to criticisms based on STRONG CORE and LEVERING CORE. Even if Rowe's evidence statement might report fairly significant evidence for atheism if the probability of atheism prior to considering that evidence turns out by some enormous coincidence to be near enough to .42, it can't report strong evidence for atheism or *very* significant evidence for atheism—certainly not levering evidence—precisely because, given theism and E1 and E2 (and our background information), which together imply that an *omniscient* God has a good reason to permit E1 and E2, it isn't antecedently likely that we would know what that reason is and thus isn't antecedently likely that Rowe's evidence statement FAILURE is false. This appears to be devastating for Rowe's arguments.

Rowe disagrees, believing that FAILURE actually satisfies the condition of CORNEA's core. He seems to think that, even if we should not expect to be able to figure out *on our own* God's reasons for allowing E1 and E2, we have good reason to expect God to reveal those reasons to us. Unfortunately for

---

[4] Martin's (1978) argument refers to the statement, which he calls "R," that either God has a sufficient reason for allowing the existence of evil in great abundance or evil in great abundance is logically necessary. A key premise is that repeated attempts to establish R (and in particular its first disjunct) have failed. Thus, Martin's argument is also an argument from the failure of theodicy and so is vulnerable to CORNEA's core.

Rowe, however, what we should expect God to reveal to us depends on our background information, which in the case of Rowe's arguments includes the fact that, if God exists, then God is a hidden God who reveals very little to us about divine plans and purposes and who for whatever reason severely limits the joy, comfort, and other pleasure we feel in this life. Relative to this background information, there seems to be little reason to expect God to *comfort* us with an *explanation* of why God produces or permits E1 and E2. If that is right, then it would seem that Rowe's evidence fails to satisfy the condition of STRONG CORE and LEVERING CORE, and so is neither strong nor levering evidence for the denial of theism.

6. THE LIMITATIONS OF CORNEA

If Wykstra were to conclude that Rowe's arguments from evil fail (or even more generally that all arguments from the failure of theodicy fail) and stop there, I would have little reason to disagree with his position.[5] Unfortunately, like many others since the publication of his very influential 1984 paper, he mistakenly takes his criticisms of Rowe's arguments to show that no evidential argument from evil succeeds. The last section of his first (1984) paper on CORNEA is called (ironically) "Etiology of an Error." He begins that section by saying that his "critique of Rowe may seem to show too much. Can it really be," he asks, "that vast suffering in our world... does not even weakly disconfirm theism?" (p. 90) (Although his current position is the more modest one that there may be weak disconfirmation but not levering disconfirmation, that improvement is irrelevant to the criticism I am about to make.)

He then (p. 90) quotes Basil Mitchell, who says that the theologian recognizes "the fact of pain as counting against" theism, but denies that it "counts decisively against it." Mitchell refers to this evidential problem of evil as "intractable." Wykstra (pp. 90–1) responds as follows:

> Perhaps Mitchell's argument here is less than compelling: for what theologians may generally have found intractable is the project of theodicy—of giving an *account* of the goods by virtue of which God allows pain; and if they go on to take *this* as evidence against theism—well, even theologians are not exempt from conceptual confusions.

---

[5] I say "little" here instead of "no" because failing to satisfy the condition of Wykstra and Perrine's version of CORE (LEVERING CORE) does not, for the reasons given earlier, entail the complete failure of an argument from evil.

Notice that Wykstra's italicized "this" refers to the failure of theodicy, while his original question was about the "vast suffering in our world." Further, Mitchell's evidence was the pain itself, not the failure of theism to explain that pain. Mitchell should reply, "I never said that the failure of theodicy is evidence against theism." Next Wykstra (p. 91) says: "Nevertheless, it is—among believers as well as non-believers—a persistent intuition that the inscrutable suffering in our world in some sense disconfirms theism." Notice the shift back from the failure of theodicy to the (inscrutable) suffering in our world. Clearly Wykstra is not seeing the importance of the distinction between the issue of whether *the suffering* in our world disconfirms theism and the issue of whether *its inscrutability* (i.e. the failure of theodicy) disconfirms theism.

Wykstra (p. 91; my italics) goes on to say (falsely) that, if his critique of Rowe is to be convincing, it should show why this intuition is false—"why such *suffering* should strike so many as disconfirming evidence if, as I have argued, it is not." His explanation (p. 91; my italics) is revealing:

> Rowe, I have allowed, is right in claiming that a wholly good God must be "against" suffering in this sense: such a being would allow suffering only if there were an outweighing good served by so doing. Rowe is also correct in seeing that such goods are, in a great many cases, nowhere within our ken. The linchpin of my critique has been that if theism is true, *this* is just what one would expect: for if we think carefully about the sort of being theism proposes for our belief, it is entirely expectable—given what we know of our cognitive limits—that the goods by virtue of which this Being allows known suffering should very often be beyond our ken.

Notice that the "this" in the middle of this passage—the one I italicized—refers to the fact that no God-justifying goods for many instances of suffering are within our ken. Given the suffering in the world and given theism, this fact is, as Wykstra says, "entirely expectable." But this in no way shows that the suffering *itself* is entirely expectable given theism and it certainly doesn't show that that suffering is not more expectable *given the denial of theism* (or given a specific alternative to theism like naturalism).

Wykstra (p. 91) adds in the next sentence that "Since this state of affairs is just what one should expect if theism were true, how can its obtaining be evidence against theism?" Clearly the phrase "this state of affairs" must refer only to the failure of theodicy and not to the suffering itself since only a good theodicy could show that the suffering itself is just what one should expect if theism were true. To draw a conclusion here, which Wykstra unfortunately does, about the suffering itself (or even about the suffering conjoined with our inability to explain it in terms of theism) is to make a mistake that unfortunately has been repeated time and again in the past quarter of a century by philosophers of religion. Because Wykstra has not refuted or really even attempted to argue against the claim that the evils we observe are antecedently far more likely to exist given theism's denial than given theism, he has not shown that those evils do not satisfy the condition of CORE and so has not shown that those evils are not strong, significant, and levering evidence against theism.[6]

[6] It is worth noting that what are sometimes called Humean arguments from evil often do not use the denial of theism as their alternative to theism. For example, one of David Hume's (1993, Part XI) own arguments from evil compares the likelihood given theism of what he calls "the strange mixture of good and ill which appears in life" (p.113) to its likelihood given what he takes to be the equally plausible hypothesis that the cause or causes of the universe are indifferent to the well-being of sentient life on earth. From the fact that the former likelihood is smaller than the latter, he concluded, not that his alternative hypothesis is probably true, but that theism is (other evidence held equal) less probable than the alternative and so (other evidence held equal) probably false. Humean arguments do not depend for their success on showing that the data of good and evil to which they appeal are evidence against theism in the sense of lowering the probability of theism. They do depend on its being the case that such data lower the ratio of the probability of theism to the probability of whatever alternative hypothesis they use. Again, since nothing Wykstra has written about CORNEA or CORE shows either explicitly or implicitly that this is not the case, it follows that he is not entitled to conclude from his critique of Rowe's arguments that Humean arguments from evil do not succeed.

11

Skeptical Theism, Abductive Atheology, and Theory Versioning[*]

Timothy Perrine and Stephen J. Wykstra

What we call "*the* evidential argument from evil" is not one argument but—like the Mafia—a *family* of them; its members go back to the formulations of William Rowe—the godfather of the family—in his 1979 "The Problem of Evil and some Varieties of Atheism." Wykstra's early versions of skeptical theism emerged in response to Rowe's evidential arguments. But, as they say in The Family, you've come a long way, baby. What sufficed as a response to Rowe may not suffice against later more sophisticated versions—in particular, those along the lines pioneered by Paul Draper.[1]

The atheological sophistication has increased in both data and norms. Whereas Rowe's data consists largely of "noseeum" features of suffering in our world, Draper appeals to a richer body of data—to, as Hume puts it, "that strange mixture of good and evil which appears in life." And whereas Rowe's inferences from this data relied on relatively simple *inductive* norms, Draper relies on the more complex *abductive* norms implicit in how we evaluate rival scientific hypotheses by their simplicity, their degree of "predictive fit" with the empirical data, and so on. Draper's case thus illustrates what we may call *abductive atheology*.

Our chief aim here is to make an earlier version of skeptical theism more responsive to the type of abductive atheology pioneered by Draper. Like most versions of skeptical theism, Wykstra's version relied on two types of principles. The first, broadly epistemological, is the principle formerly known as CORNEA—an unprincipled acronym for the *Condition of ReasoNable Epistemic Access*. In Delphic phrasing, CORNEA says that what we can't see

[*] Thanks to Ric Otte, an anonymous reviewer, and members of Calvin College's Tuesday colloquium for helpful comments.
[1] See Draper (1989, 2009) and Draper and Dougherty (2013).

can't hurt your theory, so long as it's something you shouldn't expect to see even if it's there. The second principle is broadly *theological*: that the theistic God, if such a being exists, often acts with a view to goods of such ontological depth as to be beyond our ken.

These principles seem to us—as to Draper[2]—to undercut any simple inductive inference from Rowe-style noseeum data. But, as Draper does not hesitate to point out, they seem to make theism all the more vulnerable to a Draper-style *abductive* argument. For that "strange mixture of good and evil" that we actually find in the world seems far more predictable on a suitable rival non-theistic hypothesis than on a skeptical version of theism that, by emphasizing divine inscrutability, undercuts our ability to form any expectations about that "strange mixture"—in amount, types, and distribution—of good and evil that we find in the world.

In Section 1, we review both a recent formulation of Draper's abductive argument and a recent dispute between Richard Otte and Draper about a key feature of Draper's argument. Otte faults Draper for basing the argument on a highly generic version of theism; this, Otte thinks, makes the argument irrelevant to those ordinary theists who embrace theism in some more specific version—say, that standard version of Christian theism that C. S. Lewis calls "Mere Christianity." Our analysis shows that in the dispute as formulated so far Draper has the upper hand: his abductive atheological argument, though indeed generic, cannot be deemed irrelevant by "special theists," for if its premises are true, then insofar as they make generic theism prima facie improbable, they do the same for any special version of expanded theism.

Section 2, however, finds in Otte an embryonic insight that, nurtured by an *en passant* concession of Draper's, allows a phoenix to rise from the ashes of Otte's first formulation. Expanding this concession, we bring out a key way in which the progressive *versioning* of a generic hypothesis allows one to identify relevant background information that, under specific probabilistic conditions, gives some versions of theism ascendancy over other versions. This versioning depends on updating theism in the light of the full range of relevant evidence, but doing this intimately interacts with our evaluation of whether so-called "generic" theism fits the range of data to which abductive atheologians are calling our attention. This *interactive* aspect, we argue, is crucial to correct conduct of the abductive investigation to which Draper's challenge calls us.

In Section 3, we put the methodological insight to substantive use in two ways. First, we argue that any good abductive inferences need thick data—both quantitatively and qualitatively thick—and that the abductive atheologian has yet to provide such thick data. Secondly, and more importantly, we argue that understanding the "versioning" of theism requires avoiding extreme versions

---

[2] See Draper's contribution to this volume.

of skeptical theism, opting instead for certain theses that define a *moderate* skeptical theism that affords not merely a defensive resource against the premises of some abductive atheological arguments, but also a constructive, positive project by which we may slowly discern—as if seeing through a mist—more of God's purposes in the surprising complexity of the world in which we find ourselves.

1. THE NEW ABDUCTIVE ATHEOLOGY: DRAPER'S HUMEAN APPROACH

We take abductive atheology to be a species of abductive metaphysics, seeking to harness abductive inference—the inferential engine that drives theoretical discovery in science—as a means of evaluating metaphysical hypotheses like naturalism or theism. Abductive inference—broadly speaking, inference to the best explanation—is here understood as both *explanatory* and *contrastive*. It is explanatory in that it moves from judgments about the degree of explanatory fit with data to conclusions about the probable truth or falsity of a hypothesis. It is contrastive in that these judgments concern two or more rival hypothesis, using comparisons of explanatory fit to lower or raise the relative probabilities. Draper, like Richard Swinburne, sees abductive confirmation and disconfirmation as conforming to, or at least illuminated by, the probability calculus—and in particular Bayes's theorem. He also, like Swinburne, sees explanatory fit as involving both simplicity considerations and predictive fit with data.

1.1 Draper's Humean Case

Draper's case applies abductive inference to metaphysical hypotheses that he calls "theism," "supernaturalism," and "naturalism," defined as follows: [3]

> Theism = df. There exists a divine mind that is wholly good, omniscient, and omnipotent, and on whom the physical world is asymmetrically dependent for its origin and continuing existence.

> Supernaturalism = df. The physical world either doesn't exist, or does exist but is asymmetrically dependent on the existence of the mental world.

> Naturalism = df. The mental world either doesn't exist, or it does exist but is asymmetrically dependent on the existence of the physical world.

The relevant data that Draper uses for his abductive inference is what he calls "the data of good and evil," which he explains as follows:

---

[3] Here we draw on Draper's recent formulations in Draper and Dougherty (2013).

The Humean data (of good and evil) = df. What we know about the "distribution and relative quantities of (physical) pain and pleasure, flourishing and floundering, virtue and vice, and triumph and tragedy."

Using these definitions, Draper formulates his argument (with our own premise-labels) as follows:

P1 [SIMPLER]   Naturalism is a much simpler hypothesis than theism.

P2 [FITTER]   Naturalism has a better predictive fit than theism regarding the data of good and evil.

P3 [NO-OFFSETTER]   There are no epistemic advantages that theism has over naturalism such that those features, when combined, suffice to offset the epistemic advantage naturalism has over theism if (P1) and (P2) are true.

C1 [FALSER]   So, theism is probably false.

Our focus will be especially on Draper's FITTER. But three overall features of Draper's argument merit comment.

First, we note that while Draper's premises are all positive—about the relative merits of naturalism—his conclusion is negative, claiming not that naturalism is probably true, but only that theism is probably false. While Draper's argument is thus an inference against the non-best explanation rather than an inference to the best explanation, it remains subject to the same abductive standards

Second, we note that his conclusion—FALSER—claims only that theism is disconfirmed by the data of good and evil in the sense of being "probably false," which he elsewhere puts by saying that theism has a probability of below .5.[4]

Third, we note that Draper's agenda allows him to give only a promissory-note defense of his NO-OFFSETTER premise. For Draper's real agenda, on our reading, is to establish that his "data of good and evil" are potent prima facie disconfirming evidence—that this data-basis does constitute weighty abductive evidence against theism, such that *unless* there is even more weighty offsetting evidence favoring theism, theism is out of the alethic running—or at

---

[4] As he formulates it here, Draper's conclusion does not make explicit what role or force FITTER has in sustaining the conclusion: the conclusion here is not that theism is made less probable by the data, but only that theism is improbable on the data and its lack of relative simplicity. However, he gives other formulations (e.g. Draper 1989: 331) that make explicit the probability-lowering power he attributes to Humean data: the data is strong evidence in that it increases by many times the ratio of the probabilities of a non-theistic hypothesis to that of theism. His most important and formidable claim is that the Humean data is in this sense an important type of "levering evidence." While this is not strictly part of, or entailed by, FALSER, we regard it as his most important and formidable claim, and take FALSER to be piggy-backing on it. Draper's distinction between "strength" and "significance" of evidence illuminates how his type of levering evidence is distinct from a related type of evidence, as staked out in Wykstra and Perrine (2012: 380–2).

least not in first place. While Draper sketches his reasons to think that theism gets no offsetting advantage from natural theology or a Calvinistic *sensus divinitatis*, we take his real aim to be showing the prima facie relevance of his Humean data.[5]

1.2 Draper's Case for FITTER

Draper's FITTER premise claims that naturalism fits "the data of good and evil" better than does theism. This empirical data, he says, consists of "what we know" about the "distribution and relative quantities of (physical) pain and pleasure, flourishing and floundering, virtue and vice, and triumph and tragedy." While this data is presumably empirical, he does not specify what it is that we do know about these things, or rely on any quantitative studies of such relative quantities or distribution. Moreover, facts about goods and evils that seem to fit theism better than naturalism—the capacity to find pleasure in the aesthetic beauty, for example—are, he says, relevant to the NO OFF-SETTER premise but not to FITTER.[6] This may seem to reduce FITTER to the tautological claim that naturalism has a better fit than theism with that body of data about good and evil that does not fit theism better than does naturalism. Regardless of how we should settle what is contained in the data of good and evil, we take Draper's point to be that the body of data is quite sizeable.

To support FITTER, Draper asks us to consider imaginatively two alien beings who are "much like us in intellectual ability" and very long-lived. One of these aliens—Natty—is a naturalist; the other—Theo—is a theist. By direct observation, they watch the entire course of biotic evolution on our planet, and in this way gradually acquire the same (but no more) empirical knowledge as we humans have acquired by our empirical sciences. At various stages of evolution, Natty and Theo make predictions about what is likely, by way of various goods and evils and their distribution, at the next evolutionary stage. Draper's claim is that at each stage *Natty's* predictions will be much superior to Theo's.

---

[5] Indeed, in previous formulations of his argument (1989, 2009), Draper does not have a NO-OFFSETTER premise, merely concluding that "other evidence held equal, theism is very probably false" (2009: 343).

[6] For instance, Draper writes, "Theists might also object to [FITTER] by pointing out that the data of good and evil entail the existence of complexity, life, consciousness, moral agency, etc., and that these things are evidence favoring theism over naturalism. This objection, however, is based on a misunderstanding of the argument. I assume that the existence of these things is part of the background information relative to which naturalism's and theism's predictive power with respect to the data of good and evil is assessed. In other words, Natty and Theo acquired such data before they begin making the predictions discussed above. Thus, these other data are relevant to [NO-OFFSETTER], not [FITTER]" (Draper and Dougherty 2013: 74).

Thus, suppose that Natty and Theo have, over millions of years, observed the slow evolution of plant life, and know the ratios of flourishing and languishing of seed-bearing plants. They now observe the first emergence of *sentient* life—life able to experience sensations, pain, and pleasure. What will they each predict about its flourishing and languishing? Draper claims that Natty—but not Theo—will predict that in sentient life, one will find about the same range of flourish-to-perish ratios as already observed in the plant kingdom, where, as most gardeners well know, this ratio tends to be depressingly small. For other things being equal, we should inductively project those same depressing ratios for sentient life as for plant life.

Now, for Natty, other things *are* equal, for as a naturalist, Natty accepts a "hypothesis of indifference,"[7] that there is no guiding mind behind the universe that seeks to promote the good or hinder the bad. Theo, by contrast, sees the material universe as created and sustained by a Mind that cares about good and evil. Since sentient beings have the capacity for the great good of having moral standing, and God will or may *see* this as a great good, Theo will have far less confidence in any prediction that flourishing-to-perishing ratio among sentient life will be as low as that found in the plant kingdom. The rough idea, we take it, is that since a sparrow is of much more value than an ant or a maple seedling, Theo (but not Natty) will be rather diffident about predicting that baby sparrows will languish (or perish) to the same extent as do baby ants or maple seedlings. In such ways—not necessarily in content, as we read Draper, but in degree of confidence—many of Theo's predictions will differ from Natty's. And since Natty's confident predictions will at each successive stage turn out true (or so Draper's argument supposes), Natty's hypothesis will again and again prove to fit the facts better than does Theo's.

The same, Draper argues, occurs with respect to predictions of Natty and Theo at other stages of evolution. As each new grade of life emerges, the background information about earlier grades of life will itself sanction certain probabilistic predictions about how goods and evils will be distributed; and theism—but not naturalism—will again and again give one reason to hedge on these background predictions. As Draper puts it, "the assumption that theism is true, but not the assumption that naturalism is true, undermines the justification for certain (accurate) predictions based on Theo's and Natty's shared background information."[8] After this disparity in predictive power is repeated for four or five rounds, those rooting for Theo will beg for the towel to be thrown in; Natty will be left standing (in this particular ring) alone.

But, as it goes for Natty and Theo, so also for us, for Draper's imaginative scenario aims to bring out the important logical differential in the predictive bearing of naturalism and theism. Draper's thesis is even if a hypothesis of

[7] For the hypothesis of indifference, see Draper (1989: 332f.), (2009: 343), and (2013).
[8] Draper and Dougherty (2013).

indifference does not *of itself* predict much, it acquires superior predictive fit to theism by not reducing or interfering with—as does theism—the considerable probability one can place in straight projections from empirical background information.

1.3 The Standoff over "Special Theism"

In Draper's abductive argument, the explicit objects of his abductive evaluation are theism *simpliciter* and naturalism *simpliciter*. His abductive approach is, in this sense, a highly *generic* one. But a vast legion of theistic believers—the varied stripes of Christian (or Jewish or Islamic) theists—are what we might call "special theists." What they embrace is a theistic core claim supplemented with further specifying claims—claims about human nature, about God's disposition toward humans, about God's manner of working in the universe, and so on. One tempting objection is that Draper's argument is irrelevant to any expanded version of theism that, by conjoining theism with specifying claims (such as the fallenness of nature, the depravity of humanity, the importance of free will, etc.), is able to fit Draper's Humean data just as well as does naturalism. The charge, on this line, is that Draper's abductive argument poses an evidential challenge only to "generic theists"—those holding to an ecumenical theism unalloyed with, and unencumbered by, any more specific doctrines.

Something like this idea is found in Richard Otte's critique of Draper's Humean case.[9] One of Otte's claims, at least on Draper's reading (2009: 347), is thus that:

> while the Bayesian arguments may create epistemic problems for generic the- ists (i.e. for theists who do not accept any specific revealed religion), they do not create any epistemic[10] problems for Christian or Jewish or Muslim theists, especially since the evidence statements to which Bayesian arguments typically appeal are entailed by (and thus antecedently certain on) these sectarian religious hypotheses.

A rationale for this idea might even be found in Bayes's theorem. Applied to this case,[11] Bayes's theorem says that the probability of special theism on the data of good and evil—"$P(ST \mid O \& k)$"—is equal to the probability of special theism alone—"$P(ST \mid k)$"—multiplied by the Keynesian relevance quotient— "$P(O \mid ST \& k) / P(O \mid k)$"—which is the hypothetical probability of O on

---

[9] Whether or not Otte holds the view we intend to criticize is an exegetical issue we need not settle here.

[10] We think that by "epistemic problem" here Draper means "alethic problem"—as opposed to other epistemic problems one might raise for theism (see Draper 2009: 333).

[11] On this usage of Bayes's theorem, see Wykstra and Perrine (2012: 386).

hypothesis H divided by its "background expectability" on our background knowledge alone:

$$P(ST \mid O \& k) = P(ST \mid k) * \left[\frac{P(O \mid ST \& k)}{P(O \mid k)} \right]$$

Now, if special theism (ST) "contains" or "implies" the data of good and evil (O),[12] then the probability of O on ST is 1:

$$P(ST \mid O \& k) = P(ST \mid k) * \left[\frac{1}{P(O \mid k)} \right]$$

But O can *decrease* the probability of ST only if the value of the Keynes's quotient is *less than* 1. This can't happen when the numerator is 1, for in that event, even when the denominator is at its maximum of 1, the quotient will be 1, so that probability of ST on O and k will be equal to its probability on k alone:

$$P(ST \mid O \& k) = P(ST \mid k) * \left[\frac{1}{1} \right]$$

So, it might appear that Draper's data of good and evil cannot (we might say) "make improbable" some such special version of theism—or, putting it more precisely, cannot make special theism any more improbable than special theism was to begin with. So, one might conclude, Draper's argument, with its appeal to the data of good and evil, leaves untouched any special theism of the sort Otte describes.

Draper finds this response otiose, claiming that as long as the "generic argument" has true premises and no faulty steps, and so gives us strong reason to think that *generic* theism is improbable, then it *also* gives us—*thereby*—equally strong reason to think that any *expanded version* of theism—in our terms, any special theism—is *just as* (or more) improbable.[13] This rejoinder, we think, has its strongest rationale in the Special Consequence Condition of the probability calculus. The Special Consequence Condition says that if any proposition A entails, as a consequence, proposition B, then if B has a low probability on some evidence, A has probability that is equally low or lower.[14] From this it

---

[12] It is, of course, unlikely that any version of theism held by actual theists entails O in all its details (including, say, that Tim's cat Bourbon had a particularly painful flea infestation in the summer of 2012). In countering Draper, the special theist may more modestly claim that such details in the data of good and evil, while perhaps improbable on her version of theism, are about equally improbable on non-theistic rivals that are live contenders.

[13] Draper (2009: 347).   [14] See, for discussion, Wykstra and Perrine (2012: 380–2).

follows that if we concede the Draper's premises are accepted, their conclusion applies as much to special versions of theism as to generic theism.

We find Draper's response right. To be sure, Otte is right that if some special theism "contains" the data of good and evil, then that version of theism is not made less probable *by* that data: the special version is not any less probable on that data than it is to begin with. But if Draper's premises do show that generic theism is—other information, as he likes to say, "held equal"—improbable *on* that data, then they also show the special version is similarly improbable. In one of the earliest Wykstra–Rowe skirmishes, this point was illustrated as follows.[15] Imagine that while on sabbatical at Notre Dame, Wykstra occasionally attends a mid-week Mass. This leads a graduate student to surmise that Wykstra is Roman Catholic. The student then learns that Wykstra teaches at Calvin, and each Sunday worships and takes communion at a local Christian Reformed Church. The student realizes this new data seems to greatly lower the probability of the hypothesis that Wykstra is a Roman Catholic. But to protect the hypothesis, the student adds the auxiliary claim that Wykstra has a secret mission from the Vatican to cause yet further dissension and splitting within the Christian Reformed Church. This expanded hypothesis may now perfectly "fit" the data, making entirely predictable that Wykstra goes to a CRC church each week. So the hypothesis is no longer made less probable by this data. Nevertheless, this gain is really no gain it all, for the expanded version of the Catholic hypothesis, compared with the restricted hypothesis, is hugely less probable *on* our background evidence alone. What we've gained with our right hand, we've taken away with our left. As Rowe put it, it seems that as in economics, so also here: there's no such thing as a free lunch.

2. PROBABILISTIC FOUNDATIONS
OF THEORY VERSIONING

But if Otte's objection is too easy, it's also too easy to draw the wrong moral from Draper's objection to it. For one might think the moral is that in abductive theorizing, one should stick to generic theories—that it is always a vice (indulged in only by those foolishly seeking a free lunch) to cope with challenging data by expanding through the addition of specifying claims.

If we've learned anything from science, it is that this moral cannot be the right one to draw here. In science, expansion is essential: it is how vague theoretical hunches become both explanatorily illuminating and empirically testable. While scientific theories start from what Hempel calls "general theoretical

---

[15] See Wykstra (2008).

conceptions"—of light as a particle or as a wave, for example—such generic core conceptions get their explanatory power only as they are fleshed out with further *specifying* hypotheses about the sizes and motions of light particles (or waves), their interaction with the forces exerted by ordinary matter, and so on. We make theoretical progress only by the sustained effort, under the empirical and conceptual pressures that characterize science, to add specifying hypotheses to a core conception, so as to yield expanded theories from which we identify the best *current expanded versions* of a generic core conception, running these against the best versions of rival core conceptions. What keeps such expansive *theory-versioning* from lust for free lunching is that new versions both redirect the search for relevant empirical data and increase the area and precision for contact—whether in concinnity or in conflict—between theory and experience.

Behind Otte's objection, we thus think, is the sound intuition that theory-versioning will be crucial to evaluating how Humean evidence bears abductively on theism. The challenge is to deploy this insight more perspicuously against Draper's abductive challenge.[16]

2.1 Draper's Concession

Our response to this challenge can be seen as an expansion of a point made by Draper. For in his discussions of Otte,[17] Draper concedes that it is in principle *possible* that some expanded version of theism might enable a theist to refute the Humean generic argument. This is, he says, because an expanded version of theism

> may be relevant to the issue of whether [FITTER] is true.

But to successfully challenge his argument in this way, Draper thinks the theist would need to use the "precise method" of weighted averaging, expanding theism by adding some auxiliary doctrine S which, by meeting certain special constraints, is able to show—by the weighted average method[18]—the falsity of FITTER. Draper[19] illustrates this by imagining the theist discovering some auxiliary hypothesis like

(L)   There is life after death

[16] For the importance of theory versioning in the philosophy of religion, see Wykstra (2008, 2011) and Wykstra and Perrine (2008), in scientific theorizing, Wykstra (1996a).

[17] Draper (2004) and (2009: 347–8).

[18] By the "weighted average method," we take Draper to refer to the total probability theorem, on which the total probability P(H/k) of some hypothesis H is equivalent to the some disjunctive set of logically independent versions of H.

[19] Draper (2004: 49f.).

such that two conditions are met. The two conditions, put in our own notation, are as follows:[20]

(C1)   P(L/T & k) is very high, and

(C2)   P(O/L & T & k) is much greater than P(O/HI & k)

where "k" is the relevant[21] background information. Otherwise put, the two conditions are: the auxiliary doctrine is very probable on theism (and our background information), and the atheological Humean data O are much more probable on theism conjoined with L (and our background information) than on the hypothesis of indifference (and our background information).[22] Such a discovery would allow the theist, using the weighted average method, to show that Draper's FITTER is false.

Draper does not, of course, think the prospect of finding any auxiliary doctrine meeting (C1) and (C2) is bright. This pessimism, however, may be inflated by his formulation of these two conditions. While Draper no doubt does not envision these conditions as necessary, but as either merely sufficient or perhaps just illustrative, we must note that they are considerably more than sufficient: L could show FITTER to be false by meeting far less stringent conditions. In particular, to show that FITTER is false, it will suffice if one finds a doctrine or set of doctrines L that meets condition C1 along with the much less onerous condition C2′:

(C2′)   P(O/L & T & k) is roughly the same as P(O/HI & k)

Nevertheless, on the key point of dispute with Otte, we find Draper correct. The possible theistic response identified by Draper's concession differs fundamentally from the one that Draper finds Otte urging. For instead of dismissing the generic Humean argument as irrelevant to the special theist, the approach counseled by Draper grants that the generic argument, if sound, is as damning for special theists as for generic theists. It thus undertakes to find a version

---

[20] In his (2009), Draper formulates the conditions without including background information k. But we take him to be regarding P as what he, in other discussions such as (2004), refers to "epistemic probabilities," which on his conception reflect a person's entire "epistemic background situation" including the person's k. We prefer using a notation that gives k an explicit place in the probability expression.

[21] In the context of using Bayes's theorem to evaluate incremental confirmation by some observed fact O, the "relevant" background knowledge k will not include O; instead it will—as Draper likes to put it—"abstract from" both O, and the experience, testimony, and evidence on which O is based. Draper here adopts a standard Bayesian approach to "the problem of old evidence" that, while not without critics, seems to us fundamentally right: see Howson and Urbach (2006: 297–301).

[22] We do not mean to suggest that Draper claims that satisfying (C1) and (C2) are necessary conditions for showing the falsity of FITTER. He does not. His point is just that if L did in fact satisfy C1 and C2, this would enable one to argue that FITTER is false, and that arguing this would require using the weighted average method.

of special theism that, by meeting conditions like C1 and C2 or C1 and C2′, allows the theist to contest in a direct way the truth of one or more premises in the generic argument.

2.2 Non-Monotonic Interplay: On the Importance of Being a Version

But behind Draper's correct point here, we believe, there is a new fundamental issue about how to conduct and evaluate the atheological abductive argument. In evaluating this argument, it will seem natural—especially for anyone raised on the milk of deductive arguments—to approach the premises in a one-at-a-time fashion. Taking that approach, one might first evaluate FITTER as true—holding that an atheistic hypothesis fits the data of good and evil much better than does theism—while postponing until later the task of determining whether NO OFF-SETTER is also true, which will require scrutinizing other data to see if it contains any "off-setting" evidence favoring theism sufficiently to offset whatever degree of unfavorable evidence is rightly alleged by FITTER.[23] This approach, however, is fundamentally wrong. The so-called second task cannot be so postponed, for close scrutiny of the "other" data is essential to evaluating whether FITTER itself is true. And it is essential precisely because of the importance of theory versioning.

To see why, an illustration from toy history of science seems to us *à propos*. Imagine two physicists, Smooth and Grain, who—perhaps around 1880—disagree about the ultimate continuity of matter. Smooth thinks that matter is fundamentally continuous: any portion of a solid or liquid is at bottom continuous, or "smooth," so that in any sample, however small, one can always slice the sample through any cross section one chooses. Grain, in contrast, thinks solids and liquids are ultimately granular—made up, at bottom, of small "grains" such that physical slicing will always be between the grains, rather than through them.

Now suppose Smooth adduces, in support of his theory, the stages of experience we've had in physically seeing and slicing matter at increasingly fine levels (call this data "e1"). For we have been able to slice a sample at any point down to the finest portions our technology allows us to see and manipulate, and

---

[23] We're not implying that Draper would disagree with any of this; neither, however, have we any sense that he agrees with it. Draper's concession to Otte, and the important things he has to say about theodicies elsewhere, certainly put him in close range of the line we're taking here. At the same time, other things he says—Draper (2009: 339)—seem in stark tension with it, and are easily read as entailing a one-step-at-a-time approach on which we can first determine whether or not the data of good and evil provides good prima facie reason for rejecting theism, treating this as independent of the evaluation of other evidence that bears favorably on theism. His comment (2013: 74) seems especially consonant with this "one thing at a time" approach.

this has been so at each stage of development. At each stage, our background information will predict the same will hold for the next stage, and Smoothism does not at all undercut this prediction. Granularism, in contrast, gives reason to think that at some stage—perhaps the next one—this will not be so, and thus time after time dampens the confidence of such predictions. The empirical data thus has better predictive fit with Smoothism than with Granularism.

FITTER$_S$[24]:   The Smoothist hypothesis has, given k, very much better predictive fit with e1 than the Granular hypothesis.

Now this argument for FITTER$_S$ is not to be sneezed at. It gains its force, however, from the fact that granular hypothesis, being stated generically, gives no specification at all of how small the ultimate grains of matter are. Considered a priori, after all, any size is possible. Suppose, however, that in our evaluating evidence favoring Granularism, we find (as indeed actually happened!) a body of data e2 that supports Granularism by way of supporting a specific version of it, one that adds specificity to the size of the "grains" of matter. For example, inspired by observations by Ben Franklin, Lord Rayleigh in the late 1800s calculated the thickness of a layer of olive oil spread over a pond, and found it to be on the order of a nanometer (a scant 10^{-9} m—one billionth of a meter!) thick. Thus, e2 gives strong support to the *conditional* claim

D: *If* Granularism is true, then the ultimate grains must be far tinier than any technology we can imagine will be able to see or manipulate.[25]

Here then is the key point. Data pool e2, supporting Granularism by way of supporting D, can rightly lead us to reject FITTER$_S$ as false. For once Granularism is expanded by, on good evidence, adding Doctrine D to it, we see that Granularism has[26] equally good predictive fit with the slicing data as does the Smoothist hypothesis: for we see that neither hypothesis "interferes" with the successful predictions arising from past projections from the different stages of our slicing operations. Data e2, by helping specify one version of Granularism as more probable than all other versions together, makes slicing data e1 something that does not even *need* to be offset—for it shows that FITTER$_S$ is not in fact true.

We thus see that in the conduct of an abductive argument like Draper's, any evaluation of FITTER *cannot* shunt to a later stage the "other evidence"

---

[24]   In this section the premise names are understood to take a subscript "$_S$" since they are the abductive-schema premises as applied to the generic Smoothist hypothesis in relation to its granularist rival.

[25]   If it is *more* than one grain thick, then "grains" are even smaller. Other empirical data from widely different sources supported the same conditional.

[26]   This is *toy* history of science. Readers can easily flesh out possible-world details that give a model of how "other data" wrongly shunted to "NO-OFFSETTER$_S$" evaluation turns out, by strongly supporting one version of granularism to expose the falsity of FITTER$_S$.

relevant only (it will be said) to evaluation of NO OFF-SETTER. And this is precisely because that "other evidence" favoring the alleged underdog hypothesis is vital to determining what versions of that hypothesis are the *leading* versions, the most probable versions, of the underdog theory. To the extent that one does have—or has not evaluated—relevant evidence about *this* matter, any judgment one makes as to the truth of FITTER will have little evidential *weight*.[27] In abductive inference—as is characteristic of non-monotonic reasoning[28]—the evaluation of the premises is interactive: evidence one might be tempted to shunt off to NO-OFFSETTER is intimately connected with evaluating the truth of FITTER.

3. THE VERSIONING OF THEISM: TOWARD A SENSIBLY SKEPTICAL THEISM

The question motivating this chapter is whether skeptical theism[29] is relevant, not just to Rowe-style arguments from evil, but also to abductive challenges of the sort posed by Draper's abductive atheology. Against Rowe-style arguments, the relevance was obvious. For there, the basic argument was that our *not seeing* any good justifying a theistic God in permitting various evils is strong evidence for there *not being* any such good. In response to such inferences, the skeptical theist presses:

> Look, if the theistic God exists, it's entirely expectable that we'd often be unable to see the goods for which many evils are allowed. To see these reasons, we'd need to see at least three things. First, we'd need to see the actual (or potential) Goods and Bads[30] that he seeks to further or inhibit. Second, we'd need an accurate grasp of God's weighting of these Goods and Bads. And third, we'd need an accurate sense of their connections with this particular event of suffering, as well as any other connected events that instantiate these Goods and Bads. But given the limitations of our own cognitive powers, and in view of what sort of being it would take to create and sustain our universe, it is entirely expectable that we'd often be not see such things.[31] And this—by the well-known principle formerly known as CORNEA—means that our *not seeing* them there is counts little for their *not being* there.

---

[27] Compare Keynes (1921: chapter 8).   [28] Compare Adams (1998: 8).

[29] Or, more cautiously, versions of skeptical theism by which Wykstra resisted Rowe-style arguments.

[30] We use uppercase "Goods" (and "Bads") to signal that we're talking about types, not tokens that instantiate these types in specific events, relationships, activities, and the like.

[31] Given the possible axiological depth of a world created and sustained by a theistic God, we should be pretty diffident about how fully and clearly we'd see any of these three things, much less all of them. On the "axiological depth" rationale see especially Russell and Wykstra (1988) and Wykstra (1996: 139ff).

Note that this response rests on two sorts of claims. The first are broadly *epistemological*, averring particular epistemological principles like CORNEA, which are urged as plausible for a wide range of cases. The second fall in the domain of philosophy of religion—or perhaps more aptly, philosophical theology: these claims address questions that are in a broad sense *ontological*, about the existence and nature of goods and evils *and* about the degree of access that we, as finite human beings, have to such things. To ask how skeptical theism is relevant to Draper-style evidence is to ask how both sorts of principles is relevant to them. Section 3.1 addresses how the first sort is relevant; Sections 3.2 and 3.3 do the same for the second.

3.1 Non-Monotonic Interaction, Thin Data, and the Burden of Argument

Rowe's argument from evil appealed to a piece of data that was relatively simple and that many of us are familiar with. (Indeed, this was part of the power of Rowe's argument.) By contrast, Draper's argument does not focus on such a simple feature of evil. Rather, Draper's data, O, is *the* data of good evil; O reports "what we know about the facts of good and evil." We take him to mean this seriously, so that O contains all we know about pain and pleasure among sentient animals, about tragedy and victory in human life, about flourishing and languishing among plants, insects, animals, humans, and so on. So taken, the information in O would, we surmise, perhaps fill a Britannica-sized set of volumes labeled *EGE: The Encyclopedia of Good and Evil, w*ith entries on the Boxer Rebellion, the first Woodstock festival, research on the behavior of fish with cut lips when offered food containing pain-killers, and of humans and other creatures lethally burned in firestorms, whether arising accidentally as in the of Mann Gulch forest fire of August 5 1949, or produced deliberately, as by the air-bombing of Dresden by the British on February 14 1945, or of Tokyo by the Americans less than a month later.[32]

When we turn to Draper's arguments, however, we find nothing like this. We find nothing very specific about the distribution of tragedy or triumph among the plant, animal, and human population—no concrete data regarding, say, the percentage of baby ants that perish before their prime, compared with the number of fawns that do so; or, for most human beings, the overall number of minutes of intense pain compare with the number of minutes of well-being and even pleasure; or of how often the sustained effort to cultivate a moral virtue leads to increased flourishing, compared with how often it leads to tragedy

---

[32] On pain and lethal burn injuries, see Maclean (1992: pp. xx–xxx, on using firestorms to deliberately incinerate cities of civilians, see Logan (2012: 162–6).

and suffering. So far, what data Draper offers seems to us very thin data—a modest assortment of armchair science generalizations that would perhaps take up but a paragraph or two in the *Encyclopedia of Good and Evil (EGE)*.[33]

But if we lack thick data, it seems to us clear that any empirical judgment we make about the truth of FITTER will have little evidential weight, for we have then little basis for a relevant "weighted-versioning" (using the weighted average principle) of the disjuncts within the two generic hypotheses that are mentioned by FITTER. The degree to which we are well-situated to evaluate FITTER, we think, depends heavily on how extensively we have collected and used background information so as to formulate the best disjunctive versions of generic theism (and naturalism), *and* to estimate the probabilities of each on our background information, *and* to determine the conditional probability of O on each of them. For each of these things is needful if we are, by the weighted average principle, to make any well-founded judgment about how likely O is on either theism or on naturalism.

Furthermore, a critical issue in the dialectical situation, we think, is whether the burden is here on the theistic defender, to find some version of theism that—perhaps by meeting constraints like C1 and C2 or C2′—gives good reason to think that FITTER is false. Once this issue is raised, we think the obvious answer is absolutely not. So long as it is abductive atheologians who are propounding a positive argument here, it is *they* who must be well-situated to assert a premise like FITTER. If they are not in a position to say whether some version of theism receives the lion's share of theism's background probability (and whether O has a high, middling, or low probability on that version), then they are in no position to aver that FITTER is true. A judgment based on data too thin to partition theism into theoretically fruitful disjuncts will have little evidential weight.[34]

3.2 Theory Versioning and Moderate Skeptical Theism

But some theists—especially evidentialist theists, including evidentialist *skeptical* theists—may well want here to be proactive here. They will want to

---

[33] Perhaps this is because his papers so far are meant as sketches of the form to be taken of a forthcoming more substantial cumulative argument from the detailed data, from the *Encyclopedia of Good and Evil*, that he takes to be most relevant.

[34] It is here important to bear in mind that while logical omniscient cognizers may have all possible disjuncts of a core theory lined up in their minds, and so may simply reorder them by re-conditionalizing on new data as it comes in, things are entirely different for finite *human* cognizers like *us*. For us, theoretical insight comes as new versions of a theory slowly swim into view. For us, reality typically discloses itself through conceptual breakthroughs (or masks itself through our conceptual muddles) by which new and verisimilitudinous surprising theory-versions swim into (or remain out of) view.

investigate what "versioning" of theism might most illuminate and absorb the type of Humean data toward which Draperian abductive atheology is gesturing. Without pretending to do more than sketch a project, we here indicate the type of theistic versioning that seems the most promising.

The versioning of generic theism—as for any broad core conception—will turn on what sorts of specifying auxiliary claims can be found which, when conjoined with the core theistic claim, partition theism so as to yield theoretically fruitful disjuncts. This quest will not merely conjoin the *empirical* data O with the theistic core claim, for this has no explanatory value, and falls immediately to the Secret Vatican Agent casuistry described earlier. Instead, it will seek auxiliary *theoretical* claims that, when conjoined with the core claim, yield special versions of theism that illuminate and fit the data we already apprehend, while also anticipating those portions of the data of good and evil that we have not yet investigated.

We can usefully distinguish some of these auxiliary claims into two broad categories—ontological and epistemological. The broadly ontological auxiliary claims will be about such things as the following: the purposes of God in creating and sustaining the world and in bringing about organic life of all sorts (but especially of human beings and other living creatures); the source of both human goodness and of human depravity; the need and possibility of redemption; God's mode of self-revelation to humankind; etc.

The "epistemological" auxiliary claims will posit appropriate cognitive attitudes to such ontological claims and their accessibility to us. This is not an all-or-nothing matter: here there will be a multidimensional continuum of possibilities, for these can range over a whole continuum (from the acidly skeptical to the naively non-skeptical) *over* a number of different sorts of "objects" to which we may have more or less epistemic access. Some of the object-dimensions are indicated by the following questions:

Q1)   What are the actual or potential Goods and Bads that God takes measure of in the divine actions and allowings?

Q2)   What, in God's correct reckoning, are the moral "weights" of these potential Goods and Bads?

Q3)   What are the relevant connections, from the divine point of view, between instances of suffering and the correctly weighted Goods and Bads to which they (or the decision of whether to allow them) are connected?

For each of these ontological questions (as well as others lurking in the neighborhood) there will be a continuum of options concerning types and degrees of limitations conditioning our ability to answer these questions by discerning how things stand, both at a particular time and as new information is made available to us. Without putting too fine a point on it degree-wise, we can see the options in a rough way as follows:

	1. Unlimited Scope	2. Limited Scope.
A. No Access	1A. We should regard *all* answers to these questions as utterly inscrutable or aprobable. That is, we should not assign any probabilistic value to any answers to the questions (Q1)–(Q3).	2A. We should regard *only some* answers to these questions as utterly inscrutable or aprobable. That is, we should not assign any probabilistic values to some answers to these questions (Q1)–(Q3), but we can assign some to other answers.
B. Limited Access	1B. We should regard as very improbable our ability to answer *any* of the questions (Q1)–(Q3). That is, we should give a very low probability to any answer to questions (Q1)–(Q3).	2B. We should regard as very improbable our ability to answer *only some* of the questions (Q1)–(Q3). That is, we should give a very low probabilistic answer to some of the questions (Q1)–(Q3). But we could give much higher probabilistic answers to others of those questions.

With this family of versions of skeptical theism in view, we can now ask what sort of version gives promise of being theoretically resilient, even fruitful, with respect to Humean data. We propose a skeptical theism that falls in quadrant 2B—a version within the "limited access and scope" quadrant.[35] More specifically, this "moderate" skeptical theism—perhaps better called *diffident* theism—will conjoin with theism (specified ontologically in some way) the following four *epistemic* theses:

(T1)   We should be very confident in our ability to discern some of the Goods that God values. (Perhaps these include doing what is right, taking pleasure in the appropriate things, relating to God properly, respecting others, etc.[36]) Similarly, we should be very confident that God disvalues certain evils. (Perhaps these include doing what is wrong, taking pleasure in the pain of others, disvaluing human life, hate, etc.) That is, we should assign a very high probability that these are actual Goods (and Bads), that God values (disvalues) them, and that, for that reason, God wants us to do our part in helping instantiate them (or keeping them from being instantiated).

(T2)   We should have middling to low confidence in our ability to discern the connections between the Goods we discern God as valuing, and

---

[35] Part of the reason why we are drawn to this particular version of skeptical theism is that it seems to allow for the possibility of learning and updating one's theism—a feature we think is important for theism to have. Indeed, we are fearful that a "no access, unlimited scope" version of theism will have difficulty handling the FITTER premise.

[36] We take these as illustrative. As we formulate moderate skeptical theism, it is, by itself, neutral with regard to these "ontological questions." (Though, of course, its success to responding to Draper might eventually require specifying answers to those questions.)

his acts of allowing specific instances of suffering or evil. That is, we should have *some* confidence that there are connections that we should expect to see, but not be *too* confident to see all of them or even many of them.

(T3)   We should be maximally *uncertain* that we can discern *all* the Goods that God values, and the relative weights of those we can discern and those we can't. (We should be very diffident about our ability to discern how the weight of those God-valued Goods we can discern compares with the weight of those we cannot discern.)

(T4)   We should be maximally *uncertain* that we can discern all the connections holding between all the Goods God values and all God's allowings of actual suffering.

In light of these moderate claims, perhaps Wykstra's earlier "infant/parent" analogy should be reconsidered.[37] Perhaps the paradigmatic analogy for moderate skeptical theism is not an *infant*/parent analogy but *a young child*/parent analogy. A young child can appreciate some of the values of their parents ("they love me") and even participate in some of the projects of their parents ("it's good for me to watch my younger sibling while my parents cook dinner"). Nevertheless, the young child is in no position to understand or know *all* his parents' values, what their weights are, or even what their connections are to possible suffering (such as when the child's parents permit a painful stomach pump after the child has accidentally ingesting something poisonous).

3.3 The Bearing on "Updating" and C1 and C2

It is, we think, some such *moderate* skeptical theism that is best suited to the project of addressing data of the sort that abductive atheology brings to our attention. How moderate skeptical theism provides a context for this project is intimately related to the role of updating conditional probabilities in light of new evidence. In particular, it is important to see how, in Draper's earth-watching scenario, Theo might update his auxiliary claims in light of fulfilled or unfulfilled predictions at the various stages of his observations of Earth's biosphere.

Suppose, for example, that Theo, prior to his observation of the rise of sentient life on Earth, gives a low probabilistic value to any version of skeptical theism, instead giving a high probabilistic value to (what we'll call) "naïve theism"—the view that we have, on a little reflection, ready access to—as they figure in divine decisions about what to allow and what to prevent—all possible

---

[37] See Wykstra (1984, 1996b). For discussion of the "infant/parent" analogy, see Dougherty (2012).

goods, their weights, and their connections to actual suffering.[38] Theo treats
theism as equivalent to a disjunctive set of versions of theism, each version
having a different probabilistic weight.[39] Letting T be theism and "t_x" some
specific version of theism,

$$T = t_1 \text{ or } t_2 \text{ or } t_3 \text{ or } t_4 \ldots \text{ or } t_n$$

Suppose we let the first disjunct, t_1, be naïve theism, to which Theo initially
gives a much probability (say, .48) much higher than assigned to the other
disjuncts (weighted at, say, .001).

$$T = .48 \text{ v } .001 \text{ v } .001 \text{ v } .001 \ldots .001.$$

Now if Theo begins as a naïve theist, his initial prediction regarding the first
forms of conscious life may well be along the lines Draper suggests: he'll think
that since consciousness—including the capacity to feel pleasure and pain—is
morally relevant to God, God will see to it that the distribution of flourishing
and languishing among the first conscious beings would be importantly different from the distribution of flourishing and languishing among plants (for
which "languishing" does not, we suppose, involve pain). Given this, Theo's
predictions will not, in the initial round of predictions, fit the data as well as
Natty's.[40] This means that Theo's naïve theism will receive quite a beating.

But how should Theo respond to this? Here's one such story as to how he
might rightly reason:

> I initially believed that God would think that suffering and pleasure are important,
> and are the main things relevantly connected to the distribution of flourishing
> and languishing among these newly arrived sentient organisms. Now this seemed
> to get me in trouble. But this doesn't mean I should now become utterly skeptical
> about what it is that God values and disvalues. It suggests instead that I was naïve
> in thinking I could see all the relevant goods and all the relevant connections.
> Chastened by my failed predictions, I now find two things much more likely than
> before. Epistemically, I see it is likely that we do not have such easy access to all
> the goods God values, and to all of their connections with present divine allow-
> ings. Some goods may be ones humans can't cognitively access at all; others may,
> in themselves or in their connections to present events, require patient strenuous
> inquiry for us to discern. And ontologically, I give greatly increased likelihood to
> the auxiliary claim that God values, in ways I didn't see before, a world governed

---

[38] Dougherty, in Draper and Dougherty (2013), seems to suggest that there are various a priori
considerations that Theo might very well have, and that given these considerations, Theo might
not begin as a naïve theist. ("Seems to suggest" since Dougherty does not use the concept of a
naïve theist.) This is an interesting suggestion, and while we are not necessarily opposed to the
role of a priori reasoning affecting the versioning of theism, we do not have space to provide a
full discussion of how a priori considerations—like the ones Dougherty raises—might impact
versioning theism.

[39] The notation here is intended merely as a visual heuristic.

[40] Again, we reminder the reader that we do not think that Draper is yet entitled to this conclusion since he has yet to provide thick-enough data. We here only assume, for sake of discussion, that he is right.

by regular laws of nature, and a world with strong continuity in how organisms evolve from one level to another, so that there is a certain "functional integrity" to creation—either because such law-like continuity is good in itself, or because it is connected in ways I can't see to other great goods, whether ones I see or ones I don't see. Given my commitment to theism, and my new background information, I now see that a version of theism specified by auxiliary claims along these lines is far more likely than my earlier naïve theism.

Suppose that on some such reflections as this, Theo shifts much of the probability he had assigned to naïve theism to a form of moderate skeptical theism. Very roughly, we can represent such a shift as follows, where the fourth disjunct is a form of moderate skeptical theism:

$$T = .001 \text{ v } .001 \text{ v } .001 \text{ v } .48 \dots .001.$$

On this story, then, Theo's moderate skeptical theism becomes the best version of theism to be tested against.

Suppose that Theo comes to accept moderate skeptical theism; how then will he make predictions, given theism? Since moderate skeptical theism has the most probability of the different versions of theism, the predictions of theism will be close to the predictions of moderate skeptical theism. And it seems that, in that case, his predictions will differ from his first round of predictions. His predictions will now put more weight on things like the new exhibiting continuity with the old, and will thus show little difference in content or confidence from the predictions of Natty (though some difference may remain). Thus, *theism's* predictions—and not just *moderate skeptical theism's* predictions—may very well mirror closely those predictions of Natty. (C2′) will thus be met; the abductive data will be handled by Theo's moderate skeptical theism. But if Theo's predictions are similar to those of Natty, then it won't be that Natty's predictions have a better "fit" than Theo's—they won't have a better fit at that stage or subsequent stages.

By such versioning, theism need not seek to *predict* the data of good and evil in the way that old-fashioned theodicies sought to do: skeptical theists can thus remain significantly skeptical. But their theism will leave background predictions intact much as does the non-theistic hypothesis of indifference—which on Draper's argument also does not, of course, itself pretend to explain or predict the data of good and evil. And insofar as it can do this, FITTER will be found false.[41,42]

---

[41] This criticism should be kept distinct from van Inwagen's challenge (1991) to a premise similar to FITTER. Van Inwagen's criticism can be put (more or less) like this: FITTER is true only if there is an epistemic probability of the data of good and evil on theism, and that epistemic probability is less than the epistemic probability of the data of good and evil on naturalism. But we are in no position to determine what the epistemic probability of the data of good and evil is on theism, and so we are in no position to say that *its* probability is less than the probability of the data of good and evil on naturalism. Thus, we are in no position to evaluate whether or not FITTER is true.

[42] In his (2009: 344), Draper considers something like this response from skeptical theists, objecting that "contrary to what the skeptical theist would have us believe, the possibility of

So goes, at any rate, our story here—a story, we think, that has more than a few grains of truth to it. But what's important to note is that the real burden here is not on the theists, but on any bold abductive atheologian purporting to have a weighty abductive argument against theism. For if our account here is right, it is the abductive atheologians who must, in making any case for FITTER worth its salt, show that given our background information, it is improbable that any special version of theism meets (C1) and (C2'). Relegating relevant data here to OFF-SETTER leaves any endorsement of FITTER in an evidential vacuum.

At the same time, theists have more reason to be proactive than the demands of negative apologetics. The theoretical life of theism comes from versions of expanded theism, and here we theists should view our theism, while grounded in the past, as also *dynamic,* and as needing better specification as we learn more and more, individually and communally, about ourselves and the world we live in, so as to refine theism into its best and truest versions. If the core claims of generic theism are true, it is not vain to hope that a theistic research program will, in the long run, display a certain empirically and theoretically progressive character. Whether *we* should expect to see such progressive shifts is however another matter, for as John Maynard Keynes aptly observed, in the long run—indeed, a good ways short of it—*we* shall all be dead. If generic theism is true, we may thus also hope it is true in a version on which God has given us, in the short run allotted to us, other less theoretical ways to know Him.[43]

God having moral reasons *unknown* to us to permit O does not undermine my case for [FITTER], because God's having reasons to permit O that are unknown to us is no more likely *antecedently* than God's having reasons to prevent O that are unknown to us." Note that the skeptical theist Draper is considering does not update her (epistemological and ontological) auxiliary claims at successive stages of inquiry. This difference between his skeptical theist and ours provides, we think, promising resources for addressing this objection.

[43] Wykstra (1990b, 2002).

12

Meet the New Skeptical Theism, Same as the Old Skeptical Theism

Paul Draper

The Who's classic rock anthem "Won't Get Fooled Again" is not necessarily opposed to political revolution, but it wisely encourages wariness about such change. In the end, a new regime may be very different from the old one, but just as oppressive—hence the lyric, "meet the new boss, same as the old boss." With this song in mind (let's pretend), I read Timothy Perrine and Stephen J. Wykstra's attempt in Chapter 11 of this volume to revolutionize or at least retool skeptical theism so that it applies to so-called Humean arguments from evil.

The need for change of some sort is established in Chapter 10 where I make the following point. Suppose Wykstra is right that, if there is a God, then we shouldn't expect to know what God's reasons for producing or allowing certain evils are. Then it follows that our ignorance of those reasons (i.e. the failure of the project of theodicy) is not strong evidence against theism. It does not follow, however, that the evils themselves (or other things we know about them) are not strong evidence against theism, nor does it follow that the Humean is mistaken in claiming that the observed distribution of benefits and harms to sentient beings is much more to be expected given some serious atheistic hypothesis like naturalism than it is given theism. Thus, while Wykstra's previous work on skeptical theism threatens Rowe's arguments, which take our inability to conceive of "God-justifying reasons" for certain horrific evils to be the crucial evidence, it does not, contrary to what many philosophers of religion have thought since Wykstra's 1984 paper, threaten evidential arguments from evil like mine (or David Hume's or Charles Darwin's or Michael Tooley's[1]),

---

[1] I refer of course to the evidential argument from evil Hume formulates in part XI of the *Dialogues* (1993). Darwin's argument can be found in his *Autobiography* (1958). For an interpretation and defense of that argument, see Draper (2011). Tooley's most recent formulations of his argument are defended in Plantinga and Tooley (2008: 108–46) and Tooley (2012).

which are based on various things we know about the evils in our world quite apart from any effort (and subsequent failure) to explain them theistically.[2]

The principle Wykstra (1984) called CORNEA is of no help here, and Perrine and Wykstra make no use of it. I contend, however, that while Wykstra's brand of skeptical theism undergoes radical change in their chapter, it remains ineffective as a response to arguments from evil like mine. Their criticisms of my most recent formulation of a Humean argument from evil are based on a mixture of misunderstandings of my work and subtle mistakes in reasoning. My goal is to establish this immediately so that, in the immortal words of Pete Townshend, "we don't get fooled again."[3]

1. MISUNDERSTANDINGS

Perrine and Wykstra (henceforth "P&W" for short) focus primarily on two of my papers on the problem of evil: an entry (Draper and Dougherty 2013) for a reference work on the problem of evil that I recently coauthored with Trent Dougherty and a reply (Draper 2004) to a paper by Ric Otte (2004) criticizing an earlier argument from evil of mine (1989). In the 2013 paper, I identify the defining features of a "Humean argument from evil," provide an example of such an argument, and sketch a defense of its first two premises. Dougherty then raises some objections to the argument in the part of the paper that he authored. The argument in question proceeds as follows:

1. Naturalism is much simpler than theism.

2. Naturalism has much more predictive power than theism does with respect to "the data of good and evil"—that is, with respect to what we know about the distribution and relative quantities of (physical) pleasure and pain, flourishing and floundering, virtue and vice, and triumph and tragedy.

3. Any epistemic advantages that theism has over naturalism do not, even when combined, suffice to offset the advantages that naturalism has over theism if premises 1 and 2 are true.

It follows from 1–3 that

4. Theism is probably false.

---

[2] A successful theodicy would, of course, be a threat to non-Rowean arguments from evil, but the absence of a successful theodicy is not the evidence to which non-Rowean arguments appeal.

[3] I do not mean to imply that Wykstra intentionally tried to fool anyone. Nor do I mean to disparage his brilliant work on CORNEA and its application to Rowean arguments from evil. In my opinion, this work was an exceptionally important contribution to the literature on the problem of evil.

I emphasize in the paper that nothing close to a full defense of the argument's three premises can be attempted in the available space. For what it's worth, a book-length defense of a similar argument is in progress. What concerns me, however, is not P&W's choice of target (I guess I can forgive them for not responding to a book that does not yet exist), but instead their faulty description of that target, especially their mischaracterization of my argument for premise 2. Accordingly, I begin by identifying four ways in which they have misunderstood my work. I have no doubt that I am partly responsible for these misunderstandings, and I am grateful for this opportunity to clarify my views.

1.1

The first misunderstanding concerns both how and why I divide up the data the way I do in my argument. P&W say, "facts about goods and evils that seem to fit theism better than naturalism—the capacity to find pleasure in aesthetic beauty, for example—are, [Draper] says, relevant to the [third] premise but not to the [second]" (p. 146). I don't actually say that. In fact, I intend to include aesthetic pleasure in the data of good and evil as well as many other facts that seem to fit theism better than naturalism. P&W are correct, however, in claiming that I do not include all goods and evils in the "data of good and evil." I only included facts about pleasure and pain, flourishing and languishing, moral virtue and moral vice, and triumph and tragedy. This means, for example, that I exclude facts about the existence or complexity of the universe, the order and beauty it exhibits, and the existence of consciousness. Those facts would be treated as *data* for the purposes of evaluating my third premise, but they are (and this will be important in Section 2.1) included in the background information relative to which the predictive powers of theism and naturalism are compared in the second premise. I recognize that such facts form the basis for the sort of theistic arguments to which natural theologians typically appeal. Following Swinburne and most other philosophers of religion, however, I believe it is better, for the purposes of assessing the evidence for and against theism, to separate facts about the quality of the lives led by sentient beings on earth from more general facts about the nature of those lives and the conditions that make them possible. I have no doubt that some of the latter facts favor theism over naturalism, but I also believe that some of them favor naturalism over theism (e.g. the high degree of dependence of consciousness on the brain and the success of methodological naturalism). So I'm certainly not trying to stack the deck.

I have no reason to do that, since, contrary to what P&W repeatedly say or imply about my motivations, I am not an atheologian. I am a philosopher. My goal is to engage in philosophical *inquiry* about whether or not God exists, not to justify a negative answer to that question. I also object to P&W's

uncharacteristically uncharitable suggestion that my second premise is just "the tautological claim that naturalism has a better fit than theism with that body of data about good and evil that does not fit theism better than [it] does naturalism" (p. 146). That suggestion is plainly false (not to mention that the claim it conflates with my second premise is not tautologous).

1.2

A second misunderstanding of my work, and this may be the most important of the four, concerns the structure of my cumulative case for the second premise of my argument. I defend this premise by imagining visitors to earth who learn what we know about our biosphere, though not in the order that we learn it. In particular, the data they acquire last are the data of good and evil. As they acquire these data, they make predictions—with varying degrees of confidence—based on either naturalism or theism (together with increasing background information) about what they will discover about the quality of sentient life on earth. First they make predictions about pain and pleasure. Second, taking into account what they learned about pain and pleasure, they make predictions about flourishing and languishing. Third, taking into account what they know about pleasure, pain, flourishing, and languishing, they make predictions about virtue and vice. Finally, after adding what they learn about virtue and vice to their increasing background information, they make predictions about triumph and tragedy. I defend the second premise of my argument from evil by arguing that the predictions of these alien visitors will on the whole be much more accurate when they base them on naturalism than when they base them on theism.

P&W's description of how my aliens acquire information and what they make predictions about is importantly different from my own. They say that the alien visitors simply observe the development of life on Earth from its first origins up until the present time. This is why they say that these visitors are "very long-lived" even though I never mention anything about their life span in my paper. They then attribute to me the position that at each new stage in the development of different forms of sentient life, naturalism successfully predicts what these alien beings observe while theism doesn't. This is not my position, and for good reason. The different data obtained at each historical stage are not sufficiently independent in the relevant probabilistic sense.[4] For example, *given theism*, knowing that one sort of vertebrate (amphibians, let's say) suffer and languish in huge numbers dramatically affects the probability

---

[4] "Independence" as standardly defined is an all-or-nothing concept. Here I understand it to admit of degrees. I trust the context should suffice to make clear what I have in mind without a formal definition.

(again given theism) that another sort (reptiles, for example) fare no better. Specifically, it raises it—a lot. Roughly, this is because, if God has a good reason for producing a world containing the suffering and languishing of amphibians, then it is not unlikely that God also has a good reason for producing a world in which reptiles suffer and languish too. Thus, I would seriously overestimate the severity of the evidential problem faced by theism if I were to claim that at each new stage in the development of life the alien visitors acquire new evidence that strongly favors naturalism over theism.

This is why I divide the evils (and goods) I discuss into categories based on important moral differences between those evils (and goods) instead of on morally irrelevant temporal or biological differences. My goal is to ensure that the crucial facts to which I appeal are sufficiently independent to generate distinct "predictive" problems for theism as compared to naturalism. For example, God's having good reason to cause or allow sentient beings to experience significant amounts of intense physical pain does not make it likely that God has good reason to cause or allow many of these beings never to flourish; and God's having good reason to cause or allow some sentient beings to feel physical pain and to languish does not make it likely that God has good reason to create a world full of moral vice or a world in which many human beings, whether they flourish in the biological sense or not, tragically fail to obtain the desires of their hearts. This is crucial for understanding how my cumulative case for my second premise is supposed to work.

1.3

A third misunderstanding concerns the specificity of the data of good and evil to which my argument appeals. I intend to base my argument from evil on general global facts about the existence and distribution of goods and evils, not on specific or local facts. Thus, contrary to what P&W say, in defending my second premise I do not compare theism's and naturalism's ability to predict or retrodict specific "flourish-to-perish" ratios or ranges of such ratios. Like most of us, my imaginary alien beings don't even know what the values of such ratios are, and even if they did, it would be of little relevance. Are we to suppose, for example, that the data favors theism over naturalism just because the ratio of sentient beings that flourish to sentient beings that die young is higher than the ratio of plants that flourish to plants that die young? Surely what is more important is the more general fact that both ratios are relatively low or, even more generally, that huge numbers of sentient beings, just like huge numbers of plants, die young or survive but languish. In general, very specific facts will rarely add much of relevance when the hypotheses being compared are broad metaphysical theories like theism and naturalism.

1.4

Finally, P&W say that I make an "en passant concession" (p. 143) to Otte, namely, that it is in principle possible for an expanded version of theism to refute the second premise of my argument. That is my position, but it is neither a concession nor *en passant*. In the very first paper I published on the problem of evil (Draper 1989), long before I had a chance to "concede" anything to Otte, I emphasized that theodicies and other "expansions" or "versions" of theism could potentially affect the predictive power of theism with respect to various data (i.e. they could potentially affect the *antecedent* probability of various data given theism). Following Robert M. Adams (1985: 252), I also claimed that the proper way to evaluate that effect—that is, the proper way to evaluate the effect of what P&W call "theory versioning"—on a claim like my second premise is to use the "weighted average principle" ("WAP" for short), which is a consequence of what P&W (following others) call the rule of total probability.

Using the language of "predictive power," WAP says that the predictive power of a theory T with respect to some datum D is a probability weighted average of its power to predict D assuming some specific version V of that theory is true and its power to predict D assuming that V is false. What makes this an average is that the weights given to the two quantities being averaged sum to 1. What makes it a weighted average instead of just a straight average is that more weight may be given to one of the quantities being averaged than to the other. The relevant weights are, respectively, the antecedent probability of V given T and the antecedent probability of V's denial given T. Notice that these weights are *antecedent* probabilities—they are calculated independent of the observations and testimony upon which our knowledge of the datum is based. So one cannot use V's ability to account for D to justify assigning a high value to V's probability given T.

A crucial implication of WAP is that the greater the antecedent probability of V given T, the closer T's predictive power will be to V's predictive power. In that same 1989 paper, I used WAP to argue that three distinct expansions or versions of theism (two versions of the free will theodicy and a version of skeptical theism that I called the "infinite intellect defense") fail to provide the resources for challenging my claim that the atheistic "hypothesis of indifference" has much more predictive power than theism does with respect to what we know about pleasure and pain. Thus, I completely agree with P&W that "theory versioning [is] crucial to evaluating how Humean evidence bears abductively on theism" (p. 151). That "sound intuition" [allegedly] "behind Otte's objection" (p. 151) is something I have been defending and applying for some time.

As we shall soon see, however, P&W take this intuition beyond what WAP implies and for that reason get into trouble, or so I will argue. One thing they are right about, however, is that according to WAP, if some version of theism is antecedently very likely given theism, then that version needn't have much more predictive power (with respect to the relevant data) than the relevant atheistic alternative hypothesis in order to refute the central premise of a Humean argument from evil.[5] Indeed, it need not even have as much predictive power if the goal is just to show that the atheistic alternative does not have *much* more predictive power than theism.

2. MISTAKES

P&W raise three objections concerning the second premise of my recent Humean argument from evil. The first is that I defend the second premise independently of the third, which they think represents a failure to recognize that abductive reasoning is non-monotonic. The second is that my case for my second premise fails to meet what they take to be my "burden of proof," and the third is that a skeptical expansion or version of theism can be formulated that undermines my second premise. All three of these objections fail, partly because P&W make some subtle and interesting logical mistakes. Exposing these mistakes will, I hope, lead to a deeper understanding of Humean arguments from evil.

2.1

Unlike inductive reasoning, deductive reasoning is monotonic. Adding true premises to a good inductive argument can turn it into a bad argument, but adding true premises to a sound deduction cannot make it unsound. Although P&W call my reasoning abductive and they are right that any abductive logic would have to be non-monotonic, I contend that my argument is (informally) valid and hence that my reasoning is deductive, not abductive.

In support of this contention, I offer here a mathematical model of my argument. In this model, at least one significant idealization is made, namely, that the epistemic probability of a statement can be represented as the logical probability of that statement conditional on another statement representing one's "total evidence." The argument uses the following abbreviations: "N" and "T" stand for naturalism and theism, respectively, "D" stands for the data of good

---

[5] In my 2004 reply to Otte I incomprehensibly suggest, though thankfully I don't assert, otherwise. Given how easy it is to deduce the implications of WAP, I have no idea why I did this. P&W very charitably attribute this to my only trying to state sufficient conditions for refuting the crucial Humean premise instead of necessary conditions. But why state absurdly strong sufficient conditions? More likely some kind of cut and paste accident is involved here, but it is still embarrassing (for my editor who did not catch the mistake).

and evil, and "b" stands for the background evidence (so that the total evidence is the conjunction of b and the "new evidence" D). Also, ">>" stands for "is at least one hundred times greater than," and ">>>" stands for "is at least ten thousand times greater than." Of course, the choice of this particular pair of numbers (one hundred and ten thousand) is somewhat arbitrary, but keep in mind that the following argument is a *model* of my argument and not an *interpretation* of it.

1. $Pr(N) \gg Pr(T)$.

2. $Pr(D/N\&b) \gg Pr(D/T\&b)$.

3. $Pr(b/T)$ has a value, $Pr(b/N) > 0$, and it is not the case that $Pr(b/T) \ggg Pr(b/N)$.

So, 4. $Pr(T/D\&b) < \frac{1}{2}$.

Since N entails that T is false and since the probabilities in the argument, we may suppose, necessarily conform to certain key theorems of mathematical probability (e.g. Bayes's theorem, the negation theorem, and the theorem that a statement is at least as probable as any statement that entails it), it follows that this argument is valid. Further, if the argument is sound—that is, if it is valid and its premises are true—then acquiring new information cannot render it unsound.

I suspect, however, that P&W's first objection does not really depend on challenging the validity of my argument (or the monotonicity of deductive logic). What that objection really amounts to, I think, is just the charge that my argument's second premise cannot be evaluated independently of the third. They seem to infer this conclusion from the premise that theism's predictive power with respect to the data of good and evil depends on which version or versions of theism are (antecedently) most likely to be true and that in turn depends on other evidence besides the data of good and evil—evidence that I allegedly "shunt off" to the third premise.

This argument, however, is confused. What is "shunted off" to the third premise is the issue of whether the background evidence favors (in the relevant sense) theism *over naturalism* and, if so, how strongly. Whether the background evidence favors one version of theism over another does not depend on how that issue is resolved and is in fact taken into account in my second premise (as the "b" in "$Pr(D/T\&b)$" in my mathematical model hopefully helps to make clear). Similarly, in P&W's example of "granularism" versus "smoothism," if e2 is known, then it is part of the background evidence and so will be taken into account in evaluating the antecedent probability of e1 given granularism quite independently of the issue of which if either of smoothism and granularism e2 favors. P&W seem to forget here (but not in other parts of their chapter) that the likelihoods evaluated in my second premise are not evaluated independently of background evidence. If (and this is a big "if") some known version of theism is not only more likely *on the background evidence* than other versions but also "predicts" D better than those other versions, then that fact must be taken into account in any proper evaluation of my second premise. Thus, determining whether any version of theism is like that does not, contrary to what P&W think, require evaluating the third premise of the argument.

2.2

P&W's second objection to my argument is that my case for premise 2 is insufficient to meet my burden of proof and that this is so for two reasons: first, the set of data to which I appeal is too thin, and second, proving the truth of my second premise requires doing something that I have not done, namely, showing that no expansions of theism significantly boost theism's predictive power with respect to the data of good and evil.

Concerning P&W's first reason, I agree that in the particular paper P&W target, I did not have enough space to examine the data of good and evil in sufficient detail. In several other papers, however, I offer considerably more detail. P&W might reply, however, that the data of good and evil are far too "thick" (that is, far too numerous and diverse) to address completely in a few papers or even a few books. I do not believe, however, that an adequate defense of my second premise requires explicitly addressing most everything we know about good and evil. As mentioned above, there is no need to focus on *very* specific facts when comparing broad metaphysical hypotheses, not to mention that much of the data is, in effect, redundant (recall what I said earlier about amphibian pain and reptile pain). Thus, almost all of what P&W call "The Encyclopedia of Good and Evil" can legitimately be ignored.

P&W's second reason, *taken literally*, sets the standard for meeting my burden of proof unreasonably high. To demand that I consider every possible version of theism, *including ones that have yet to be formulated*, is to overlook the fact that the probabilities in my argument are epistemic. If there is a good theodicy out there in logical space that we have not yet discovered, then its discovery would *increase* the predictive power of theism; it wouldn't prove that our previous assessment of theism's predictive power is mistaken. (This point famously creates a "problem of new hypotheses" for ultra-orthodox subjective Bayesians who naïvely think that Bayes's rule or some generalization of it like Jeffrey's rule is the sole requirement of reason when it comes to updating one's credences.) In addition, theists have for centuries been offering expansions of theism in an attempt to deal with the lack of fit between theism and the facts of evil. These efforts are widely recognized to have been failures, which is one reason for all the attention currently being given to skeptical theism. Further, I have carefully analyzed and criticized (in 2001 and 2011) what I believe are the two best contemporary attempts to expand theism so that it accounts for evil. So while philosophers rarely meet their burden of proof, this may be a rare exception. Granted, I've had centuries of help from other philosophers and theologians, but given that help it's hard to imagine a substantial burden of proof in philosophy that has been met more thoroughly than the burden to show that the project of theodicy is a failure—that attempts to use auxiliary hypotheses about God's purposes to significantly boost the predictive power of theism with respect to the facts of evil have not been successful.

Of course, not all specific versions of theism that might help refute my second premise are theodicies. Some expand theism, not by offering an auxiliary hypothesis about God's possible purposes for allowing evil, but instead by offering various versions of skeptical theism. For example, one could add to theism an auxiliary hypothesis pointing out the vast distance between human and divine knowledge about goods, evils, and the broadly logical relations they bear to each other. This is the "infinite intellect defense" that I evaluated using WAP in my 1989 paper. I also wrote papers (1996 and 2013) defending my arguments from evil against Peter van Inwagen's and Michael Bergmann's versions of skeptical theism, and in my other chapter in this volume I deal with Wykstra's CORNEA-based version of skeptical theism.

P&W are free, of course, to challenge my arguments in these papers (or in my writings on theodicy), but until they do, I don't know what more they expect me to do to meet my burden of proof. Further, while it is possible that there are more effective versions of skeptical theism (or more effective theodicies) of which I am unaware (perhaps because no one has yet formulated them or perhaps because I haven't read every paper and book ever written on theodicy and skeptical theism), the probabilities in my argument are epistemic ones. Thus, as I have already pointed out, logical omniscience is not required in order to assess them. Further, my ultimate goal is to determine whether my argument is sound relative to my own epistemic situation and to relevantly similar epistemic situations. If I were an atheologian trying to use my argument to prove that theism is improbable relative to the epistemic situations of everyone on earth (or even of every philosopher of religion in the Midwest), then P&W's second objection would have much more force.

2.3

P&W's third objection involves formulating a new version of skeptical theism designed specifically to undermine my second premise. This "moderately" skeptical version of theism adds to theism a number of theses about what degree of confidence we rationally should have in certain claims about our cognitive abilities. Roughly, moderate skeptical theists believe that (i) we should have great confidence that we can discern some of the goods and evils that God values and disvalues, (ii) we should have middling to low confidence that we can discern how these goods and evils might be connected, and (iii) we should have no confidence at all that we can discern all of the goods God values and all of the ways in which the goods God values are connected to various evils.

It's not clear, however, how these theses are supposed to help, even if they are antecedently likely given theism. An inability to discern certain goods, evils, and connections between goods and evils is no more likely to result in ignorance of reasons why God would produce or allow various evils than it is to result in ignorance of reasons (in addition to the known ones) of why God would prevent them. Further, these "skeptical" theses, even if true, provide no reason at all to deny that states of affairs that are prima facie bad are likely to be ultima facie bad, and that suffices to show that various evils are less expected given theism and background information than given naturalism and background information.

P&W give a second version of moderate skeptical theism, however, one that adds an ontological thesis to these epistemic theses. They also explain in some detail how this second version of moderate skeptical theism is supposed to undermine my argument. Their explanation makes use of my imaginary alien visitors and in particular of the one named "Theo," who is a theist. They suggest that Theo won't initially be a moderate skeptical theist. Instead, he will be a "naïve theist": he will naïvely expect to have "ready access to—as they figure in divine decisions about what to allow and what to prevent—all possible goods, their weights, and their connections to actual suffering" (pp. 160–161). This will lead him, again initially, to make some seriously overconfident predictions about how pain, pleasure, flourishing, and languishing will be distributed among the sentient beings on earth.

I hope P&W don't mean to imply that the Theo in my argument would be so foolish as to be a naïve theist. My argument doesn't depend on naïve theism being antecedently likely given theism because my points are essentially contrastive. My claim is that theists have significantly less reason than naturalists have to expect the distribution of certain goods and evils that we find. I don't need to claim that Theo would make confident but incorrect predictions about how in fact good and evil is distributed. So once again, there may be some misunderstanding of my argument here, or perhaps "naïve theism" isn't supposed to describe the position held by my Theo. I'll assume the latter. In any case, I think P&W could make their point no less effectively even if, initially, Theo is just uninformed instead of naïve.

P&W go on to say that, because Theo is *initially* a naïve theist, he will fail to predict the *initial* data about good and evil as well as his naturalist alien colleague, Natty. But once some of those data come in, he will come to believe a more skeptical version of theism, presumably adopting the skeptical theses mentioned above. In addition, he will assign a much higher probability than he did before to the ontological thesis that God values 'a world governed by regular laws of nature, and a world with strong continuity in how organisms evolve from one level to another, so that there is a certain "functional integrity" to creation—either because such law-like continuity is a good in itself, or because it is connected in ways [we] can't see to other great goods...' (pp. 161–162). P&W claim that these revisions of Theo's theistic perspective will lead him to make essentially the same predictions that Natty does with respect to any further data. From this they conclude that my second premise "will be found false" (p. 162).

One flaw in this argument, if I am interpreting it correctly, is that its conclusion does not follow from its premises. So long as naturalism has much more predictive power than theism does with respect to the initial data—and P&W emphasize that in the first round of predictions "Theo's naïve realism will receive quite a beating" (p. 161)—the fact that the remaining data won't favor one of the two theories over the other leads to the conclusion that my second premise is true, not that it is false! The obviousness of this mistake suggests that I must be misinterpreting P&W's argument. I can think of two plausible alternative interpretations. On each of these alternative interpretations, P&W's argument avoids the non sequitur just pointed out but fails to establish its conclusion for other more subtle reasons.

The first alternative interpretation is suggested by P&W's claim that "if Theo's predictions are similar to those of Natty, then it won't be that Natty's predictions have a better "fit" than Theo's—they won't have a better fit *at that stage or subsequent stages*" (p. 162, italics are mine). Since this passage follows passages like "[Theo's] predictions will differ from his first round of predictions" (p. 162), I originally interpreted "at that stage" to refer to the second stage, the one following the first stage when Theo was still a naïve theist. Perhaps, however, P&W intend it to refer to the initial stage. On this interpretation, as soon as Theo realizes that his original less skeptical version of theism is a predictive failure, he doesn't just adopt a skeptical version of theism for the purposes of making subsequent predictions. Instead, he in effect allows himself a complete do-over, now basing his predictions about all the data, including the initial data, on his new skeptical version of theism. That avoids the non sequitur in question, but the argument still makes a serious logical mistake.

Consider the following analogy. Suppose three balls are randomly drawn from one of four urns. Perhaps a card is randomly drawn from a standard 52-card deck and the suit of that card determines from which of the four urns the ball is drawn. According to theory-12, the balls all came from either the first urn or the second urn. According to theory-34, the balls all came from either the third urn or the fourth urn. Now suppose that the first, third, and fourth urns each contain 900 yellow balls and 100 purple balls, while the second urn contains three yellow balls and 997 purple balls. Further, it is observed that all three of the balls drawn are yellow. Notice that there are two versions of each of the two theories. According to first version of theory-12, all of the balls came from the first urn. According to the second version, they all came from the second urn. Similarly, theory-34 can also be divided into two versions. Obviously, the fact that the first ball drawn is yellow "favors" theory-34 over theory-12 (in the sense of raising the ratio of the probability of the one theory to the probability of the other) because that ball is almost twice as likely to be yellow if theory-34 is true than if theory-12 is true. Of course, once a defender of theory-12 sees that first yellow ball, he will have good reason to believe that the first version of his theory is more probable than the second version and so, if he clings to his theory, he will base his predictions about the color of the next two balls on that version of his theory. Of course, when the next two balls turn out, as predicted, to be yellow, the defender of theory-12 should not conclude that the first ball's being yellow did not favor theory-34 over theory-12. That would be analogous to the non sequitur in P&W's argument on my original interpretation of it. It would be no less mistaken, however, for a defender of theory-12 to think she has no evidential problem on the grounds that she now knows that the first version of her theory is the most likely to be true and that version can predict the color of all three balls, including the first, just as well as theory-34. Such a mistake is analogous to the mistake that P&W's argument makes on my first alternative interpretation of it (or it would be analogous if one corrected for P&W's attributing irrationality to Theo by making him start out as a naïve theist as opposed to just an uninformed one).

According to a second alternative interpretation, my original interpretation of P&W's argument is correct in all respects except one, namely, that it over-looks the fact that the argument is enthymematic, the implicit premise being that naturalism does not have much more predictive power than theism with respect to the initial data. On this interpretation, P&W's argument does not make any logical mistakes, but it depends on a controversial premise that is unstated and undefended (and that appears to be denied). Further, defending that premise would be very difficult, even if P&W had correctly interpreted what my initial data actually are, so that Theo's initial round of predictions would just be about pleasure and pain. (On their interpretation, Theo's first round of predictions would be about the pleasure, pain, flourishing, and lan-guishing of primitive sentient life.) Minimally, P&W would have to refute my 1989 paper, where I focused solely on facts about pain and pleasure and argued that a serious atheistic hypothesis similar to naturalism has much more pre-dictive power with respect to those facts than theism does.

Assume for the sake of argument, however, that my 1989 paper was a fail-ure and that in fact the implicit premise in P&W's argument on the second alternative interpretation is true. Then P&W would still lack a good argument for the falsity of my second premise, for at least two reasons. First, the epis-temic theses in P&W's moderately skeptical version of theism have, as I have already pointed out, little effect on theism's predictive power with respect to the remaining data of good and evil (that is, the data about flourishing and languishing, virtue and vice, and triumph and tragedy). Second, even if the ontological thesis in P&W's moderately skeptical version of theism is antecedently likely given theism and what we know about pain and pleasure, that thesis (either by itself or in combination with the epistemic theses) would not significantly boost the predictive power of theism with respect to the data of good and evil. After all, we have no good *antecedent* reason (i.e. no reason that is independent of the observations and testimony upon which our knowledge of the data of good and evil is based) to believe that a better balance of flourishing over languishing or virtue over vice or triumph over tragedy would somehow prevent God from creating a world with regular laws or with continuity between biological levels or with "functional integrity."

I conclude that none of P&W's three objections succeeds. The new skeptical theism, same as the old skeptical theism, is powerless in the face of a carefully formulated and defended Humean argument from evil.[6]

---

[6] I am grateful to Trent Dougherty and an anonymous referee for helpful comments on an earlier draft of this chapter.

13

Learning Not to be Naïve: A Comment on the Exchange between Perrine/Wykstra and Draper

Lara Buchak

Does postulating *skeptical theism* undermine the claim that the amount and type of evil in our world is evidence (strong or weak) against God's existence? Participants in this debate are ultimately interested in the relative probability of theism and atheism; whether evil confirms atheism over theism; and if it does, to what degree. A crucial issue is how the probabilities of these two hypotheses shift when we come to believe, through trying to construct a theodicy, that no satisfying positive account of why God permits the amount of evil in our world is forthcoming: that *naïve theism* is false and thus that skeptical theism is the only viable version of theism.[1] According to Timothy Perrine and Stephen Wykstra, the relevant comparison is between the best version of each theory, and comparing skeptical theism with (the best version of) atheism will show that evil does not strongly confirm atheism over theism. According to Paul Draper, the relevant comparison is between atheism and theism full stop, and comparing these will show that evil does strongly confirm atheism over theism. Their disagreement is spelled out in a particular example of belief updating which they both discuss.[2] Examining how the probability facts change in this example will help us see what the disagreement ultimately rests on, and whether there is a way forward for the skeptical theist.

Here is the example. Consider two aliens, Natty (a naturalist) and Theo (a theist), who learn the empirical facts about our world in a particular order,

---

[1] What participants in this debate typically hold is that naïve theism is *very unlikely* to be true, given that we lack a positive account of why God allows evil. It will simplify the discussion to assume that naïve theism has been ruled out entirely, and that skeptical theism is the only theistic alternative.

[2] Original example Draper. Here I follow Draper (2014: 167).

while making some predictions on the basis of their theories N and T (I will use TS to stand for skeptical theism and $\overline{TS}$ to stand for naïve theism, making the simplifying assumption that these are the only two theistic options). They first "make predictions about pain and pleasure. Second, taking into account what they learned about pain and pleasure, they make predictions about flourishing and languishing ... Finally ... they make predictions about triumph and tragedy" (Draper 2014: 167). According to Draper, Natty's predictions will be on the whole more accurate than Theo's.[3] In probabilistic terms, if $E_1, E_2, \ldots, E_n$ are the data, and b is the background information, then $p(E_1 \mid N \& b) \gg p(E_1 \mid T \& b)$, $p(E_2 \mid E_1 \& N \& b) \gg p(E_2 \mid E_1 \& T \& b)$, and so on for successive data points (though Natty's predictions needn't all be *much* more accurate). If D, the total data of good and evil, is the conjunction of $E_1, E_2, \ldots, E_n$, then $p(D \mid N \& b) \gg p(D \mid T \& b)$. And as long as we don't have $p(T \mid b) \ggg p(N \mid b)$,[4] application of Bayes's Theorem shows that $p(T \mid D \& b) < \frac{1}{2}$. None of this is controversial to participants in the debate if the only theistic possibility on the table is naïve theism.

What difference could skeptical theism make to this scenario? According to Perrine and Wykstra, Theo could develop as follows.[5] He begins as a naïve theist—or, more accurately, assigns most of theism's probability to naïve theism and only a tiny amount to alternative precisifications of theism—but then notices that his initial assumptions about what God values get him into trouble. As a result, "chastened by [his] failed predictions" and "given [his] commitment to theism" he now "shifts much of the probability he had assigned to naïve theism to a form of moderate skeptical theism."[6] Of course, once he has shifted most of theism's probability to skeptical theism, then his theism predicts the data just as well as Natty's naturalism.

What is Perrine's and Wykstra's claim here, in probabilistic terms, and how is it supposed to undermine the above argument that $p(T \mid D \& b) < \frac{1}{2}$? Draper mentions three interpretive possibilities, two of which are important for our purposes.[7] The first is that Theo's initial predictions remain the same and are inaccurate ($p(E_1 \mid N \& b) \gg p(E_1 \mid T \& b)$), but thereafter Theo's theism

[3] On p. 161, Perrine and Wykstra (2014) assign a particular probability distribution to Theo, though unfortunately p(T) is not given. One might assume from the particular values they assign that they mean to imply p(T) = .5. However, if, in parallel, Natty assigns p(N) = .5, this seems to imply that Theo and Natty assign the same probability as each other to N and T, obscuring the sense in which Theo is a theist (in Perrine's and Wkystra's words, *committed* to theism) and Natty a naturalist. Therefore, I will assume that Theo assigns p(T) = 1 and Natty p(N) = 1, since this seems to better capture the assumptions that both sets of authors are making. Since what matters are the probabilities the *observer* assigns to each hypothesis at the end of the experiment, it won't make a difference to the debate. I will also assume for simplicity that T and N are mutually exclusive and exhaustive.

[4] See Draper (2014: 171).   [5] Perrine and Wykstra (2014: 160–2)

[6] Perrine and Wykstra (2014: 161–2) I will hereafter drop the modifier "moderate" from "moderate skeptical theism."

[7] Draper (2014: 174–5)

becomes skeptical theism and his subsequent predictions are in line with those of naturalism ($p(E_2 \mid E_1 \& N \& b) = p(E_2 \mid E_1 \& T \& b)$ and so forth). As Draper also points out, however, this set of probabilities still implies that $p(D \mid N \& b) \gg p(D \mid T \& b)$. The second interpretation, which Draper also argues against, is more interesting: upon realizing that naïve theism is not viable, Theo adopts skeptical theism,[8] and then predicts all of the data anew (including the initial data point). Since all participants in this debate agree that $p(D \mid TS \& b) = p(D \mid N \& b)$, then if $p(TS \mid T \& b) \approx 1$, it follows that $p(D \mid T \& b) \approx p(D \mid N \& b)$, and so D is not evidence for atheism over theism, strong evidence or otherwise.

Draper suggests a problem for this version of Perrine's and Wykstra's argument, by way of analogy. Suppose we have four urns, three of which (#1, #3, #4) contain many more yellow balls than purple balls, and one of which (#2) contains more purple balls than yellow balls. Balls are being drawn from one of the urns, and we are interested in how our probabilities about the urn they were drawn from should change in response to seeing the colors of these balls. Theory T12 says the balls are being drawn from urn #1 or urn #2, and comes in two versions: T1, which says they are drawn from urn #1, and T2, which says they are drawn from urn #2. Theory T34 says the balls are being drawn from urn #3 or urn #4. Upon seeing a yellow ball (Y), two things ought to happen. First, a defender of T12 ought to shift probability from T2 to T1: on the assumption that T12 is correct, T1 is much more likely to be correct than T2. For the same reason, an impartial observer should raise her conditional probability $p(T1 \mid T12)$. But second, and crucially, an impartial observer should *also* shift some of her probability from T12 to T34: as Draper puts it, the data favors T34 over T12.[9] And, according to Draper, these same two facts hold in the case of Theo and Natty. While Theo should raise his probability for skeptical theism

---

[8] Or he assigns most of his probability to skeptical theism, as in Perrine's and Wykstra's discussion: again, for mathematical simplicity I am assuming that alternatives to skeptical theism have been completely ruled out.

[9] As an example: let's say our antecedent probabilities are $p(T1) = p(T2) = p(T3) = p(T4) = .25$, and so $p(T12) = p(T34) = .5$ and $p(T1 \mid T12) = p(T2 \mid T12) = .5$. Let us also assume, following Draper, that $p(Y \mid T1) = p(Y \mid T3) = p(Y \mid T4) = .9$, and $p(Y \mid T2) = .003$. Then we have:

$$p(Y) = p(Y|T1)p(T1) + p(Y|T2)p(T2) + p(Y|T3)p(T3) + p(Y|T4)p(T4) = .67575.$$
$$p(T1|Y) = p(Y|T1)p(T1)/p(Y) = .333 \text{ (and similarly for } p(T3 \mid Y) \text{ and } p(T4 \mid Y).$$
$$p(T2|Y) = p(Y|T2)p(T2)/p(Y) = .001$$
$$p(Y|T12) = p(Y|T1)p(T1|T12) + p(Y|T2)p(T2|T12) = .4515$$
$$p(Y|T34) = p(Y|T3)p(T3|T34) + p(Y|T4)p(T4|T34) = .9 .$$
$$p(T12|Y) = p(Y|T12)p(T12)/p(Y) = .334 \text{ (another way to see this is that}$$
$$p(T12|Y) = p(T1 \text{ v } T2|Y) = p(T1|Y) + p(T2|Y)$$
$$p(T34|Y) = .666$$
$$p(Y \& T12 \mid T12 \& T1) = p(Y \mid T1)$$
$$p(T1 \mid Y \& T12) = p(Y \& T12 \mid T12 \& T1)p(T1 \mid T12)/p(Y \mid T12) = .997$$

(and we the observer should raise our conditional probability for skeptical theism given theism), we the observer should *also* lower our probability for theism overall: the data supports atheism over theism.

Draper's conclusion that the data supports T34 over T12 in the urn example is clearly correct. So what exact mistake is being made by the adherent of T12 who says "I now know that T1 is the best version of my theory, and the data does not support T34 over T1, so the data does not support T34 over T12"? (This is supposed to be analogous to Perrine's and Wykstra's claim that the data does not support atheism over theism *in general*, once we notice that skeptical theism is the best version of theism.) The move of letting the adherent make his view more specific in response to the data, and the thought that the question of which general theory the data supports is answered by looking at his prediction on the more specific theory, obscure an important point. When we learn that T2 is likely false, this has an effect not just on the relative probabilities of T1 and T2 conditional on the assumption that T12 is true, but also on the relative unconditional probabilities of T12 and T34—and it has an effect precisely by eliminating a previously viable possibility for one theory without doing the same for the other theory. (Technically, it lowers the probability of a previously higher-probability possibility, but let us assume for the sake of discussion that it eliminates the possibility altogether.)

A better picture of how the probabilities of the theories shift, according to Bayesianism, is the following (it assumes both that T12 and T34 are initially given equal probability by the observer, and that the disjuncts of T12 are initially given equal probability by the observer, but the analogy can be made more general). We begin with two representatives of T12, one who adheres to T1 and one who adheres to T2, and two representatives of T34—so that the relative number of representatives is equal to the relative probability we assign to each theory. When the data comes in, the representative of T2 is eliminated. So while the spokesperson for T12 will now be our T1 representative, there will be more spokespeople for T34 overall. If the situation between Theo and Natty when they learn D is like the situation between the defenders of T12 and the defenders of T34 when they learn Y, then the correct analogy for what happens in response to discovering that naïve theism isn't viable would mirror the analogy here, with the relative size of the voice in favor of theism decreasing.[10]

Upon learning Y, we conditionalize on Y, and so $p_{new}(T1 \mid T12) = .997$ and $p_{new}(T12) = .334$.

The antecedent probabilities of the theories here are not crucial. As long as $p(T2) > 0$, we will have $p_{new}(T1 \mid T12) > p(T1 \mid T12)$ and $p_{new}(T12) < p(T12)$.

[10] A similar point holds if we are meant to interpret Theo as assigning $p(T) = .5$ rather than $p(T) = 1$ (see footnote 3): as he rules out non-skeptical theism, $p(TS \mid T)$ increases, but $p(T)$ decreases.

Therefore, if what we are interested in is how conditionalizing on D impacts the relative probability of theism and atheism, then Draper is correct: even though conditionalizing on D should make theists become skeptical theists, D is evidence for atheism over theism.

Is there anything then to be said for Perrine's and Wykstra's position? Might there be other legitimate ways of updating on the data? Yes. We can model Natty's and Theo's situation in such a way that the evidence doesn't support atheism over theism—so that the observer ought not to lower her probability for theism. (Which model—this model or Draper's—is *accurate* will ultimately depend on certain further facts, as we will see.) The mathematical details aren't explicitly spelled out by Perrine and Wykstra, but this model makes good on what seems to be the primary point driving their argument: that what the data about evil supports is the *conditional claim* that if theism is true then skeptical theism is true.[11] The existence of such a model shows that, indeed, the question of whether the data of good and evil supports atheism even in light of the skeptical theist hypothesis turns not primarily on a mathematical question about what follows from the probability calculus and Bayesian updating, but on a more fundamental question about how to appropriately characterize the role of skeptical theism in the argument.

Let us step back and consider the general phenomenon of how probability shifts in response to evidence. A helpful way to think about this phenomenon comes from van Fraassen (1989: 161–2). Think of the entire space of hypotheses as a Venn diagram, where each region in the diagram specifies the truth-value of all the propositions we care about. We have a unit's worth of "mud" to distribute across the space, and the amount of mud in each region is the probability assigned to the proposition describing that region. So, for example, in the diagrams below (Figure 13.1), the amount of mud in the shaded region represents the probability of $H\overline{E}$ and of $A\overline{B}$, respectively; the amount of mud surrounded by the thick line represents the probability of H and of A, respectively. If we think of unconditional probability as a primitive, and define conditional probability in terms of it,[12] then conditional probability can be read off the diagram as well: the conditional probability of $\overline{E}$ given H is the ratio of the amount of mud in the $H\overline{E}$ region to the total amount of mud in the H region (the proportion of the thick-lined region that is shaded).

We can now consider how one's probability distribution could change in response to new facts coming to light. Learning new facts can be represented by moving mud around in the diagram. Here are two ways that one could move mud around, that each correspond to a particular way of ruling out the possibility that $A\overline{B}$. The first is that one could remove all the mud from

[11] See, for example, claim "D" about Granularism on p. 154.

[12] There may be good philosophical reasons to think of conditional probability as primitive (see Hájek (2003) and Pruss (2012)). Nonetheless, this won't matter to our discussion.

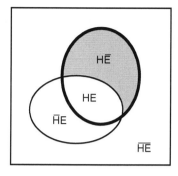 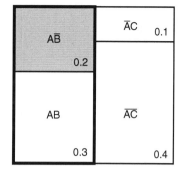

Fig. 13.1 Muddy Venn Diagrams

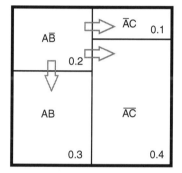 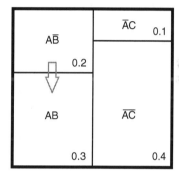

Fig. 13.2 Two responses to ruling out A$\overline{\text{B}}$

the A$\overline{\text{B}}$ region and distribute it to the rest of the diagram while preserving facts about the *proportions* of the remaining mud (as in the left-hand side of Figure 2 and Figure 3). The probabilities of AB, $\overline{\text{AC}}$, and $\overline{\text{A}}$C are .3, .4, and .1, respectively, and so to maintain the 3:4:1 ratio, we distribute probability so that p(AB) = .375, p($\overline{\text{AC}}$) = .5, and p($\overline{\text{A}}$C) = .125. (This is equivalent to "removing" the A$\overline{\text{B}}$ mud and renormalizing, as van Fraassen describes the procedure.) This procedure preserves the probability ratio of the remaining possibilities, and corresponds to the familiar updating rule known as (classical) *condition-alization*. Indeed, Bayes's Rule is a formal characterization of the operation of this procedure when we learn some evidence E (i.e. rule out H$\overline{\text{E}}$ and $\overline{\text{HE}}$). So, the first way to move mud around is to *maintain the ratios between the unconditional probabilities of the remaining options*. One obvious effect of con-ditionalizing by eliminating A$\overline{\text{B}}$ is to lower the probability of A relative to $\overline{\text{A}}$: since one of the "A" regions is eliminated, and the remaining regions retain their ratios with each other, the probability of A can only go down. This is what

Cell	Before	Change	After	Cell	Before	Change	After
$A\bar{B}$	0.2	−0.2	0	$A\bar{B}$	0.2	−0.2	0
AB	0.3	0.2(0.3/0.8) = .075	0.375	AB	0.3	0.2	0.5
$\bar{A}C$	0.1	0.2(0.1/0.8) = .025	0.125	$\bar{A}C$	0.1	0	0.1
$\bar{A}\bar{C}$	0.4	0.2(0.4/0.8) = .1	0.5	$\bar{A}\bar{C}$	0.4	0	0.4
SUM	1	0	1		1	0	1

Fig. 13.3 Two ways of redistributing credences

happened in the case of the urns: T12 was (nearly) ruled out, and the mud previously assigned to that region was redistributed to the remaining hypotheses in proportion to their previous probability. Similarly, to borrow another example from the skeptical theism literature, the same result should obtain when you find yourself in the following situation.[13] You are not sure whether your friend is in town (A) or out of town ($\bar{A}$), but if he is in town there are a limited number of possibilities. You check the concert hall ($A\bar{B}$), and he is not there. In this situation, the probability you assign to "he is in town" ought to decrease. You've learned that he is not at the concert hall, and conditionalized on that fact. *Purely incidentally*, you've also learned the (material) conditional <If he is in town, he is not at the concert hall>.

A second way that one could move mud around in the diagram while ruling out the possibility that $A\bar{B}$ is to take all of the mud from $A\bar{B}$ and move it to AB (as in the right-hand side of Figure 13.2 and Figure 13.3). This procedure preserves the ratio between p(A) and p($\bar{A}$), since mud is moved around only within the "A" region, not between the two regions. But it does not preserve the ratio between AB and any of the other regions: the probability of AB increases relative to the probability of $\bar{A}C$, for example. What type of learning, if any, could result in such a change? One example is learning the indicative conditional <If A then B> in a situation in which learning this conditional is irrelevant to the probability of its antecedent. For example, you assign equal probability to the hypothesis that your friend is in town (A) and the hypothesis that he is out of town ($\bar{A}$). There are five coffee shops in town, three Pete's and two Starbucks, and knowing nothing else, you assign equal probability to his being at each (with AB representing his being in town at a Pete's and $A\bar{B}$ his being in town at a Starbucks). You then learn that he hates Starbucks, so if he's in town, he won't be there—therefore, you can rule out $A\bar{B}$. Intuitively, though, learning this fact shouldn't make you think it more

---

[13] Rowe (2004).

likely that he is out of town. Whereas the first procedure captured updating by conditionalization, this procedure captures *updating on an indicative conditional* without lowering the probability of the antecedent. In both cases, you've ruled out a version of one of the more general hypotheses: but in the first case, you've ruled it out in such a way as to make the general hypothesis less likely, and in the second, you haven't.

How should this second kind of updating be formalized? And, moreover, how do we know when learning a conditional <If A then B> is a case of learning that $A\overline{B}$ is false that can be handled by conditionalizing on not-($A\overline{B}$), and when it is a case in which the probability of the antecedent ought to be preserved? That is, how do we know when we're in an updating situation in which we ought to set $p(A\overline{B}) = 0$ while preserving the ratios of unconditional probabilities, and when we're in an updating situation in which we ought to set $p(A\overline{B}) = 0$ while preserving the antecedent probability of A? Unfortunately, there is currently no consensus.[14] Bradley (2005) argues that updating on a conditional without changing the antecedent probability can be modeled using what he calls "Adams conditioning," a special case of Jeffrey conditioning. He adds that how to update in a particular case requires a judgment call about "the epistemic standing of both our conditional and unconditional beliefs." Douven and Romeijn (2011) expand on Bradley's suggestion by suggesting a procedure for deciding which probability facts to preserve, a procedure that takes into account which probability facts are more "epistemically entrenched." Lukits (2013) argues for a rule known as MAXENT, which delivers the verdict that when updating on a conditional, the probability of the antecedent is preserved if the antecedent is causally independent of the consequent. And Bovens and Ferreira (2010) claim that standard Bayesian conditionalizing allows us to retain the prior probability of a conditional's antecedent as long as we include the fact that we learned the conditional in the set of facts we conditionalize on (this is a standard solution to the Monty Hall problem).

Despite the lack of consensus, three things are clear. First, there *are* cases of learning a conditional in which the probability of the antecedent ought to be preserved. Second, updating on a conditional <If A then B> in these cases cannot be modeled by conditionalizing exclusively on the material conditional (or on its truth-functional equivalent not-($A\overline{B}$)): either we will have to take into account additional information or we will have to use a different updating rule. Finally, knowing whether we are in one of these cases—whether the probability of the antecedent ought to be preserved—requires more than knowing which conditional we are updating on: it requires knowing which antecedent probabilities we are more committed to or how we came to receive the information that the conditional is true.

---

[14] Douven and Romeijn (2011: 6) point out that it is not merely that there is no consensus, but that the question has received very little attention in the literature.

Is some scientific progress best modeled as learning a conditional while preserving the probability of its antecedent? One case of this might be that of a scientist adopting a research program and trying to discover some of its commitments, on the assumption that it is true, and for reasons independent of what its rivals can explain. This describes Perrine's and Wykstra's physicist "Grain," who gathers independent evidence (e2) for his conditional claim that if Granularism is true, then a particular version of it must be true. Learning which precisification of a general theory is the most plausible needn't always make the general theory less likely relative to the alternatives.

Now we can see what the key question for this debate is: when we take ourselves to learn that naïve theism is false—because we learn the data of good and evil and conclude that a theodicy won't work—should we conditionalize on not-(T$\bar{\text{S}}$), thereby preserving the ratios between the remaining unconditional probabilities, or should we update on the conditional <If T then S> in such a way as to preserve the probability of T?[15] What those who reject theodicy (everyone in this debate) agree to is *at least* that no or very low probability should be assigned to T$\bar{\text{S}}$ (let's assume no probability, for the sake of argument). But should that probability be redistributed evenly across the remaining space, thus preserving the antecedent ratio between TS and N; or should it be redistributed to T, thus preserving the antecedent ratio between T and N? The answer to this question depends on how exactly to characterize the data of good and evil, the failure of theodicy, and, perhaps, how we've come to learn these facts. Is what we take ourselves to have learned appropriately characterized as supporting not-(T$\bar{\text{S}}$), or appropriately characterized as supporting the conditional <If T then S>?

Draper's urn example suggests that what we learn is exactly that a certain alternative (non-skeptical theism) is off the table—and if this is all we learn, then he is right that according to standard Bayesianism the evidence from evil supports atheism over theism, even when skeptical theism is on the table. Perrine's and Wykstra's Granularism example suggests that what we learn is the conditional <If theism, then skeptical theism>. Notice that Perrine and Wykstra take Theo's absorption of the facts to primarily be a way of refining his theory. *Within* theism, he is considering what the best hypothesis is: he is considering, if theism is true, in what way is it most likely to be true? And he

[15] Just to be clear: the *data* itself isn't "naïve theism is false." The data is some set of facts (D plus the supposed failure of theodicy) which has very low probability on naïve theism (I assume for simplicity: no probability), and higher probability on the remaining hypotheses, probability that is equal for all three hypotheses. This mirrors the structure of the above examples, in which the data were "I drew a yellow ball," "I checked the concert and my friend wasn't there," "a reliable third party said my friend hates Starbucks," and e1; this data has low or no probability on the hypotheses T2, my friend is at the concert, my friend is at Starbucks, and a very coarse version of Granularism; and this data has higher probability on both T1 and T34, on both my friend is in town but not at the concert and my friend is out of town, both my friend is in town but not at Starbucks and my friend is out of town, and both fine-grained Granularism and Smoothism.

learns that skeptical theism is the best version of theism. If this is all *we* learn, then evil supports skeptical theism over other brands of theism but does not support atheism over theism.

We've already mentioned some situations that require conditionalizing on not-$(A\bar{B})$ and some that require updating on the conditional <If A then B> while preserving the probability of A. While I cannot give a precise characterization of features that distinguish when ruling out $A\bar{B}$ ought to be characterized as conditionalizing on not-$(A\bar{B})$ and when doing so ought to be characterized as updating on a conditional, here are a few general thoughts. The first is that, as several of the authors mentioned above point out, one ought to consider how one came to be in possession of the evidence that rules out $A\bar{B}$. What exactly do we learn *about our own learning* when we learn that naïve theism is false? In the scientific case, Grain started with a supposition and determined what followed from it: he asked, assuming Granularism is true, what's the best version of it? That the conditional was learned was independent of which general theory is true. This was also true in the second friend-locating case. In the urn case, one sampled randomly from the environment without regard to the assumptions of the general theories in question. This was also true in the first friend-locating case. The second thought (also pointed out by the above authors) is that when figuring out whether to conditionalize on not-$(A\bar{B})$ or update on the conditional <If A then B>, one ought to think about which "probability facts" are more epistemically entrenched. For example, are we theists first and specific theists second, or does theism get its support from the initial plausibility of some of its specific versions?

I will close by pointing out that the general question discussed here reappears in a parallel debate: that about whether fine-tuning is evidence for theism. In particular, we might wonder whether the naturalist's invocation of the possibility of multiple universes blocks the claim that fine-tuning strongly supports theism over atheism. And we can approach this question by considering: when one learns that the physical constants are extremely unlikely to support life on single-universe atheism, is what one learns more accurately characterized as "If atheism, then multi-universe atheism" or as "Not single-universe atheism"? In both of these debates, the difference between the two ways of ruling out $A\bar{B}$ (naïve theism in the case of the argument from evil and single-universe atheism in the case of the fine-tuning argument) may explain why the proposed response (skeptical theism and multi-universe atheism, respectively) can seem ad hoc to those on the side of $\bar{A}$. The defender of A thinks of the data as supporting <If A then B>, whereas the defender of the claim that the datum undermines A thinks of the data as supporting not-$(A\bar{B})$.

Examining the differences between Perrine/Wykstra and Draper reveals the way forward in the debate about whether skeptical theism undermines the argument from evil: we need to consider how to appropriately characterize the evidence, and which updating procedure to use to take it into account.

Those who reject theodicy agree that we should assign no (or very low) probability to naïve theism in light of the evidence from evil and the history of theodicy. And if the evidence from evil and the history of theodicy is appropriately characterized as exactly "A theism according to which we know what goods there are is incompatible with the level and type of evil in our world" (in short: naïve theism is incompatible with evil), then introducing skeptical theism as a potential hypothesis cannot blunt the force of the blow for the theist, since the initially most plausible specification of theism is ruled out without changing the relative probability of other versions of theism as compared with atheism. However, if the evidence is appropriately characterized as "If God exists, then our knowing the goods there are is incompatible with the level and type of evil in our world," then hope remains for the skeptical theist.

Part III

Skeptical Theism's Implications for Theism

14

Skeptical Theism and Skeptical Atheism

J. L. Schellenberg

At the heart of skeptical theism are claims such as these three, defended by Michael Bergmann (2009):

S1   We have no good reason for thinking that the possible goods we know of are representative, relative to the property of figuring in a (potentially) God-justifying reason for permitting such things as hiddenness or horrors, of the possible goods there are.[1]

S2   We have no good reason for thinking that the possible evils we know of are representative, relative to the property of figuring in a (potentially) God-justifying reason for permitting such things as hiddenness or horrors, of the possible evils there are.

S3   We have no good reason for thinking that the entailment relations we know of between possible goods and the permission of possible evils are representative, relative to the property of figuring in a (potentially) God-justifying reason for permitting such things as hiddenness or horrors, of the entailment relations there are between possible goods and the permission of possible evils.[2]

Bergmann and other skeptical theists find claims like these to be very plausible—even commonsensical. They think, moreover, that the atheist who is

---

[1] Skeptical theism began with a focus on the problem of evil. But its defenders have recently sought to extend it to the hiddenness argument—see Bergmann (2009).

[2] This statement of Bergmann's three theses is in some places fuller than his, but the additional material comes right out of his explanation of how the term 'representative' is to be taken. (See Bergmann 2001 and 2009.)

promoting one or another argument from hiddenness or horrors should see them in the same way, and thereby be led to give up his argument. The central idea of skeptical theism is regarded as non-discriminatory, no respecter of persons, available to just any reasoning person at all.

Skeptical theism is thought by its advocates to be non-discriminatory in another way, too. As already suggested, it is supposed to work for just any argument from hiddenness or horrors. In a recent piece, Bergmann applies his skeptical theses to arguments from William Rowe, Paul Draper, and myself, arguing in each case that, given such truths as S1–S3, we are simply "in the dark" about something we need to know if the argument is to be successful (2009).

It seems to me that skeptical theism had better have this reach if it wants to do important work for theism in philosophy, for a theistic device that deactivates some threatening arguments from hiddenness or horrors but not all of them will leave atheism untroubled (the atheist, after all, only needs one argument to work). But I believe that it lacks this reach. Some robust forms of atheistic reasoning from hiddenness or horrors are untouched by it, at least to this extent: that they are not prevented by it from providing justification for the atheist to be an atheist.[3] This is argued in Section I. In Section II we see that skeptical theism is non-discriminatory in a way that might not be welcomed by its advocates, in that it suggests a new way for the atheist to question the *theist's* support for his own belief. If skeptical theism undermines some ways of justifying atheistic belief, *skeptical atheism* undermines perhaps the most important way of trying to justify theistic belief, using the theist's own form of reasoning to do so, while leaving the aforementioned atheistic arguments unscathed. Finally, in Section III, I expose another way in which we might speak of a "skeptical atheism" alongside skeptical theism, growing out of the discussion of the previous section. Paradoxical as it may seem, an *investigative* atheism may be embedded in a wider skepticism, and may use the form of reasoning employed by skeptical theists to realize new ways of perpetuating at least doubt about theism and, more positively, to communicate an urgent message: that a very great deal of investigation remains to be done into alternatives to theism as an understanding of the divine. The upshot? Skeptical theism utilizes a form of reasoning that not only lacks the reach that would make it really powerful in the hands of theistic philosophers, but potentially possesses quite formidable investigative powers when placed in the hands of atheists.

---

[3] I believe they also provide justification for a conversion from theism to atheism, but I will not argue for this claim here.

I

Let's begin by considering how atheistic reasoning may acquire immunity to skeptical theism. I suggest that the atheist should allow that skepticism is indeed often appropriate, but follow up with the observation that belief and confidence are sometimes appropriate, too, and that some of the propositions available to an atheist concerned with hiddenness or horrors (a) are ones about which she is appropriately believing and confident and (b) clearly entail that no God-justifying reason of the needed sort exists.

Notice that we can illustrate the first part of this answer with what the skeptical theist himself is confident and believing about, despite his skepticism: propositions about how he should live his life, for example, or about not being a brain-in-a-vat (Bergmann 2009). And presumably he is—at least in the present dialectical situation—not inclined to question the idea that the atheist is likewise rightly confident about various such things.

Well, in the same way, I would suggest, it begs to be noted that although certainly not equipped with a comprehensive grasp of the domains of value and modality, and quite in the dark about many things, we may nonetheless be the recipients of various *specific* insights about value and modality that generate premises and inferences which an atheist can employ. As inquirers, desiring to achieve fundamental understanding, whether that be theistic in nature or not, we should *look* for such stray instances where light pierces the darkness. Certainly we should not delight in darkness! And I would suggest that if we seek, we will find.

There is some a priori reason to suspect that such will turn out to be the case in the present area of concern. This is because the claim of traditional theism is that the ultimate reality is a *person*, very different from us in various ways, certainly, but in many ways similar too. I don't think this is always remembered by skeptical theists, who sometimes write as though we were talking about the more general idea I have elsewhere called ultimism, instead of about theism; as though we were forced to operate without much of an idea as to how metaphysical, axiological, and soteriological ultimacy are instantiated if there is a God. Given the *quite detailed filling out* of ultimism that theism represents, we do have a few ideas about such things that should be regarded as reliable. Theism describes the ultimate in familiar terms, and so even if there may be much that we are quite unfamiliar with in the realms of value and modality, and even if a God would be familiar with many such things while we are not, what we *do* know on relevant matters may strongly seem to us to entail that things would in some way be different, in respect of hiddenness and horrors, than in fact they are, if there were a God.

I have defended such claims in various places. Because of our access to truths about, among other things, the love of persons, we can learn that a perfectly loving personal God would never permit nonresistant nonbelief, which manifestly exists. And because of our access to truths about, among other things, the empathy of persons, we can learn that a perfectly empathetic personal God would never permit horrors, which also manifestly exist. I will not repeat all the details of the arguments, but they include reference to such obvious-seeming propositions as: *Because God is unsurpassable greatness personified, persons who grow ever deeper into God realize their deepest good* and *Because God is infinitely deep and rich and exclusively good, endless opportunities for persons to grow ever deeper into God arise even where God has prevented horrors altogether* and also *If finite persons can achieve their deepest good without horrors being permitted, then an unsurpassably empathetic God will not permit horrors.*

Now in response to such claims the skeptical theist may want to suggest that some unknown valuable dimension of growth into God might, for all we know, require that horrors be permitted. But this may seem to the atheist a case of implausible reaching, which reason alone can no longer be said to support (see Schellenberg 2007: 254–6). Or perhaps the skeptical theist will want to argue for the possibility of relevant goods *external* to any such relationship which God might find attractive. But here again it may seem to the atheist that we have to forget what theism has got us talking about in the first place—an ultimate person—to be impressed.

Consider by way of analogy a single man who marries and has children: Does this behavior not rightly constrain the goods he is willing to pursue, at least insofar as he is a loving husband and father? Though when he was on his own he spent time with many female friends and was otherwise preoccupied with his own wide-ranging pursuits, traveling to Europe for months at a time, shifting from place to place and from one activity to another, now things are different, and quite naturally and rightly so. Now he has a family to help provide for, to support in emotional and financial ways. He can't just leave for Greece or Spain any time he wants to indulge his own interests—better, he has *new* interests which lead him happily to say no when invitations to do such things arise. Similarly with God, if God is to be regarded as a loving person—an *ultimately* loving person—who has created vulnerable finite persons to be the object of divine love. The God described by skeptical theists who may, for all we know, have purposes quite unrelated to us that require hiddenness *from* us or horrors *for* us is not an ultimately loving and kind and empathetic being. If a person at all, such a God would be comparable to a delinquent father or mother who simply can't or won't live up to the demands taken on board when the commitments of marriage and family are entered into.

The atheist, in my view, should say that there is a *large medley* of such things to be said in which may be found propositions concerning horrors or hiddenness entailing the nonexistence of a personal God—propositions and entailments that seem as obvious to him, that are as much a matter of common sense, perhaps (if we can think of the latter as extending to necessary truths), the longer and the more intently he reflects on them, as the claim that we may be in the dark on many things regarding modality and value. There is therefore absolutely nothing immodest or unduly cognizant of our cognitive limitations in his endorsing those views. Indeed, by accepting both those views and the most general and plausible content of the skeptical theist's cautions, the atheist can claim to come out further ahead, in the world of inquiry, with a more balanced stance and one more sensitive to the results of wide reflection than would otherwise be possible.[4]

In his (2009) Bergmann says that he doesn't see how love or infinite resourcefulness, which I have also emphasized, are relevant to whether there is an outweighing good that might successfully draw God's attention, given that there being such a good would not be a contingent but a necessary state of affairs. In my view the strongest atheistic arguments make such an observation irrelevant when, against the backdrop of undeniable claims about God's love and empathy, they distinguish outweighing goods from our deepest good in relationship with God, or when, in connection with the infinite richness and resourcefulness of God, they distinguish the goods emphasized by critics from the broader types of good they instantiate, all of which can be met with in relationship with God. But however that may be, in the present context the demurral of skeptical theists is compatible with the failure of their argument. For what Bergmann and others don't see needn't prevent the *atheist* from being convinced, and justifiedly so, if he thinks he clearly sees that God would not permit horrors or hiddenness, in the context of *both* the skeptical theist's arguments *and* such reflections as were outlined earlier in this section. These reflections, it is worth noting, take us far beyond the famous "noseeum" inferences of William Rowe's original arguments, to which skeptical theism was originally directed (see Rowe 1979).

Suppose the skeptical theist grants, for reasons of the sort I have given, that his reasoning may not remove the atheist's justification for believing that atheism is true. This is at the same time an admission that skeptical theism lacks, as I have put it, the reach that would make it really powerful as a theistic form of reasoning in philosophy. For it cannot entirely stamp out the blaze of atheistic reasoning. Skeptical theism, I suggest, is going to seem most powerful where one or other of three conditions is realized: (a) where the atheistic reasoning examined is exclusively probabilistic, perhaps depending on simple inductive inferences about reasons for evil unsupplemented by additional truths about the divine nature, of the sort once found in Rowe; (b) where parties to the

---

[4] It seems unlikely that S1–S3 can be accepted by the atheist compatibly with his accepting the moves in atheistic reasoning I have described. What the atheist will conclude, if the incompatibility obtains, is that what his moves give him reason to believe makes S1–S3 false in his case. But, of course, even then he can go along with a more general caution about how much one should claim to know in matters of value and modality.

debate share an undernourished conception of God, without sufficient content to entail such a thing as that a God would have an aversion of the relevant sort to horrors or hiddenness; or (c) where the conception of God that dominates is nourished by ideas from theistic religious traditions reflecting centuries of thinking about God on the assumption that God exists, and therefore on the assumption that a God would permit both horrors and hiddenness. Philosophers of religion who examine atheistic reasoning should resist all three of these conditions, at least within the precincts of philosophy. What we have seen, in effect, is that if they do, they will find the philosophical force of skeptical theism against such reasoning greatly attenuated.

II

Suppose that the claim defended in the previous section is correct. This is compatible with the *theist* for one reason or another being justified in rejecting *for herself* the arguments from horrors or hiddenness that, I have said, may justify the atheist's belief. Let's suppose that she is so justified. Still, there is a problem for the theist's belief that arises in this connection. For if there is a skeptical theism that undermines certain ways of justifying atheistic belief for the atheist, such as Rowe's original evidential argument from evil, there is also a skeptical *atheism* that can undermine the *theist's* ways of justifying theistic belief for herself. This, then, is the second point to be made in an assessment of the force of skeptical theism. Skeptical theism succeeds, to the extent that it does, only by empowering skeptical atheism, giving to the atheist an argument form she can use against the theist's own basis or grounds for being a theist.

I want to focus here on experiences apparently of God. In his (2009) Bergmann concedes that design arguments for theism are imperilled by skeptical theism. Perhaps other theistic arguments will be similarly affected. I will leave this for others to consider. For all such results in relation to theistic *arguments* only give skeptical theists an extra reason to do what perhaps most theists in philosophy are already doing: emphasize *non-propositional* sources of justification for belief. What I have in mind, in particular, are the sorts of justification for theistic belief defended by William P. Alston in his influential (1991) and by Alvin Plantinga in his equally influential (2000). Experiential accounts of theistic belief and its justification of the sort defended here have become more and more common in theistic philosophy in recent decades.

So how can we bring skeptical theism into conversation with them? One way would be to propose a new skeptical thesis, which the atheist may say should be as acceptable to the theist as she claims S1–S3 ought to be to Rowe:

S4   We have no good reason for thinking that the considerations opposing
the epistemic force of religious experience we know of are representative, relative to the property of (potentially) figuring in an undefeatable defeater of religious experience as justification for theistic belief,
of the considerations opposing the epistemic force of religious experience there are.

There is, I suggest, no non-arbitrary way for the theist to discriminate between
the matters addressed by S1–S3 and those addressed by S4 in relation to what
she has reason to believe. If we are cognitively limited in a way that would
make the first three propositions true, then the fourth is true as well: the cognitive limitations in question affect all the matters under considerations here if
they affect any. Notice also, in this connection, that S4 is as "theism-friendly"
as Begmann's own theses, mentioned earlier, are "atheism-friendly."[5] Good
reason to believe in God is no more good reason to affirm representativeness
here than good reason to believe in the nonexistence of God was good reason
to affirm it there.

Let's look a bit more closely now at how Rowe can return the favor when the
skeptical theist hands him her argument, thus becoming, in effect, a skeptical
atheist. The bearing of facts about value and modality, which the skeptical theist already regards as rightfully generating skepticism, may be harder to see in
this case. But it is there. It might be, for example (so the skeptical theist should
reflect to herself), that what certain unknown truths would clearly show to
anyone who beheld them is that great evils would necessarily be generated
were God to be present to traditional theists in the ways they believe to be
the case, at least at the present stage of human development—evils sufficiently
impressive to prevent any God there may be from being present in those ways
at this time.

On the basis of very similar reasoning, skeptical theists make their own case
against atheistic arguments. Indeed, the skeptical theist may think it's enough
just to say that a God's reasons would not be transparent to us. For example,
in his response to divine hiddenness Bergmann writes that "we're simply in
the dark about whether (and how likely it is that) there are any God-justifying
reasons for permitting a period of divine hiddenness" (2009: 382–3). Now
we've already seen how an atheist might successfully resist such a move—at
least for herself. But the skeptical theist, naturally enough, accepts it. So we
can respond: How long a period of divine hiddenness might God tolerate?
Might the notion of divine hiddenness appropriately be broadened so as to
include theists, in the sense that their experiences apparently of God, because
of unknown divine purposes requiring it and/or their own spiritual immaturity, are not of God at all? Suppose they are *not* of God in the relevant sense. If

---

[5] I owe these terms to discussion with Paul Draper.

persistently and clearly presented with such a truth, any theist relying on religious experience would have an undefeatable undercutting defeater for such experience as justification for her theistic belief. As it is, she is in the dark about whether the relevant proposition is true. So she is in the dark as well about whether, more adequately positioned, she would have such a defeater. But surely to justifiedly believe that God exists in response to religious experience, she must believe that the facts of the case would not support such a defeater. If she cannot so believe, then this *itself* defeats her justification. It follows that she cannot justifiedly believe that God exists in this way.

Of course there is nothing to require that we restrict ourselves to unknown truths about value or modality in this connection. If there may be unknown truths about such things, it is hard to see why there might not be unknown truths in certain other, relevantly similar domains as well: should we expect our cognitive limitations to be so narrowly circumscribed as to prohibit this? Here it may be apropos to mention that, according to the best science, which theistic philosophers will wish to accommodate, we presently exist at a very early stage in the total period that may see intelligent life on our planet. We have at most 50,000 years of anything approaching careful thought about religion under our belts, and another billion years remain in which we—or species that come after us—may continue to think about such things (see Schellenberg 2013). Hence there may be many subjects on which we not only could but *will* do better than we have.

Perhaps—so the skeptical theist should reflect to herself—developments in psychology or neurophysiology, emerging long after we are gone, will reveal facts about the current human mind and/or brain inconsistent with such religious experiences as traditional theists today describe being veridical (undercutting defeater). Another possibility within a skeptically theistic frame of reference is that new and even more powerful and convincing theistic religious experiences, which advanced techniques of the future show to be veridical but inconsistent with God having been present to anyone in our own day in the way that God was thought to be present, will arise in the deep future (another undercutting defeater). Perhaps veridical experiences of God of sufficient clarity and intensity to justify belief in God are reserved for our more fully developed descendants. I would judge that any theist who believes such propositions as S1–S3 after fully making the transition from human to scientific timescales and properly appreciating the epistemic weight of distantly future Earthly possibilities will believe as well, insofar as reason has its way with her, that we have no good reason for thinking that events of the sort I have just described will never occur. S1–S3 describe what is the case for theists only if S4 does too.

How might the skeptical theist respond? Well, I suppose she might claim that her experience apparently of God is so intense and clear and enduring as to make it impossible for her not to respond to it believingly in the way that she does. One is inclined to think of *excuse* rather than *justification* in such a case. But we need not sort this out. For the religious experiences of theists in the actual world are almost never of that type. Plantinga admits as much in his (2000). Even where forceful, they are commonly not enduring. Nor are they frequently so discriminating as to have, precisely and clearly, theistic content alone, yielding to no other interpretation. Thus, there is the opportunity to consider and be influenced by the defeater we have constructed from skeptical theistic materials. To the extent that such a defeater is resisted, we must wonder how seriously we should take the skeptical theist's criticisms of Rowe and others.

Perhaps the skeptical theist will at this point seek to defeat my argument by *reductio*. S4 appeals explicitly to the epistemic possibility of unknown evidence incompatible with the epistemic force of evidence (broadly construed) that theists might seek to use today. The skeptical theist may claim that a crucial shift is made when we transition from something like "unknown goods" to something like "unknown evidence." The former is precise and localized, whereas the latter threatens to balloon out into a skepticism consuming all our beliefs. For which beliefs will *not* be impugned if we always have to worry about completely unknown counterarguments and experiences? Since the argument employing S4 implies the acceptability of such an unacceptable general skepticism, we have good reason to reject that argument.

I would suggest that there is indeed a broader skepticism to be developed here (it is the elephant in the room), and instead of fleeing from it, we should embrace it. I call it *total evidence skepticism*. To get a basic idea of this skepticism's distinguishing features, notice first that the total evidence relevant to a proposition, as here understood, is not my total relevant evidence or the total relevant evidence available or the total relevant evidence thus far assessed by human beings, or anything of the sort, but rather the total relevant evidence *simpliciter*: everything in the world that bears on the truth of that proposition (with the "bears on" relation defined in such a way that a proposition cannot evidentially bear on itself)—in other words, the evidence relevant to its truth as it would be seen from a God's-eye view, from the perspective of omniscience.

With that as background, we may say that total evidence skepticism is the claim that, for many a proposition expressing a belief or potential belief of ours, we have reason to be in doubt, or skeptical, about whether the total relevant evidence supports that proposition. Even if *our* relevant evidence—the relevant evidence we have actually examined—supports the proposition, our evidence may not be representative of the *total* relevant evidence: for all we know, although the former supports it, the latter does not. Now a proposition is true only if the total evidence in my sense does support it. Thus where we have reason to be in doubt about whether the total evidence supports some proposition, we also have reason to be in doubt as to whether that proposition is true.

I have had something to say about this sort of skepticism elsewhere (Schellenberg 2007, 2013). And much more needs to be said. In particular, the related points about the deep future and our place in time touched on earlier in this chapter need to be unravelled further. Here it will suffice to point out that if through investigation the skeptical theist comes to feel the force of something like total evidence skepticism, she will also see that the apparently troublesome feature of S4, treated here as paving the way for a *reductio*, ought rather to be embraced.

But we need to preempt a certain sort of response to this reasoning, a somewhat unsubtle response lurking already in the way I earlier phrased the objection here addressed. This response repeats the concern that it's "all or nothing"—total evidence skepticism is also *total skepticism*, and should be expected to consume all our beliefs. Here I would urge calm. There is no reason to expect at the outset of such a discussion that no way of discriminating among propositions in respect of belief-worthiness, no criteria for sensible discrimination, can ever be found. Especially is this the case since total evidence skepticism, if linked to a proper appreciation of our place in scientific time, has to be seen as arising *within* inquiry. It is part of an attempt to further discovery of truths about the world by means compatible with our present primitivity. The inquiry to which it sees itself as attached springs not from belief of some controversial proposition to which it might itself be applied but from a love of understanding by which many of us are gripped, even in our primitivity. And although such love presupposes certain beliefs, such as the belief that understanding is of great value and worth pursuing, such beliefs are ones that serious inquirers will regard as evidently true.

Thus although total evidence skepticism is opposed to the blithe confidence about complex matters we may have felt in the absence of respect for the future, and so can be experienced as initially jarring or disillusioning, the vulnerability of the propositions it places in question is quite compatible with the intellectual safety of many others. We may have learned, through investigation in science, that we are still at the very beginning of organized inquiry on this planet, and that quite possibly there are many more—and also radically different and better justified—ideas to come, and this particularly in our most ambitious inquiries, focused on the more profound and complex matters. But we also see that a balance must be struck. The parameters of inquiry themselves require that we reject the idea that in our short time on the scene we have learned *nothing* of importance. How to strike the balance therefore should become an object of inquiry in its own right, replacing any alarm over the possibility of a descent into global skepticism (see Schellenberg 2013).[6]

---

[6] A tempting thought that needs to be avoided as we seek such a balance is that the further our questions are from matters of pressing human concern, the less we should expect to know about them. As Martin Rees points out (2012), some of the best understood subjects concern celestial objects existing far from "where we live," and some of the least well understood, such as the best diet or how to predict and control the weather, are quite "close to home," affecting our lives in obvious ways.

Having said that, it does seem that the claim that theistic belief is justified by experiences apparently of God is going to be among the more vulnerable here. It certainly faces total evidence skepticism much more clearly than do the claims of the atheistic arguments I defended against skeptical theism in Section I. Although there are plenty of questions about how and when such skepticism ought to be deemed applicable, it will be hard to deny that what seems most obvious to us upon reflection should be given a pass. And there don't seem to be any obvious-seeming truths in the neighborhood that the theist could turn to her advantage in the way that I have suggested the atheist may turn to her advantage certain apparent necessary truths about horrors and hiddenness.

If this assessment is correct, then although I have not insisted that any atheistic argument should convince the theist, we can use the very sort of skeptical reasoning against which we defended the *atheist's* right to believe his argument sound to argue that what *does* convince many a theist—experiences apparently of God—ought not to do so. Even should Rowe's argument or some other probabilistic argument from horrors or hiddenness fall to skeptical theism, such an event can be made the occasion of learning all-round when the atheist, in return, hands something like S4 to the theist and thus removes what may be essential grounds for her belief in God. Skeptical theism invites skeptical atheism.

III

As just suggested, the atheism I defend arises in the context of total evidence skepticism and so (given my particular way of developing that skepticism) with an awareness of human immaturity in scientific time. And so we have another way of understanding that term "skeptical atheism." The seeming paradoxicality of this idea is erased when we notice that total evidence skepticism may be accepted for the purposes of deeper *inquiry* and so along with the aim to make what progress we can, even at our relatively primitive stage of development, by reference to (among other things) what seems to us most obviously true. The atheist will think her own position may represent such progress. But skepticism still marks the larger context in which she operates, if she behaves as I think she ought. Thus, for example, my sort of atheist will note how much more ambitious metaphysical *naturalism* is than atheism, and how many interesting options are ruled out if one is a naturalist. And so she will not immediately endorse naturalism along with her atheism. Hers is an *investigative* atheism, not the sort of *reactionary* atheism that is unfortunately all too common in our culture today, which is as firmly wed to naturalism as many theists are to theism, reacting to the latter from a prior commitment to the former.[7]

Against this background I will be understood when I say that an investigative atheism may take some interest in showing how the skeptical theistic way of reasoning, brought into the larger flow of total evidence skepticism, can be used to expose certain additional sources of doubt about theism sufficient to prevent overhasty migration to theism on the part of those left unconvinced by atheism. Moreover, and more positively, it can be used to inspire a greater openness to new religiously-relevant investigative results in the future. With these thoughts in mind, let's add two more skeptical theses to our list:

S5   We have no good reason for thinking that the arguments from horrors or hiddenness against theism we know of are representative, relative to the property of (potentially) constituting a successful proof that theism is false, of the arguments from horrors or hiddenness against theism there are.

S6   We have no good reason for thinking that the possible goods we know of are representative, relative to the property of consistency with a person being axiologically ultimate, of the possible goods there are.

Unlike S4, these two theses are not theism-friendly: good reason to believe theism true is good reason to believe that the arguments from horrors and possible goods we know of *are* representative (in the relevant senses) of the arguments from horrors and possible goods there are. So the theist will say that we have to show that he lacks good reason to believe theism true before we can expect him to go along with S5 and S6. Now if the "good reason to believe theism true" that the theist takes himself to have depends on religious experience in any way, then perhaps we have already done so. But my main purpose here is to show what atheists can do for investigation in philosophy by defending atheism in a context where certain skeptical theses are also defended, and for that purpose no judgment on this matter is needed. So while here noting

---

[7] It is important to note here the epistemic asymmetry between atheism and naturalism. Atheism makes only the negative claim that there is no person-like divine. This has many fewer metaphysical consequences than the positive claim of naturalism, and so is much less profound. Think also of the relative number of *alternatives* to theism and naturalism—the number of different ways in which these propositions can be false. Specifically, naturalism has many *more* alternatives than atheism, all of which must be false if it (naturalism) is true. Similar points arise in a comparison of atheism and theism. And so it will not be surprising if atheism does much better in a context of total evidence skepticism than either of the other propositions. Here it may also be useful to notice that if the existence of God requires that there be a person who is all powerful, all knowing, all good and all loving, as well as the creator of the universe, then theistic arguments have the task of showing that *all* those conditions are *satisfied*. But an atheistic argument need only show that *one* such condition is *not satisfied*. For such general reasons as these, atheists may be expected to have an easier time than theists resisting total evidence skepticism.

this consequence of our work in the previous section, I shall from here on disregard it.

Suppose, then, that we are engaging someone who is left unconvinced by atheistic reasoning and wondering what to make of theism—someone, moreover, who accepts S1–S3. I suggest that, when presented with S5 and S6, she will realize that there is no non-arbitrary way of discriminating between the matters addressed by these propositions and those addressed by S1–S3 in relation to what we have reason to believe. If we are cognitively limited in a way that would make the first three propositions true, then the fifth and sixth are true as well: the cognitive limitations in question affect all the matters under consideration here if they affect any. But what S5 and S6 represent are some new sources of at least doubt about theism. What this means is that by a skeptical theistic sort of reasoning, our questing non-theist has just been provided with good reason to *remain* a non-theist.

S5

Consider how this works in the case of S5. We easily assume that all of the relevant arguments in this or that domain have already been made, and that new authors, striving for innovation, just end up recycling old moves. This is a rather cynical view—one that is, I think, belied by the facts. However that may be, it seems clear that any non-theist impressed by skeptical theism, given even the apparently modest skepticism of S1–S3, is in no position to endorse it in relation to hiddenness or horrors. If S1–S3 are correct, then the cynical view is false for those domains, for then there may well be unknown facts about value or modality enabling deductive arguments from horrors or hiddenness to be made that would strike us as very novel—and also as sound, even if all previous efforts have left us unimpressed. How could this be denied, if indeed we are in the dark about the subjects in question? Perhaps what we are in the dark about is just what would enable such arguments to be made. If significant goods and evils and logical connections might be unknown to us, then we cannot legislate which way their implications would point. Then it might be that, were we to have a God's-eye view of such things, what we would see is that there is no good providing a morally sufficient reason for horrors, or that hiddenness entails the absence of some good (or the existence of some other evil) that would certainly be present (or absent) were there a perfectly good and loving God. Imagining what a God might see is indeed helpful here, as skeptical theism suggests, though what a God might see—it would have to be from some other possible world!—is that there is no God.

Someone lacking independent reason to believe in God may of course think that such arguments as I defended in Section I themselves illustrate how new investigations can reveal novel and sound arguments from horrors or hiddenness. But my main point here is that even if she does not think this, or even if she *ceases* to think this, the skeptical theistic form of reasoning can, ironically, be used to show that she should remain a non-theist.

S6

Let's consider next the link between skepticism about value of the sort promoted by S1 and the skepticism of S6. Since the latter skepticism may seem a bit unusual, and since it is tied up with what might be called the positive message of skeptical atheism, which can easily go unheeded, I propose to consider it somewhat more fully.

If there might be a good quite unknown to us that, were we to become aware of it and see things clearly, would strike us as providing a good reason for God to permit horrors, then our picture of value must be very partial indeed. Our understanding of value-related facts might have to be completely reconfigured to accommodate such a good—if an unsurpassably good and loving person would have a good reason to permit millions of horrors over a period of many millennia then the realm of value must be very strange. But then there is no non-arbitrary way for our non-theist to deny that she lacks good reason for thinking that a divine reality would be a person in the first place. For if the realm of value might be that strange, then our understanding of value *ultimacy* might be mistaken. Then the *greatest possible* value—which is what I am taking axiological ultimacy to entail—might seem very strange to us too.

There is another way of getting at this point. We have no good reason for thinking we can identify what has the greatest possible value if the most *fundamental* truths about value might be out of reach for us. The most fundamental truths in any domain obviously have a bearing on all the others, and might here be expected to determine how "greatest" or "least" in matters of value comes to apply. And it seems that the most fundamental truths about value may be obscured, and indeed the most deeply obscured of value truths, if skeptical theism is on the right track about value. Now perhaps we could know the deepest truths about value even if many other significant value truths were entirely beyond our ken, but the skeptical theist will surely have a hard time convincing us that we do: if some significant value truths might be beyond our ken because of relevant cognitive limitations, then the deepest might be beyond our ken too. Consider only how so many investigative enterprises have floundered for want of the most fundamental truths in their domain— or because of regularly changing views on what these are. Even the delivery of *more* fundamental truths would please many inquirers! Take, for example, physics. Physicists would be very happy if they found truths that unify quantum mechanics and general relativity, and they might consider themselves to have done so even while remaining doubtful as to whether they had struck absolute bedrock explanatorily. The claim to know the most fundamental truths in some domain is generally the most ambitious claim one can make. Thus if anything should come under the glare of value skepticism on account of our cognitive limitations, surely it is the suggestion that one has accessed the most fundamental truths about value. But then without the immunity to skepticism about such matters that a theist may take herself to have, our non-theist is stuck with the consequent of the conditional mentioned at the beginning of this paragraph, which says that we are in the dark about what would instantiate the greatest possible value.

Now if we are thus in the dark, then even if the possible goods we know of are consistent with some characterization of axiological ultimacy, we have no good reason for thinking similarly about the possible goods there are. (Notice how modality comes into play here along with value.) It follows that even if the possible goods we know of are consistent with a person being axiologically ultimate, as perhaps most theists and non-theists today would affirm, we have no good reason for thinking that the same is true of the possible goods there are. Despite what the goods we know of seem to indicate, there may, if we are in the dark about the greatest possible value, be unknown goods belonging to axiological ultimacy that no person could instantiate. And, of course, this is just as S6 would have it.[8]

Now perhaps the skeptical theist will wish to relieve the non-theist of such doubts. What options does she have? Well, perhaps it will seem that even if *theism* can't properly be used by the non-theist to ground a deductive inference to the conclusion that S6 is false in her own case, some other proposition can be thus employed—and can be thus employed while still leaving S1–S3 in the clear. It may, in particular, seem to the skeptical theist that it is just *evident* that no non-person could be axiologically ultimate. One skeptical theist, Peter van Inwagen, actually claims as much in his recent Gifford Lectures. As he puts it: "I myself would say, without the least immodesty, that I am greater than any possible non-person—simply because I am a person" (2006: 158). Just what van Inwagen is claiming here is a bit unclear since he doesn't wish to give an analysis of the concept of a person. Intending only to "fix the concept," he says this: "By a person, I mean a being who may be, in the most straightforward and literal sense, *addressed*—a being whom one may call 'thou'" (2006: 20). But it seems clear that he and other skeptical theists who hold that no non-person could be axiologically ultimate would be willing to fill out this explication in terms of the presence of beliefs, desires, values, rational capacities, and so forth, if only because these are things van Inwagen will surely mention if asked

---

[8] It may be thought that there is an important distinction between "greatest possible reality" and "greatest possible being" that is relevant here. Perhaps the theistic God realizes the latter property while not needing to realize the former. Suppose this is so. It poses no problem for the argument, which can be phrased, without loss of plausibility, in terms of either property.

to explain what makes *him* a person and thereby makes him greater than any non-person, and because these are properties presupposed by the properties of omnipotence, omniscience, omnibenevolence, and so on as understood by traditional theists, who invariably ascribe them to God. So let us assume that this somewhat enlarged depiction of a person is applicable here. I will also assume that personal qualities are defining qualities, in the case of God, in such a way that no other properties God may possess are more fundamental— no other properties subsume the personal ones either explanatorily or evaluatively. This seems required by the notion that God *is* a person, which implies that the most fundamental features of Godhood are personal ones.

On these assumptions, what is to be said for the claim that it is evident that no non-person could be axiologically ultimate? Van Inwagen himself admits that what we have here is a "substantive metaphysical thesis" (2006: 158). As such, it is hard to see how a *skeptical* theist could be justified in regarding the notion as evidently true. It is, of course, a notion very familiar to us, presupposed in much Western religious thought. But anyone who recognizes such facts about our place in time as I mentioned earlier, and who thinks, within this frame of reference, about how we in the West are only now starting to acquaint ourselves with non-theistic religious thought, will regard the observation about familiarity as damaging to the case a skeptical theist is here required to make rather than helpful. Add to this what we are just now beginning to learn from the fledgling field of study known as the cognitive science of religion about how evolution may have predisposed us to find agency especially significant in matters religious (Barrett 2004, Boyer 2001, Tremlin 2006), and we will conclude that it would be wise to back away from the claim that it is just evident that only a person could be axiologically ultimate. Here it is also important to remember that the idea that a non-person could be axiologically ultimate need not deny that personal qualities (or properties analogous thereto) would necessarily have some place in an ultimate divine reality. Perhaps they are allotted a lesser role in some larger mix defined by valuable properties of which we have, as yet, no inkling (Schellenberg 2009, 2013). Against this background, the idea that an axiologically ultimate reality evidently could only be a person must seem quite evidently unavailable to a skeptical theist seeking to remove, for non-theists, the new source of doubt about theism represented by S6.

For some this new source of doubt may be disquieting. But within the context of a total evidence skepticism sensitive to our place in time it may easily come to appear exhilarating instead. Of course if what seems most important to us is that we figure everything out, as swiftly as possible, or if a central aim of ours is to protect an understanding (perhaps theistic, perhaps naturalistic) that we've already arrived at, then such doubt may not seem very attractive. But if we allow our imaginations to linger in the thought of an understanding of the world beheld by finite beings but so magnificently deep that all our present thinking, even if it contains much truth, is just the tip of the proverbial iceberg, we may be attracted to a different stance. In any case, it seems clear that skeptical reasoning of the sort employed by the skeptical theist can be used to show that, whatever the religious diversity displayed by the world as we know it, much deeply significant religious diversity may not yet have come to light. Because of our early place in time, we need to be open to the possibility that our best religious ideas—including our best ideas about what is axiologically ultimate—are still ahead of us. This is the positive message of a skeptical atheism, a message designed to stir us from our complacency and prompt us to begin a deeper investigation into things divine.

IV

So what options are open or live for skeptical theists who accept my arguments—if any such there should be? Well, if the arguments of Section II are accepted, then of course a wider religious skepticism might be expected to replace the skeptical theist's theism. But I imagine this outcome will, at least for the time being, be resisted by theistic philosophers. I expect there will be opposition to the skeptical atheist's attempt to show that the skeptical theist is "hoist by his own petard." What success might attend such efforts only time will tell. The skeptical theist might also rightly point out how an examination of the consequences of theism for a wide array of philosophical and religious problems, presently being undertaken by, for example, Christian philosophers in America, can make for an investigative *theism*. This is certainly true, and I can imagine a scenario in which skeptical theists and skeptical atheists, both investigatively minded, together enlarge our field of vision on many matters that are or ought to be under inquiry. But if the fuller doubts that I have argued should come with skeptical theism eventually take hold, then a much stronger emphasis on non-theistic pictures of the divine (or on non-theistic fillings for ultimism) might be expected to appear in Western philosophy of religion. After all, we have devoted centuries and millennia of intense effort to the exploration of theism. One wonders what might come of a few millennia of equally rigorous attention to non-theistic ideas, both known and (presently) unknown.

There is also a very different alternative for skeptical theists that at least deserves mention. Seeing that whatever supports such theses as S1–S3 supports, in the right circumstances, S4–S6 as well, the skeptical theist might regard this as providing what amounts to a *reductio* for the former theses and so come to reject them. Of course, this would mean rejecting skeptical theism, too, but it is certainly one of the responses a theist might make.

Someone who responds in this way will perhaps be inclined to say: "You're right—if I accept the first three theses on the grounds that make them attractive, then I should find myself drawn to the other three as well. But on reflection it seems to me that the other three are false—and this even while leaving the possibility of an inference to their falsehood from a prior conviction that theism is true entirely to one side! I *can* use what I presently know about value to rule out a non-personal ultimate, and I *can* infer from careful research into available arguments from horrors and purported defeaters of religious experience as justification for theistic belief that no such arguments are successful. Thank you for helping me to see this clearly. Of course, now I have to write William Rowe a letter of apology—and maybe also send one to all those journals that have published my papers on skeptical theism...."

I suspect that few skeptical theists will experience such a sudden conversion. But what we see here is still a way of responding to the arguments of this chapter. I do not believe that it is the best response, but if on reflection it seems the right move to make, then our skeptical theist can avoid the feasible response I myself would promote, which means giving up theistic belief. Of course, to make it, our skeptical theist must cease to be a "skeptical" theist. And I would suggest that if she wants to avoid giving up "theist" too, she had better start writing papers on theodicy—fast.

15

Skeptical Theism, Atheism, and Total Evidence Skepticism

Michael Bergmann

In his "Skeptical Theism and Skeptical Atheism," John Schellenberg presses a number of interesting objections and challenges to theistic belief, which are supposed to cause special trouble for *skeptical* theists.[1] In this short chapter I will not be able to address all of his remarks, but I will address some of the most important concerns he raises. I'll begin, in Section I, by offering some clarificatory comments concerning skeptical theism. In Section II, I will evaluate an atheistic argument that Schellenberg finds particularly impressive. In Section III, I'll examine the view Schellenberg calls "total evidence skepticism" and consider its bearing on theistic belief. In the final section I'll consider whether Schellenberg is right in thinking that skeptical theism commits one to total evidence skepticism and to some of the other skeptical theses he proposes.

I CLARIFYING THE SKEPTICAL THEIST'S SKEPTICISM

Skeptical theism has a skeptical component and a theistic component.[2] Schellenberg begins his chapter by describing the skeptical component of skeptical theism (which can be endorsed by both agnostics and atheists as well as by theists) as the endorsement of the following three skeptical theses:

S1 We have no good reason for thinking that the possible goods we know of are representative, relative to the property of figuring in a (potentially)

---

[1] This chapter appears in this volume. Unless otherwise noted, page references are to this chapter.
[2] The theistic component is just the traditional view that God, a supreme and perfect personal being, exists.

God-justifying reason for permitting such things as hiddenness or horrors, of the possible goods there are.

S2 We have no good reason for thinking that the possible evils we know of are representative, relative to the property of figuring in a (potentially) God-justifying reason for permitting such things as hiddenness or horrors, of the possible evils there are.

S3 We have no good reason for thinking that the entailment relations we know of between possible goods and the permission of possible evils are representative, relative to the property of figuring in a (potentially) God-justifying reason for permitting such things as hiddenness or horrors, of the entailment relations there are between possible goods and the permission of possible evils.[3]

To this description of the skeptical component, which is fine as far as it goes, I would like to add two clarificatory remarks.[4]

First, skeptical theists don't claim that their skeptical theses undermine all arguments from evil. S1–S3 say that we don't have good reason for thinking the goods, evils, and entailments between them (or GEEs) that we know of are representative of the GEEs that there are. These skeptical theses are used by the skeptical theist to target inductive inferences from God-justifying reasons we can think of (by reflection on known GEEs) to the conclusion that there are no God-justifying reasons for permitting the evils we know of. Some arguments from evil explicitly rely on such an inference.[5] Others try to avoid relying on such an inference but arguably fail to avoid so doing.[6] But this doesn't show that *all* arguments from evil rely on inductive inferences based on known GEEs. In previous work, I have explicitly refrained from saying that they all do and I'm inclined to think that some don't.[7] So Schellenberg is mistaken when he says (p. 192) that the skeptical theist's skepticism "is supposed to work for just any argument from hiddenness or horrors."[8]

---

[3] As he notes, his S1–S3 include more than my formulation of the skeptical theist's skeptical theses ST1–ST3, but the extra material included in S1–S3 is an accurate statement of how I think they should be understood, so I have no objection to them.

[4] For further clarificatory comments, see Bergmann (2009: 376–81). For an account of skeptical theism that isn't tied so closely to the skeptical theses mentioned here, see McBrayer (2010a).

[5] See Rowe (1979, 1988, and 1991).

[6] In Bergmann (2009: 382–5), I contend that arguments from evil proposed by Draper and by Schellenberg fall into this category.

[7] See Bergmann (2009: 381) where I set the question issue aside. And see Howard-Snyder and Bergmann (2004: 23–5) where we note that Tooley's argument from evil seems not to be undermined by the skeptical theist's skepticism.

[8] Schellenberg tells us (pp. 192 & 195) that the skeptical theist's skepticism had better work against *every* argument from evil "if it wants to do important work for theism in philosophy" or be "really powerful as a theistic form of reasoning." That seems a rather high standard. If an insight or objection is plausible and useful for undermining many atheistic arguments,

Second, the skeptical theses support only a limited skepticism about certain kinds of access to God's reasons. (This will be important in Section IV.) One way to discover what reasons might be available to God for permitting evils is to reflect on the GEEs that we can think of, trying to piece together from such material potential God-justifying reasons for permitting horrific suffering or divine hiddenness.[9] If, in doing that, one can't think of any God-justifying reasons for permitting such evils, one might inductively infer (from the sample of possible reasons considered) that no reasons for permitting such evils are God-justifying. The skeptical theses tell us that *that* is not a good way to discover reasons God might have for permitting evil because we should have doubts about whether the sample (on which the inductive inference would be based) is relevantly representative. But the fact that we can't tell *just by reflecting on the GEEs that we know of*[10] what God's reasons are doesn't imply that we have no way at all of discovering various things about God's reasons. For example, since I know that I exist, I know that God (if God exists) didn't have an all-things-considered good reason to permanently annihilate me a short time ago (if he did, I wouldn't be here). Likewise, if you knew that some action was intrinsically wrong for anyone to perform, regardless of the consequences, then you could thereby know that a morally perfect being like God would have an all-things-considered good reason not to perform such an act.[11] Even if we can't tell these things about God's reasons using the method described at the beginning of this paragraph, that doesn't mean that we can't tell them in other ways.

Another way to put this point is to say that S1–S3 are claiming that we have no *induction-friendly* good reasons for thinking that the GEEs that we know of are relevantly representative of the GEEs that there are. Such reasons (for thinking known GEEs are relevantly representative) are induction-friendly only if they aren't dependent on previous knowledge of the conclusion one is trying to reach inductively (via inference from those known GEEs). So, for example, if we knew on independent grounds (e.g. moral intuition about what

---

that makes it important and powerful. It's true that, as I've mentioned before (see Bergmann [2009: 380–1]), the skeptical theist's skepticism doesn't show that theism is true. But it can do important and powerful work for theism without showing that theism is true; it can do this by undermining a large number of reasons for thinking that theism is false. It seems rather demanding and implausible to say that no important work for theism can be done unless one shows that atheism is false or unreasonable.

[9] The idea here is that, although God hates evil, he would permit it if doing so were not intrinsically wrong or unloving and the overall consequences of doing so were sufficiently positive. Whether the overall consequences of doing so are sufficiently positive will depend, in part, on what possible goods and possible evils there are and on what entailments hold between them.

[10] This italicized phrase refers to the method just described of reflecting on consequences of permitting evils in order to discover (via induction from the reasons we're aware of) whether God has a reason to permit evils that aren't intrinsically wrong to permit.

[11] Similar points are made in Bergmann (2001: n. 27), Bergmann (2009: 391), and more extensively in my Bergmann (2012: 14–16).

is intrinsically wrong, no matter what the consequences) that it was impossible for there to be a God-justifying reason to permit some evil E, and we also knew (by trying) that we couldn't think of any such reason when we reflected on the GEEs we know of, then we'd know that the GEEs we know of *were* representative of the GEEs there are (in terms of whether they feature in a God-justifying reason for permitting E). But this reason for thinking the GEEs we know of are representative of the GEEs there are would not be induction-friendly, because it depends on previous knowledge that there are no God-justifying reasons for permitting E. Hence, this reason couldn't help us *discover*, via induction from the GEEs we know of, that there are no God-justifying reasons for permitting E. The upshot is that, although the skeptical theist's skepticism says that we can't know via inductive inference from known GEEs that there are no God-justifying reasons for permitting the evils that trouble us, it doesn't say we can't discover in some other way whether there are such reasons.[12]

II SCHELLENBERG'S ARGUMENT FOR ATHEISM

Schellenberg draws our attention to the following argument from evil:

1. People can have endless opportunities to grow ever deeper into God[13] even if God has prevented horrors altogether. (This is because God is infinitely deep and rich and exclusively good.)
2. People who grow ever deeper into God realize their deepest good. (This is because God is unsurpassable greatness personified.)
3. Therefore, people can achieve their deepest good without horrors being permitted. [from 1 and 2]
4. If people can achieve their deepest good without horrors being permitted, then God will not permit horrors. (This is because God is unsurpassably empathetic.)
5. Therefore, God (if he exists) will not permit horrors. [from 3 and 4]
6. But there are horrors.
7. Therefore, God does not exist. [from 5 and 6]

[12] Nor is it saying that we can discover or that we, in fact, have some other way of knowing that there are no such God-justifying reasons.

[13] I'm not sure I know what it means to grow deeper into God. Since Schellenberg doesn't explain it in his chapter, I'll just go with what I take to be one natural construal of the phrase—a construal according to which "growing deeper into God" means becoming more like God in moral character, understanding God better, or having an improved and closer interpersonal relationship with God. To grow *ever* deeper is to *always* be improving in one or more of these ways.

I agree that premise 6 is obviously true. But Schellenberg says (p. 194) that premises 1, 2, and 4 are obviously true too. I beg to differ. Premise 2 is doubtful because it ignores the possibility of people perpetually and asymptotically approaching, without ever reaching, a limit to their depth of growth—where this limit is insufficient for achieving their deepest good. Premise 1 is doubtful because there may be limits to how deep one can grow into God—limits that can be surpassed (for some person or other) only if God permits horrors.[14] Perhaps we can't think of any reason why permitting horrors is required for opportunities to grow ever deeper into God. But given S1–S3, it's not reasonable to conclude from this that we can see (or that it's reasonable to believe) that there isn't, or isn't likely to be, any such reason.[15] After all, it may be that there are entailment relations we aren't aware of between *inter alia* possible goods (including the good of certain people growing ever deeper into God) and possible evils (including the permissions of horrors). Given our limited grasp of the realm of GEEs, it is implausible that we can just see that this is false or unlikely.[16] Schellenberg suggests (p. 194) that this sort of response is "a case of implausible reaching, which reason alone can no longer be said to support." On the contrary, I'd say it is just a sensible sober assessment of our capacities for modal insight into the realm of possible goods, evils, and the logical relations between them.[17]

Premise 4 is also doubtful. To see why, consider these questions: Could an unsurpassably empathetic God permit a person S to suffer horrors even if permitting those horrors isn't required for achieving S's deepest good? Could there be a reason that would justifiedly motivate such a God to permit such a

---

[14] Schellenberg argues (2007: 244) that traditional theists are committed to thinking that some humans realize their deepest good without suffering horrors and suggests that this implies that all humans can realize their deepest good without God permitting horrors. But it's not clear that traditional theists are committed to that premise: perhaps all who will eventually enjoy everlasting union with God will also undergo horrific suffering (after death if not before). In any case, even if some humans can realize their deepest good without suffering horrors, it doesn't follow that (a) they can do so without being *permitted* to suffer horrors that they don't in fact suffer or that (b) all humans can realize their deepest good without suffering horrors.

[15] It's possible that Schellenberg would agree with this sentence given that he says (note 4) that it "seems unlikely that S1–S3 can be accepted by the atheist compatibly with his accepting" the atheistic argument under discussion.

[16] I should emphasize that although I think our grasp of the realm of GEEs is limited, I also think we have a significant grasp of that realm. Thus, I agree with Schellenberg when he says (p. 193) that "we may nonetheless be the recipients of various *specific* insights about value and modality" and that "we should not delight in darkness."

[17] His reference (p. 194) to Schellenberg (2007: 254–6) doesn't help. In Schellenberg (2007: 256) he says that it's "inconceivable" that a manifestation of God's infinite attractiveness (without the permission of any horrors—which, he thinks, are more likely to embitter us than attract us) would fail to enable a person to progress ever deeper into relationship with God. According to Schellenberg, God's manifestation of his infinite attractiveness (without permitting horrors) "can immediately be seen by us to be the sort of thing capable of" enabling us to achieve our greatest good. In my view, it is remarks like these about what is inconceivable and what we can immediately see, not any doubts about these remarks that count as implausible reaching.

thing? I don't see why not. God might permit a person S to suffer horrors in order to achieve some other very great good, perhaps to enable some other person to achieve her greatest good. We can agree that God wouldn't permit S to suffer horrors for that reason if doing so involved God treating S merely as a means. But there's no good reason to think God couldn't do this without treating S merely as a means. Suppose that (a) in permitting S to suffer horrors (in order for God to achieve some purpose other than bringing about S's achievement of her deepest good), God ensures that he can also bring some great good to S out of that permitted suffering, even though that isn't God's reason for permitting the suffering and that (b) God knows that if S were aware of the relevant facts and S's affections were rightly ordered toward the good, then S would willingly agree to suffer the horrors in question in order to work with God in achieving the purpose God has in mind. Then it's not at all clear that God wouldn't permit S to suffer horrors if those horrors weren't *required* to achieve S's deepest good.[18] Instead, whether God will permit people to suffer horrors (even if this is not required for them to achieve their deepest good), will depend on what GEEs there are, and this is something we can't see just by reflecting on the GEEs we can think of. These considerations give us ample reason to have serious doubts about premise 4.

Notice that in giving these replies to Schellenberg's argument from evil, I didn't rely solely on the skeptical theist's skepticism. That's because his argument relies in places on some moves and premises that aren't undermined by the skeptical theist's skepticism. Unfortunately, some of these other moves and premises fall prey to other objections, in the ways noted in this section.

III TOTAL EVIDENCE SKEPTICISM AND THEISTIC BELIEF

Total evidence skepticism raises skeptical concerns based on worries about our access to the total evidence. The total evidence relative to a proposition is everything (other than the proposition itself) that bears on the truth of that proposition—everything relevant as it would be seen from a God's-eye perspective. The modus operandi of total evidence skepticism (TES) is to point out that we don't have reflective access (i.e. access on reflection alone) to the total evidence relative to some proposition p and to claim that, in light of that fact, we are rationally required to withhold judgment about p. Although this claim might initially seem plausible, the problem is that for *every* proposition p, we lack reflective access to the total evidence relative to p, including the

---

[18] See Plantinga (2000: 493–4) for further discussion.

case where p is the proposition that *if we don't have reflective access to the total evidence relative to a proposition, then we are rationally required to withhold judgment about that proposition.* If TES is going to have significant, persuasive, and yet limited skeptical force, it needs to be formulated in a way that makes it clear when our lack of reflective access to the total evidence causes skeptical problems and when it doesn't.

Schellenberg formulates his favored version of TES as follows: "for many a proposition expressing a belief or potential belief of ours, we have reason to be in doubt or skeptical, about whether the total relevant evidence supports that proposition."[19] An important question for Schellenberg's TES is this: under what conditions does our recognition that we lack reflective access to the total evidence bearing on p rationally require us to be skeptical about whether the total evidence bearing on p supports p? It's clear that Schellenberg thinks that in some cases it does require us to be skeptical (otherwise his version of TES is uninteresting) and in other cases it doesn't. But it is not clear from his chapter in this volume what makes for this difference.

In my view, TES does not give rise to a compelling skeptical worry. It's true that I don't have reflective access to the total evidence bearing on whether I exist or on whether I have hands or on whether I had orange juice for breakfast today or on whether 2 + 2 = 4 or on whether I'm currently in extreme pain. But in each of these cases I have knowledge or reasonable belief from which I can infer certain facts about the total evidence bearing on these propositions. For example, I reasonably believe that the total evidence supports the claim that 2 + 2 = 4. I reasonably believe this even though I don't have reflective access to the total evidence bearing on that claim. The reason I can reasonably believe this about the total evidence is that I know that, for any proposition p, the total evidence bearing on p supports p, if p is true; likewise, it supports ~p, if p is false. From that knowledge, together with my knowledge that it's true that 2 + 2 = 4, I can conclude that the total evidence supports the claim that 2 + 2 = 4. Something similar applies to the claim that *it's false that my current evidential basis for my belief that 2 + 2 = 4 is without epistemic force.* When I consider it, I reasonably believe that my belief that 2 + 2 = 4 is a reasonable one. From that I conclude that it's false that its evidential basis is without epistemic force. And from that I conclude that the total evidence supports the claim that *it's false that my current evidential basis for my belief that 2 + 2 = 4 is without epistemic force.* In his chapter in this volume, Schellenberg doesn't say, of any proposition, that he reasonably believes that the total evidence supports it. But since he doesn't find TES to be a compelling skeptical worry across the

---

[19] The use of "many" make this statement of TES a little vague. Suppose there were 100 or 200 propositions of which this was true. Would that make Schellenberg's version of TES true? Does it matter what those propositions are?

board, my guess is that he would have no objection to the sort of response to TES that I've outlined here.

How does this bear on theistic belief? Schellenberg's S4[20] suggests that we should acknowledge that we are in the dark about whether the total evidence supports the claim that *it's false that my evidential basis for my belief that God exists is without epistemic force.* I think a rational theist, one whose theistic beliefs are justified in something like the ways suggested by Alston (1991) or Plantinga (2000),[21] could sensibly respond by saying the following: "When I consider the matter, I reasonably believe that my belief that God exists is a rational one. From that I conclude that it's false that its evidential basis is without epistemic force. And from that I reasonably conclude that the total evidence supports the claim that *it's false that my evidential basis for my belief that God exists is without epistemic force.*"[22] In short, a rational theist could respond to Schellenberg's S4 in the same way one responds when defending any rational belief against objections based on TES.

Similar remarks apply to S5,[23] a principle that suggests that we should acknowledge that we're in the dark about whether the total evidence includes successful proofs of atheism. Just as those who rationally believe that there is an external world and that the universe has been around a long time can rationally infer from these propositions that the total evidence (to which they, admittedly, lack reflective access) does not include any successful proofs that

---

[20] S4 says:

> We have no good reason for thinking that the considerations opposing the epistemic force of religious experience we know of are representative, relative to the property of (potentially) figuring in an undefeatable defeater of religious experience as justification for theistic belief, of the considerations opposing the epistemic force of religious experience there are.

[21] Throughout this chapter, when I talk about a rational theist, I'll have in mind someone whose theistic beliefs are justified in this manner.

[22] A rational theist might be less sure about what the evidential basis is for her belief that God exists than she is about the rationality of her belief that God exists, just as a person might be less sure about what the evidential basis is for her belief that $2 + 2 = 4$ than she is about the rationality of her belief that $2 + 2 = 4$. But even in that case, the theist could rationally conclude that (a) it's plausible to think her belief that God exists is based on religious experience (e.g. on theistic seemings) and (b) if her belief that God exists is in fact based on religious experience, then the total evidence supports the claim that *it's false that the religious experience on which her belief that God exists is based is without epistemic force.* Likewise, the person who rationally believes that $2 + 2 = 4$ could rationally conclude that (a) it's plausible to think her belief that $2 + 2 = 4$ is based on a mathematical seeming and (b) if her belief that $2 + 2 = 4$ is in fact based on a mathematical seeming, then the total evidence supports the claim that *it's false that the mathematical seeming on which her belief that $2 + 2 = 4$ is based is without epistemic force.*

[23] S5 says:

> We have no good reason for thinking that the arguments from horrors or hiddenness against theism we know of are representative, relative to the property of (potentially) constituting a successful proof that theism is false, of the arguments from horrors or hiddenness against theism there are.

there is no external world or that the universe came into existence only five minutes ago, so also rational theists can rationally infer that the total evidence does not include any successful proofs of atheism, either from horrors or hiddenness. This doesn't mean one could never come across compelling and persuasive evidence that it's false that there is an external world or that it's false that the universe came into existence only five minutes ago (or that theism is false). I'm not arguing that such things are impossible. The point is just that from reasonable belief that p, one can infer that the total evidence does not include a successful proof that p is false (since if p is true, the total evidence supports p, in which case it does not include a *successful* proof that p is false). The rational theist is simply joining the many others who use this style of reasoning in response to TES when she infers that the total evidence does not include any successful atheistic arguments. She is responding to S5 in the way people respond to TES-based worries about as yet unknown successful proofs that there is no external world or that the universe came into existence only five minutes ago.

Schellenberg's view, as I understand it, is that a response to TES, of the sort that I have given above, is just fine when it is applied to a belief such as 2 + 2 = 4, but it doesn't work when it is applied to the belief that God exists. Why not? As was mentioned earlier, the answer isn't clear from his chapter.[24] But elsewhere he suggests that our beliefs can escape TES only in cases where (a) the evidence for the beliefs is "so strong" that it leaves "no room" for skeptical doubt or (b) the beliefs are "universal and unavoidable," in part because (practically speaking) we can't get started on inquiry unless we "take the plunge" somewhere in trusting our inclinations to believe, even if it's "only where we have to."[25] This proposal gives rise to many questions. For starters, we need to know what precisely it means for there to be no room for skeptical doubt.[26] Likewise, what does it mean to say we can trust our belief inclinations

---

[24] In his chapter, he says that beliefs that are "evidently true" (p. 200) escape the force of TES and that "what seems most obvious to us upon reflection should be given a pass" (p. 201). And he seems to think belief in God's existence doesn't escape the force of TES because the experience on which it is based is not "so intense and clear and enduring as to make it impossible ... not to respond to it believingly" (p. 198). He also seems to think (p. 200) that the premises of his argument for atheism, discussed in Section II, escape TES (it would, of course, make sense for him to think that, given that he seems to put weight on that argument; but, for the reasons mentioned in Section II, it's a mistake to think this of the premises of his argument for atheism). There are hints, in these remarks, of a standard he has in mind, but no clear statement.

[25] The condition specified in (a) is discussed in Schellenberg (2007: 31–2) and the condition specified in (b) in Schellenberg (2007: 169–75). He seems to acknowledge, in the latter passage, that condition (b) might be satisfied when condition (a) is not; that's why he calls it "taking the plunge" when one goes with condition (b) upon being reminded that our basic picture of reality "might be fundamentally flawed" (p. 173).

[26] There is certainly room to ask standard skeptical questions, even regarding the beliefs about which we are most certain (e.g. "couldn't one feel absolutely certain that one sees p's truth clearly, even when p is false?"). Does the fact that one can ask such a question count as having room for skeptical doubt?

but only when "we have to"? In what sense must the beliefs be unavoidable and universal? Answering such questions will help us to get clear on what this principle is saying. But then further questions arise: Is this quasi-Cartesian epistemic requirement plausible? Do Schellenberg's own beliefs, on which he relies in defending his views, satisfy this requirement? And is he able to formulate a principle stating the conditions under which beliefs escape TES—one such that belief in that principle satisfies the very conditions it specifies? I would say that the answer is "No" to each of these three questions, just as it is if we focus, instead, on parallel questions in connection with Descartes's rather demanding epistemic requirements. But if that's right, then there is no compelling reason for thinking that Schellenberg's proposed principle causes any trouble for the responses given in this section to the TES-based worries that Schellenberg raises for theistic belief.

Unfortunately, I don't have the space here to examine Schellenberg's proposed epistemic principle in any detail. So I'll just say this for now. Schellenberg could insist on a strict Cartesian standard for justification. But given that standard, very few of our beliefs are going to be justified and Schellenberg's religious skepticism would be uninteresting. Or he could go with some other standard, less demanding than a strict Cartesian one. But then he will need to argue persuasively *both* that theistic belief doesn't satisfy that less demanding standard *and* that his particular less demanding standard (rather than some other one that the defender of theistic belief finds plausible) is the correct standard. In my view, Schellenberg has not done this, either in his chapter in this volume or in his 2007. I expect that theistic philosophers sympathetic to Alston (1991) and Plantinga (2000) will find the background epistemological views espoused by Schellenberg significantly less well-developed and less compelling by comparison.

IV SKEPTICAL THEISM AND TOTAL EVIDENCE SKEPTICISM

Can a skeptical theist consistently respond to S4, S5, and TES in the way I just recommended in the previous section? Or is Schellenberg right when he says (p. 198) that the skeptical theist's endorsement of S1–S3 rationally commits her to S4 as well?[27] S1–S3 tell us that we can't tell *just by reflecting on the GEEs*

---

[27] He also claims (p. 203) that those who endorse S1–S3 are committed to S5, mentioned in note 23, and S6, which runs as follows:

S6 We have no good reason for thinking that the possible goods we know of are representative, relative to the property of consistency with a person being axiologically ultimate, of the possible goods there are.

we know of that there are no God-justifying reasons for permitting the horrors and hiddenness that are appealed to in atheistic arguments from evil. Does accepting this commit a theist to thinking that she can't tell that there are no all-things-considered God-justifying reasons for allowing her previous belief in God to be based on grounds that are without epistemic force? No. At most, it commits her to thinking that we can't tell *just by reflecting on the GEEs we know of* that there are no God-justifying reasons for allowing her previous belief in God to be based on grounds that are without epistemic force. But, as noted in my second clarificatory remark about skeptical theism in Section I, her having that thought is consistent with her knowing about God's reasons in some other way. In particular, a theist might know in the way described in Section III that *it's false that the evidential basis for her previous belief that God exists is without epistemic force*; and she can sensibly conclude from this that God did not have an all-things-considered good reason to make it the case that the evidential basis for her previous belief that God exists is without epistemic force.

Similar points can be made about S5. It may be true that we can't tell *just by reflecting on the attempted proofs of atheism that we know of* that the total relevant evidence includes no successful proofs of atheism. But this doesn't mean that we can't know this in some other way. For example, a rational theist could know this in the way described in the previous section—i.e. by inferring from the fact that God exists (something she reasonably believes) that the total evidence does not include any successful proofs of atheism, either from horrors or hiddenness.[28]

Of course, as I've noted before,[29] the skeptical theist's skepticism doesn't itself justify the belief that God exists or the belief that the evidential basis of one's belief that God exists is not without epistemic force or that the total evidence doesn't include any successful proofs of atheism. Agnostics and atheists can accept the skeptical theist's skepticism without accepting these other things. The point is, rather, that the skeptical theist's skepticism is *consistent with* rational belief that God exists and with rational belief that the evidential basis of one's theistic belief has epistemic force and with rational belief that there are no successful proofs of atheism.

Some readers might still have the following lingering worry: If the skeptical theist's skepticism causes no trouble for theistic belief, why does it cause trouble for atheistic arguments from evil? It causes trouble for atheistic arguments

---

[28] Although I don't have the space to go into it here in any detail, similar points could also be made about S6 (which is given in the previous note). The rational theist can reasonably believe that God is a personal being (i.e. a being capable of things such as loving and knowing and acting). From that she can infer that (a) the total evidence supports the view that God is a personal being and that (b) the claim that God is a personal being is consistent with all the facts, including all the facts about what possible goods there are.

[29] See Bergmann (2009: 380–1).

from evil that rely (explicitly or implicitly) on inductive arguments from the GEEs we know of to all the GEEs there are, concluding from our inability to discern any God-justifying reasons for permitting a certain evil that it's false or unlikely that there are any such reasons. Non-theists might try, in their atheistic arguments from horrors or hiddenness, to avoid relying on such inductive inferences. They might, for example, suggest that we can just see, of some actual horror or instance of hiddenness that we know of, that it is intrinsically wrong for God to permit it, no matter how beneficial the consequences of permitting it (for the sufferer or for others). But it's quite implausible to think, of any of the actual horrors or instances of hiddenness that we know of, that we can *just see* (i.e. that we are non-inferentially justified in believing on the basis of intuition) that it is intrinsically wrong for God to temporarily permit them, no matter how beneficial the consequences.[30] Given that it's obviously possible for there to be things far worse than the actual horrors and hiddenness that we know of and that God has to us the relationship of divine creator, master, and caregiver to beloved subject and creature, it's not plausible that it would be *intrinsically wrong* for God to permit such suffering, no matter how beneficial it would be for his creatures to avoid far worse horrors.

Or one might think instead that, just as we can have non-inferentially justified perceptual or memory or introspective or mathematical beliefs, we can have a non-inferentially justified belief that it's false or unlikely that there are any God-justifying reasons for the permission of certain evils. But once one acknowledges that it's false that *temporarily permitting the horrors or instances of hiddenness that we know of is intrinsically wrong (no matter how beneficial the consequences)*, one should admit that God would permit such things if he had a good reason to do so. S1–S3 give us excellent reason to think we can't tell just by reflecting on the GEEs we know of *that it's false or unlikely that there is a God-justifying reason to permit such things*. Nor is it plausible to think we can tell such things intuitively and directly, on the basis of seemings. Given S1–S3 and that it's not *intrinsically* wrong to permit the horrors and hiddenness we know of, one should be doubtful of the reliability of any seeming that it's false or unlikely that there is a God-justifying reason to permit such things. How could minds as inferior as ours tell, intuitively and directly, whether God has good reasons for permitting such things?[31]

---

[30] For example, suppose that temporarily permitting God's hiddenness from a particular human was necessary for (a) making future everlasting union between that person and God possible and (b) avoiding future everlasting separation between that person and God. It's quite implausible to suggest that we can *just see* that permitting divine hiddenness in such a situation would be intrinsically wrong. It is irrelevant whether permitting temporary divine hiddenness *is in fact* necessary for (a) and (b). The point is that if it were necessary, permitting it wouldn't be wrong, which shows that it's not intrinsically wrong. Schellenberg (2002: 47–8) seems to think otherwise. For a discussion of his argument given there, see Bergmann (2009: 382–3).

[31] Thanks to Justin P. McBrayer, Phil Osborne, Michael Rea, and especially Ross Parker for helpful comments on previous drafts.

16

Skeptical Demonism: A Failed Response to a Humean Challenge

Wes Morriston

Our sense of music, harmony, and indeed beauty of all kinds, gives satisfaction, without being absolutely necessary to the preservation and propagation of the species. But what racking pains, on the other hand, arise from gouts, gravels, megrims, toothaches, rheumatisms, where the injury to the animal machinery is either small or incurable? Mirth, laughter, play, frolic, seem gratuitous satisfactions, which have no further tendency: spleen, melancholy, discontent, superstition, are pains of the same nature. How then does the Divine benevolence display itself, in the sense of you Anthropomorphites? None but we Mystics, as you were pleased to call us, can account for this strange mixture of phenomena ...

—*David Hume*[1]

The beauties and benefits that grace our lives are often said to show God's goodness to creatures, bearing witness to his love and care for them. Some theists even find in them an argument for God's goodness and wisdom. But a moment's reflection shows this to be hopelessly one-sided. If we are to infer anything about God's moral character from our experience of the world, then—as Hume so clearly saw—we must consider the *mixture* of good *and* ill, of beauty *and* ugliness, of benefit *and* harm that characterizes life in our world.

---

[1] Hume (1947: 198). All page references are to this edition. Referred to hereafter as *Dialogues*.

1. HUME'S CHALLENGE

In Part XI of the *Dialogues Concerning Natural Religion*, Hume has Philo[2] briefly consider four different hypotheses about the moral character of the "first causes" of the universe, with a view to deciding which of them best fits the "mixed phenomena" we experience.

> There may four hypotheses be framed concerning the first causes of the universe: that they are endowed with perfect goodness; that they have perfect malice; that they are opposite, and have both goodness and malice; that they have neither goodness nor malice. Mixed phenomena can never prove the two former unmixed principles; and the uniformity and steadiness of general laws seem to oppose the third. The fourth, therefore, seems by far the most probable (212).

Hume here leaves open the possibility that the universe has two or more "first causes." Given that we have no a priori information about its (or their) moral character, he holds that if we are to form any opinion on this subject, we must do so by "looking around the world" and considering how likely its general features are, given each of the four hypotheses. When we do so, he thinks we can effectively rule out all but the fourth. The two "unmixed" hypotheses do a poor job of explaining the mixture of good and ill we find in the world. If the ultimate source of things were perfectly good, we would expect things to be far better. If it were perfectly malicious, we would expect things to be far worse.

For reasons that need not detain us, Hume sets aside the third hypothesis,[3] but he seems more favorably disposed to the fourth, according to which the ultimate source is "entirely indifferent" to the welfare of creatures, having "no more regard to good above ill, than to heat above cold, or to drought above moisture, or to light above heavy" (211). This, Hume has Philo say, is the "true conclusion"—not because it gives us a reason to expect anything in particular, but because (unlike the other hypotheses) it gives us no reason to expect a world different from the one revealed to us by experience.

Does Hume really mean to endorse the indifference hypothesis? It's not clear that he does. Elsewhere he has Philo defend the more modest thesis that there are no empirical grounds for drawing any definite conclusion about the moral character of the first causes of the universe.[4] It's not entirely clear how all this is meant to fit together, but perhaps we can smooth things out by reading

---

[2] For ease of exposition, I make the plausible assumption that Philo speaks for Hume in this matter, and I shall often refer to Hume's position without mentioning Philo.

[3] He equates it with the Manichaean hypothesis that the world is a battleground in which the forces of light are arrayed against the forces of darkness, which he dismisses from consideration on the ground that it makes the "the perfect uniformity and agreement of the parts of the universe" rather surprising Hume (1947: 211).

[4] "What then shall we pronounce on this occasion? Shall we say that these circumstances are not necessary, and that they might easily have been altered in the contrivance of the universe? This decision seems too presumptuous for creatures so blind and ignorant" (1947: 210).

Hume as saying that one should not endorse any hypothesis about the moral character of the first causes, but that the indifference hypothesis is significantly more likely than any *one* of the others. That would give Hume's view a modest tilt toward indifference, since indifference would be the *least unlikely* of the four. But such a tilt would be entirely consistent with his overall skepticism.

Whether or not this is the right way to read Hume, I believe that his *Dialogues* provide materials with which we can mount quite an interesting challenge to the claim that "perfect goodness" (in a sense that entails perfect benevolence toward creatures) rules our world. The trick is to view it as one of several hypotheses, and then to show that the mixture of good and ill we find in the world is much less likely given either of the two "unmixed" hypotheses (perfect goodness or perfect malice) than it is given the indifference hypothesis. That will provide a reason for *not accepting* either of the unmixed hypotheses—that is, for refraining from judging either of them to be true (or especially likely).[5] Such a position would of course be entirely consistent with a complete suspense of judgment.[6]

By actively considering *both* "unmixed" hypotheses (perfect goodness *and* perfect malice) we can sharpen the challenge to the standard theistic view that a perfectly good deity rules the world. If the latter hypothesis fares no better than the former against our Humean challenge, that's already a problem for traditional theists. And if it should turn out that the observed mixture of good and ill makes it unreasonable to accept the perfect malice hypothesis, then theists have the non-trivial burden of explaining why it does not also make it unreasonable to accept the perfect goodness hypothesis.

To get a feel for how this sort of argument might go, it will help to pit very specific versions of the perfect goodness and perfect malice hypotheses against a very specific version of Hume's *indifference* hypothesis. Then we can consider how well a Hume-style argument for not accepting either of the two "unmixed" hypotheses holds up against the challenge of *skeptical theism* and its evil twin, *skeptical demonism*.

2. DEMONISM VS. INDIFFERENCE

Since I want to focus attention primarily on the *moral character* of the ultimate source of things, I shall assume—at least for the sake of argument—that there

---

[5] Among contemporary philosophers, Paul Draper has done more than anyone else to develop this sort of challenge. The argument I'll be considering is inspired by Draper's original argument. See Draper (1989). Referred to hereafter as *Draper*.

[6] One might, of course, have pragmatic reasons for betting one's life on a hypothesis that she does not "accept" in my sense. I take no position here on the rationality of such Pascalian wagering.

is a single creator and ruler of the universe, and that it has the maximum possible degree of knowledge, intelligence, and power.[7] I shall also assume that its preference structure gives high priority to certain aesthetic values—that it could be expected to appreciate a great variety of different kinds of being, including a prodigious variety of different and interrelated types of living things. It will be convenient to treat these points as part of our background information, as we consider various hypotheses about the moral character of this being, particularly with respect to its attitude toward (and treatment of) sentient creatures.

Also included as part of our background information is the "uniformity and steadiness of general laws," as well as the fact that the universe contains sentient creatures who can experience pleasure and pain and are capable of being benefited or harmed in many other ways, and that some of these creatures are rational animals, who can form social bonds and can make and carry out long-term plans. *Explicitly excluded* from background information is the mixture of goods and ills actually experienced by these creatures, the degree to which they flourish or flounder, and the distribution of pleasure and pain in their lives. Observations of this mixture will count as "new evidence" as we evaluate various hypotheses about the moral character of the creator and governor of the universe.

Just three such hypotheses will be considered: (i) that the creator is perfectly *benevolent*, (ii) that it is perfectly *malicious*, and (iii) that it is completely *indifferent* to the welfare of individual creatures. An inventive philosopher might frame any number of "mixed" moral character hypotheses, but it will not be necessary to consider any of them here.

The first hypothesis is endorsed by classical theism; I'll refer to it as the theistic view, or *theism* for short. Few (if any) people ever give serious consideration to the second hypothesis. But since the thought that the world is ruled by a maximally powerful, intelligent, and *malevolent* being will figure prominently in what follows, let's give it a name. I'll call it *supreme demonism*—or simply *demonism*. Demonists (if there are any) believe in what I shall refer to as *the Demon*.

The third hypothesis may be referred to as *the indifference hypothesis*, or simply as *indifference*. It is much more specific than Hume's indifference hypothesis, since it concerns the moral character of a single maximally powerful and intelligent person.[8] But it does have this much in common with Hume's

---

[7] Here I depart from Hume. In Part XI of the *Dialogues*, Cleanthes and Philo are considering the hypothesis that the universe is the product of a *finitely* powerful, good, and wise being.

[8] Nor is it identical to Paul Draper's "Hypothesis of Indifference," according to which "neither the nature nor the condition of sentient beings on earth is the result of benevolent or malevolent actions performed by non-human persons" (1989: 339). On the other hand, it is very close to what Draper calls "the Indifferent Deity Hypothesis" (1989: 347).

idea: it says that the creator and ruler of the universe is not concerned with what's good or bad for individual creatures.

So how do these hypotheses fare when we consider the "mixed phenomena" of good and ill in our world? Beginning with *demonism*, let's do a thought-experiment of the kind suggested by another passage of the *Dialogues*.[9] Imagine someone of "very limited intelligence" (intelligence on, roughly, the human scale) who pays a "visit" to our world. Prior to this visit, she is given all the background information specified above. But she is also informed that the Demon is the creator and governor of the world she is about to observe. That's all she knows before taking into account the "mixed phenomena" of good and ill to be found there. Here, then, is the question. Should this visitor not be surprised—should she not be very surprised—to discover that the mixture isn't worse than she finds it to be? To find so much, and so many varieties of goodness in the mix? Think, for example, of heart-melting sunsets, of babies' smiles, of Mozart and Beethoven, of the feeling you have when you're simply glad to be alive. These and other experienced goods too numerous to mention are not in scarce supply. As Hume's Cleanthes says, "Health is more common than sickness; pleasure than pain; happiness than misery. And for one vexation which we meet with, we attain, upon computation, a hundred enjoyments" (200). Cleanthes may be stretching things a bit here, but he has a point.

So, then, our imaginary visitor must be quite surprised to discover so much pleasure and well-being and good cheer mixed in with all the misery that she must surely have expected to find. All the same, she knows that the Demon is the creator and ruler of this world, and she rightly concludes that he has a suitably malevolent reason for putting up with this profusion of goodness. No doubt, she reasons, the Demon has to permit great goods for the sake of yet greater evils or to prevent even greater goods.

Now imagine a second such visitor to our world—a person of limited intelligence who has the same background information as the first visitor, with one important exception. This visitor has been informed that the creator and ruler of the world he is about to observe is perfectly good and benevolent. He will be surprised by all the pain and misery and failure mixed in with all the pleasure and flourishing that he expected to find. But for reasons parallel to those cited above, he rightly concludes that the deity must have a suitably benevolent (though to him unknown) reason for including so much misery in the mix. He doesn't know what that reason is, but he rightly concludes that there must be one.

Imagine, finally, a third visitor—one who has been given no prior information about the *moral character* of the creator and ruler of the world he is about to visit, but who has all the background information specified earlier.

---

[9] Hume (1947: 203).

The exquisite beauty of nature and the prodigious variety of living things will not surprise him given what he's been told about the creator's aesthetic preferences. Nor will the mixture of good and ill experienced by the creatures surprise him, since it's well within the range of what might be expected in a world of the kind specified by his background information. "If every thing in the universe be conducted by general laws, and if animals be rendered susceptible of pain," he reasons, "it scarcely seems possible but some ill must arise in the various shocks of matter."[10] But once our third visitor has taken a look around, it may occur to him to wonder if anything can be said about the moral character of the creator and governor of this world. He inquires into the matter, and *demonism, theism,* and *indifference* are among the hypotheses that he considers and compares. He might, I suggest, give the following argument for preferring the indifference hypothesis, and so for not accepting either of the others. "Indifference makes no difference," he reasons. "That is, it makes no difference to what we should expect just on background information. But the mixture of good and ill that I've discovered would be very surprising indeed given either demonism or theism. If the Demon were in charge, one should expect things to be far worse for creatures. If a benevolent God were in charge, one would expect a vastly more favorable mixture of good and ill. The mixture that I've discovered is antecedently *much* less likely on either demonism or theism than it is on the indifference hypothesis, and this is a reason of considerable weight for preferring it to the others. Given that there is nothing (other than the abundance of evil in the mixture, of course) to be said in favor of demonism, and nothing (other than the abundance of goodness in the mixture) to be said in favor of theism, it would be quite unreasonable for me to accept either of those hypotheses."

The third visitor's reasoning is not an argument to the best explanation, since he does not conclude that the indifference hypothesis is true, or even that it is particularly likely to be true. He doesn't claim to have considered all the possibilities—for example, he hasn't considered the possibility that the ultimate source of this world has a mixed moral character. But he does claim to have discovered a strong reason for preferring indifference to each of the other hypotheses he has considered, and so for not accepting either of them.

It will be useful to distinguish two arguments here—one for not accepting demonism, and one for not accepting theism. We can exhibit their common structure as follows. Let O be a set of uncontested observation statements, let H1 and H2 be a pair of logically incompatible hypotheses, and let B be everything we know that's logically independent of the statements in O. We can then argue as follows.

---

[10] Hume (1947: 207).

1. The (epistemic[11]) probability of O given H2 and B is significantly higher than that of O given H1 and B.
2. The (epistemic) probability of H2 given B is not lower than that of H1 given B.
3. If 1 and 2 are both true, then O makes it unreasonable to accept H1.
4. So O makes it unreasonable to accept H1.

Substitute the mixture of good and ill we find in the world for O, indifference for H2, and demonism for H1, and you have a Hume-inspired argument for concluding that the mixture makes it unreasonable to accept demonism. And, mutatis mutandis, you have a Hume-inspired argument for concluding that the mixture makes it unreasonable to accept theism. I shall refer to each of these arguments as *the Humean Argument*, leaving it to the context to make clear which of them I am referring to.[12]

So how might a demonist (or a theist) respond to the Humean Argument? One possibility, of course, would be to give strong reasons for believing that demonism (or theism) is highly likely given only background information. Then premise 2 would be false, and we'd be in the position of the first (or the second) Humean visitor to our world. Another possibility would be to defend a theory about reasons the Demon (or God) would likely have for causing or permitting the mixed phenomena disclosed by experience—or, as we may put it, to provide a "demonadicy" (or a theodicy). If the probability of some comprehensive demonadicy (or theodicy) given demonism (or theism) were high enough, this would undercut the claim that the mixture of good and ill is surprising on that hypothesis.

But there is a third possibility—the one I shall attempt to evaluate in this chapter. Demonists (or theists) may argue that it is unreasonable to form any expectation whatever about the mixture of good and ill given demonism (or theism). They may say that the probability of the mixture we've discovered given demonism (and also given theism) is inscrutable—that it is neither high nor low nor middling nor a bit above middling nor a bit below. In order to see why they might think this, we need to take a quick look at what has come to be known as the "skeptical theist" response to evidential arguments from evil.[13]

---

[11] By the epistemic probability of a proposition, I mean the degree of credence that should be given by a rational person. In this case, I am concerned with a conditional epistemic probability—with the degree to which a rational person should expect the observed mixture of good and ill given theism (or demonism). I'll be concerned exclusively with epistemic probabilities throughout, but won't always flag them as such.

[12] I call them Humean arguments in deference to their original inspiration, but they also bear a strong resemblance to the argument given by Paul Draper in the article referenced in note 5.

[13] Interestingly, it was a non-theist who first gave the position this apt name. See Draper (1996).

3. SKEPTICAL THEISM AND THE "NOSEEUM" INFERENCE

Skeptical theism was originally developed in response to a rather different sort of evidential argument—one that explicitly relies on what Stephen Wykstra has aptly dubbed a "noseeum" inference—an inference from our failure to discover (to "see") a morally sufficient reason for God's permitting some terrible evil to the conclusion that there is no such reason.[14] Here is a generic version of the argument.

5. Despite our best efforts, we have been unable to discover reasons that would justify God in permitting some of the worst evils.

6. So it's quite likely that there is no such reason.

7. But God (if he exists) wouldn't permit the worst evils unless he had a justifying reason.

8. So it's quite unlikely that God exists.

Since this argument bears a strong resemblance to William Rowe's 1979 version of the evidential argument from evil, I'll refer to it as a "Rowe-style argument."[15]

Skeptical theists accept premises 5 and 7 of the Rowe-style argument, but reject the noseeum inference from 5 to 6. Some try to block it by developing "just-so" stories in which God has morally sufficient reasons for permitting various evils. They don't claim that any of these stories is especially likely to be true, but merely that one of them might, for all we know, be true—in which case, there is (for all we know) a God-justifying reason even though we have been unable to discover it.

Suppose, for example, that libertarian free will is necessary for moral responsibility and moral goodness. And suppose further that for each possible person there is a fact of the matter about what that person would freely do in any possible situation in which she was made free. For all we know, the truth-values for these "counterfactuals of creaturely freedom" (as they have come to be called) might be such that not even God could achieve a better overall balance of *moral* good and evil. Arguably, this would provide a God-justifying reason for permitting all the evil that exists. So then, for all we know, there is such a reason.[16]

---

[14] Wykstra (1996b).   [15] Rowe (1979).

[16] See Plantinga (1996). Once it's granted that the counterfactuals of creaturely freedom have definite truth-values at all, they seem to provide theistic defenders with a kind of wild card. These peculiar counterfactuals may (for all *we* know) have whatever truth-values they need to have in order to get the theist out of trouble. There was never any real need for Plantinga to bring in the possibility that "Satan and his cohorts" are responsible for natural evil, since the counterfactuals of *human* freedom might (for all we know) be such that a difference in the amount or distribution of natural evil would have resulted in a less favorable balance of moral good over moral evil.

Some of the details of this story (especially the part about the counterfactuals of creaturely freedom) are highly controversial. But if you think it might (for all we know) be true, then you have a reason to reject the noseeum inference at the heart of the Rowe-style evidential argument. If, on the other hand, you think this particular story is too implausible to take seriously, you may wish to consider other stories designed to do the same job. As long as we can't discredit *all* such stories, a skeptical theist may insist that we are in no position to make the noseeum inference from 5 to 6 of the Rowe-style argument.[17]

However, many skeptical theists think we don't need a just-so story in order to see that this particular noseeum inference is fallacious. It is unreasonable, they think, to expect finite creatures like us to discover *God*-sized reasons for permitting evil. And this, they say, is all it takes to derail the move from 5 to 6. Stephen Wykstra, one of the pioneers of this view, puts the matter succinctly: "If God does exist, it's not surprising that we often cannot see these goods God sees. God being God (and us being us), this is just what one should expect."[18] But if it's unsurprising that we don't see the goods for the sake of which God permits terrible evils, then the fact that we don't see them constitutes little evidence for thinking that they're not there.[19]

Michael Bergmann, another prominent skeptical theist, builds a formidable case against Rowe's noseeum inference. His argument deploys several much-discussed "skeptical theses," which can perhaps be summarized in one sentence: we have no good reason to think that the possible goods and evils and entailment relations we know of are a representative sample of all that there are.[20] Bergmann thinks his skeptical theses are plausible, that the burden of proof is on anyone who rejects them, and that together they provide a strong "commonsensical" reason for rejecting the noseeum inference at the heart of the Rowe-style argument.[21]

To see how this works, let H be some horrific evil for which we can think of no God-satisfying reason. Then for all we know, there might be some great *unknown good* that God cannot achieve without permitting H; or there might be some even greater *unknown evil* that God cannot prevent without permitting H; or there might be some *unknown entailment relation* such that one or the other of these things holds with respect to some *known goods or evils*. In any or all of these ways, God might (for all we know) have a morally sufficient reason for permitting H that is utterly beyond our ken. The fact that we can't see what *God's* reasons are is therefore utterly unsurprising.

---

[17] For additional just-so stories, see van Inwagen (1988) and (1991). Another excellent source is Alston (1996b).
[18] Wykstra (2012: 30–1).
[19] For Wykstra's most recent attempt to formulate and defend a general epistemological principle that has the desired implication, see Wykstra and Perrine (2012).
[20] Bergmann (2009: 376). Referred to hereafter as *Bergmann*.
[21] See Bergmann (2012: 28).

4. IMPLICATIONS FOR THE HUMEAN ARGUMENT

Even if reflections like these derail the Rowe-style argument, they seem at first glance to be entirely irrelevant to the Humean Argument, since it doesn't make the noseeum inference that skeptical theists seek to undermine. The Humean Argument says that the observed mixture of good and evil is surprising given theism. That, and *not* the fact that no one has come up with a plausible God-justifying reason for permitting evil, is said to make the observed mixture count as evidence against theism.[22] It's true, of course, that a highly plausible God-justifying reason would blunt the force of the argument by raising the probability of the observed mixture given theism. But that's not much of an objection unless and until somebody actually provides such an account—or, more precisely, until somebody comes up with one that is quite likely given theism.

Skeptical theists disagree. They think this places the burden of proof in the wrong place. What we should say about the probability of the mixture of good and ill given theism, they say, depends on the correct assessment of the probability of God-justifying reasons for permitting so much evil in the mixture. Before concluding that the probability of the mixture given theism is low, we must first establish that the probability of a God-justifying reason is low.[23] But since we cannot avail ourselves of a noseeum inference, we are unable to do that. We are simply "in the dark" about the probability of a God-justifying reason—in which case (so it is claimed) we are *also* completely "in the dark" about the probability of the observed mixture of good and ill given theism. We can't say that it's high or low or middling or a bit above middling or a bit below—it's simply inscrutable. Therefore (it is alleged) we cannot meaningfully compare it to the probability of the observed mixture given indifference, and the first premise of our Humean Argument for not accepting theism must be rejected.

I do not think that this is an adequate response to the Humean Argument, but I'll hold my fire until we've seen how the issue plays out in the context of the parallel Humean challenge to *demonism*. If all goes according to plan, it will be obvious to the reader that the skeptical theist's general strategy works just as well (or poorly) for demonism as it does for theism. So what I have to say in defense of premise 1 of the Humean Argument for not accepting demonism will apply, mutatis mutandis, to the parallel argument for not accepting theism.

---

[22] The Humean Argument is *not* an argument from the failure of theodicy. Two papers by Paul Draper have helped me understand this crucial point. See Draper (2013) and "Confirmation and the Truth about CORNEA" (in this volume).

[23] This is my best attempt to understand Bergmann's response to the Draper argument cited in note 5. See Bergmann (2009: 383).

5. SKEPTICAL DEMONISM

If a perfectly malicious Demon rules the universe, he must have suitably malevolent reasons for permitting creatures to experience so much goodness and for permitting them to flourish as often and for as long as they do. At this point, someone might be tempted by a Rowe-style "argument from goodness" against demonism. Letting G stand for the amount and variety of goodness we find in the lives of creatures in our world, the argument might go something like this:

9. Despite our best efforts, we have been unable to discover a demonically sufficient reason for permitting G.

10. So it's quite likely that there is no such reason.

11. But the Demon (if he exists) would not permit G unless he had a demonically sufficient reason for so doing.

12. So it's quite likely that the Demon does not exist.

We are now ready to add a *skeptical demonist* to our cast of characters. The skeptical demonist grants premises 9 and 11, but she rejects the noseeum inference of 10 from 9. She may argue that it is fallacious by developing a just-so story about the Demon's reasons for permitting creatures to experience so much goodness. To take just one example, she might provide a Molinist-style free will defense. For all we know, the Demon strongly prefers harms that are *freely inflicted* to those that aren't. A vast amount of harm is freely inflicted on creatures by other creatures, and of course the Demon rejoices in such harm. If you ask why the Demon permits so much goodness, our skeptical demonist may reply: "Well, for all we know, the Demon's preferences and the truth-values of the counterfactuals of creaturely freedom are such that the Demon is most fully satisfied by a policy that permits many animals to flourish and to experience many goods." As far as I can see, this move works just as well (or poorly) for a demonist as it does for a theist.

If you don't think this story is plausible enough to do the job, the skeptical demonist should be able to come up with others—stories featuring heartbreak and loss (which obviously presuppose hearts to be broken and goods to be lost), or perhaps stories about an afterlife in which creatures who were happy on earth come to wish they'd never been born and in which the evils they then experience are intensified by the memory of goods experienced in their pre-mortem lives. The skeptical demonist will then demand that we rule out *all* such stories before concluding that there is no demonically sufficient reason.

Alternatively, the skeptical demonist may claim that no such story is required. If the Demon exists, he possesses the maximum possible degree of knowledge and intelligence and power, and from this alone she may conclude that it is to be expected that *Demon*-sized reasons would be utterly beyond our ken. Our failure to discern them therefore provides little or no evidence for saying that there are none.

Suppose (at least for the sake of argument) that this is right. How might it be relevant to the *Humean* line of argument developed earlier? Once again, the skeptical demonist may borrow from the skeptical theist's playbook. She may insist that the probability of the observed mixture given demonism *depends on* the probability of a demonically sufficient reason for causing or permitting the observed mixture. In order to conclude that the probability of the mixture given demonism is low, one must first establish that the probability of a demonically sufficient reason is low. But without a noseeum inference of the sort that's just been demolished, it's not easy to see how that could be done.

Our skeptical demonist may also borrow from Bergmann's way of making the skeptical theist's case, working with suitable demonic analogues of his skeptical theses. For all we know, she may say, there are unknown goods and evils and entailment relations, such that the demon cannot prevent the goods we celebrate without giving up great (known or unknown) evils or permitting even greater (known or unknown) goods. We have been given no reason to rule out these possibilities.

Since we're so completely "in the dark" about these matters, we must refrain from making any judgment at all about the probability of a demonically sufficient reason. It is simply inscrutable. But then the probability of the observed mixture given demonism must also be inscrutable. In which case, we can't compare it to the probability of the observed mixture given indifference, and premise 1 of the Humean Argument must be rejected. Thus reasons our skeptical demonist.

5.1 The Failure of Skeptical Demonism

Does this take care of business for the demonist? I think not. Let's begin by recalling that the Humean Argument compares a pair of conditional *epistemic* probabilities. To what degree, it asks, should demonism lead a rational person to expect a mixture of good and ill like the one we find in our world? And how does that compare with the degree to which one should expect such a mixture given the indifference hypothesis? To answer these questions we do *not* need to assess the "objective probability" of a demonically satisfying reason within some large and uncharted space of logically possible goods and evils and entailments. We can find significant support for premise 1 without attempting anything as ambitious as that.

Think about it this way. The Demon (if he exists) is perfectly malicious. He hates the goods in life that we celebrate, and rejoices in the horrors we lament. Causing horror and misery and preventing happiness and pleasure are among his highest priorities. Given such a perfectly malevolent preference structure, he has *a* reason—indeed a very powerful reason—for producing a much less "friendly" mixture of good and ill. And this (I say) gives us quite a strong reason to expect a less favorable mixture given demonism. By contrast, we have no reason at all to find the observed mixture of good and ill especially surprising given the indifference hypothesis. (Indifference, we've said, makes no difference.) So in the absence of positive evidence for thinking otherwise, we should conclude that the mixture is significantly *more* surprising given demonism than given indifference, which is all that premise 1 of the Humean Argument says.

The skeptical demonist may reply that without knowing more about the "space" of goods and evils and entailments that would be known to the Demon, we have no reason to deny that there are demonically satisfying reasons for causing/permitting the mixture, and (therefore) no reason to form any expectation about the mixture given demonism. But I think this would be to misread the dialectical situation. The case I have made for premise 1 does not depend on a prior judgment about the probability of a demonically satisfying reason. The perfect malevolence of the Demon's preference structure already gives us *a* reason for expecting a much nastier mixture of good and ill on demonism than the one we've observed. There is room for disagreement about just *how* strong this reason is, but it doesn't cease to be *a* strong reason just because the skeptical demonist has reminded us that there *might* be an unknown something that should, if we knew of it, lead us to expect a mixture no worse than the one we've actually found. There might, after all, be an unknown something such that, if we knew of it, would give us even more reason to expect a far worse mixture. As far as I can see, these competing "unknowns" cancel one another out, leaving us exactly where we started, with quite a strong—and as yet undefeated—reason for expecting to discover a much nastier mixture of good and ill.

All the same, one might wonder where this leaves the epistemic probability of a demonically sufficient reason for causing/permitting the observed mixture. Well, it cannot be denied that if (A) the epistemic probability of the mixture given demonism is low (low enough to make it significantly lower than the probability of the mixture given indifference), then (B) the epistemic probability of a demonically satisfying reason must also be low. But it doesn't follow that we must establish (B) on independent grounds and use it to help establish (A). Indeed, this way of thinking about (A) and (B) seems to me to get things exactly backwards. If we accept (B), it is because we think we already have an undefeated reason for accepting (A), and not the other way around.

Does this mean that we are, after all, making an unwarranted judgment about the probable contents of a vast and uncharted "space" of logical possibilities? This charge might have merit if we were making a claim about some sort of descriptive objective probability. But that's not what we're doing. We're merely trying to determine what a reasonable person should say given the evidence available to her.[24] It is (I say) entirely reasonable for her to find the mixture quite surprising given demonism. Unless and until she is given a positive reason to think otherwise, she should give little credence to the thought that there is a demonically satisfying reason for causing/permitting a mixture no "worse" than this one. In arriving at this position, she has not relied on a noseeum inference. Nor has she drawn an inductive inference from a possibly unrepresentative sample of goods and evils and entailments. Good Humean that she is, she has dropped every "arbitrary supposition or conjecture" and reasoned "merely from the known phenomena"[25]—from what she knows about sentient creatures and the world they inhabit and from what might be expected if the world is ruled by perfect malice.

5.2 Application

The foregoing remarks apply mutatis mutandis to theism. *As far as the observed mixture of good and ill in the world is concerned*, theism is epistemically on a par with demonism. *If* the observed mixture were all we had to go on, it would be unreasonable to accept either of these hypotheses about the moral character of the creator and ruler of the universe.

I do not say that this is all we have to go on or that theism and demonism are epistemically on a par *all things considered*. *Hume* may have thought the observed mixture was all we have to go on in trying to make a judgment about the moral character of the first cause(s), but I make no such claim. For all I've said here, we may be justified in believing on other grounds that theism is true, or that demonism is false, or both.[26] Without further investigation, therefore, one should not claim that theism and demonism are epistemically on a par all things considered.

But even if they were, and even if both of them could be decisively ruled out, it would be a mistake to jump to the conclusion that the indifference hypothesis is especially likely to be true, since we haven't considered the full range of

---

[24] Paul Draper (2013) puts the point succinctly: "being completely in the dark about whether the probability of J [that there is a God-justifying reason for permitting observed evils] is high in some non-epistemic sense of the word 'probability' does not imply being completely in the dark about whether the epistemic probability of J is high".

[25] Hume (1947: 202).

[26] Plausible arguments for saying that an omnipotent and omniscient being must be perfectly benevolent are in short supply. But the following argument for rejecting demonism seems promising to me. Suppose it is necessarily true (all else equal) that one ought to promote the welfare of others. Then an *omniscient* being would know that this is so, and would (if we can assume a fairly modest version of moral internalism) have at least *some* inclination to promote the good of creatures. But a perfectly malicious demon would have no such inclination. It follows that the Demon (as defined above) does not exist. (This line of argument might also be deployed against the indifference hypothesis.)

hypotheses about the moral character of the supposed creator and ruler of the universe. In particular, we've said nothing about the multitude of *mixed* moral character hypotheses that might be framed by an inventive philosopher. For all we've said, the observed mixture of good and ill might be more likely given one of them than it is given indifference. But that's not a problem for the Humean Argument. It's just more grist for the mill: if one or more of the mixed character hypotheses can't be ruled out, this gives us even more reason *not to accept* the view that the world is ruled by perfect benevolence (or by perfect malice).

6. CONCLUDING REMARKS

As developed here, the Humean Argument focuses on just a tiny sliver of logical space. It asks about the moral character of a personal ultimate who is just assumed to exist and to possess maximal power and knowledge. These points were treated as given—as background information shared by all three "visitors" to our world. Obviously, many other possibilities might have been considered. The ultimate cause(s) might be limited in power or knowledge, but not in benevolence. Or it (they) might be impersonal. Or there might no first cause(s). But despite its narrow focus, the Humean Argument has real bite. Demonists may be in short supply, but there are many theists whose view of God's moral nature falls well within the slice of logical space under consideration here. If the Humean Argument is successful, it shows that one should *not accept* their view that God is perfectly benevolent.

I have not here attempted to show that the argument is successful or that it can be defended against every objection that might be raised. *My* project is much less ambitious than that. It is merely to show that *skeptical theism fails to provide an adequate response*. To see why this is so, I thought it would be useful to work out the logic of the situation in connection with a hypothesis nobody believes. That's why I brought demonism into the discussion and gave an imaginary skeptical demonist a run for her money.

It is well to be reminded of our cognitive limitations, and a degree of epistemic humility is no doubt advisable. But one wonders whether skeptical theists have picked the right thing to be skeptical about. *If* the choice is between suspending judgment about God's moral character, and suspending judgment about the probability of the observed mixture of good and ill given perfect benevolence—*and* given perfect malice!—then (I say) their skepticism is misplaced.[27]

---

[27] My debt to the work of Paul Draper is evident throughout. I would also like to thank two anonymous reviewers for Oxford University Press for vigorous and insightful comments and criticisms, Kate Rogers for her stimulating comments at the 2013 meeting of the Society for the Philosophy of Religion, and Beth Seacord for making numerous corrections and helpful suggestions.

17

Divine Deception

Erik J. Wielenberg

1. INTRODUCTION

The dominant view within Christianity has it that God does not deceive. Descartes famously maintains that God is perfect and "the light of nature teaches us that deception must always be the result of some deficiency" (1960: 108). More recently, Paul Helm remarks that "[t]he thought that God might be less than utterly trustworthy is surely abhorrent to [Christians]" (2002: 245). There is, however, a minority tradition within Christianity according to which God sometimes engages in intentional deception and is morally justified in doing so.[1] I draw on this minority tradition, together with skeptical theism, to raise doubts about the following thesis:

> (T) God's testimony that all who believe in Jesus will have eternal life provides recipients of that testimony with a knowledge-sufficient degree of warrant for the belief that all who believe in Jesus will have eternal life.

I understand warrant to be whatever makes the difference between mere true belief and knowledge. I take it that warrant comes in degrees. (T) says that anyone who receives God's testimony that all who believe in Jesus will have eternal life is thereby warranted in believing that proposition, and is warranted to such a degree that, if she actually believes that proposition, she knows it. I take it that something like (T) is at least suggested by Christianity's creedal commitments and that if (T) is false it is hard to see what could provide warrant for the belief that all who believe in Jesus will have eternal life.[2]

---

[1] For helpful discussion of these two traditions, see Ramsey (1985).

[2] I do not claim that (T) itself is part of traditional Christianity. As William Abraham points out, a claim like (T) that employs concepts from contemporary epistemology is unlikely to be part of traditional Christianity itself: "the church offers no formal theory as to how it knows that it possesses the truth about God" (2006: 17).

In what follows I first argue that there are possible situations in which divine deception is morally permissible (Section 2). Next, I consider four apparent cases of divine deception found in scripture (Section 3). I draw on the results of Sections 2 and 3 to develop a prima facie case against (T) (Section 4). Finally, I address an important objection to my argument (Section 5). My overall aim is not to provide a decisive proof for the falsity of (T) but rather to develop a weighty prima face case against (T), thereby creating a burden of proof for those who wish to endorse (T).

2. THE POSSIBILITY OF MORALLY PERMISSIBLE DIVINE DECEPTION

Sometimes the only available means of preventing some great evil or of attaining some great good requires deception. In some cases of this sort, deception is morally permissible. Suppose you are hiding an innocent person in your home. A murderer who wants to kill the innocent person appears at your doorstep and demands to know whether the innocent person is in your house. This case constitutes what Sissela Bok calls "an acute crisis" where "[t]here seems no way to prevent the misdeed without the lie, and time is running out" (1998: 108). The case illustrates that whatever moral considerations there are against the permissibility of deceit can be outweighed if the consequences of not deceiving are sufficiently bad. This is not to say that consequences of action are the *only* morally relevant considerations. Instead, it is to say that consequences of actions are *among* the morally relevant considerations—and, in extreme cases, consequences of actions can trump or outweigh the other morally relevant considerations.

In the murderer case, the fact that the situation springs itself upon you with no warning is morally significant in that it prevents you from finding ways of protecting the victim that do not involve deception. But lack of time to identify alternatives is not the only factor that can make deception permissible. A lack of knowledge, inability to understand, or emotional immaturity in one's listener can also make deception necessary in order to prevent a great evil or achieve a great good. These factors can justify parental deception of children. Bok says:

> In talking to [children], one may hope to produce, for their own good, as adequate an idea of what is at stake as possible, so that they will be able to respond "appropriately"—neither too casually nor too intensely if it is a present danger, and without excessive worry if it is a future danger. The truth will then be bent precisely so as to convey what the speaker thinks is the right "picture"; it will compensate for the inexperience or the fears of the listener ... [Additionally,] [s]uch "translation" into language the child can understand ... can ... be mixed with deception—to

play down, for instance, dangers about which nothing can be done, or to create conversely, some terror in the child to make sure he stays away from dangers he *can* do something to avoid. (1998: 208)

Lee Basham describes a case of the second kind. He reports that as a child he was obsessed with tortoises and was convinced that there were tortoises in the forest behind his house. His parents tried a variety of means to keep him from going into the forest to look for tortoises: they explained the real dangers to him and they imposed increasingly severe punishments for entering the forest. However, "[t]hey didn't understand, we are talking about tortoises. Tortoises are worth it" (2002: 237). Finally, his parents told him that a horrible beast that eats children lived in the forest, just waiting for tortoise-seeking morsels. This deception finally did the trick.

The 1997 film *Life is Beautiful* depicts a parental deception that plays both roles described by Bok above. In the film, a father and son are placed in a Nazi concentration camp. In order to shield his son from the horrors of the camp as well as help him survive, the father convinces his son that their situation is actually a game in which the first team to earn 1000 points wins a tank. By assigning point increases to behaviors that make survival in the concentration camp more likely and point decreases to behaviors that make survival less likely, the father manages to keep his son alive and in relatively good spirits through the entire ordeal.

The biblical account of the binding of Isaac also seems to sanction parental deception. A natural reading of the account suggests that Abraham sincerely believed that he would have to kill Isaac. An important element of the story is God's declaration (by way of an angel) that "now I know that you fear God, since you have not withheld your son, your only son, from me" (Genesis 22:12).[3] This line suggests that Abraham's willingness to sacrifice Isaac is an indication of the depth of Abraham's devotion to God: Abraham is so devoted to God that he is willing to kill his only beloved son if God commands him to do so. The story most powerfully illustrates such devotion if Abraham believed that he really would have to sacrifice Isaac from the moment God commanded Abraham to take Isaac to Moriah and "offer him there as a burnt offering" (Genesis 22:2).[4] As Kierkegaard says, "given the task as assigned to Abraham, he himself has to act; consequently, he has to know in the crucial moment what he himself will do, and consequently, he has to know that Isaac is going to be sacrificed" (1983: 119). However, when Isaac asks, "[t]he fire and wood

---

[3] Unless otherwise noted, all biblical references are to the NRSV.

[4] Other interpretations are available; for example, perhaps Abraham hoped he wouldn't have to go through with the sacrifice, despite God's command. Or perhaps Abraham was utterly confused and believed neither that he would have to sacrifice Isaac nor that he would not have to sacrifice Isaac. But a drawback of such interpretations is if Abraham never really thought that he would have to go through with the sacrifice, then the story is far less effective as an illustration of the depth of Abraham's devotion to God.

are here, but where is the lamb for a burnt offering?" Abraham replies: "God himself will provide the lamb for a burnt offering, my son" (Genesis 22:7–8). Assuming that Abraham believed that he would have to sacrifice Isaac, his response to Isaac's question is intentionally deceptive. Whatever interpretation readers of the account may place on Abraham's answer, it is clear—both to us and to Abraham—that *Isaac* understood Abraham to be saying that God was going to give them an actual lamb for the sacrifice.

Kierkegaard maintains that when Abraham answers Isaac's question "he does not speak an untruth, but neither does he say anything, for he is speaking in a strange tongue" (1983: 119). But this will not do; Abraham knows that Isaac will not take him to be speaking a strange tongue. The first of Kierkegaard's four retellings of the binding of Isaac explains why Abraham deceives Isaac. In that retelling, Abraham tells Isaac the truth:

> But Abraham said to himself, "I will not hide from Isaac where this walk is taking him." He stood still, he laid his hand on Isaac's head in blessing, and Isaac kneeled to receive it. And Abraham's face epitomized fatherliness; his gaze was gentle, his words admonishing. But Isaac could not understand him, his soul could not be uplifted; he clasped Abraham's knees, he pleaded at his feet, he begged for his young life. (1983: 10)

Abraham intentionally deceived Isaac, and Kierkegaard's retelling explains why: telling Isaac the truth would have brought only anguish.

Here, then, is the argument for the possibility of situations in which divine deception is morally permissible:

1. Deception in the sorts of cases discussed in this section is morally permissible.
2. Possibly, God is sometimes in relevantly similar situations with respect to human beings.
3. Therefore, possibly, it is sometimes morally permissible for God to deceive human beings.[5]

The case for (1) was given above. The case for (2) rests on the conceivability of situations in which God faces a dilemma like those faced by the deceptive parents discussed above. Consider these remarks by Origen:

> [W]e deceive children when we frighten children in order that it may halt the lack of education in youth. And we frighten children when we speak through words of deceit on account of what is basic to their infancy, in order that through the deceit we may cause them to be afraid and to resort to teachers both to declare and to do what is applicable for the progress of children. We are all children of God and

---

[5] The sort of possibility I have in mind here is metaphysical or broadly logical possibility; see Plantinga (1974: 44–5).

we need the discipline of children. Because of this, God, since he cares about us, deceives us. (1998: 217)

Origen also says: "Perhaps, then, as a father wishes to deceive a son in his own interest while he is still a boy, since he cannot be helped any other way unless the boy is deceived ... so it is also for the God of the universe" (1998: 226).[6] Origen holds that God, like a loving parent, sometimes deceives human beings because it is the only way He can attain some important benefit for them.[7] I take it that the conceivability of such scenarios, while it does not constitute decisive proof that such scenarios are possible, is at least prima facie evidence for their possibility.

An important objection to (2) has it that while human parents may find themselves in situations in which the only available means of preventing some great evil or attaining some great good involves deception; God's omnipotence precludes Him ever facing such a predicament.

Human free will makes trouble for this objection. Alvin Plantinga (1998) has persuasively argued that because of the nature of human free will, it is possible that God faces a predicament in which He is unable to create beings with free will without also introducing some evil into the world. Others have argued that the existence of human free will means that God may face a predicament in which He is able to achieve some great good for us only by causing us to suffer. For example, C. S. Lewis (2001b) argues that it is precisely because He loves us that God sometimes causes us to suffer. This idea is strikingly similar to Origen's suggestion that "God, since he cares about us, deceives us" (1998: 217).

Our world contains instances of horrendous suffering. Apparently, then, despite His omnipotence, God found Himself in a predicament that made it morally permissible for Him to permit these horrendous sufferings. While that does not *entail* that it is possible that God faces a situation in which it is morally permissible for Him to deceive us, it does show that the defender of the omnipotence-based objection to premise 2 above has some work to do to motivate the claim that God's omnipotence implies that it's impossible for him to face a situation in which He can achieve some great good only by deceiving us. In particular, the proponent of this objection needs to explain why God's omnipotence makes it impossible for Him to face that kind of predicament without also making it impossible for Him to face a predicament in which He can achieve some great good only by allowing us to suffer greatly.

In fact, there is reason to believe that the range of cases in which it is morally permissible for God to deceive human beings is broader than the range of cases in which it is morally permissible for human parents to deceive their

[6] Some criticized Descartes's view that God could not deceive by appealing to justified parental deceit of their children; see Haldane and Ross (1967: 27, 77–8).

[7] Henry Home (Lord Kames) controversially suggested that God deceives us for our own good by providing us with a "delusive sense of liberty" (2005: 252–6).

children. In her discussion of paternalistic lies, Bok notes that while there are cases in which parents are justified in deceiving their children, this sort of deceit carries with it serious dangers that ought to limit its use. One danger is that those who engage in such deceit may be self-deceived about their own motives, believing themselves to have benevolent motives while in reality deceiving out of a desire to protect themselves or retain control over the situation (Bok 1998: 212). This worry about hidden motives is a danger that human parents face but a perfect God does not. The same holds for some other risks associated with paternalistic lies:

> [P]aternalistic lies, while they are easy to understand and to sympathize with at times, also carry very special risks: risks to the liar himself from having to lie more and more in order to keep up the appearance among people he lives with or sees often, and thus from the greater likelihood of discovery and loss of credibility; risks to the relationship in which the deception takes place; and risks of exploitation of every kind for the deceived. (Bok 1998: 218–19)

The fact that human agents are unable perfectly to predict these and other risks of paternalistic deceit imposes moral limits on the use of such deceit to which God is not subject. This is another respect in which deceit is similar to inflicting pain. Some theistic writers have proposed that God sometimes inflicts suffering upon us in order to improve our moral characters (see Lewis 2001b: 90–3, and Hick 1974: 279–97). But surely similar actions on the part of human agents are rarely (if ever) morally permissible. Why? A likely answer is that human beings are rarely (or never) in a position to know how to use pain properly to achieve this goal. Unlike God, we are not qualified to use pain to build others' character. Consequently, the range of cases in which God may inflict suffering on humans is far broader than the range of cases in which humans may inflict suffering upon each other. The same is true of deceit.[8]

3. DIVINE DECEPTION IN SCRIPTURE

There are episodes in scripture that appear to depict divine deception. Of course, how one interprets scripture depends in part on one's philosophical and theological commitments. Thus, the scriptural case for the reality of divine deception is supported by the philosophical case for the possibility of permissible divine deception. Once we see that divine deception may be morally permissible, we should be open to interpretations of scripture that posit such deception. The presence of divine deception in scripture is significant in that it makes divine deception more than a mere metaphysical possibility. If

---

[8] For somewhat similar ideas, see Coope (2001: 389–90).

God's actual track record includes instances of deception of human beings, then we should take seriously the possibility that God deceives us in heretofore unrecognized ways.

Consider again the binding of Isaac. God commands Abraham: "Take your son, your only son Isaac, whom you love, and go to the land of Moriah, and offer him there as a burnt offering on one of the mountains that I shall show you" (Genesis 22:2). As I suggested above, the most natural reading of the story has it that God's command creates in Abraham the belief that God is going to make him sacrifice Isaac. If this is right, then God knew both that (i) His command to Abraham would cause Abraham to believe (reasonably) that Abraham was going to sacrifice Isaac and (ii) Abraham was not going to sacrifice Isaac. I agree with Hubert Martin's assessment that "in testing Abraham, God … deceives him" (1987: 8).

Consider as well the Genesis account of Adam and Eve in the Garden of Eden. God tells Adam that "of the tree of the knowledge of good and evil you shall not eat, for in the day that you eat of it you shall die" (or: "you shall *surely* die") (Genesis 2:17). According to biblical scholar James Barr, "*all* cases of the phrase 'you (he, they) will surely die' [in the Old Testament] refer to an imminent death, all 40 or so of them" (2006: 12).[9] Yet after Adam and Eve eat the forbidden fruit they are punished but do not die. Interestingly, the serpent is more truthful about the consequences of disobedience than God is: "[T]he serpent said to the woman, 'You will not die; for God knows that when you eat of it your eyes will be opened, and you will be like God, knowing good and evil'" (Genesis 3:4–5).[10] It might be suggested that Adam and Eve die in that they are ejected from the garden and condemned to mortality (Genesis 3:22–4).[11] However, just as becoming fragile is not the same thing as breaking, becoming mortal is not the same thing as dying.[12] Still another suggestion is that Adam and Eve died *spiritually* in that they became separated from God as a consequence of their disobedience. However, there is no support in the text itself for construing God's initial declaration in this way (Toy 1891: 5).

A third example of divine deception occurs in the book of Jeremiah. After Jeremiah the prophet is imprisoned for predicting the destruction of Jerusalem and Judah at the hands of the Babylonians, he declares: "Thou has deceived me, O lord, and I was deceived" (Jeremiah 20:7).[13] Origen sees this as an example of justified divine deception. Joseph Trigg explains Origen's view this way:

---

[9] Against the suggestion that "day" here should be interpreted as a "day of God" (i.e. 1000 years), see Moberly (1988).

[10] On the serpent's truthfulness, see French (1982: 25–6), and Moberly (1998: 8–9).

[11] For a critique of this interpretation, see Moberly (1988: 14–15).

[12] It is also not plausible to suppose that God's words in Genesis 2:17 should be understood as imposing becoming mortal as the punishment for eating from the tree; see Toy (1891: 4–5) and Moberly (2008: 34).

[13] This translation is from Trigg (1988: 147). The NRSV renders the passage this way: "O Lord, you have enticed me, and I was enticed."

God had a prophecy of judgment for Jeremiah to make against his own people. God knew, however, that although Jeremiah would not willingly prophesy against his own people, he would have no qualms about prophesying against other people. God therefore, deceived Jeremiah. He says to him, "Take from my hand the cup of this unmixed wine, and make all the nations to whom I send you drink from it." Jeremiah understood God to be asking him to make all the other nations drink from the cup of God's wrath and punishment, without imagining that his own would be the first nation to drink from it. Having accepted the cup, he realized he had been deceived when God said, "And you shall first make Jerusalem drink from it." (1988: 154)

Some commentators are reluctant to acknowledge this episode as involving divine deception.[14] One alternative proposal has it that the beginning of Jeremiah's lament in this passage should be translated this way: "You tried to persuade me [to be a prophet], and I was persuaded; You [i.e. your arguments] proved too strong for me, and you overpowered me" (Clines and Gunn 1978: 22). Perhaps, then, we should say that Jeremiah was persuaded rather than deceived.

One problem with this proposal is that the "arguments" that God offers Jeremiah after Jeremiah's initial reluctance to serve as a prophet consist of (i) God repeatedly insisting that Jeremiah become a prophet and (ii) God assuring Jeremiah that it won't be so bad. Specifically, God tells Jeremiah that "I am with you to deliver you" (Jeremiah 1:8) and that "today I appoint you over nations and over kingdoms, to pluck up and to pull down" (Jeremiah 1:10). Together, these words surely leave Jeremiah (who is at this time "only a boy" [Jeremiah 1:6]) with a misleading impression of what is in store for him: predicting the destruction of his own people and consequently becoming reviled, threatened with death, and imprisoned. The best description of what God has done to Jeremiah here is not "persuasion" but rather "seduction," "enticement," or "deception."

The final example of divine deception that I will consider appears in the New Testament. In the Gospel of John, Jesus's brothers encourage him to go to the Festival of Booths in Judea and "show yourself to the world" (John 7:4). Jesus appears to respond with deceit:

> Jesus said to them, "My time is not yet come, but your time is always here. The world cannot hate you, but it hates me because I testify against it that its works are evil. Go to the festival yourselves. I am not going to this festival, for my time has not yet fully come." After saying this, he remained in Galilee. But after his brothers had gone to the festival, then he also went, not publicly but as it were in secret. (John 7:6–10)

Again, some commentators seek to avoid attributing intentional deception to Jesus. Ben Witherington III suggests that "[w]hat [Jesus] had said to the brothers he sincerely meant, but he received a late word from God shortly thereafter that changed his plans" (1995: 171). But this interpretation posits

---

[14] Calvin implausibly claims that Jeremiah's language "is ironical" and that "when he says that he was deceived [h]e assumes the character of his enemies" (2007: 19).

an event—indeed, a crucially important event—that is not depicted in the text. Unlike Witherington, Charles Giblin strives to avoid an interpretation according to which Jesus changed his mind. He argues that Jesus's actions are consistent with his declaration that "I am not going to this festival" as follows:

> [W]hereas [the evangelist] implies that Jesus' brethren go up for ... the feast, the evangelist does not say that Jesus goes up for the feast, much less for *this* feast ... As events work out, Jesus attends the feast with a certain dramatic reservation; he arrives when the feast is already half-over ... When he does arrive, he goes up to the temple to teach. Thus, he does not celebrate the feast or 'go up for it' as others would—and would expect him to do. (1980: 208)

On Giblin's interpretation, Jesus plans all along to attend the festival but does not deceive his brothers because, while he attends the festival, he arrives late and attends not to celebrate but rather to teach. To see that these distinctions will not help Jesus evade the charge of deception here, consider the matter from the perspective of Jesus's brothers. Given the exchange between Jesus and his brothers, it would be entirely predictable (and reasonable) that the brothers would understand Jesus to be saying that he would not be attending the festival at all, for any purpose. The most natural interpretation of the episode is that Jesus planned to attend the festival all along but wanted to do so in secret. He intentionally gave his brothers the false impression that he would not attend the festival so that he could do so in secret.

Of course, interpreting scripture is a tricky business and, in the case of each of the four episodes in scripture discussed in this section, interpretations according to which divine deception does not occur have been proposed. In light of this, it might be suggested that the most reasonable thing to do is not to assent to any particular interpretation on offer and to be agnostic about whether any of these passages depict divine deception.

In response, I claim that the interpretations of these four episodes according to which each involves divine deception are the most plausible interpretations on offer. In each case, the interpretations that don't involve divine deception are somewhat forced and unnatural in comparison with the interpretations I favor. I do not think that we are in a situation in which there are multiple equally plausible interpretations, some of which involve divine deception and some of which do not. Rather, the interpretations that involve divine deception are more plausible than the others, so much so that we ought to accept them unless and until a persuasive case is made against these interpretations.[15]

---

[15] Other possible examples of divine deception in scripture include: Exodus 3:18 and 5:1–3; 1 Kings 22; Ezekiel 14:9; Jeremiah 4:10; 1 Samuel 16:1–3. For helpful discussion of some of these (and other) passages, see Chisholm (1998).

4. DIVINE DECEPTION AND ESCHATOLOGY

It is widely recognized that to cast doubt on a claim to know p, more is required than merely noting the metaphysical possibility of some claim incompatible with p. As James Cargile puts it, "[d]escribing an incompatible possibility does not constitute any basis for criticism of my claim to know something incompatible with that possibility obtaining unless there is some reason to think there is a real chance that it does obtain" (2000: 165; see also Guleserian 2001: 298–9). The following remarks by van Inwagen shed some light on the distinction between a mere possibility and a real chance:

> Your friend Clarissa, a single mother, left her two very young children alone in her flat for several hours very late last night. Your Aunt Harriet, a maiden lady of strong moral principles, learns of this and declares that Clarissa is unfit to raise children. You spring to your friend's defense: "Now, Aunt Harriet, don't go jumping to conclusions. There's probably a perfectly good explanation. Maybe Billy or Annie was ill, and she decided to go over to the clinic for help. You know she hasn't got a phone or a car and no one in that neighborhood of hers would come to the door at two o'clock in the morning." ... [Y]ou're not claiming to have said anything that shows that Clarissa really is a good mother.... [W]hat you're trying to establish is that for all you or Aunt Harriet know, she had some good reason for what she did.... What you're trying to convince Aunt Harriet of is that there is ... *a very real possibility* that Clarissa had a good reason for leaving her children alone. (2006: 66)

I claim that a scenario in which God's declaration that all who believe in Jesus will have eternal life is a divine deception is not just metaphysically possible; rather, there is a real chance—a very real possibility in van Inwagen's sense—that this scenario obtains. To support this claim fully, I must introduce one additional idea: skeptical theism.

Consider the well-known declaration in Isaiah that "[f]or as the heavens are higher than the earth, so are [God's] ways higher than your ways and [God's] thoughts higher than your thoughts" (Isaiah 55:9) as well as Paul's remark that God's judgments are "unsearchable" and His ways "inscrutable" (Romans 11:33).[16] Such passages suggest a substantial gap between human and divine knowledge. Stephen Wykstra says: "A modest proposal might be that [God's] wisdom is to ours, roughly as an adult human's is to a one-month old infant's" (1984: 88). Our knowledge of good and evil in particular may fall well short of God's knowledge. Michael Bergmann suggests that "it wouldn't be the least bit surprising if [axiological] reality far outstripped our understanding of it" (2001: 284) and that for all we know, there are lots of goods, evils, and connections between good and evil of which human beings are unaware (2009).

---

[16] Also relevant here are Job and Ecclesiastes 8:17.

In each of the four cases of divine deception discussed in the previous section, God deceives people about what the future has in store for them. He causes Abraham to believe that he will have to sacrifice Isaac; He causes Adam and Eve to believe that if they eat from the tree of knowledge of good and evil, they will die on that very day; He causes Jeremiah to believe that being a prophet won't be so bad; and He causes the disciples to believe that Jesus will not attend the festival. In each case, there is presumably some justification for the divine deception—a justification that is (at least prior to their discovery of the deception) beyond the ken of those being deceived.

Consider, then, the possibility that there is, unknown to us, some great good that God can attain (or some great evil that He can avoid) only by employing the deception that all who believe in the Son will have eternal life; call this the "Great Deception Scenario" (GDS). The argument of Section 2 together with skeptical theism supports the conclusion that GDS is metaphysically possible. I submit that the arguments of the preceding section, suggesting the presence in the actual world of divine deception with a certain structure, moves GDS from the realm of mere metaphysically possibility to the sort of thing that we ought to believe has a real chance of happening. Of particular salience is the fact that the divine deception in GDS has the same basic structure as the four cases of divine deception discussed in the preceding section. In all five cases, God deceives human beings and is justified in doing so by something beyond the ken of the deceived. We may be in something like Abraham's situation before God tells him not to sacrifice Isaac or the boy's situation in *Life is Beautiful* before he discovers the truth. Because we should believe that there is a real chance that GDS is actual, we ought not accept (T).[17]

Another route to the same conclusion employs Wykstra's much-discussed Condition of Reasonable Epistemic Access (CORNEA):

> On the basis of cognized situation s, human H is entitled to claim "It appears that p" only if it is reasonable for H to believe that, given her cognitive faculties and the use she has made of them, if p were not the case, s would likely be different than it is in some way discernible by her. (1984: 85)

Let p = the proposition that all who believe in Jesus will have eternal life, and let H = a human familiar with the argument of this chapter to this point. Wykstra has indicated that CORNEA applies only to what he calls "dynamic" epistemic operators (2007: 91–2). Thus, the relevant question here is the following. Suppose that H does not know that God has declared that all who believe in the Son will have eternal life; would adding this knowledge to H's

---

[17] Some readers might be attracted to this thought: Perhaps God could deceive in the ways alleged in my discussion of the four episodes from scripture in the previous section—but surely God wouldn't deceive us about something as important as what's involved in (T)! For a helpful critical discussion of this thought, see Hudson (2014: 125–6).

total evidence entitle H to claim that it appears to him that all who believe in the Son will have eternal life?

CORNEA tells us that to answer that question, we must consider this one: is it reasonable for H to believe that if it were not the case that all who believe in the Son will have eternal life, H's cognized situation would likely be different than it is in some way discernible by H? I say no. There are various possible worlds in which p (all who believe in the Son will have eternal life) is false. For example, p is false in all worlds in which God does not exist. However, assuming that God does exist, those worlds are quite distant from the actual world and can be ignored. In some nearby worlds in which p is false, God exists but has not declared that p is true (call these "A-worlds"). However, it is reasonable to believe that there are nearby possible worlds in which p is false and yet God has declared that p is true. Consider, for instance, a world in which p is false and there is some great good beyond our ken that can be attained only if God deceives us into thinking that p is true (call such worlds "B-worlds").

Assuming that H is familiar with my argument so far, it is not reasonable for H to believe that it is likely that the nearest not-p world is an A-world rather than a B-world. Therefore, it follows from CORNEA that adding the knowledge that God has declared p to be true to H's total evidence does not entitle H to claim that p appears to be true.

My case against (T), then, rests on a three-part foundation: (i) the section two argument for the metaphysical possibility of permissible divine deception, (ii) passages in scripture that are naturally read as describing deception of human beings by God about what the future has in store for them, where such deception is justified by factors beyond the ken of those being deceived, and (iii) the likelihood of a gap between our knowledge of good and evil and God's knowledge of good and evil.

Jennifer Lackey highlights an important fact about testimony:

> [T]estimony is quite unlike other sources of belief precisely because it is so wildly *heterogeneous* epistemically—there is, for instance, all the difference in the world between reading *The National Enquirer* and reading *The New York Times*. Moreover, this heterogeneity requires subjects to be much more discriminating when accepting testimony than when trusting, say, sense perception. (2008: 192)

One consequence of the epistemic heterogeneity of testimony is that "hearers *do* have some positive work to do for testimonial knowledge" (2008: 168). Included in this positive work is consideration of a given speaker's track record. Lackey emphasizes heterogeneity across sources, but a single source can also be heterogeneous. Erik the philosopher may be a reliable testifier with respect to Plato's theory of forms but not with respect to what an MRI of your lungs reveals, whereas Aaron the radiologist may be a reliable testifier with respect to the latter but not the former. In the case of God, His track record with respect to what the future holds is decidedly mixed. Consequently, His testimony to the effect that all who believe in the Son will have eternal life does not enable us to know that it is so.

5. FALSE OR MERELY CRYPTIC?

In at least some of the cases of divine deception in scripture that I have discussed, God does not assert any falsehoods. God never explicitly declares that Abraham will have to sacrifice Isaac; similarly, God deceives Jeremiah without asserting any actual falsehoods. In the other two examples I considered, it seems harder to make the case that God speaks no falsehood.[18] But suppose for the sake of argument that such a case can be made. Suppose, in fact, that God has never uttered a falsehood. Suppose further that we know that God *couldn't* assert a falsehood. What impact would this have on my central argument?

My case that God sometimes intentionally *deceives* would remain intact. If God never speaks falsely, what follows is that He sometimes deceives without asserting falsehoods. Sometimes He deceives by issuing misleading commands, as in the binding of Isaac. In other cases He deceives by asserting things that, while technically true, turn out to be true in surprising or unexpected ways. Sometimes God deceives by making assertions that are true but *cryptic*.[19]

If we know that God never asserts falsehood, then what my argument shows is that there is a real chance that God's declaration that all who believe in the Son will have eternal life is *true but cryptic*. Though perhaps less troubling than the conclusion that (T) is false, this remains a problematic result. To see why, suppose that what God means by "having eternal life" turns out to mean nothing more than being remembered by God in a special way. Thus, believers "live on" forever in God's mind in a particular way; yet, their deaths mark the permanent end of their actions and experiences. This scenario is a far cry from the one Christians typically envision when they think of the declaration that all who believe in Jesus will have eternal life.[20]

6. CONCLUSION

The upshot of the argument I have given is that Christians ought to take the possibility of divine deception seriously. There is a strong case to be made that

---

[18] Moberly (2008) defends an interpretation of Genesis 2–3 according to which God speaks truthfully but metaphorically. Barr rejects Moberly's interpretation (2006: 12).

[19] For example, a literal reading of Joshua 10:12–13 suggests a geocentric model of the universe, but most contemporary Christians reject such a model (thanks to an anonymous reader for this point).

[20] Thanks to Michael Bergmann for discussion of divine crypticness.

the Christian God is a loving father who sometimes allows His children to suffer horribly and sometimes deceives them. He does these things not in spite of His love but because of it. Consequently, divine deception about the fate of believers is more than a metaphysical possibility; there is a real chance that it is real.

As I noted at the outset, my aim is not to refute (T) decisively but rather to provide a weighty prima facie case against (T). There are various stages at which my argument might be resisted. The case for the possibility of permissible divine deception might be resisted by arguing that divine omnipotence is incompatible with the possibility of such deception. The case for the plausibility of actual divine deception might be resisted by convincing arguments against my interpretations of the relevant episodes from scripture. And the case for the claim that there is a real chance that GDS is actual might be undermined by the identification of important salient differences between GDS and the four episodes of divine deception discussed in Section 3. My hope, then, is to have shown that there is a good case to be made against (T). Contrary to popular contemporary belief, the impossibility or implausibility of divine deception cannot be taken for granted, and those who would endorse (T) face the challenge of answering the argument of this chapter. [21]

[21] This chapter represents a (hopefully) improved discussion of some ideas explored in my 2010. Hud Hudson (2014) independently discusses similar ideas. Shorter versions of this chapter were presented at the 2011 Midwest Conference of the Society of Christian Philosophers at Hope College and the 2011 Australasian Philosophy of Religion Associating meeting at the University of Auckland; I thank those audiences for their helpful comments. I also thank Michael Bergmann, Andrew Cullison, Luke Gelinas, and Charles Pigden. Robert Garcia, Trent Dougherty, and an anonymous reader provided extremely helpful comments on an earlier version of this chapter; I thank them for their careful comments even while recognizing that I have not been able adequately to address all of their concerns.

18

Two New Versions of Skeptical Theism

Andrew Cullison

In this chapter, I will present and defend two new versions of skeptical theism with the aim of solving what I call the *Reasoning about God* Problem. Skeptical theists hold that a premise in standard formulations of the problem of evil is unjustified, because it is supported by a fallacious kind of inference. The premise is that there are evils that God would have no justifying reason to permit. Skeptical theists, maintain that the mere fact that there do not seem to be any goods that God might want that outweigh the horrendous evil in the world is insufficient to conclude that there must be no such reason. For all you know, there could be a reason that is beyond your ken.[1]

However, skeptical theism, understood this way, has a serious problem. It threatens to undermine *all reasoning* about what God will or won't do. The most notable examples include versions of theism that hold that God has made certain promises. Suppose you think that God made a promise and will keep it. If you embrace skeptical theism, you seem to be committed to being skeptical about whether or not God would keep promises. What possible grounds could you have for thinking that God will keep that promise? You're not in a position to judge whether or not God would have a sufficiently good reason to break that promise. For all you know, God could have a reason to break his promise that is also beyond your ken. In fact, any attempt to reason about what God would do is in jeopardy. Call this objection the *Reasoning about God Problem.*[2]

In Section 1 of this chapter, I outline the skeptical theist challenge to the of evil and The Reasoning about God Problem. In Section 2, I develop the first new version of skeptical theism by offering a plausible epistemic principle that (a) gives us the resources to appeal to the skeptical theist strategy when

---

[1] It is worth noting that "skeptical theism" is a bit of a misnomer. One could be an atheist or an agnostic (for reasons other than the problem of evil) and agree that the core inference in the problem of evil is problematic.

[2] See Wielenberg (2010), Hudson (2014), and Segal (2011) for examples of this problem.

confronted with the evidential of evil, but (b) does not deprive us of the ability to reason about what God will do in other matters (such as keeping promises). I call this a new version of skeptical theism because it offers a different motivation for being skeptical about the inference noted above.

In Section 3, I develop another version of skeptical theism. This version is a more radical departure from traditional skeptical theism. I show that there is a kind of axiological skepticism open to the theist with respect to the *other* premise, the premise that states that God would not permit unnecessary evils. I classify this as a *new* version of skeptical theism because while it involves suspending judgment about a premise in the problem of evil, based on needing to suspend judgment about what kinds of axiological options are open to God, a theist could consistently embrace this response while completely rejecting the classical skeptical theist strategy with respect to the first premise of the of evil.

1. SKEPTICAL THEISM AND THE REASONING ABOUT GOD PROBLEM

Here is a standard way to formulate the of evil.[3]

1.1 The Problem of Evil

1. There exist horrendous evils that God would have no justifying reason to permit.
2. God would not permit horrendous evil unless God had a justifying reason to permit it.
3. There is no God.

Skeptical theists resist premise (1) by noting that it relies on a suspicious kind of inference. The motivation for premise (1) is something like this:

(A) I can't think of a possible reason that would outweigh this evil. So, there must not be one.

Inferences that conform to the pattern of reasoning in (A) are called "*noseeum*" *inferences*. Sometimes, these are good inferences. If I can't see a tiger in the room, I should conclude that there isn't one. But sometimes these are bad inferences. For example, if I can't see bacteria on my hand, I should not conclude

---

[3] Readers familiar with skeptical theism and the Reasoning about God problem who have been reading other chapters in this volume can most likely go straight to the next section.

that there are not any bacteria on my hand. When you diagnose the difference between good noseeum inferences and bad noseeum inferences, skeptical theists think that the noseeum inference in the problem of evil argument falls on the bad side.

Here is a simple account of what makes something a bad noseeum inference. Bacteria are, by their nature, the sorts of things you wouldn't detect with your ordinary cognitive faculties and you know this, so you can't appeal to the fact that you can't see them (using your ordinary cognitive faculties) to conclude that there are no bacteria on your hands. Reasons that God might have to allow horrendous evils are like bacteria in this regard. Skeptical theists maintain that, for all you know, there are reasons that God might have for allowing any particular evil, and you lack the right sort of perspective to know if the range of goods that you're aware of is representative of the range of possible outweighing goods that God might have. Because of this possibility, the fact that you can't detect a possible reason with your cognitive faculties is insufficient to conclude that God couldn't have one.

But skeptical theism faces a serious difficulty. It threatens to undermine any reasoning about divine activity, and this has serious implications. Many theists think that they have good reasons to believe something is true, simply because God promised, or because they think that God is good and this is what a good being would do. This kind of reasoning seems to be blocked for the skeptical theist. After all, for all you know God might have reasons not to keep the promise or *not* to do the thing that you think a good being would do. You're not a God, and you lack the right kind of perspective to rule out possible outweighing reasons that God might have to lie to you or do something seemingly contrary to what you think a good being would do. Call this the *Reasoning about God Problem*.

In the remainder of this chapter, I will explore two possible solutions to the Reasoning about God Problem. Both solutions involve developing what I think is appropriate to describe as new versions of skeptical theism.

2. VERSION ONE: A NEW MOTIVATION FOR RESISTING PREMISE ONE

The first strategy I will pursue involves attempting to find a principled way to establish an asymmetry between suspending judgment about whether a person had a good reason to allow some evil on the one hand and suspending judgment about whether they'll keep promises, or other seemingly good things in the future. Fortunately, we can isolate some cases that are prima facie parallel to the counterpart cases involving Reasoning about God. Here are two cases that will serve as a useful warm-up exercise.

2.1 Case One: Father Kills Someone

I discover that my dad has killed someone and it doesn't seem to me that there is any morally overriding reason. But I think to myself, "This is weird. Perhaps my dad really did have some good reason that I'm unaware of. I don't know enough about this situation. I better not judge that there isn't one until I get some more information."

2.2 Case Two: Father Promises to Pick Me Up

On my way to discuss the recent events with my father, he calls me and says he'd like to meet at a local coffee shop. He says, "I promise, I'll meet you there." It seems that I could be reasonable in believing that my father will keep his promise.

Here we have an instance of a relevantly similar asymmetry. It is true that in Case Two, there may be overriding moral reasons that might mitigate against my father meeting me. It also may be true that I would not be in a position to judge whether or not there were any. But it still seems reasonable to believe that my father will keep his promise. So there are possible cases, where I should be skeptical about whether or not a person had a good reason to do something prima facie evil because for all I know they had some reason beyond my ken, but I should not be skeptical about whether or not they will keep a future promise despite the fact that *for all I know* they might have some reason beyond my ken to break the promise.[4]

So it isn't *always* the case that reasonably suspending judgment about whether a person has some hidden reason for allowing for some particular evil entails that you must be skeptical about whether or not that person will do good in other circumstances or keep promises. A proponent of the Reasoning about God objection needs some reason to think that the case with respect to God is *unlike* the Father case in a way that makes an *epistemic difference.*

The problem here is that there are clearly differences that are relevant. Here is one. I have evidence that my father is good. The evidence that my father is good provides me (a) with reason to think that he'll keep his promises and (b) with reasons to suspend judgment (until I get all the facts) in cases where he apparently does something harmful.

One could argue that we *do* have evidence for thinking that there is a God, and thereby claim that these two cases are analogous to the cases that motivate the Reasoning about God problem, but for the purposes of discussing the problem of evil, we should not be so quick. First, it's dialectically odd. What is at issue is whether or not there is a God that is loving. We don't want to appeal

---

[4] This seems similar to something that Segal (2011) suggests as a possible reply to the problem.

to the fact that God is loving in order to make this case parallel. Second, the original spirit of the skeptical theist response was to try and argue that *in no way* is evil evidence against the existence of God. This strategy, as it stands, seems to concede that evil is evidence, but that it is simply outweighed by other considerations, namely evidence that there is a loving God.

However, the above cases should give the skeptical theist a little hope that we might be able to find a more parallel case, and I think we can. It involves first stripping away some of the features of the above case, and thinking carefully through the skeptical theist's original motivation for arguing that we should be skeptical about the first premise in the problem of evil.

To do this, I first need to introduce some terminology from the literature on epistemic disagreement, an *epistemic peer* and *epistemic superior*. An epistemic peer is someone who is on an epistemic par with respect to a particular question. They have been exposed to all of the same evidence and they are equals with respect to various epistemic virtues such as intelligence, honesty, and thoughtfulness. An *epistemic superior* is someone who exceeds you with respect to evidence with respect to all questions and intellectual virtues.[5]

I now want to introduce parallel notions in the moral domain, *moral peer* and *moral superior*. A moral peer is someone who is (roughly) as good as you, morally speaking. They do the right thing about as often as you do, exhibit the same virtuous character to the roughly the same degree, etc. A moral superior is someone who is better than you on both scales. A moral superior acts rightly more often than you do and exhibits more virtuous character traits to higher degrees. Now call someone a *normative peer* who is both an epistemic and moral peer. And call someone a *normative superior* who is both an epistemic superior with respect to every domain, and a moral superior.

Now we are in a position to consider a modified motivation for being skeptical about the first premise in the problem of evil that preserves the asymmetry we're looking for.

2.3 Case Three

Suppose you are traveling and you see a dog caught in a bear trap, and the situation seems like a horrendous evil. As you start to help the dog, you might start to consider whether there was anyone who was a *normative peer* with respect to this situation that had the means to assist the dog.

Is there someone who is both an epistemic peer and a moral peer aware of this situation? After a while, you might reasonably come to believe that there must not be. Maybe there is someone around with more evidence that bears

⁵ I take this characterization from Kelly (2005).

on this, but you might reasonably think that there is no one around who is a *normative peer.*

However, should you judge that there is no *normative superior* who is aware of this situation who could help if they wanted to *based solely on the evidence you have that this is all things considered bad?* I think the answer to that is no. Consider two epistemic principles.

2.4 No Peer Principle

If it seems to you that A is wrong and that there could be no justifying reason to permit it, then (absent defeaters) it is reasonable to infer that there are/were no normative peers with the power, knowledge, and desire to prevent evil who had an overriding reason to allow this.

2.5 No Superior Principle

If it seems to you that A is wrong and that there could be no justifying reason to permit it, then (absent defeaters) it is reasonable to infer that there are/were no normative superiors who had the power, knowledge, and desire to prevent A who had an overriding reason to allow this.

I think that we should accept something like the No Peer Principle, but we should not accept the No Superior Principle. We should reject the No Superior Principle, because it conflicts with the following more general epistemic principle.

(E) Evidence that P is not evidence that no one else has weightier evidence that not-P.

Your evidence that P *alone* wouldn't be enough to conclude that there was no one who didn't have evidence to the contrary. You would need to bring other evidence to bear on this question, other facts about the situation that bear on whether or not other people have disconfirming evidence. We can look at situations like the dog in pain and rule out the existence of normative peers. Normative peers by hypothesis have all of the same evidence that I do, so there must be no one with exactly all of the information that I have who is also a moral peer.

But if we were to ask ourselves, "*Is there a normative superior?*" matters are different. We can't use the evidence of evil as evidence that there isn't a normative superior because some possible normative superiors *by hypothesis* have evidence that we don't have. To rule out all normative superiors we would effectively be concluding on the basis of our evidence that this is evil, that there must not be anyone with weightier evidence that this is not-evil. But this is precisely what's at issue, whether evil alone is evidence against the existence of God. Evil alone cannot be evidence against the existence of a normative superior, because (E) is true. Other considerations would need to be added.[6]

This yields an alternative rationale for being skeptical about the claim that there exist evils that God would have no justifying reason to permit. Accepting that premise would be tantamount to accepting the No Superior Principle. But we shouldn't accept that. The crucial claims motivating skepticism between classical skeptical theism and what I am proposing are importantly different.

2.6 Original Crucial Claim

For all I know, there are possible goods that outweigh these bads, and so I should be skeptical about the thesis that there are no goods that outweigh these bads.

2.7 Revised Crucial Claim

Evidence that some event E is an unjustified horrendous evil, is not evidence that no one (including possible normative superiors) has weightier evidence that E is not an unjustified horrendous evil.

Four points are worth noting. First, the revised crucial claim is compatible with accepting or rejecting the original crucial claim. Second, it is also compatible with accepting or rejecting the thesis that the original crucial claim entails that we should be skeptical about whether or not there are evils that no God would have a justifying reason to permit. Third, the revised crucial claim still gives us a reason to suspend judgment about the first premise of the problem of evil, because it makes it reasonable to think that we should not rule out the existence of some possible normative superiors when we encounter a horrendous evil. This may not be sufficient to call this a *new* version of skeptical theism, but these are still important differences worth highlighting.

---

[6] It's been suggested to me that perhaps evidence for P, really is evidence that no one has evidence that not-P based on some plausible assumptions about some of the probabilities involved. Suppose the probability that there is evidence against P is lower if P is true rather than not true. One might think that we should conditionalize in the face of evidence for P and increase our credence that someone doesn't have evidence for P. Two brief points about this are in order. I doubt this is true for people who are not aware of these facts about probability distributions and also have good reason to believe them. But more importantly, I suspect there is a stronger principle we could appeal to that sidesteps this issue. If you have sufficient evidence to believe P, you do not have sufficient evidence to believe that no one else has sufficient evidence to believe that not-P. Even if we should increase our credence that no one has evidence that against P, it is very implausible to suppose that it is to some degree that warrants full acceptance. This stronger principle would enable us to still resist the first premise in the problem of evil.

The last point to note is that, because we have offered this alternative way to motivate skepticism about the first premise we are free to make predictions about what a normative superior would do in certain future situations. If I thought some normative superior made a promise to me I could still be reasonable in thinking that she would keep it. Nothing about the revised crucial claim, threatens predictions about future behavior. The revised crucial claim only commits us to being cautious about concluding that there is no normative superior in the case of an actual evil.

To bolster this last point, consider the following analogy. If I have a perception of a stop sign, I shouldn't think that there isn't someone who doesn't have reason to think that there is no stop sign present (based solely on my perceptions that there is a stop sign). But this doesn't prevent me from thinking that people in general will tend to see what I see in future situations.[7] The same can be said about moral matters. A particular action might seem all things considered wrong to me, but I shouldn't think that someone else (particularly a normative superior) doesn't have some weightier evidence to the contrary. This fact, does not bar me from thinking that normative superiors will tend to think roughly what I think about a wide range of future moral matters.

Notice that this seems perfectly reasonable in other cases of disagreement with epistemic superiors. Suppose I am in the room with a brilliant mathematician, and we're both looking at the problem on the board to which the answer seems to me to be 5. I can be justified in believing that he will write 5 on the board as the solution, but suppose he writes a 7. Here, I should suspend judgment about the answer being 5. At the very least, I shouldn't conclude that he doesn't have some good conflicting evidence that I do not have. Maybe he sees something I don't. But I can *still* make reasonable predictions about what he will do for the next set of problems. When dealing with *known* epistemic

---

[7] This analogy is important for the following reason. It has been suggested to me that the Reasoning about God problem might resurface. Suppose I have evidence that some normative superior will keep a promise. That doesn't entail that I have evidence that no one else has weightier evidence that the normative superior in question will not keep their promise. This is true. I don't have that evidence. But this does not mean I cannot rely on my evidence that they will keep their promise, in much the same way I can rely on my evidence that there is a stop sign. There is an important asymmetry between these cases and the proponent of the problem of evil. The problem of evil assumes that there is an entailment relationship between two kinds of evidence. I make no such assumption, and I am not committed to it when I maintain that you can be justified in believing that normative superiors will keep promises. The analogy is important for another reason. It has been suggested to me that suspending judgment about whether or not a normative superior believes not-P, is effectively a suspension of judgment about whether the total evidence supports P, which gives me a defeater for P. I don't think that's true. What's relevant for justification is what my total evidence supports, and it seems reasonable to proceed in forming judgments on the basis of my evidence but withhold belief about whether or not there is better evidence to the contrary available to someone else. The stop sign case is a good example of this.

superiors, there is a big difference between an actual case of disagreement and making predictions about future agreement.[8]

In the case of an actual evil, the issue is whether or not you can judge that there is no *normative superior* with whom you are having an epistemic disagreement. In the case of thinking about future goods, the issues are quite a bit different. If we frame the motivation for being skeptical in this way, then we may have a way to suspend judgment about whether or not there is a normative superior with whom we are having a disagreement. Let's turn our attention to some possible objections.

2.8 Objections

Objection One: Suspending judgment about the existence of possible normative superiors leads to moral paralysis.

Above I said that a particular action might seem all things considered wrong to me, but I shouldn't think that someone else (particularly a normative superior) doesn't have some weightier evidence to the contrary. One might argue that this leads to moral paralysis.[9] We simply will not know how we should act.

I don't think this is an issue here. It has been argued that skeptical theism is committed to *moral skepticism,* and I take this to be a separate issue from the Reasoning about God problem. One could, for example, think they have an adequate response to the charge of moral skepticism without having a response to the Reasoning about God problem, and vice versa. Furthermore, there are interesting, promising responses to the charge of moral skepticism. So one could embrace my response to the Reasoning about God problem, and embrace a different response to the charge of moral skepticism.[10]

Second, it's not clear that my response *does* lead to moral paralysis in the way that traditional skeptical theism might. Merely not being in a position to know if someone else has weightier evidence concerning a moral matter, does not by itself leads to moral paralysis.

Consider the analogy above concerning the stop sign. Suppose I was going to act on my stop sign belief. I can reasonably judge that there is a stop sign. Reasonably judge that I can't know whether or not someone has weightier

---

[8] Note that matters are not different if you are entertaining the possibility of a math superior anonymously observing you. Suppose you are doing math problems in a room with a video camera. You may think that a math superior would likely agree with you on this problem, but you are not justified in believing that there isn't a math superior watching you that has evidence you've missed.

[9] Thanks to an anonymous referee for this suggestion.

[10] See Howard-Snyder for one example.

evidence that there is not a stop sign, and yet still rationally act on my stop sign beliefs. I should stop my car, even though I am not willing to conclude that there is no one else out there that doesn't have weightier evidence that there is no stop sign present. I see no reason to treat moral beliefs differently.

Objection Two: A new kind of morals —a defeater for moral beliefs

There is another kind of skeptical worry lurking. One might argue as follows:

If I believe P, but suspend judgment about whether I have a normative superior who

believes ~P, then aren't I in effect suspending judgment about whether the total

available evidence supports P? And if I suspend judgment about whether the total

available evidence supports P, might I have a defeater for P?[11]

However, here we must be careful about what the extension of "total evidence" is. In this situation, I would not (for example) be suspending judgment about whether the total evidence available to me supports thinking P. So, if we mean *my* total evidence, then the answer is: No. We do not have a defeater, because I am not suspending judgment about the evidential relation that is an essential component of justification.

The objector might mean something broader by "total evidence" such as the fusion of everyone's evidence. But if you suspend judgment about whether or not the total evidence in *that* sense supports P, we don't have a defeater. Again, consider the stop sign analogy. I can suspend judgment about whether there are other people with weightier evidence that there is not a stop sign, and effectively suspend judgment about whether the fusion of everyone's total evidence supports P, but I don't have a defeater for my belief that there is a stop sign. I should still believe there is a stop sign.

Objection Three: The Atheist can make claims about whether or not a normative superior would agree with them some particular evil being unjustified.

I noted that we can in general still make predictions about whether or not a normative superior will (in general) agree with us on future moral matters, but if we say this don't we leave open the following bit of reasoning? Can't the proponent of the problem of evil say: the normative superior would agree with me on this particular evil being unjustified? Can't the atheist then judge that there must not be any normative superior who had the power to stop this particular evil? Suprisingly, perhaps, the answer to the first question is "Yes"—the

---

[11] Thanks to another anonymous referee for this excellent point.

atheist probably *can* judge that most normative superiors would likely agree with me on this particular evil, but they also should not judge that there are no normative superiors with weightier evidence to the contrary.

    Objection Four: The revised claim is a double-edged sword: return of the Reasoning about God problem

If we accept (E), then we must accept the following instance of it.

    (E*)   Evidence that some normative superior N will keep a promise does not entail that we have evidence that no one else has weightier evidence that N will not keep that promise.

One might worry that the Reasoning about God problem has returned. The truth of (E*), it has been suggested, threatens to undermine Reasoning about God. Presumably, the assumption here is that a lack of evidence concerning whether or not someone else has evidence in a case of future promise keeping functions as a kind of defeater.

   But, again, the stop sign analogy is helpful here. Evidence that something is a stop sign, does not entail that I have evidence that no one else has weightier evidence to the contrary, I'm still entitled to believe there is a stop sign. The relevant difference is that the problem of evil explicitly assumes that evidence of one kind, entails that we have evidence of another kind. When I assume that an agent will keep their promise, I'm not assuming that there is evidence of some other kind, so I'm not making the same kind of epistemic error that a proponent of the problem of evil is making. Furthermore, as I noted above, the mere fact that I *lack* evidence concerning possible weightier evidence that someone else might have for the denial of P does not entail that *I* have a defeater for P.

3. VERSION TWO: A NEW KIND OF SKEPTICAL THEISM

In this section, I will introduce and explore another new version of skeptical theism. It departs from what is traditionally classified as skeptical theism by focusing on the second premise of the problem of evil, but as we shall see, I think it is still appropriate to label this a kind of skeptical theism.

   Understanding this version depends on first understanding Peter van Inwagen's main reason for rejecting the second premise in the problem of evil. Van Inwagen has argued against this premise by noting that it is committed to the thesis that there is some minimum amount of evil that is sufficient for God's purposes. Van Inwagen rejects this assumption and argues for *The No-Minimum Claim:*

3.1 The No-Minimum Claim

For any amount of pain and suffering which serves God's purposes there
is some lesser amount of pain and suffering that also would serve God's
purposes.[12]

Part of what van Inwagen seems to have in mind is that pain can be divided
up into smaller and smaller units ad infinitum in ways that might still be sufficient for God's purposes. If the no-minimum claim is true, there will always be
some world with less evil that God could have realized that would be sufficient
for God's purposes. What is God to do in a situation like this? It seems that it
would permissible for God to simply pick a world and create it knowing that
some of the evil in that world will be gratuitous.

Jeff Jordan has recently argued against van Inwagen. While Jordan is willing to concede that we could divide units of pain and suffering in this fashion,
however, he argues that it is implausible to suppose that we could do so in a
manner that would be detectable by human beings. At some point the changes
in the amount of pain and suffering would not be detectable by human beings,
and so we would have some kind of minimum for all practical purposes with
respect to human beings[13]

In a previous paper, I argued against Jordan. I conceded that while we may
actually have a threshold on the minimum amount of pain we can experience,
God could have made us with more and more fine-grained pain detection discriminating abilities ad infinitum. So van Inwagen can still plausibly defend
the no-minimum claim[14] In his reply to my objection, Jordan insists that there
would still be some practical limit.[15] It remains unclear to me why, as a matter
of metaphysical necessity, the space of worlds must be laid out the way Jordan
insists. What I have described seems like a possibility, but for those who are
resistant perhaps *skepticism* is the best option here.

Van Inwagen does not need to *accept* the no-minimum claim to undermine
the problem of evil. Proponents of the problem of evil are committed denying
the no-minimum claim, and so all we need to do is maintain that we should
not believe that it's false. We should be skeptical about its denial.

For starters, we have no idea what levels of pain would be sufficient for
God's purposes, and more importantly we should say that we simply have
no idea if God would not have an infinite array of worlds with less and less
pain. So, we should *at minimum* be skeptical about whether or not there is a
minimum amount of evil that would be sufficient for a God's purposes, and
whether there would be a practical limit on our pain detection capacities.
But if we should be skeptical about whether or not there is some minimum

---

[12] Van Inwagen (1991).   [13] Jordan (2009).   [14] Cullison (2011).
[15] Jordan (2011).

amount, then we should be skeptical about whether or not God would permit gratuitous evils; i.e. we should be skeptical about the second premise of the problem of evil.

I think it's appropriate to call this a kind of skeptical theism. It is a kind of skepticism about what axiological options would be open to God, and it puts pressure on us to suspend judgment about a premise in the problem of evil argument. However, instead of saying that we should be skeptical about whether or not these evils are gratuitous, we can say we should be skeptical about whether God has an infinite array of worlds open to him that involve less and less pain and still achieve her purposes.

And what's interesting about this kind of skeptical theism is that it *also* avoids the Reasoning about God problem. This kind of skepticism is compatible with insisting that we know that God wouldn't have a justifying reason to permit some of the evil we observe, and we still could make predictions about what God would or would not do when he makes a promise.

One might object that van Inwagen's no-minimum claim fairs no better in preserving our ability to reason about what God would or would not do. After all, if God is just arbitrarily choosing from an infinite array of worlds, what hope do we really have in relying on a promise that we think God has made?

However, there's an important difference between God allowing some number of deaths, or some number of natural disasters that cause some level of pain and God breaking promises. Those are the sorts of evils that the no-minimum claim is responding to and those evils seem importantly different from the evil of God breaking a promise. So, there is conceptual room to maintain we don't know what options are open to God in terms of pain detecting capacities and lesser and lesser evils while being confident that if there is a God that made a promise, that God would keep it.

Second, the infinite array of worlds could all have *some* features in common if they are the sorts of things that are *best* no matter what. For example, one might think that it is all things considered *best* for there to be a world that contains free creatures capable of forming loving relationships with each other and their creator. If one thought that, then they could consistently reason that there may be an infinite array of worlds each involving less and less pain that is sufficient for God's purposes, while maintaining that *all* of those worlds would have free creatures capable of forming loving relationships, and also being worlds in which God kept promises.

You might not think that this *is* all things considered best, but this is only to serve as an example to illustrate that one could consistently embrace skepticism with respect to rejecting the no-minimum claim and also reason that there are some features of this world that it is reasonable to expect God would realize.

4. CONCLUSION

I have offered two ways to be a skeptical theist and solve the Reasoning about God problem. The first is to embrace a related, but importantly different motivation for being skeptical about the first premise. This strategy relies on thinking about what our evidence for a proposition supports (or in this case doesn't support) concerning other persons' evidence against that proposition and some analogies to thinking about cases of epistemic disagreement. When encountering actual evils you should be skeptical about whether there is an normative superior provided there are no other reasons to think that such a being doesn't exist. But the actual evil by itself is not evidence against the existence of an epistemic superior. The second version invites us to embrace skepticism about the second premise, by showing that we should (at minimum) be skeptical about a thesis that the second premise is committed to, namely that there is some minimum amount of suffering that would be sufficient for God's purposes.

My hope is that theists might find, at least, one of these new versions attractive, but it's also worth noting that these solutions are compatible with each other. Theists could be doubly skeptical regarding the problem of evil and argue that we should suspend judgment about both premises. Theists would still be in a position to form reasonable judgments about what God might do, particularly with respect to promise keeping.[16]

[16] Acknowledgements omitted: Neil Fei; Dale Tuggy; Tomas Bogardus (plus students); Joshua Spencer; John Shoemaker; Justin Snedegar; and Mindy Newton.

19

Trust, Silence, and Liturgical Acts

Kevin Timpe

INTRODUCTION

It is widely acknowledged that skeptical theism, if true, would provide a forceful reply to the evidential problem of evil. Many of the leading objections to skeptical theism (hereafter, *ST*) take the form of showing unacceptable consequences of endorsing *ST* in response to the evidential problem of evil. This "Unacceptable Consequences" argument, as I shall refer to it, comes in a number of forms:

Global Skepticism: If *ST* were true and a satisfactory response to the evidential problem of evil, then by parity of reasons we would be committed to all sorts of wide-ranging skeptical conclusions, perhaps even global skepticism.[1]

Moral Skepticism: If *ST* were true and a satisfactory response to the evidential problem of evil, then by parity of reasons it would lead to a kind of moral skepticism.

Moral Paralysis: If *ST* were true and a satisfactory response to the evidential problem of evil, then by parity of reasons it would undermine moral deliberation.[2]

Lack of Trust: If *ST* were true and a satisfactory response to the evidential problem of evil, then it would undermine our trust in God.[3]

In the present chapter, I offer a defense of ST against one version of the Unacceptable Consequences argument, specifically the *Lack of Trust* argument. One might think that endorsing *ST* would make it more difficult for the individual to trust that God is working toward the good; my goal is to show why this is not the case.

---

[1] See, for example, McBrayer (2012), particularly section III; and Dougherty (2008).

[2] See, among others, McBrayer (2012), Jordan (2006), and Piper (2007).

[3] For an objection to *ST* along these lines, see Wielenberg (2010) and Maitzen (2007).

I argue that the motivation for adopting *ST* can be seen as a way of responding not only to the problem of evil, but also the problem of divine hiddenness.[4] Below, I address the relationship between *ST* and another problem—the problem of divine silence. As with discussions of the problem of evil, the problem of divine silence can focus either on divine silence in general or on the divine silence to a particular kind of suffering; I adopt the latter approach. I argue that how silence should be interpreted depends on what other beliefs we have about the character of the agent who is silent. Given a Christian understanding of the nature of God, divine silence need not give reason to doubt God's trustworthiness. Silence would only justify *Lack of Trust* if God did not provide an accessible way of experiencing His presence despite His silence. But divine silence is compatible with divine self-disclosure, and such self-disclosure can help sustain one's trust in God, despite God's silence.

I argue that the liturgical life of the Church—specifically Eucharistic celebration—can provide a basis of maintaining one's trust in God even if those practices do not result in propositional knowledge regarding His justification for evil. I end by considering what this argument does, and does not, establish. I do not seek to prove that skeptical theism is true, or that belief in God is rational. However, for one who is already disposed towards theistic belief of a certain sort, the presence of evils for which one does not know the reason or for which God does not provide any answer need not undermine one's trust in God.

I EVIL AND SILENCE

Most philosophers of religion who invoke *ST* do so in response to the problem of evil. Given that the "problem of evil" is not a single problem or argument, it is more accurate to say that most philosophers of religion who invoke skeptical theism do so in response to evidential versions of the problem of evil. According to these sorts of arguments, the amounts and kinds of evil the world contains give us reason or evidence to believe in the nonexistence of God even if they are not logically incompatible with his existence. Evidence of God's existence is, in a sense, hidden from us and our inability to understand what reasons He has for allowing evil, many claim, count against the rationality of belief in His existence.[5] And so while the problem of evil and the problem of

---

[4] It is not my intention to argue for skeptical theism in this chapter. For arguments of that sort, see McBrayer (2010b) and (2012) (as well as other chapters in this book).

[5] Since I'm primarily concerned with evidential versions of the problem of evil in this chapter, what is at issue is not God's existence but the rationality of belief in such.

divine hiddenness might be formally distinct,[6] many people take the hiddenness of God to be an evil that God must have a justifying reason for, given that
it is precisely God's hiddenness that leads to individuals not believing in and
uniting themselves to Him. So it is natural to see skeptical theism as a line
of response not just to the problem of evil, but also to the problem of divine
hiddenness.

In a recent article, Michael Rea argues that divine hiddenness does not cast
doubt on the belief that God strongly desires to promote the well-being of
all of His rational creatures, despite what many proponents—as well as some
opponents—of the argument from divine hiddenness have supposed (Rea
2009). Rea thinks that what is usually thought of as the problem of divine hiddenness is best thought of instead as involving silence, rather than hiddenness.
The reason for this is that the considerations used to motivate the claim that
God is hidden—specifically, that the evidence in support of God's existence is
inconclusive and that many individuals rarely if ever have an experience that
seems to them to involve direct experience of the love or presence of God—
does not establish the claim that God is hidden. Instead, it only establishes
the weaker claim that God is silent: "that God hasn't made a special effort to
ensure that most of his rational creatures detect (as such) whatever signs of his
existence there might be" (Rea 2009: 80). However, even if a being isn't hidden,
it may still be that he is silent in a way that calls into question his goodness:

> A man who chooses to whisper rather than shout instructions to his children,
> knowing all the while that they cannot (yet) hear him over the racket they are
> making, is being silent toward his children in the sense that I have in mind. . ..
> Henceforth, when I speak of divine silence I will be speaking simply of the fact
> that inconclusive evidence and absence of religious experience both obtain. As
> I understand it, then, divine silence is compatible with God's having provided
> some widely and readily accessible way for his creatures to find him and to experi-
> ence his presence, albeit indirectly, despite his silence. (Rea 2009: 81)

This leads Rea to ask the following question: "Assuming divine silence doesn't
contribute to our well-being or to any greater human good, does the fact of
divine silence give us any reason to doubt that God cares about us?" (Rea
2009: 81). Divine silence, Rea argues, is compatible with the love and goodness
of God if He provides an accessible way of experiencing His presence despite
His silence. Such a way can be found in the liturgical life of the Church.

Below, I extend the general contours of Rea's response to the problem of
divine silence to the closely related issues of *ST*. While Rea argues that divine
silence is compatible with divine presence and love, I hope to place Rea's point
within the context of a discussion about the implications of *ST*. *ST* arises in
response to our not knowing what justifying reason God has for allowing

---

[6] See, for example, van Inwagen (2009); for a contrary position, see Schellenberg (2010).

certain evils to occur. I argue that the motivation for adopting *ST* need not be undermined by divine silence. As Rea's argument makes clear, how silence should be interpreted depends on what other beliefs we have about the character of the agent who is silent. Given a Christian understanding of the nature of God, divine silence does not give reason to believe in a *deus abscondus*. Liturgical practices can provide a way of responding to divine silence even if those practices do not result in propositional knowledge regarding the justification for evil. In particular, I show how liturgical acts can provide an opportunity for maintaining trust and faith in the face of God's apparent silence in the face of evil.

II SUFFERING IN SILENCE

Before moving to the argument, it will be helpful for us to have a particular case in mind. This is particularly true given that I'm interested in showing not how God's silence is no threat to a believer's trust in Him in the face of particular instances of suffering rather than in the face of evil in general.[7] One reason for focusing on a particular case, rather than evil in general, is that it helps avoid a problem that Michael Levine says plagues many contemporary analytic treatments of evil, namely "opting for an antiseptic approach to the problem of evil" (Levine 2000: 99). And others have raised a similar criticism that abstract treatments of evil are problematic because they tend to devalue the suffering of those who are experiencing the evil.[8] So my goal in this section is to give an example of evil that I'll be working with in what follows. And while this will be the only example that I'll be directly addressing, I think it should be obvious how many of the considerations below would also be relevant to other instances of suffering.

Consider the case of Lee. Lee is a theist who is justified in his theistic beliefs. He has considered the plethora of arguments for and against the existence of God. He thinks that a cumulative case—one based on, say, the modal ontological argument, the contingency-based cosmological argument, and the fine-tuning argument—can be made for the rationality of belief in God's existence. While he thinks that the logical problem of evil fails, he does think that the evidential problem of evil lowers the rationality of belief in God. That is, his subjective probability for the proposition "God exists" is lowered when he considers the existence, kinds, magnitude, and distribution of evil

---

[7] For a worthwhile discussion of what is particularly troubling about the problem of evil is suffering, see Stump (2010: 4ff).

[8] See, for instance, the discussion in Stump (2010).

in the world.[9] Yet, for him at least, the subjective probability is still above .5. More specifically, Lee is a Christian. He thinks that specific Christian doctrines—most notably the Incarnation and the Sacramental life of the Church—give reasons to think that God is not hidden to such a degree that it makes it irrational for him to believe in God's existence.

Lee is also a first-time father. Shortly after his son Cooper is born, Lee learns that Cooper suffers from a previously unknown genetic abnormality. Because no one has been previously diagnosed with the same abnormality, there is no prognosis for what the abnormality will mean for Cooper's life and future. But in the first few years of Cooper's life, it becomes clear that the abnormality causes myriad problems: gross motor delays, vestibular disorientation, coordination problems, and a significant speech delay, which perhaps masks a cognitive delay. These various problems cause suffering not only for Cooper (he is, for example, aware that he's unable to communicate effectively with others) but also for Lee, who loves and cares for the flourishing of his son. As Eleonore Stump has argued elsewhere, "what is bad about the evil a human being suffers is that it undermines (partly or entirely) her flourishing" (Stump 2010: 11).

The initial uncertainty of his son's illness causes Lee to go into depression for a while, for which he seeks therapy. Over the first few years of Cooper's life, Lee comes to function better under the uncertainty caused by Cooper's illness, but the situation still takes a toll on him. He takes a less-desirable job in another part of the country with a lower cost of living, relocating his family to where he and his wife can focus more on Cooper's care and therapy. There, Cooper receives physical, occupational, and speech therapy weekly. And while Cooper makes great strides, his condition still has a significant negative impact on his life. Over the years, Lee cries out repeatedly for God to help him know how best to care for his son, to minimize his son's suffering, and to cope with his own. But he receives no divine guidance on how best to seek care for Cooper; no reassurance that Cooper will flourish in his life; no confirmation of the quality of his parenting, protection, and love for Cooper.

III TRUST AND SILENCE

We now have a particular instance of suffering—Cooper's suffering from his genetic abnormality, but also the related suffering of Lee on behalf of Cooper. Furthermore, it is unclear to Lee as to why this particular instance of suffering has occurred. It seems to be, as one doctor once described Cooper's condition,

---

[9] It may be that embracing *ST* blocks the lowering of his subjective probability entirely, or that it merely reduces the degree to which the evidential problem of evil lowers the rationality of belief in God's existence.

"a freak accident, like getting struck by lightning—twice." As Trent Dougherty writes, "One's not understanding why one's suffering is occurring is a constituent, perhaps the key constituent, of one's overall suffering which makes it almost unbearable at times" (Dougherty 2012: 21). It's not that Lee thinks God doesn't have a good reason for allowing his son to suffer; rather, it's that he's asked God to help him understand what he can best do to alleviate and mitigate that suffering in a way that hasn't met with a reply. Lee, we might say, isn't looking for a theodicy; he's looking for a response. And instead he's met with silence.

We are now in a position to see how being in such a situation might incline a person towards endorsing *ST*. As David James Anderson writes, "Skeptical theists claim that this fact (the fact that we cannot see any possible reasons for divine permission of evil) is not at all surprising on theism, and does not count as a reason (at least not a strong reason) against it" (Anderson 2012: 27). Lee's awareness of the evidential problem of evil and the various theistic responses to it, especially when coupled with his own situation, is what inclines him to endorse *ST*. For example, he find himself agreeing with the words of Alvin Plantinga: "Our grasp of the fundamental ways of things is at best limited; there is no reason to think that if God *did* have a reason for permitting the evil in question, we would be the first to know" (Plantinga 1996: 70). But even if one grants this, it might seem that God's not giving an individual any indication what His reason is for allowing a particular instance of suffering might make it harder for that individual to trust God.

At this point, it would be helpful to have an account of the nature of trust. Annett Baier (1995) and Linda Zagzebski (2014) suggest that trust is a three-place relation. According to Zagzebski,

> trust combines epistemic, affective, and behavioral components, each of which is a three-place relation. When X trusts Y for purpose Z, (1) X *believes* that Y will get Z and that X may be harmed if Y does not do so. (2) X *feels* trusting towards Y for purpose Z, and (3) X *treats* Y as if it will get Z. I do not claim that all three components of trust are necessary in every instance, but I think that they are present in standard cases. (Zagzebski 2014: 2f in manuscript)

In the present context, we might say that Lee trusts God with Cooper's flourishing just in case (1) Lee believes that God is, in fact, working toward Cooper's flourishing; (2) Lee feels trusting toward God with respect to Cooper's flourishing; and (3) Lee treats God as if He will, to the best of his ability and consistent with His other aims, bring about Cooper's flourishing.[10] Cooper's genetic abnormality, and the suffering it causes, could of course impact any of these three elements, and it may impact them all. And these aspects of trust are

---

[10] Although Lee may hope for Cooper's flourishing, and the healing that it requires, in this life, he trusts that even if that doesn't happen here it will happen in the life to come.

also related to the theological virtue of faith, which requires trust in the one
who is the object of one's faith. By faith, "man freely commits his entire self to
God" (Aquinas 1954: 5) a commitment which could not be done unless the
individual trusted God and His promises. According to the writer of the Letter
to the Hebrews, "faith is the substance of things to be hoped for, the certainty
of things that appear not." So Lee's trust in God is part of his faith in God and
God's loving-kindness towards Cooper. The question, then, is how Lee can
maintain trust and faith in God regarding Cooper despite his son's suffering.

As mentioned above, Michael Rea has recently argued that the bulk of the
reasons usually given for divine hiddenness is better understood as supporting
divine silence. Rea interprets the problem of divine hiddenness in terms of the
following biconditional:

H1:   God is hidden ↔ God permits INCONCLUSIVE EVIDENCE & ABSENCE OF
       RELIGIOUS EXPERIENCE to obtain (Rea 2009, 78),

where inconclusive evidence and absence of religious experience are understood as follows:

INCONCLUSIVE EVIDENCE: For many people, the available a priori and empiri-
    cal evidence in support of God's existence is inconclusive: one can be
    fully aware of it and at the same time rationally believe that God does
    not exist.

ABSENCE OF RELIGIOUS EXPERIENCE: Many people—believers and unbelievers
    alike—have never had an experience that seems to them to be a direct
    experience or awareness of the love or presence of God; and those who
    do have such experiences have them rarely. (Rea 2009: 76)

Rea grants that the left-to-right conditional involved in H1 is true; but he
thinks that the right-to-left conditional is false, for the mere fact that God permits INCONCLUSIVE EVIDENCE and ABSENCE OF RELIGIOUS EXPERIENCE doesn't mean
that he is hidden. To support his claim, Rea makes the following analogy:

Suppose there's an object—a car, perhaps—that is in plain sight in Wilma's driveway but which Wilma can't see because her eyes are closed. The car isn't hidden
from her; she's just not looking. Indeed, even if someone had put the car in her
driveway knowing that she wouldn't be looking, we wouldn't want to say that the
person had hidden the car from her. (Rea 2009: 79)

Rea's suggestion is that, for all we know, "there's something analogous to 'open-
ing our eyes' that we all can do that would allow us to receive experiences
or other evidence of the presence of God" (Rea 2009: 79). Given that many,
perhaps even most, people haven't done this, most people may have good reason for thinking that God doesn't exist insofar as they don't see any justifying reason God could have for allowing INCONCLUSIVE EVIDENCE and ABSENCE
OF RELIGIOUS EXPERIENCE. But Rea thinks it false to think of this as involving

hiddenness, which suggests that God is intentionally making it difficult for humans to figure out his presence:

> The term I would prefer to use in characterizing what we seem to know about God's self-disclosure to the bulk of humanity is, therefore, not hiddenness but rather silence. To say that something is hidden implies either that it has been deliberately concealed or that it has been concealed (deliberately or not) to such a degree that those from whom it is hidden can't reasonably be expected to find it. This is why divine hiddenness would seem to require justification. If God cares about our well-being, one would think that, absent special reasons for doing otherwise, he would put us in circumstances such that we could reasonably be expected eventually to find him. But inconclusive evidence and absence of religious experience don't imply that God is deliberately concealing his existence from us; nor do they imply, on their own, that we can't reasonably be expected eventually to find him. What they do imply is that God hasn't made a special effort to ensure that most of his rational creatures detect (as such) whatever signs of his existence there might be or whatever messages he might be sending us. (Rea 2009: 80).[11]

By divine silence, then, Rea means to refer to the fact that both INCONCLUSIVE EVIDENCE and ABSENCE OF RELIGIOUS EXPERIENCE obtain, when God could disclose himself in a way that they fail to obtain.

Rea then raises the following question: "Assuming divine silence doesn't contribute to our well-being or to any greater human good, does the fact of divine silence give us any reason to doubt that God cares about us?" (Rea 2009: 81). The parallel between this question and the evidential problem of evil should be obvious (and if one thinks that divine silence is itself an evil, Rea's question becomes a version of the evidential problem of evil). While Rea thinks this question is "natural," he also thinks the reasoning behind it is flawed insofar as silence can be interpreted in different ways:

> It is flawed in just the same way in which complaints about the behavior of human persons are often flawed: it depends on a particular interpretation of behavior that can in fact be interpreted in any of a number of different ways, depending upon what assumptions we make about the person's beliefs, desires, motives, dispositions, and overall personality.... Silence is an interpretable kind of behavior; and, as with any other person, God's behavior doesn't wear its interpretation on its sleeve—it can be understood only in the light of substantial background information. (Rea 2009: 82f)

For Rea, divine silence would only give us reason to question God's love for us if "we had good reason to think that God had provided no way for us to find him or to experience his presence in the midst of his silence" (Rea 2009: 83). But, as Rea points out, many theists think it is false to say that they have no way

---

[11] Rea grants that further facts, when coupled with INCONCLUSIVE EVIDENCE and ABSENCE OF RELI- GIOUS EXPERIENCE, may in fact justify the claim that God is hidden; but he doesn't think we yet have reason to think there are such further facts.

to experience God in the midst of His silence; that is, for many theists there are reasons to think that God has in fact provided other means to draw people into His presence. In the next section, I want to show how Christians in particular think that God has in fact provided other such means to show His love and solidarity with humans despite what might be interpreted as divine silence.[12]

IV THE INCARNATION AND THE TABLE

Above, I have summarized Rea's argument as to why divine silence need not conflict with God's love and care for His creation. Rea ends his article by considering and defending the following claim:

> DIVINE SELF-DISCLOSURE: God has provided some widely and readily accessible
> way of finding him and experiencing his presence despite his silence.

If a person, such as Lee, had reason to think that DIVINE SELF-DISCLOSURE were true, then the mere fact (or even what would look like to that individual as a fact) that God is silent in the face of suffering would not by itself give reason to question God's concern for him. Rea in fact argues that we have some reason to think that DIVINE SELF-DISCLOSURE is plausibly true, as least for adherents of some religious traditions. Rea suggests the liturgical actions and practices "can be ways of experiencing the mediated presence of God" (Rea 2009: 92). It will, of course, be easier to proceed if we have a particular religious tradition, and a set of liturgical practices, in mind. In what follows, I'll explore Rea's suggestion along the lines of Christianity. But it should be clear from the treatment below how similar considerations might also be made within other religious and liturgical traditions.

At the heart of the Christian tradition is the belief that God became incarnate in human flesh in order to reconcile us with God and so that we might know God's love.[13] Furthermore, many Christians believe that the divine blessing is fully revealed and communicated in the Church's liturgy. The liturgy not only recalls the events of God's salvation of humans, but makes them present to those who participate in it. The Church's liturgy finds its most intense expression and culminates in the sacrament of the Eucharist, which confers efficacious grace for the redemption of God's creation.[14] Furthermore, "by the Eucharistic

---

[12] Russell asks the following question: "if God is good, and cares about us, wouldn't he want us to be apprised of his game plan? Wouldn't he want the universe to be morally transparent. . . to sensitive creatures like ourselves?" (Russell and Wykstra 1988: 147). Rea's article also gives an answer to this question; though it is an answer that I here do not have the space to investigate. See Rea (2009: 84–87).

[13] There are, of course, further reasons for the incarnation; see Beaudoin (2003: 457–60).

[14] I am not here arguing that the Eucharist is the only liturgical practice which can serve the role of preserving one's trust in God in the face of apparent divine silence, but only that it is one—perhaps even the best—liturgical practice to serve that role. By partaking of the Eucharist, one is

celebration we already unite ourselves with the heavenly liturgy and anticipate eternal life, when God will be all in all" (Beaudoin 2003: 1326). By participating in this sacrament, the believer augments his union with God and finds a fore-taste of the perfected union with God that is to come. The Eucharist thus points beyond the suffering of this present life toward the beatific vision. "For now we see in a mirror [a]dimly, but then face to face; now I know in part, but then I will know fully just as I also have been fully known" (1 Corinthians 13:12).

When Lee participates in the Church's liturgy, and most specifically when he partakes of the Eucharist, Lee may find faith and trust in God to be sus-tainable despite Cooper's suffering. To be clear, the sacrament does not give Lee answers to his questions about God's reason for allowing Cooper to suf-fer. What he finds is compassion and presence, a presence which means that God is not silent to Lee's concerns. When partaking of the Eucharist, Lee feels God's presence more palpably than any other time, and there can trust that God *is* working toward the flourishing of all His people, including Cooper, even if he is not able to understand *how* that is. God may give no answers, but He gives Himself. And this, more than answers or reasons, is what Lee ulti-mately needs.[15] During the Eucharist, it is thus false that ABSENCE OF RELIGIOUS EXPERIENCE obtains for Lee, and thus false that he experiences divine silence despite neither knowing God's reasons for allowing his son's suffering nor hav-ing guidance from God on best to care for Cooper.

V CONCLUSION

Above, I've suggested that the failure to understand why God allows a par-ticular instance of suffering need not mean that God is silent with respect to that suffering. Drawing on Rea's work, I've argued that the liturgical life of the Church—specifically the Eucharistic celebration—can provide a basis of maintaining one's trust in God even if it does not result in propositional knowledge regarding His justification for evil. I have not attempted to argue that skeptical theism is true, or that believe in God is rational (although I have assumed that such believe can be rational, at least for some individuals). But

---

participating in the very Incarnation of God Himself, and the justification and sanctification that His atoning life, death, and resurrection make possible.

[15] Joshua Thurow has noted that if the *Moral Skepticism* version of *Unacceptable Consequences* succeeds, then the response I've given here to *Lack of Trust* will fail, since "if the moral skepticism problem goes through, then it seems like I wouldn't know that God is doing something good for me by providing the liturgy, and so I may still rightly not trust God." This seems to be true. But note that if this were the case, then it would be *Moral Skepticism* that was doing all the work, and not *Lack of Trust*. Keep in mind also that my goal in the present chapter is only to deal with the latter objection to *ST*.

for some individuals who are already disposed toward certain kinds of theistic belief, the presence of evils for which one does not know the reason or for which God does not provide any answer need not undermine one's trust in God. Justin P. McBrayer has recently argued that the skepticism of skeptical theism is context sensitive (McBrayer 2012). His conclusion sits well with what I've argued above. For some individuals, not knowing God's reason for allowing a particular evil might give them reason for doubting the existence or trustworthiness of God. But for other individuals who already have robust religious beliefs, particularly when they are in certain contexts—at the Table, for example—God's silence need not undermine their trust and faith.

Of course, whether or not the epistemic response to suffering outlined above will succeed for a particular individual will depend upon a number of factors: the suffering involved, the reasons the individual has which count in favor of her religious belief, the liturgical practices associated with those religious beliefs, etc.... Orthodoxy is, at least etymologically, about right worship rather than just mere right belief. And so it should not be surprising that a person's liturgical practices, and not just propositional beliefs, may be relevant to the individual's ability to trust God in the face of suffering.[16]

[16] I am very grateful to Brent Peterson, Joshua Thurow, and Leigh Vicens for very helpful and thorough sets of comments on an earlier draft of this chapter. I'd also like to thank Justin P. McBrayer and Trent Dougherty for inviting me to contribute to this project and allowing me to reflect on issues that are at least as much autobiographical as academic for me.

Part IV

Skeptical Theism's Implications for Morality

20

Agnosticism, Skeptical Theism, and Moral Obligation

Stephen Maitzen

1. EVIL, THEODICY, AND SKEPTICAL THEISM

In his influential essay "Epistemic Humility, Arguments from Evil, and Moral Skepticism," Daniel Howard-Snyder relates the story of Ashley Jones, a twelve-year-old girl "who, while babysitting her neighbor's children, was raped and bludgeoned to death by an escapee from a local juvenile detention center" in the state of Washington.[1] He uses the phrase "Ashley's suffering" to denote "the evil done to ... Ashley ... and what she suffered and lost" as a result of that evil (18).

If God exists as portrayed by traditional monotheism—a being perfect in knowledge, power, and goodness—then why did God let Ashley's suffering occur? To answer that question on God's behalf is to offer a theodicy. A theodicy aims to justify God's permission of Ashley's suffering on the grounds that such permission (i) achieves some particular outweighing good that not even a perfect being could achieve at less cost, or (ii) prevents some even worse particular outcome that not even a perfect being could prevent at less cost, or else (iii) is an unfortunate side-effect of some good that's too good to give up (such as unchecked libertarian free will on the part of human agents) and furthermore a side-effect that not even a perfect being could prevent.

In my experience, the most popular theodicies belong to type (iii). By far the most popular token of that type, judging from my experience in front of university classrooms and in front of audiences at both public and academic forums, is one that invokes libertarian (i.e., contracausal) free will—hereafter, "LFW." This theodicy claims that the possession of LFW by human

---

[1] Howard-Snyder (2009: 18). To avoid needless clutter in what follows, further citations of this particular work will give page number only.

agents—crucially, LFW totally unconstrained by God—is a good that's too good to give up, even if it has the unavoidable side-effect of Ashley's suffering at the hands of someone exercising LFW. I frankly don't understand the popularity of this indefensible theodicy, especially among philosophers who ought to know better.[2] Because of its relentless prevalence, I feel justified in singling it out for criticism. It fails on several grounds; space here allows me to mention just four of them.

First, the theodicy assumes that LFW is both a coherent notion and also the only kind of freedom that makes possible the moral agency we value as human beings; both assumptions are highly contentious, to put it mildly. It's far from clear that LFW can be explained coherently and, even if it can, it's far from clear that any morally responsible agent must possess LFW that not even God may ever constrain.[3]

Second, it assumes that LFW has so much intrinsic positive *value* that God would rightly refrain from ever constraining it, an assumption that overstates the value we assign to freedom in general, including LFW if indeed we have it. As Derk Pereboom notes, from the commonsense moral perspective "the evildoer's freedom is a weightless consideration, not merely an outweighed consideration" (Pereboom [2005: 84], citing Lewis [1993: 155]).[4] In assessing the escapee's rape and murder of Ashley, our commonsense moral attitude assigns no discernible positive value to the escapee's having freely committed those crimes. Indeed, nothing could be more obvious than the fact that we don't regard a serious wrongdoer's freedom as a value that stands in the way of our preventing his wrongdoing; on the contrary, we often regard ourselves as not just permitted but *obligated* to interfere with the wrongdoer's freedom. Hence the totally hands-off policy that the LFW theodicy attributes to God has no analogue at all in our moral practice.

Third, in claiming that God would never interfere with human LFW, the theodicy runs up against the scriptural portrayal of God as having manipulated human decisions such as Pharaoh's: "The LORD hardened the heart of Pharaoh, the king of Egypt, so he chased after the people of Israel ..." (Exodus 14:8a, NLT). Indeed, according to scripture God may well have a regular *practice* of "hardening hearts" and thereby interfering with human free choice: "So you see, God chooses to show mercy to some, and he chooses to harden the

---

[2] For example, when I presented Maitzen (2009b) as a colloquium paper at the American Philosophical Association Eastern Division Meeting in 2006, my commentator, a noted philosopher of religion, relied almost entirely on the LFW theodicy in his public response.

[3] See, for example, Fischer et al. (2007), in which Robert Kane's three co-contributors aim telling objections at his libertarian theory of free will. In my judgment, Kane's replies to those objections only highlight the implausibility (arguably, the incoherence) of his theory.

[4] Howard-Snyder wisely doubts that "being free" has intrinsic positive value: "I doubt that my being free [to perform a particular good action] is a state of affairs that is good *in itself*" (23, emphasis in original).

hearts of others so they refuse to listen" (Romans 9:18, NLT). In any case, if God's hardening of hearts is consistent with the inviolable nature of human LFW, then so too would be God's softening the heart of the escapee so that he refrains from raping and killing Ashley.[5]

Fourth, there's evidence that the theodicy errs in assuming that our every-day moral judgments care *at all* about the existence of LFW. If we can regard Anglo-American criminal jurisprudence as accurately reflecting our commonsense moral practice—if, in other words, the criminal law doesn't war with commonsense morality on this issue—then it's clear that we routinely hold agents morally responsible *without regard* to whether they possess LFW. Juries routinely convict defendants without even asking, let alone ascer-taining, whether the defendants' actions were causally determined by prior states of the universe. Likewise judges never, as far as I know, instruct jurors to satisfy themselves of the defendant's LFW before they issue a verdict. One might explain this omission by insisting that the law simply presupposes the defendant's LFW and regards the presupposition as too obvious to need say-ing. But this explanation misunderstands the law's attitude toward obvious presuppositions. Judges' instructions to juries routinely include platitudes so obvious that only lawyers would bother to make them explicit, such as the admonition that witnesses don't always tell the truth.[6] In such a context, the persistent failure to mention LFW would be inexplicable if LFW were relevant, especially since the libertarian holds that defendants are *blameless* if they lack LFW when they commit the crimes of which they're accused. In short, to the extent to which the criminal law reflects them, our actual moral judgments pay no attention to LFW.

Given the abject failure of this most popular of theodicies, I can understand why skeptical theists don't hold out much hope for the enterprise of theodicy. I share their dim view of its prospects. Skeptical theists don't like our chances of explaining, in any way that would satisfy most reasonable people, why God allowed Ashley to be raped and killed. They recognize that, even after think-ing hard about it, we come up empty when we try to identify (i) a particular outweighing good that not even God could achieve without allowing Ashley's suffering; or (ii) an even worse particular outcome that not even God could

---

[5] Christian philosopher Peter van Inwagen (1995: 54) declares it to be *obvious* that God's hard-ening an agent's heart deprives the agent of LFW on that occasion.

[6] Indeed, when the issue of LFW does come up in the criminal law, appellate courts tend to remind trial courts that the issue isn't relevant to criminal responsibility. See, for instance, the much-cited holding in *State v. Sikora*, 44 N.J. 453, 210 A.2d 193 (1965: 202–3): "Criminal responsibility must be judged at the level of the conscious. If a person thinks, plans, and executes the plan at that level, the criminality of his act cannot be denied, wholly or partially, because, although he did not realize it, his conscious [mind] was influenced to think, to plan and to exe-cute the plan by unconscious influences which were the product of his genes and his lifelong environment. [C]riminal guilt cannot be denied or confined... because [the defendant] was una-ware that his decisions and conduct were mechanistically directed by unconscious influences."

prevent without allowing Ashley's suffering; or (iii) some good that's too good to give up, of which Ashley's suffering was a side-effect that not even God could prevent.

Skeptical theists, however, don't find it the least bit surprising that we're so bad at coming up with satisfying theodicies. According to skeptical theism, we shouldn't think that our grasp of possible goods and evils, or our grasp of what it takes to achieve those goods and avoid those evils, even remotely approaches God's perfect grasp of these matters, particularly if we can't rule out that people experience goods and evils not just in this life but also in an eternal afterlife. As the skeptical theist Michael Bergmann says, "It just doesn't seem unlikely that our understanding of the realm of value falls miserably short of capturing all that is true about that realm" (Bergmann 2001: 279). Because skeptical theists are theists, they believe that a perfect God exists, and so they believe that God *has* morally sufficient reasons for allowing whatever horrific evils occur. But they say that we have no reason to think we could discover on our own what those morally sufficient reasons are.

Indeed, I think skeptical theism denies us any reason to think that we can discover God's reasons even if God ostensibly *tells* us what they are. For deception on God's part isn't automatically wrong, all things considered, and hence skeptical theism allows that God might deceive us for morally sufficient reasons beyond our ken, including when he apparently reveals to us his reasons for allowing some evil or other.[7] In sum, skeptical theism denies us any confidence that we've *ever* managed to identify, by any means, the justification God actually relies on for any of his actions or omissions. For all we know, any justification we entertain, however compelling it might seem to us, is shallower, or at least other, than the justification that actually motivates a perfectly wise God.

Skeptical theism has an obvious implication for well-known versions of the evidential argument from evil. If we have no reason to think we would see God's morally sufficient reasons for allowing some or all of the evil in our world, then our failure to see them—our failure to find a convincing theodicy—isn't itself evidence that God *has* no such reasons (and hence doesn't exist). Now, one might accept that implication but argue that our failure to see God's morally sufficient reasons is nevertheless *best explained* by the nonexistence of those reasons even if it's not *evidence* for their nonexistence. By the same token, my *seeming* to have hands might be best explained by my *having* hands, even if my seeming to have hands isn't evidence that some undetectable skeptical scenario doesn't obtain instead, such as one in which I'm a brain-in-a-vat being deceived into thinking I have hands.[8]

---

[7] See Wielenberg (2010) for much more on the relation between skeptical theism and our inability to rule out divine deception.

[8] Russell (1996) defends both of these anti-skeptical claims on the basis of inferences to the best explanation.

But I want to focus instead on a different reply to skeptical theism. Many of its critics object that its skeptical attitude toward our grasp of the "realm of value" implies or reflects untenable moral skepticism, or induces appalling moral paralysis, or produces some equally dire result. Howard-Snyder calls this popular objection to skeptical theism "the Moral Skepticism Objection" (18). He aims to rebut the objection by rebutting it as an objection to the *skeptical* part of skeptical theism, which part he labels "Agnosticism," a label he intentionally capitalizes, presumably in order to distinguish this position from others more commonly called "agnosticism." I'm unconvinced that he succeeds in defending Agnosticism against the Moral Skepticism Objection, for reasons that I'll detail in Section 3. I'm even less convinced that he succeeds in defending skeptical theism against the objection, for reasons that I'll detail in Section 4. Skeptical theism adds theism to Agnosticism, and the addition makes a difference. If Howard-Snyder's defense of Agnosticism has any use as a defense of skeptical theism against the Moral Skepticism Objection, then the objection shouldn't become even stronger when you add theism to Agnosticism. I'll argue that it does become stronger.

2. HOWARD-SNYDER'S DEFENSE OF AGNOSTICISM

Howard-Snyder describes Agnosticism as holding that "we should be in doubt about" two issues: (a) "whether the goods we know of constitute a representative sample of all the goods there are" and (b) "whether each good we know of is such that the necessary conditions of its realization we know of are all [the necessary conditions of its realization that] there are" (18). Thus Howard-Snyder's Agnostic echoes the skeptical theist's skepticism about our grasp of "the realm of value." Indeed, in all essential respects Agnosticism *just is* the skeptical part of skeptical theism.

Howard-Snyder then applies Agnosticism to the case of Ashley's suffering. "Agnosticism," he says, "tells us that since we should be in doubt about" (a) and (b), "we should be in doubt about whether there is a reason that would justify God's nonintervention" in Ashley's case (19). By our being "in doubt about" (a) or (b), Howard-Snyder means our being "of two minds about it, ambivalent, undecided" (22). The idea is that if we're in doubt about whether there's a reason that would justify God's nonintervention in the face of Ashley's suffering, then we're in doubt about whether God had a moral obligation to intervene that God failed to live up to.

Does Agnosticism imply that we should be in doubt about whether God *did* intervene to prevent Ashley's suffering, despite our overwhelming impression that God didn't? Does Agnosticism imply that we may have missed God's intervention? Good questions. Because Howard-Snyder is concerned to defend Agnosticism against the charge that it implies an implausibly strong kind of skepticism, I presume he would reject such a radically skeptical reaction to the claim that God didn't intervene.[9] But back to the main issue. If we should be *in doubt* about whether there's a reason that would justify God's nonintervention (assuming God didn't intervene), then we shouldn't accept the conclusions reached by standard versions of the evidential argument from evil: namely, that there *is no* reason that would justify God's nonintervention and therefore (given that God *has* such a reason *if* God exists) no God.

The Moral Skepticism Objection to Agnosticism that Howard-Snyder then considers is the following three-step argument (19, emphases added):

(1) If Agnosticism is true, then we should be in doubt about whether *we* should have intervened to prevent Ashley's suffering [even if we could have done so at no real risk to ourselves].

(2) We should *not* be in doubt about whether we should have intervened.

(3) So, Agnosticism is false.

According to the objection, Agnosticism implies that we should be undecided about whether we should have intervened to prevent Ashley's suffering even if we could have done so at no cost to ourselves, a result that implies implausible moral skepticism on our part, or induces appalling moral paralysis in us, or both. Howard-Snyder's response is to argue that no type of "moral theory and principle" will make premises (1) and (2) of that three-step argument both come out true, and hence the Moral Skepticism Objection is unsound.

I want to clear out of the way a tempting rebuttal to the Moral Skepticism Objection that might occur to the reader. It goes as follows. Even if some reason justifies *God* in allowing Ashley's suffering, that alone doesn't make it likely that some reason justifies *us* in allowing Ashley's suffering. For an omniscient God can know, and thereby have, a reason to allow Ashley's suffering even when we comparatively ignorant beings don't know, and thereby don't have, that reason. Because God knows more than we do, the range of reasons that potentially justify God in allowing Ashley's suffering is *greater* than the range of reasons that potentially justify us in allowing it.

As obvious as this rebuttal may seem, it nevertheless fails. Omniscience cuts both ways here. Any reason to think that God's omniscience reveals a greater range of reasons that justify allowing Ashley's suffering is equally a reason to think that God's omniscience reveals a greater range of reasons that *prohibit* allowing Ashley's suffering. An omniscient God can know, and thereby have, reasons to

---

[9] Although I won't argue for the point here, it's not clear to me that Agnosticism can avoid endorsing this radically skeptical reaction. Bergmann (2012) argues that it can.

prevent suffering that we comparatively ignorant beings don't know and thereby don't have. Moreover, an all-powerful God will have *ways* of preventing suffering that we comparatively powerless beings lack. Given God's knowledge and power, the legitimate reasons God has to allow suffering are just as likely to be *fewer* than the legitimate reasons we have. It's a commonplace of our moral practice that the less limited the agent, the fewer the justifications we're willing to accept for the agent's permission of suffering. (As the Spider-Man Principle says, "With great power comes great responsibility.") So this tempting rebuttal to the Moral Skepticism Objection is, at best, a wash.

Before proceeding further, let me make a small but important point about the vagaries of English idiom. The statement "We should have intervened" is straightforwardly interpreted as meaning "We were *obligated* to intervene: we were wrong not to intervene or would have been wrong had we not intervened." By contrast, the statement "We should be in doubt about whether we should have intervened" is less clear-cut. It can plausibly be taken to mean (c) "We should be in doubt about whether we were obligated to intervene." But it can also plausibly be taken to mean (d) "We should be in doubt about whether we were *permitted* to intervene: we should be undecided about whether we did something *wrong* by intervening." The Moral Skepticism Objection, as I understand it, concerns only (c) and not (d): the objection alleges that Agnosticism implies (c). Therefore, a successful defense of Agnosticism against the objection must establish either that Agnosticism *doesn't imply* (c) or that (c) isn't *false* even if Agnosticism does imply (c).

Howard-Snyder aims to establish that disjunction. He proceeds by dilemma, dividing theories of moral obligation into two exhaustive categories: roughly, those that say our obligation to intervene *depends on the total consequences of our intervention*, and those that say it doesn't. For convenience, let's call those theories of moral obligation *consequentialist* and *non-consequentialist*, respectively. He argues that consequentialist theories falsify premise (2) of the Moral Skepticism Objection, because they imply that we *should* be in doubt about our obligation to intervene in Ashley's case. After all, how can we know what the *total* consequences of our intervention will be? Presumably, the total consequences of any action ramify indefinitely in space and time, far beyond what any of us can foresee. So if our obligation to intervene depends on how the total consequences of our intervention happen to shake out, then—contrary to premise (2)—we ought to admit that we're *clueless* about whether we're obligated to intervene.[10]

Howard-Snyder then argues that non-consequentialist theories, on the other hand, falsify premise (1) of the objection, because they imply that we *shouldn't* be in doubt about our obligation to intervene in Ashley's case, even if we acknowledge that we're clueless about the total consequences of our

[10] I borrow the term "clueless" from Lenman (2000), an article cited favorably by Howard-Snyder (29, n. 20).

intervention.[11] Either way, then, the Moral Skepticism Objection contains a false premise. As Howard-Snyder readily concedes, his discussion doesn't address every possible consequentialist or non-consequentialist theory of moral obligation. Still, he discusses a wide range of them, and he challenges his opponents to specify a moral "theory or principle" on which premises (1) and (2) of the Moral Skepticism Objection both come out true.

3. AGNOSTICISM AND COMMONSENSE MORAL OBLIGATION

While Howard-Snyder's point is worth making in the debate over skeptical theism, in a way his point isn't really news. As I see it, the Moral Skepticism Objection to Agnosticism reflects a worry arising from *commonsense morality*, and therefore the objection reflects the *mixture* of consequentialist and non-consequentialist elements that commonsense morality notoriously contains. Commonsense morality apparently holds that, in general, the consequences of our intervention *do and yet don't* matter to our obligation to intervene: commonsense morality is both consequentialist and non-consequentialist, or neither purely one nor purely the other.

Witness, for example, the judgments elicited from those who ponder the infamous "trolley problem," in which an agent must bring about the death of one innocent person or else allow five innocent people to be killed.[12] The problem has become infamous because the judgments we tend to make reflect the aforementioned mixture of consequentialist and non-consequentialist elements: the consequentialist's solution—sacrificing one to save five—is, we say, sometimes morally permissible, perhaps even required, and sometimes morally wrong. Nor can the philosophers who study the problem agree on a principled rationale for our diverse judgments. Indeed, it's a well-known source of embarrassment in ethics that commonsense morality, being the hodgepodge that it is, supplies counterexamples to every consequentialist or non-consequentialist theory of moral obligation on offer. That's why neither consequentialists nor their opponents can legitimately claim victory in the age-old debate between them.[13]

[11] Howard-Snyder's argument contains details and nuances that my brief summary of it ignores, but not, I think, any details or nuances that block my criticism of it.
[12] The *locus classicus* of the problem is Foot (1967), which stands at the head of a large scholarly and popular literature on it.
[13] Consider this analogy: Arguably, no economic *theory* properly so-called (Marxism, free-market capitalism, you name it) captures the attitudes held by the average adult in the developed world about how to run an economy. No economic theory accommodates the hodgepodge of views we might call "commonsense economics": every theory says something that common sense rejects.

So it shouldn't surprise us if commonsense morality seems to make our obligation to intervene in Ashley's case hinge on the total consequences of our intervention, just as premise (1) of the Moral Skepticism Objection implies, and yet seems *not* to make our obligation hinge on those consequences, just as premise (2) implies. How should we handle this apparent inconsistency? If commonsense morality is in fact self-inconsistent, then *any* theory at all conflicts with it, in which case it's no knock against Agnosticism in particular that it conflicts with commonsense morality. But I think we needn't conclude that commonsense morality is self-inconsistent, and I'll propose a way of resolving the apparent inconsistency, a way that casts doubt on Agnosticism.

I take it as obvious that commonsense morality *does* obligate us to intervene in Ashley's case, particularly if we can intervene at no risk to ourselves. I'll offer a rational reconstruction of this obligation, an explanation of it that gives it a logically consistent basis, but a basis that's incompatible with Agnosticism. I don't make the psychological claim that we actually entertain this rationale when we deliberate about intervening in cases such as Ashley's. On the contrary, in such cases we tend, I think, to act instinctively rather than deliberately and reflectively. Nor need I claim that we explicitly invoke the rationale retrospectively when we reflect on our intervention or nonintervention. I offer it as a rationale that makes the best sense possible of what commonsense morality says is our clear obligation to intervene. If we *were* to go through this reasoning, our thinking would at least make sense.

Our obligation to intervene to prevent[14] the suffering of an individual such as Ashley depends on what we predict will be the *total consequences to that individual* if we intervene or don't intervene. Ordinary language provides evidence that we restrict our focus in this way. For it would be at least odd for us to say that we owed it to Ashley's family or friends to protect her, and still more odd for us to say that we owed it to the universe or to future generations to do so. On the contrary, in circumstances of the kind that Howard-Snyder relates, we say that we owed it to Ashley herself to intervene, or at least that we owed it to her above anyone else.

But at the same time we regard ourselves as obligated to intervene on Ashley's behalf only if we at least implicitly assume that the total consequences for her will be better if we intervene than if we don't. Why do I claim that our obligation depends on this (at least implicit) assumption? Because if we thought that our intervention made, for all we could tell, *no positive difference to her overall welfare*, we could make no sense of our being morally *obligated* to intervene. We might be able to make sense of our being morally *permitted* to intervene, but permission is of course weaker than obligation.

---

[14] Of course, we also think we're obligated to *relieve* suffering in many cases, but that obligation falls under the heading of prevention for the simple reason that to relieve suffering is just to *prevent* further (or worse) suffering.

Ordinary language provides evidence for my claim here as well. Imagine someone who intervenes in Ashley's case and thereby manages to stop what surely seems to be the immediate harm that she would otherwise have suffered. Now imagine that Howard-Snyder's Agnostic tells the intervener that his having acted to protect Ashley produced foreseeable consequences for her that bear no known relation to the total consequences for her: for all any of us can tell, Ashley is *worse-off overall* for his having intervened. How might the intervener reply to the Agnostic? He might well say, to begin with, "I did what any reasonable person would have thought was best for Ashley." But this language—in particular, the term "reasonable"—is the language of someone seeking *exoneration* for what he did, not the language of someone telling us he did his *duty*.[15] We're inclined to say that no one can be *faulted* or *blamed* for intervening if he reasonably thought it would benefit an innocent person; this commonplace attitude underwrites Good Samaritan laws that protect interveners from liability if their intervention ends up causing harm. But one's being blameless for intervening doesn't at all imply that one was obligated to intervene.

Indeed, if we think the intervener ought to have seen beforehand what the Agnostic now tells him—namely, that his intervention produced foreseeable consequences for Ashley that bear no known relation to the total consequences for her—then we may not even *excuse* his conduct on the grounds that he reasonably believed it to be beneficial. For if you accept what Agnosticism says about the haphazard relationship between the consequences for Ashley that you can foresee and the consequences for her that actually obtain, why should you assign any weight at all to the consequences you can foresee? According to Agnosticism, you should regard the foreseeable consequences as no better than a coin-toss in predicting the total consequences of your intervention. Why intervene on the basis of what you can reasonably discern if you think that what you can reasonably discern bears no reliable connection to what's really the case? Indeed, I can imagine an Agnostic being motivated to criticize the intervener along these lines: "You say that you saw some reason to intervene and saw no reason not to. But you should have recognized that your failure to see a reason against intervening has *no probative value*: for all you could tell, your intervention did Ashley much more harm than good."

---

[15] Compare Eleonore Stump's use of "reasonable" here (Stump 1985: 412–13): "God can see into the minds and hearts of human beings and determine what sort and amount of suffering is likely to produce the best results; we cannot . . . Therefore, since all human suffering is *prima facie* evil, and since we do not know with any high degree of probability how much (if any) of it is likely to result in good for any particular sufferer on any particular occasion, it is reasonable for us to eliminate the suffering as much as we can." This passage fails to explain why we're obligated to eliminate suffering; at most it explains why we're morally *permitted* to (try to) eliminate suffering even if we think that God might be allowing that very suffering in order to benefit the sufferer.

Alternatively, the intervener might reply to the Agnostic this way: "From what you've told me, I now see that by intervening I took a shot in the dark, since the consequences for Ashley that I could foresee don't at all predict the overall consequences for her. But it was a shot I had to take." Unlike "reasonable," the language "had to take" does suggest obligation, but it's odd language for the intervener to use here: why "had"? Normally, when we think we *had* to take a shot in the dark it's because we think that taking a shot, while perhaps unlikely to succeed, offered us our *best chance* at success. But the Agnostic objects to thinking this way in Ashley's case. According to Agnosticism, we have no reason to think that our intervention, our taking a shot in the dark because it *seems* to offer us our best chance to benefit Ashley overall, is *in fact* how it seems to us. For it's no less probable, given what we know, that our *not* intervening offers us our best chance to benefit her overall.

Most likely of all, however, the intervener will reply to the Agnostic in something like this way: "It's absurd to say that I only *guessed* that I'd help Ashley overall if I prevented what looked to be an imminent assault on her. You say that the consequences for Ashley of my intervention that I could foresee don't reliably indicate the overall consequences for her. You say that, for all I can tell, I made her worse off overall by intervening. But that's crazy. Of course she's better off overall because I intervened. Or at the very least she's *probably* better off overall." I think a response along those lines makes the best sense of his—and our—belief that he was obligated to intervene. But it's a response that Agnosticism must reject.

On my reconstruction of it, then, commonsense morality accepts premise (2) of the Moral Skepticism Objection, because we know we ought to intervene. But it also accepts premise (1). For Agnosticism tells us we had better *not* rest our obligation to intervene on the assumption that our intervention will help Ashley overall: we should admit that we have no idea whether it will. Instead, according to Agnosticism, if our obligation to intervene stems at all from the consequences the intervention produces for Ashley, then the only consequences that it makes sense for us to regard as relevant are those that we can foresee.

Surely the consequences for Ashley do matter in *some* way to our obligation to intervene; any plausible position accepts that point, and commonsense morality certainly accepts it. Yet Agnosticism says that the consequences we can foresee are "but a drop in the ocean," as Howard-Snyder puts it (30), a negligible contribution to the total consequences for Ashley. Moreover, all we know about is the drop, and we have no reason to think that the nature of the drop represents the nature of the ocean. If we operated with that Agnostic outlook, I can't see how we would regard ourselves as obligated to add our drop to the ocean—obligated to make that negligible contribution—rather than merely allowed to add it.[16] Given what Agnosticism sees as the haphazard relation between the overall consequences and the vanishingly small fraction that we can foresee, it makes no sense to take those we can foresee *seriously* enough to ground our obligation on them. Agnostics might reply that "we have some evidence that Ashley will benefit if we intervene and none that she'll benefit if we don't intervene. So, given that we ought to follow our evidence, we ought to intervene."[17] But, again, why are we *obligated* to follow our evidence if we accept the Agnostic claim that our evidence is no better than a coin-toss in predicting whether our intervention will benefit Ashley in the way that really matters, i.e., overall? That's why I've portrayed commonsense morality as confidently assuming that our intervention *will* benefit her overall.

Agnostics may dismiss commonsense morality's confident assumption as epistemically unwarranted, but they face the challenge of explaining our obligation to intervene in way that doesn't have us making the assumption. Bear in mind, too, that the scope of the assumption is restricted to the overall consequences of our intervention for Ashley in particular. Because we restrict our focus to the overall consequences for her, we presumably deserve to be *more* confident than we would had our focus included not just Ashley but all the morally significant beings ever affected by our intervention. Nevertheless, I can't see that greater degree of confidence making any difference from the Agnostic's perspective: Agnosticism still says that we can do no better than guess that our intervention will benefit Ashley herself overall. For that reason, I've argued, Agnostics *don't* leave commonsense morality just as they found it.

In sum, I've responded to Agnosticism on behalf of commonsense morality in roughly the way G. E. Moore responds to external-world skepticism on behalf of commonsense knowledge. Commonsense morality tells us we should be confident that we're obligated to intervene in Ashley's case. But commonsense morality also recognizes that we *shouldn't* be confident of that obligation if we think that Agnosticism is true—if we think that, for all we know, we'll do Ashley much more harm than good by intervening. So we shouldn't think that Agnosticism is true. Moore notoriously dismisses the external-world skeptic's conclusion: "You might as well suggest that I do not know that I am now standing up and talking—that perhaps after all I'm not, and that it's not quite certain that I am!" (Moore 1959: 146). I'm suggesting that commonsense morality likewise dismisses the Agnostic's claim that, for all we know, we'll do Ashley much more harm than good if we intervene on her behalf.

---

[16] As David Anderson remarked in conversation, when Agnosticism tells us to intervene (or not) on the basis of foreseeable consequences despite their bearing no known relation to total consequences, it seems to be telling us "how to keep our noses clean," how to avoid being blameworthy for intervening. Again, however, we can intervene blamelessly without being obligated to intervene.

[17] An anonymous reviewer offered this reply.

4. ADDING THEISM TO AGNOSTICISM

Howard-Snyder argues (42–5) that the Moral Skepticism Objection proves no more effective against skeptical theism—i.e., no more effective against the conjunction of Agnosticism and theism—than against Agnosticism alone. He recognizes that skeptical theism may at least *appear* more vulnerable to the Moral Skepticism Objection, for skeptical theists, unlike non-theistic Agnostics, believe that

> there *really is* some reason that justifies God's non-intervention in Ashley's case, … a reason that God actively used to permit Ashley's suffering, so to speak, and if we have no idea at all what it is, then, for all we can tell, there is a reason for *us* not to intervene.… [43]

But Howard-Snyder replies that here, as elsewhere, we shouldn't trust the appearances. For two reasons, he says, skeptical theism is in fact no more vulnerable to the objection than Agnosticism is.

One of those reasons is his earlier claim that neither consequentialist nor non-consequentialist theories of moral obligation make both premises of the Moral Skepticism Objection come out true, whether or not we include theism in the mix. I conceded that claim and offered in reply a reconstruction of our commonsense moral obligation to intervene in Ashley's case on which we *take for granted* that our intervention will do her more overall good than harm. I don't claim to have provided anything that deserves to be called "a theory of moral obligation," only a reconstruction of our ordinary moral attitude. I have nothing to add here to that earlier discussion.

Howard-Snyder's other reason is that skeptical theists—theists who accept Agnosticism—can "reasonably think God has instructed humankind to prevent suffering in general and that God permits a lot of it precisely because he intends for us to try to prevent it" (43–4). This divine instruction allegedly overcomes any ambivalence about intervening that skeptical theists might otherwise feel. Elsewhere I've criticized at length the notion that skeptical theists can rely on God's commands for moral guidance, and I won't repeat all of those criticisms here.[18] But I do want to raise three objections to Howard-Snyder's claim that skeptical theists can "reasonably think God has instructed humankind to prevent suffering in general and that God permits a lot of it precisely because he intends for us to try to prevent it."

First, even if skeptical theists can reasonably conclude that God *has* commanded us to prevent suffering in general (a command, by the way, that's hard to find in the monotheistic scriptures), what does such a command mean?

---

[18] See Maitzen (2007), which Howard-Snyder cites in a footnote to his claim about God's instructions to humankind (44 n. 47) without indicating that I dispute his claim. In fact, because the footnote simply reads "Cp. Maitzen 2007," it may give readers the misimpression that I *concur* with his claim.

Presumably it doesn't mean, for instance, that we should prevent all painful childhood vaccinations, for we justifiedly believe that vaccinations *benefit* children overall despite the fact that needles can really hurt when you're a kid. It must mean, instead, that we should prevent a child's suffering *unless* we justifiedly believe that permitting the suffering will benefit the child overall. But skeptical theists say that we should never regard ourselves as justified in the belief that what we do will benefit the child *overall*: to regard ourselves as justified in that belief is to presume insight into the total consequences of our action—insight that Agnostics, including skeptical theists, say we have no right to presume. Skeptical theism, therefore, denies us the epistemic self-regard we need to *apply* the command to prevent suffering in general.

My two remaining objections concern the familiar-enough suggestion "that God permits a lot of [suffering] precisely because he intends for us to try to prevent it." First, and in the present context ironically, it doesn't apply to Ashley's suffering. According to newspaper accounts, no human agent was realistically in a position to prevent the escapee's rape and murder of Ashley. The escapee simply failed to return to his halfway house after being allowed out earlier in the day for a routine shift at his job; the five young children Ashley was babysitting were all asleep when the crime occurred. Her case is of course not unusual in this regard. Much suffering occurs in the presence of only a perpetrator and a victim, with no third human agent in a position to prevent anything.

Second, I find it incredible that a being who merits the label "perfect" could permit, or even risk, a child's horrible suffering precisely so that *we* can try to prevent it from occurring or from continuing. Indeed, no being who deserves to be called even "decent" could do that. Any human agent who acted that way would have to be depraved or deranged. Such treatment of a child can only be regarded as morally intolerable exploitation, even if it's exploitation on the part of the child's creator.[19] Any being that exploits innocent children thereby fails to merit the description "perfect" or the title of God. It follows, then, that God never risks, let alone permits, a child's horrible suffering *in order* to give us a chance to intervene.[20]

More generally, because exploiting children by its very nature implies a defect in the power, knowledge, or goodness of the exploiter, no perfect being can possibly exploit children for *any* reason. Therefore, no perfect God can possibly permit a child to endure suffering (presumably undeserved and

[19] For defense of this claim, see Maitzen (2009b) and (2010b).
[20] In correspondence, David Anderson described an "Open Notion of Providence" on which "God freely abdicates control over ... rational human agents" such as the escapee, thereby permitting the escapee to rape and kill Ashley. It's a commonplace that some abdications of control are immoral abdications of responsibility. God acts immorally if he abdicates responsibility for preventing Ashley's suffering so that (somehow) *we* become responsible for trying to prevent it.

unwanted) except as a consequence of something that's necessary for, or optimal for securing, the child's *own* greater good.[21] To apply the point to Ashley's suffering in particular, no perfect God can possibly permit Ashley's suffering unless as a consequence of something necessary for, or optimal for securing, Ashley's greater good. Otherwise, God would be exploiting Ashley for some ulterior purpose. But if God exists then God *did* permit it, or at any rate Agnosticism can't tell us to be in doubt about whether God did, for that would commit Agnostics to a degree of skepticism Howard-Snyder seems concerned to avoid. So it must have been for her own good, all things considered.

In that case, contrary to Howard-Snyder, Agnosticism isn't "at home" (42) with theism. If we believe theism, we should believe that Ashley's suffering was a consequence of something necessary or optimal for her own net benefit, whereas if we're Agnostics we should be in doubt about whether it was. Furthermore, if we believe that Ashley's suffering was a consequence of something necessary or optimal for her own net benefit, then we should be (at least) in doubt about whether we would have been obligated to *prevent* her suffering had we been able to. For if we believe that a vaccination is necessary or optimal for a child's benefit, all things considered (the pain and risks of the vaccination included), then we should be (at least) in doubt about whether we ought to prevent it even though it hurts. That's an understatement, of course: in such circumstances we believe we have no obligation to prevent the vaccination and, if anything, some obligation to bring it about. Recall that Howard-Snyder aims to show that skeptical theism—the conjunction of theism and Agnosticism—should make us no more doubtful about our obligation to intervene in Ashley's case than we are independently of it. Commonsense morality, I argued earlier, leaves us in no doubt about that obligation. Skeptical theism leaves us in serious doubt about it, or worse.

As the vaccination analogy shows, we regard ourselves as obligated to prevent suffering by a child only if we discount (or dismiss altogether, or confidently regard as unlikely) the possibility that the child will be better off if we *don't* prevent it. Nothing in our experience suggests that children benefit *in general* if allowed to suffer, or at least nothing in our experience suggests that in general we can't tell *when* they benefit if allowed to suffer. I've argued that Agnosticism and skeptical theism turn all of that on its head. Agnosticism tells us we *shouldn't* think we can tell when a child will benefit overall if allowed to

---

[21] To be clear, I intend this principle as a constraint on God's permission of such suffering in any possible world, regardless of *our* actions in that world. In Maitzen (2009b), (2010a), and (2010b), I defend the principle against objections that it may now occur to the reader to raise. I think the principle extends to any case in which God permits undeserved, involuntary human suffering, but it's clearest in the case of children because of their (absolute or comparative) lack of autonomy. Christian philosopher Eleonore Stump has long endorsed a principle of this sort; see, e.g., Stump (1985), (1990), (2010).

suffer. Skeptical theism, because it adds theism to Agnosticism, goes further: it gives us reason to think that a child *must* be better off, or at least no worse off, if allowed to suffer. If, despite my argument, that last claim strikes you as too strong to be plausible, the following comparative claim is weaker and hence more plausible: the *worse* a child's suffering, the *more reason* theism gives us for thinking that the suffering must be a consequence of something necessary or optimal for the child's own good, and hence the less reason theism gives us to prevent the suffering. We ought to prevent mild suffering first, extreme suffering later. From the perspective of commonsense morality, that weaker claim is trouble enough.

One last point in closing. Howard-Snyder argues that his rebuttal of the Moral Skepticism Objection shows that Agnosticism comports just as well with naturalism as it does with theism (43). But one reason to think it doesn't is this: theism asserts, while naturalism denies, the possibility that we'll experience goods or evils in an afterlife that lasts forever. According to naturalism, all the goods and evils Ashley will ever experience came to an end with her natural death. Clearly, then, if naturalism is true we have a more reliable grasp of those goods and evils, and of what it takes to achieve the former and avoid the latter, than we do if Ashley's experience of goods and evils continues *post mortem*. Our judgment that intervening to prevent Ashley's rape and murder is good for her overall is therefore also more reliable if naturalism is true than if theism is true. I've argued that our commonsense moral obligation to intervene hinges on that judgment, and so I count this as another reason to regard commonsense morality as more at home with naturalism than with Agnosticism, theism, or their combination.

21

Agnosticism, the Moral Skepticism Objection, and Commonsense Morality

Daniel Howard-Snyder

Many arguments from evil for atheism rely on something like the following line of thought:

> *The Inference.* On sustained reflection, we don't see how any reason we know of would justify God in permitting all the evil in the world; therefore, there probably is no such reason.

Some critics of the Inference insist that *even if* the premise is true and *even if* we lack evidential and non-evidential warrant for theism, we should not draw the Inference. You might think of these critics as "agnostics about the Inference," as I have described them elsewhere.[1] You ask them to set aside whatever might be said in favor of theism and then put a question to them: how likely is it that there is no reason that would justify God in permitting all the evil in the world given that we can't see how any reason we know of would do the trick? "Beats me," they reply; "I'm in no position to tell."

There are different versions of agnosticism about the Inference. The one I had in mind in my (2009)—which I called *Agnosticism* with a capital "A"— affirms among other relevantly similar theses that

> *Agnostic Thesis 1* (AT1). We should be in doubt about whether the goods we know of constitute a representative sample of all the goods there are.

The *Agnostic*—with a capital "A"—continues: given AT1 (and, for ease of exposition, let's set aside the relevantly similar theses), we should be in doubt about whether some good we don't know of figures in a reason that would justify

---

[1] Howard-Snyder (2009: 18).

God. But if we should be in doubt about that, then we should be in doubt about whether there is a reason that would justify God. And if we should be in doubt about that, we should *not* infer that there is no such reason, *even if* we don't see how any reason would justify God and *even if* we lack evidential and non-evidential warrant for theism. To do otherwise exhibits an unseemly lack of intellectual humility.

One objection to Agnosticism is *the Moral Skepticism Objection*—or *the Objection*, for short—a simple version of which goes like this. Let *Ashley's suffering* name the evil done to twelve-year-old Ashley Jones and what she suffered and lost in Stanwood, Washington, September 21, 1997, who while babysitting her neighbor's kids, was raped and bludgeoned to death by an escapee from a local juvenile detention center. Suppose we could have easily intervened to prevent Ashley's suffering without any cost to ourselves. In that case, it would be absurd to suppose that we should be in doubt about whether we should have intervened. *Obviously* we should have intervened. Agnosticism, however, implies otherwise. It tells us that since we should be in doubt about whether the goods we know of constitute a representative sample of all the goods there are, we should be in doubt about whether there is a reason that would justify God's nonintervention. But if that's right, then so is this: since we should be in doubt about whether the goods we know of constitute a representative sample of all the goods there are, we should also be in doubt about whether there is a reason that would justify *our* nonintervention, in which case we should be in doubt about whether *we* should have intervened. So Agnosticism implies that we should be in doubt about whether we should have intervened. But that's absurd. Obviously we should have intervened. So Agnosticism is false.

It will prove useful to summarize the main argument of the Objection:

1. If Agnosticism is true, then we should be in doubt about whether we should have intervened to prevent Ashley's suffering (if we could have).

2. We should not be in doubt about whether we should have intervened.

3. So, Agnosticism is false.

I suspect that the Objection fails. Stephen Maitzen thinks otherwise. In what follows, I will assess his defense of the Objection after I summarize my reasons for suspicion. Before I proceed, though, let me clarify some things about Agnosticism.

First, Agnosticism is not skeptical theism. It is consistent with atheism, naturalism in particular. Second, when the Agnostic says that we should be *in* doubt about something, she does not mean that we should doubt *that* it is so. For one to be *in* doubt about something is for one neither to believe nor disbelieve it as a result of one's grounds for it seeming to be roughly on a par with one's grounds for its denial. If one doubts *that* something is so, one is at least strongly inclined to disbelieve it. Being in doubt lacks that implication.

Third preliminary: according to Maitzen,

> If we believe theism, we should believe that Ashley's suffering was a consequence of something necessary or optimal for her own net benefit, whereas if we're Agnostics we should be in doubt about whether it was.[2]

This is false, and not just because theism does not entail that "Ashley's suffering was a consequence of something necessary or optimal for her own net benefit."[3] For even if it did entail that, it is not true that "if we're Agnostics we should be in doubt about whether it was." That's because of the "even if" clauses that define Agnosticism. Here's how they work. Suppose you're a theist who thinks your warrant for theism swamps that for atheism, so much so that you're virtually certain there's a God, and suppose you think that theism entails that "Ashley's suffering was a consequence of something necessary or optimal for her own net benefit." Suppose further that you take yourself to see how "Ashley's suffering was a consequence of something necessary or optimal for her own net benefit." In that case, you'll be apt to infer that we should *not* be in doubt about whether it was. Still, you might well put yourself in the shoes of those who disagree with your rosy assessment of theism and theodicy and reflect on what we should think from their perspective; and you might express the conclusion of your reflections as follows: "*even if* we don't see how any reason would justify God and *even if* there is no evidence and non-evidential warrant for God's existence, we should not infer that there is no such reason."[4] That's how an Agnostic can consistently be a theist while not being in doubt about whether "Ashley's suffering was a consequence of something necessary or optimal for her own net benefit," contrary to what Maitzen states.

Unlike the Agnostic I have just represented, in what follows the Agnostic I will represent holds that the premise of the Inference really is true, that we really don't see how any reason we know of would justify God in permitting all the evil in the world.

Fourth, when the Agnostic says that we don't see how any reason we know of would justify God in permitting all the evil in the world, she means that we don't see how any reason we know of would *fully* justify God in permitting *all* of it. This is compatible with her seeing how some reason we know of would fully justify God in permitting *some* of it, perhaps even a great deal of it; and

[2] Maitzen (This volume: 291).

[3] At the very best, all that Maitzen can properly claim here (and I don't mean to suggest that it *is* proper) is that theism entails that it is *God's permission of* Ashley's suffering, *or something comparably bad*, which is a consequence of something necessary or optimal for her own net benefit. Ashley's suffering *itself* need not be such a consequence. See Rowe (1979) and Swinburne (1998) for guidance on how to express the relevant relations between "something necessary or optimal for her own net benefit" and her suffering.

[4] Maitzen (2009b: 18), his emphasis.

it is compatible with her seeing how some reason we know of would *partially* justify God in permitting all of it.

Fifth and final preliminary: Maitzen says that I aim

> to rebut the objection by rebutting it as an objection to the skeptical part of skeptical theism, which part he [that is, me, Dan Howard-Snyder] labels "Agnosticism," a label he intentionally capitalizes, presumably in order to distinguish this position from others more commonly called "agnosticism."[5]

This is mistaken. As I said in my (2009), Agnosticism is a version of agnosticism *about the Inference*.[6] I did not use a capital "A" in order to distinguish Agnosticism from other positions more commonly called "agnosticism." I used a capital "A" to give it pride of place among other versions of agnosticism about the Inference. (Think Alston, Bergmann, Rea, Wykstra etc.) Thus, Agnosticism is not "the skeptical part of skeptical theism"; it is false that "in all essential respects Agnosticism just *is* the skeptical part of skeptical theism"; it is not true that "[s]keptical theism adds theism to Agnosticism."[7]

To illustrate the difference between Agnosticism and other versions of agnosticism about the Inference, and to underscore the importance it can make, consider a familiar variation on the Inference:

> The Inference*. No good we know of would justify God in permitting all the evil in the world; therefore, probably no good would do so.[8]

Now recall the agnostic part, or a part of the agnostic part, of Michael Bergmann's agnosticism:

> ST1.   We have no good reason for thinking that the possible goods we know of are representative of the possible goods there are.[9]

ST1 targets the Inference* via (something at least equivalent to)

> Bergmann's Specific Principle. We should believe that, probably, no good would justify God in permitting all the evil in the world on the basis of no good we know of would do so *only if* we have good reason for thinking

[5] Maitzen (This volume: 281).

[6] "Some critics, however, insist that even if the premise is true and even if there isn't better evidence or non-evidential warrant for God's existence, we should not infer that there is no justifying reason. These are the agnostics about the Inference ... There are different versions of agnosticism about the Inference. The one I have in mind—henceforth *Agnosticism* with a capital *A*—affirms. . ." (Howard-Snyder 2009: 17–18).

[7] Maitzen (This volume: 281).

[8] Cf. Rowe (1996: 263). In what follows in the text, I will be highlighting the difference between Bergmann's approach and the Agnostic's approach to the Inference*. Neither approach, however, concedes the premise of the Inference*. See Bergmann (2001: 294 n. 9), Howard-Snyder (1996a: 308 n.13), and Howard-Snyder (2009: 27–8). See also Alston (1996a: 325–16).

[9] Bergmann (2001: 279).

that the possible goods we know of are representative of the possible goods there are.

I lose sleep over Bergmann's Specific Principle. For consider the following question: what makes it the case that *no good we know of would justify God* is a truth-conducive basis for believing that *no good would justify God*? Answer: the possible goods we know of are representative of the possible goods there are. In effect, then, Bergmann's Specific Principle tells us to believe that a population has a certain property on the basis of a sample uniformly possessing it only if we have good reason to think that the latter is a truth-conducive basis for believing the former. Since there's nothing special about this belief, its epistemic status, and the basis for it, it appears that, if we affirm Bergmann's Specific Principle, we'll also have to affirm

> Bergmann's General Principle. We should believe something on the basis of something else *only if* we have good reason for thinking that the latter is a truth-conducive basis for believing the former.

Bergmann's General Principle has notoriously undesirable epistemic consequences. That's one reason why I worry about joining him in his approach to the Inference.

(I should add that Bergmann nowhere endorses the principles I have named after him. I suspect that he might respond to my worry in something like the following way: restrict the application of the General Principle to occasions on which we harbor some doubt about whether the basis of our belief is truth-conducive, and restrict the application of the Specific Principle in the same way. So restricted, I'd sleep much better—although I sometimes stay awake over ST1 itself. I mean, if we have a large enough sample that over a long period of time remains *uniformly* thus-and-so, doesn't that give us *some* reason to think that the whole population is thus-and-so, just a tiny little bit of reason? If so, then, contrary to ST1, it's not true that we have *no* reason to think that the possible goods we know of are representative of the possible goods there are.)

Now contrast Bergmann's approach with the Agnostic's approach. According to the Agnostic,

> AT1. We should be in doubt about whether the goods we know of constitute a representative sample of all the goods there are.

AT1 targets the Inference* via (something at least equivalent to)

> The Agnostic's Specific Principle. We should believe that, probably, no good would justify God in permitting all the evil in the world on the basis of no good we know of would do so *only if* it is not the case that we should be in doubt about whether the possible goods we know of are representative of the possible goods there are.

For reasons like those mentioned above, it appears that, if we affirm the Agnostic's Specific Principle, we'll also have to affirm

> The Agnostic's General Principle. We should believe something on the basis of something else *only if* it is not the case that we should be in doubt about whether the latter is a truth-conducive basis for believing the former.

None of the notoriously undesirable epistemic consequences of Bergmann's General Principle are consequences of the Agnostic's General Principle (and nothing similar to the concern I raised for ST1 itself can be raised for AT1 itself). Indeed, the Agnostic's General Principle seems quite sensible. Upshot: Agnosticism, with a capital "A," differs importantly from some other versions of agnosticism about the Inference. Moreover, it fares somewhat better than them.

I now turn to a summary of my assessment of the Objection; my reasons for suspicion about it.

I claimed that our assessment of the Objection should reflect the epistemic implications of our moral theories or principles, which come in two types: (i) those that posit right- and wrong-making features of an act that should leave us in doubt about its moral status and (ii) those that posit right- and wrong-making features of an act that should not leave us in doubt about its moral status. Any theory or principle of the first type is an instance of *Moral Inaccessibilism*; any theory or principle of the second type is an instance of *Moral Accessibilism*. If we endorse an instance of Inaccessibilism, then, prior to our assessment of the Objection, we should be prepared to deny premise (2), while if we endorse an instance of Accessibilism, then, prior to our assessment of the Objection, we should be primed to deny premise (1). Either way, the epistemic implications of our moral theories or principles imply that the Objection is unsound.

To illustrate how a moral theory or principle might prepare us to deny premise (2), I stated three theories or principles that take the total consequences of an act *very, very* seriously, and I argued that if any of them is correct, we should be in doubt about whether we should have intervened to prevent Ashley's suffering (if we could have). One of them was

> Objective Maximizing Act Consequentialism (OMAC). An agent's act is permissible solely in virtue of the fact that its total consequences are no overall worse than those of any option open to him; otherwise, it is impermissible.

I have in mind a concept of "consequence" that implies what many of my consequentialist friends say, namely that what you do among the options open to you will have ramifications until the end of time and *all* of them are morally relevant.[10] So understood, OMAC implies that we should be in doubt about

---

[10] Cf. Elinor Mason: "consequentialism demands that we make decisions that have as their justification *the whole future*" (2004: 317, emphasis added).

whether we should have intervened. For we are in no position to tell whether the unforeseeable consequences of intervention are better than nonintervention, and the unforeseeable consequences swamp the foreseeable ones; thus, we should be in doubt about whether the total consequences of our intervening are overall worse than our not intervening. In that case, we should be in doubt about whether we should have intervened and, prior to assessing the Objection, we should be prepared to deny premise (2)—*if we endorse OMAC.*

To underscore how darkness envelops us on this score, I noted how much of our behavior has massive and inscrutable causal ramifications. Killing and engendering, and refraining from killing and engendering, ramify in massive ways because they are directly identity-affecting actions. They directly "make a difference to the identities of future persons [that is, a difference to what people there will be] and these differences are apt to amplify exponentially down the generations."[11] Moreover, much of our other behavior is indirectly identity-affecting. To illustrate the general point, imagine Richard, a first-century bandit in southern Germany who, while raiding a small village, spares the life of a pregnant woman, Angie. Angie, it turns out, is the great-great- ... [add 97 'great's] ... great-grandmother of Adolf Hitler. By permitting Angie to live, Richard played a role in the occurrence of the Holocaust.[12] Moreover, anyone who refrained from killing any of the intermediate ancestors of Hitler before they engendered the relevant child, or assisted in introducing the parents of each generation, or refrained from introducing them to others, and so on, played a role as well. Which one of these people throughout the generations had any inkling that their behavior would contribute to such a horror? (For sources of massive causal ramification distinct from identity-affecting actions, see Lenman 2000: 347–8.)

As it was with Angie and Richard, so it is with Ashley and us. We are in the dark about the unforeseeable consequences of our intervening and not intervening; moreover, the foreseeable consequences are but a drop in the ocean of the total consequences, and all but that drop is inscrutable to us. So, *if we endorse OMAC*, then when we turn to assess the Objection we should already be in doubt about whether we should have intervened; we should already be prepared to deny premise (2).[13]

To illustrate the point that if we endorse an instance of Accessibilism, then, prior to our assessment of the Objection, we should already be primed to deny premise (1), I stated three moral theories or principles that take the consequences of an act *much, much* less seriously than OMAC and I argued that if any of them is correct, then we should be primed to deny that Agnosticism implies that we should be in doubt about whether we should prevent Ashley's suffering (if we could have). One of them was

---

[11] Lenman (2000: 346).   [12] Lenman (2000: 344–6).
[13] See Howard-Snyder (2009: 30–9) for my replies to objections to this argument.

Requirement R$_s$. Intervene to prevent horrific evil you can prevent, unless you believe there is better reason for you not to intervene.

My argument for concluding that, given R$_s$, Agnosticism does not imply that we should be in doubt about whether we should prevent Ashley's suffering was roughly this: given R$_s$, the presumption of intervention can be overridden only by *our believing* there is better reason for us not to intervene, and our not believing there is better reason for us to intervene is compatible with *someone else* believing there is better reason for them not to intervene. Thus, it might well be the case that we should be in doubt about whether there is some reason we don't know of that would justify someone else's permitting it, e.g. God's, even though we should not be in doubt about whether we should prevent it.

After saying a few words about how my suspicions about the Objection were unaffected by whether we assumed theism or naturalism to be true, and after arguing that the reasons motivating those suspicions undermined Almeida and Oppy's variants on (the simple version of) the Objection, I invited those who held moral theories or principles other than the six I had discussed to do two things:

> First, explain how it is that, on your theory or principles, we should not be in doubt about whether we should intervene to prevent Ashley's suffering. When you give your explanation, be sure to take into account the fact that most of what we do is either directly or indirectly identity-affecting, and thus that most of what we do has massive causal ramifications. If you deny this fact, explain why. If you don't deny it, explain how it is that, despite this fact, we should not be in doubt about whether we should intervene, given your theory or principle. If your explanation appeals to expected value, indifference, intuition, virtue, duties, or the tea leaves in your kitchen sink, explain why objections to your explanation have no force.
>
> Second, explain how it is that, given your theory or principles, Agnosticism implies that we should be in doubt about whether we should intervene to prevent Ashley's suffering. And whatever you say on that score, make it plain why it is that your own theory or principles aren't really driving the doubt and Agnosticism is just coming along for the ride.[14]

So how does Maitzen respond to this invitation?
Initially, as follows:

> While Howard-Snyder's point is worth making in the debate over skeptical the-ism, in a way his point isn't really news. As I see it, the Moral Skepticism Objection to Agnosticism reflects a worry arising from *commonsense morality*, and therefore the objection reflects the *mixture* of consequentialist and non-consequentialist elements that commonsense morality notoriously contains. Commonsense morality apparently holds that, in general, the consequences of our intervention *do and yet don't* matter to our obligation to intervene: commonsense morality is

---

[14] Howard-Snyder (2009: 53).

both consequentialist and non-consequentialist, or neither purely one nor purely the other.[15]

What should we make of this?

Suppose we go along with the idea that there is such a thing as commonsense morality. Furthermore, let's suppose that commonsense morality "holds that, in general, the consequences of our intervention *do and yet don't* matter to our obligation to intervene." In that case, we might well ask: why should the Agnostic care about a worry that arises from something obviously false? Maybe we should suppose instead that "commonsense morality is both consequential-ist and non-consequentialist." But what does that mean? According to Maitzen, "theories of moral obligation" divide into "two exhaustive categories: roughly, those that say our obligation to intervene *depends on the total consequences of our intervention*, and those that say it doesn't"; the former he calls "conse-quentialist" and the latter "non-consequentialist."[16] In that case, commonsense morality says both that our obligation to intervene depends on the total con-sequences of our intervention and that it does not. But again: why should the Agnostic care about a worry that arises from something obviously false?

(This is a good place to note another misrepresentation by Maitzen. He says that, in the course of my argument, I distinguish consequentialist and non-consequentialist theories and he represents my argument as relying on that distinction.[17] I drew no such distinction, however; and my argument does not rely on it. I distinguished Accessibilist and Inaccessibilist theories and principles; the line between Accessibilist and Inaccessibilist theories and principles runs orthogonal to the line between non-consequentialist and con-sequentialist theories and principles.[18])

Back to the main thread of discussion: Maitzen sees the contradiction in commonsense morality but, he says, "we needn't conclude that [it] is self-inconsistent" and he "propose[s] a way of resolving the apparent incon-sistency."[19] It isn't clear to me what it is to "resolve" an explicit contradiction, but it is clear to me that Maitzen's "way of resolving" *this* contradiction involves what he calls a "rational reconstruction" of our obligation to intervene in Ashley's case. According to Maitzen, that reconstruction consists of "an expla-nation" that has three features: (i) it constitutes "a logically consistent basis" for our obligation to intervene, (ii) it "makes the best sense possible of what commonsense morality tells us is our clear obligation to intervene," and (iii) it is "incompatible with Agnosticism."[20] Now, I grant that his explanation does

[15] Maitzen (this volume: 284, his emphasis).
[16] Maitzen (This volume: 283).
[17] Maitzen (This volume: 283).
[18] Moreover, I wouldn't draw the latter line the way Maitzen does; I would draw it the way Frances Howard-Snyder draws it in her (1994).
[19] Maitzen (This volume: 285).
[20] Maitzen (This volume: 285).

not contain an explicit contradiction, and so it's an improvement over what he calls "commonsense morality." But I deny that it "makes the best sense possible of what commonsense morality tells us is our clear obligation to intervene." In fact, another explanation much more in keeping with common sense makes much better sense of our obligation; moreover, that other explanation is compatible with Agnosticism.

Let's begin with a simple question: exactly what moral principle governing the prevention of suffering like Ashley's informs Maitzen's explanation of our obligation to intervene? Well, on the one hand, he says that "[s]urely the consequences for Ashley do matter in *some* way to our obligation to intervene."[21] This suggests that our obligation depends on *the consequences* to her. But, on the other hand, he says that our obligation to intervene "depends on what we predict [or "at least implicitly assume"] will be the total consequences to that individual if we intervene or don't intervene."[22] This suggests that it depends on *what we predict or assume*. These are very different suggestions. According to the first, if our not intervening to prevent someone's suffering is better for him overall, we are obligated *not* to intervene, never mind whether we predict or assume that it is overall better for him that we intervene. According to the second, if we predict or assume that it is overall better for him that we intervene, then we are obligated to intervene, never mind whether our not intervening is overall better for him. According to the first, to tell whether we are obligated we must judge alternative futures. According to the second, to tell whether we are obligated we must access our minds. So which does Maitzen intend?

I suspect it's the first. That is, I suspect that, according to Maitzen, common sense tells us that our obligation to prevent suffering depends on the consequences of our intervening or not intervening, but it does not depend on the total consequences for everyone until the end of time. When it comes to what we are obligated to do, the only consequences that matter are those for the individual, e.g. Ashley. Commonsense morality, on Maitzen's view, "restrict[s] our focus to the overall consequences *for her*."[23]

Another question: Maitzen says that our obligation "depends on" the consequences for the individual. But it could depend on the consequences in two ways: solely or just partly. Which is it? He mentions in passing a "risk to ourselves," and he intimates here and elsewhere that the suffering in question is undeserved and involuntary, all of which suggests that we are not obligated to intervene if so doing poses a significant risk to us, or if the suffering is deserved or (under certain conditions) undergone voluntarily.[24] If Maitzen has other things in mind, then, since we don't know what they are, we can't assess whether, on the principle he has in mind, we should be in doubt about

---

[21] Maitzen (This volume: 287, his emphasis).   [22] Maitzen (This volume: 285).
[23] Maitzen (This volume: 288, my emphasis).
[24] Maitzen (This volume: 285, 286) and (2009b: 109).

whether we are obligated to intervene in Ashley's case. The only way forward, therefore, is to suppose he has nothing else in mind.

So in what follows I will take it that the moral principle governing the prevention of suffering like Ashley's that informs Maitzen's explanation is

> Maitzen's Morality. One is obligated to prevent someone's undeserved suffering if and only if the total consequences for him will be better if one intervenes than if one doesn't—unless one can't intervene or there's a significant risk to oneself or he deliberately chooses to endure it.

The main thing to notice about Maitzen's Morality is that it is false, *obviously* false. (1) Suppose there are two people each of whose undeserved and involuntary suffering you can prevent without cost to yourself, but you can't prevent both. Maitzen's Morality implies that you are nevertheless obligated to prevent both. But you aren't. (2) Suppose that you can prevent a stranger's undeserved and involuntary suffering at no cost to yourself, but you can do so only at grave cost to your loved ones. Maitzen's Morality implies that you are still obligated to prevent his suffering. But you aren't. (3) Suppose that you can prevent the undeserved and involuntary suffering of an individual at no cost to yourself, but you can do so only if you fail in your special obligation to preserve the lives of thousands who are under your proper authority. Maitzen's Morality implies that you are nevertheless obligated to prevent his suffering. But you aren't. (4) Suppose that you can prevent someone's undeserved and involuntary suffering at no cost to yourself and you permit it only for the sake of some significantly outweighing good that has nothing to do with him; moreover, suppose that you know that he would choose to endure it if he were to deliberate with all the relevant information. Maitzen's Morality implies that you are still obligated to prevent his suffering. But you aren't. (5) Suppose that you can prevent someone's undeserved and involuntary suffering at no risk to yourself and you can permit it only for the sake of some significantly outweighing good that has nothing to do with him; moreover, suppose that you know that he will be properly compensated for enduring it. Maitzen's Morality implies that you are nevertheless obligated to prevent his suffering. But you aren't. And note that none of these cases requires that you exploit the sufferer or treat him as a mere means, or that you are unfair or unloving or lacking in compassion or empathy.

At this point, we might well pose a familiar question: why should the Agnostic care about a worry that arises from something obviously false?

Maitzen's Morality is not just false. It does not "[make] the best sense possible of what commonsense morality tells us is our clear obligation to intervene" in cases like Ashley's. That's because it restricts our focus in a way common sense does not. It restricts our focus to the individual and oneself. Common sense knows no such bounds. It does not turn a blind eye to others. A much better explanation of our obligation to prevent suffering like Ashley's relies on a moral principle that respects commonsense morality's concern for others in addition to the individual and oneself, a principle aptly named

> Commonsense Morality. One is obligated to prevent someone's undeserved suffering if and only if the total consequences for him will be better if one intervenes than if one doesn't—unless one has a sufficiently good reason not to intervene and one permits it for that reason.

I do not claim that Commonsense Morality is true. I only claim that it is much more in keeping with common sense than Maitzen's Morality. Moreover, Commonsense Morality is compatible with Agnosticism. For even if I am in doubt about whether some good I don't know of would figure in a reason that might justify someone else in permitting Ashley's suffering, e.g. God, it does not follow that I thereby have a sufficiently good reason not to intervene; thus, to the extent that I sensibly think that the foreseeable consequences for Ashley reliably indicate the overall consequences for her, I should conclude that I'm obligated to intervene. Consequently, if I believe Commonsense Morality, I should be primed to deny premise (1) of the Objection.

Maitzen denies that the Agnostic can sensibly think of the foreseeable consequences for Ashley as reliably indicating the total consequences for her. Indeed, he even goes so far as to represent Agnosticism *as the view that* the foreseeable consequences for Ashley do not reliably indicate the total consequences for her, *as the view that* the former "bear no known relation" to the latter, *as the view that* there's a "haphazard relation" between the two. In section 3 of his chapter, Maitzen identifies someone as "Howard-Snyder's Agnostic," who "tells the intervener that his having acted to protect Ashley produced foreseeable consequences for her that bear no known relation to the total consequences for her: for all any of us can tell, Ashley is *worse off overall* for his having intervened."[25] Maitzen then gives three replies on behalf of the intervener, the third of which is this:

> Most likely of all, however, the intervener will reply to [Howard-Snyder's] Agnostic in something like this way: "It's absurd to say that I only *guessed* that I'd help Ashley overall if I prevented what looked to be an imminent assault on her. You say that the consequences for Ashley of my intervention that I could foresee don't reliably indicate the overall consequences for her. You say that, for all I can tell, I made her worse off overall by intervening. But that's crazy. Of course she's better off overall because I intervened. Or at the very least she's *probably* better off overall." I think a response along those lines makes the best sense of his—and our—belief that he was obligated to intervene. But it's a response that Agnosticism must reject.[26]

What Maitzen calls Howard-Snyder's Agnostic," however, is not the real Agnostic. Maitzen misrepresents Agnosticism. The real Agnostic asserts that

---

[25] Maitzen (This volume: 286).   [26] Maitzen (This volume: 287).

- we should be in doubt about whether the foreseeable consequences of our intervening and not intervening reliably indicate *the total consequences for everyone until the end of time.*

Maitzen represents her as asserting that

- the foreseeable consequences of our intervening and not intervening do not reliably indicate *the total consequences for Ashley.*

But the real Agnostic said no such thing. She never restricted her focus to "the total consequences for Ashley."[27] Of course, Maitzen might wish to *argue* that the former entails the latter, but I'll consider that argument when I see it. Until then, I see no reason why the Agnostic can't affirm the former while denying the latter.

Interestingly, Maitzen does not argue that the foreseeable consequences of our intervening and not intervening reliably indicate that it's overall best for Ashley that we intervene. Instead, he says that to suppose otherwise is "crazy," and proposes that we properly "*take for granted* that our intervention will do her more overall good than harm."[28] Suppose he's right. Suppose we properly take that for granted. Why can't the Agnostic do the same? How does Agnosticism, *real* Agnosticism, and my defense of it imply that she cannot?

Let's briefly consider the bearing of naturalism and theism in all this. Is there some significant tension between, naturalism or theism, on the one hand, and Agnosticism and my defense of it, on the other? As I have been at pains to point out, to answer this question we must state what moral principles we bring to the task. Maitzen thinks that friends of common sense will bring Maitzen's Morality. I disagree. If common sense offers any moral principle relevant to the prevention of suffering like Ashley's, it is much, *much* closer to Commonsense Morality. So suppose you are a naturalist or a theist who is a friend of common sense and, as such, you endorse Commonsense Morality. Suppose you also accept premise (2) of the Objection. Does your naturalism or theism in conjunction with Commonsense Morality give you any reason to

---

[27] Nearly 20 percent of the sentences in Section 3 of Maitzen (this volume) represent the Agnostic as *asserting* something about the consequences *for Ashley*. At one point, Maitzen writes, quoting me: "Yet Agnosticism says that the consequences we can foresee are 'but a drop in the ocean,' as Howard-Snyder puts it (30), a negligible contribution to *the total consequences for Ashley*" Maitzen (This volume: 287, emphasis added). Here's what he's quoting: "the foreseeable consequences are but a drop in the ocean of *the total consequences*" (Howard-Snyder 2009: 30, emphasis added).This is a good place to point out another misrepresentation by Maitzen. The Agnostic says that *we should be in doubt about whether* the foreseeable consequences reliably indicate the total consequences, and not that the foreseeable consequences *do not* reliably indicate the total consequences. If you think you're in no position to judge whether p, you aren't going to judge that not-p.

[28] Maitzen (This volume: 287 and 289, his emphasis).

accept premise (1)? Not that I can see. For neither naturalism nor theism give you any reason to think that Agnosticism and my defense of it entails that you have sufficiently good reason not to intervene; consequently, neither naturalism nor theism give you any reason to think that Agnosticism and my defense of it entails that you should be in doubt about whether you should intervene.

"But hold on a minute," someone might retort. "Unlike a naturalist, if you're a theist, you will think that there *really is* some morally sufficient reason that justifies God's nonintervention in Ashley's case, a reason that He *actively used* in permitting it. If in addition you don't see how any reason you know of would be sufficient, then, *for all you can tell*, there is a reason that would justify *your* nonintervention in Ashley's case. Consequently, you should be in doubt about whether you are obligated to intervene."

A theist who endorses Commonsense Morality might well reply as follows: "Yes, I think that there really is some morally sufficient reason that justifies God's nonintervention in Ashley's case, one that He actively used in permitting it; and yes, I don't see how any reason I know of would be sufficient; and yes, for all I can tell, there is a reason that would justify my nonintervention in Ashley's case. But it simply doesn't follow that I should be in doubt about whether I am obligated to intervene. Whether that follows depends on what moral principle governs the prevention of suffering like Ashley's. I think Commonsense Morality does. Thus, I think that it follows that I am not obligated to intervene only if the following propositions is true: *if, for all I can tell, there is a reason that would justify my nonintervention, then I have a sufficiently good reason not to intervene*. But that propositions is false. It's being the case that, for all I can tell, there is a reason that would justify my nonintervention is *not* a sufficiently good reason for me not to intervene."[29]

I conclude that if you endorse Commonsense Morality, then, whether you are a naturalist or a theist, you have no reason to dissent from my defense of Agnosticism—at least not by virtue of your naturalism or theism. Of course, there may well be some naturalist or theist who endorses some obviously false moral principles on which my defense of Agnosticism fails. But to repeat: why should the Agnostic care about that?[30]

---

[29] Cf. Howard-Snyder (2009: 43–4), "uninstructed theism."
[30] Thanks to Frances Howard-Snyder for comments on this chapter.

22

Skeptical Theism within Reason[*]

Ted Poston

This world contains inscrutable evils, evils that when we carefully consider them we cannot see why an all-powerful, all-knowing, and perfectly good being would permit them to occur. A popular move is that the existence of inscrutable evils makes it reasonable to believe that there are gratuitous evils, evils that no reason at all justifies God in permitting the evils. This inference is a *noseeum inference*; because we do not see any justifying reason for permitting certain evils, there is not any justifying reason.

Skeptical theism questions the noseeum inference at the heart of the evidential argument from evil. Skeptical theists claim that because the data we possess and our ability to mine the data are both quite limited in comparison with the cognitive powers of a perfect being, we should be skeptical about our ability to limn the possible reasons a perfect being may have for permitting evil. For all we know, there might be goods or evils (and/or entailments between goods, evils, and permissions) we don't know about that justify a perfect being in permitting horrendous evils. Because we are in this skeptical situation, the existence of inscrutable evils does not make it reasonable to believe that there are gratuitous evils.

A powerful criticism of skeptical theism centers on its alleged skeptical implications regarding our knowledge of value and morality. First, some argue that the skeptical theist's skepticism cuts both ways. If it undermines the evidential argument from evil then it also undermines positive arguments for the existence of God.[1] Richard Swinburne rightly stresses the importance of our ability to make reasonable judgments about what kinds of states of affairs are valuable in order to determine what kinds of states of affairs a perfect being

[*] Thanks to Kenny Boyce, Andrew Cling, Nicholas Jones, Kevin Meeker, Bradley Monton, and Philip Swenson for helpful comments on an earlier draft.
[1] Beaudoin (1998).

has reason to bring about.[2] Second, some argue that a skeptical theist's skepticism is inconsistent with knowledge of our moral obligations.[3]

My aim in this chapter is to is argue for the consistency of skeptical theism with a broadly evidentialist approach to the justification of theism. An evidentialist approach to theism requires that we can make reasonable judgments about what kinds of states of affairs a perfect being will bring about. This, in turn, requires that we can make reasonable judgments about the value of some states of affairs. Thus, I will argue for a view which endorses agnosticism about the noseeum inference together with some knowledge of value. I will not discuss the application to moral principles, but the argument that skeptical theism is consistent with knowledge of some values can be parlayed into an argument that skeptical theism is consistent with knowledge of defeasible moral principles. Since, as I argue, skeptical theism doesn't undermine some values, it follows—mutatis mutandis—that skeptical theism does not undermine defeasible moral principles.

The resulting position offers a good contrast to the popular reformed epistemology espoused by many skeptical theists. These theists argue that the belief that there is a perfect being is properly basic and that the main threat to the rationality of this belief is the problem of evil. Consequently, they take the main goal of skeptical theism to undermine the power of evil to defeat theistic belief. Once the threat from the problem of evil is removed, theistic belief may enjoy its status as properly basic. By contrast, I hold that theistic belief is justified only if it is held on the basis of good evidence and that, while the problem of evil is an initial threat to theism, reflection on the kinds of considerations skeptical theists offer shows that the duration, extent, and magnitude of evil should not change one's situation with respect to what one's evidence indicates apropos the proposition that there is a perfect being.

I begin to argue for this evidentialist position by presenting a brief explanation of skeptical theism, focusing on the specific skeptical propositions. In the second section I explain the reasons skeptical theists have for being skeptical about our ability to determine theodical questions.[4] In the third section I explain the role of value considerations in Swinburne's evidentialist approach to theism and I defend the coherence of this approach with the reasons given in the second section. In the final section I examine John Beaudoin's argument that skeptical theism undermines inverse probability arguments for theism.

---

[2] See Swinburne (2004: 112–23).
[3] This argument has received careful attention by Bergmann and Rea (2005), Bergmann (2012), and Howard-Snyder, (2009).
[4] This section relies heavily on Alston's (1991) excellent article.

1. WHAT ARE SKEPTICAL THEISTS
SKEPTICAL ABOUT?

Skeptical theism aims to undermine the inference from inscrutable evils to gratuitous evils by providing reasons for thinking that we should be skeptical about whether this inference is good. Skeptical theism differs from more ordinary forms of skepticism. A normal kind of skepticism calls into question our knowledge about some broadly defined class of beliefs. For instance, there are skeptics about the past, about other minds, about the external world, and about the future. Other forms of skepticism are more local. For example, one might be a skeptic about whether the bird in yonder marsh is a Wilson's Plover. Or, one might be a skeptic about whether the Provost's decision to incentivize online teaching will increase faculty willingness to teach online courses. As I shall be urging, skeptical theism should be understood as a more local kind of skepticism in contrast to a more global skepticism.

Consider, for instance, one way to motivate skeptical theism by way of a more general global skepticism. This kind of skeptical theism assumes skepticism about the future consequences of an action. It then argues along the following lines. A person knows that an action is valuable only if she knows that, on balance, its future consequences are better than any of its competitors. But, since no one knows the future consequences of an act, no one knows that an act is valuable.

Skeptical theists do not argue this way and if they did, it would be a mistake. Rather skeptical theists focus on the specific theodical issue of whether there is a reason that justifies a perfect being in permitting inscrutable evils. Skeptical theists are skeptical about our ability to make reasonable judgments about this proposition, not because of general skeptical arguments about value or morality, but rather because of the difficulties attending this specific proposition.

Occasionally, skeptical theists can sound as if they are endorsing a general value skepticism. Michael Bergmann, for instance, writes, "It just doesn't seem *unlikely* that our understanding of the realm of value falls miserably short of capturing all that is true about that realm."[5] Consider one of Bergmann's skeptical theist theses.

[ST1]   We have no good reason for thinking that the possible goods we know of are representative of the possible goods there are with respect to the property of figuring in a (potentially) God-justifying reason for permitting the evils we see around us.[6]

This is often given in abbreviated form as "[ST1] We have no good reason for thinking that the possible goods we know of are representative of the possible goods there are," which does sound as if there's a general value skepticism

---

[5] Bergmann (2001: 279, emphasis added).   [6] Bergmann (2012: 11–12).

in the neighborhood. I contend, however, that there is a much more natural way to motivate skeptical theism without relying on any principles that raise a general skepticism about value. The key to my solution is to recognize that the inscrutability thesis is ambiguous. The claim that there are evils that we cannot scrutinize a God-justifying reason for permitting is ambiguous between,

> (Inscrutability 1) There are evils that we have surveyed all the reasons we are aware of pertaining to divine permission and we have found them inadequate.
>
> (Inscrutability 2) There are evils that we have surveyed all the reasons we are aware of pertaining to divine permission and we are unable to determine whether they are adequate.

Inscrutability 1 and Inscrutability 2 offer different explanations for our inability to scrutinize God-justifying reasons. Inscrutability 1 holds that the explanation lies in the fact that each of the reasons offered for divine permission *is* inadequate. Inscrutability 2 holds that the explanation lies in the fact that we are *unable to determine* the adequacy of the reasons. In both cases, the evils are inscrutable: we are unable to know whether there's a God-justifying reason for permitting those particular evils. The explanations of this fact differ. We are unable to know either because the reasons we are aware of *are* inadequate or because we *can't determine* whether the reasons we are aware of are inadequate. The following section defends Inscrutability 2 by considering seven skeptical problems pertaining to our ability to determine the adequacy of reasons for divine permission.

2. CONCEIVED DEFENSES AND UNCONCEIVED DEFENSES

A defense is an epistemologically possible story in which God and evil coexist. There are extant defenses that have been formulated and investigated, and there are defenses which have yet to be formulated and investigated. Let us call the first class of defenses *conceived defenses* and the second *unconceived defenses*. Skeptical theism can be motivated by a skepticism about certain details of the conceived defenses.[7] The conceived defenses posit facts for which we are unable to know whether those facts obtain. This inability is principled; in our present epistemic position, many of these facts are not accessible to us. Crucially, these facts do not threaten the truth of either defeasible value claims

---

[7] I gleaned this response from a close reading on Alston's (1991) superb essay. Many of the skeptical problems I formulate below are generalizations of points Alston makes in that essay. The development of Alston's essay I suggest is entirely of my own making. I do not know whether Alston would have approved this way of developing skeptical theism.

or defeasible moral principles. Yet, equally important, our lack of knowledge about these facts prevents us from determining the adequacy of the theodical reasons offered. In the following, I develop and defend these claims. I begin with a list and explanation of skeptical problems, and then I illustrate the problems by examining two representative defenses.

2.1 Skeptical Problems with Conceived Defenses

A defense is a story and stories have details. What makes for a good story is the intricacy of the characters, the goals to be achieved, and the interactions between psychologically compelling characters. A good story often leaves crucial issues to be guessed at or leaves crucial questions unanswered. Likewise, a good defense will leave many issues open and, depending on how the details are filled out, the defense may fall apart. But, as I shall contend, many of the details are such that we are not in a position to determine which way the details should be filled out. Below I offer seven skeptical problems that threaten our ability to scrutinize God-justifying reasons.

First, there is *the complexity problem*. Human beings face significant cognitive limitations in reliably assessing intricate situations. There are limits to the amount of information a person can hold before the mind. A defense posits some good or right that, together with other facts, may justify God in permitting evil. To determine the adequacy of a defense one must fully grasp the good, together with the arguments that it *is* a good, that *would* justify a perfect being, the arguments against that, enough moral theory to understand the relevant permissions and entailments between facts and permissions, and then understand all the relevant facts on the ground. Many of the relevant facts on the ground are such that we should be skeptical about our ability to determine them. But supposing we can settle all these questions, the complexity problem is that we have reason to think that due to the complexity of this issue, we should be skeptical about our ability to reliably judge an intricate situation.

Second, there is *the Cartesian problem*. We have some first-person privileged access to our own mental states. We lack this access to the mental states of others. While we can often know what another person is experiencing, we know little of another person's higher-order mental states apart from testimony. There can be crucial moral differences between two individuals that are not recognizable at the level of behavior. It is only an internal difference that, perhaps, no one else knows about which makes the moral difference.

Trent Dougherty and I have argued that[8] though inferences from behavior might reasonably implicate certain beliefs and desires, they will ordinarily not provide insight into higher-order states such as whether the individual believes

---

[8] The next several paragraphs are from Poston and Dougherty (2008).

his beliefs and desires to be objectionable or desires to have certain beliefs and desires. Yet both one's degrees of confidence and one's higher-order states are surely factors relevant to the assessment of moral character. To illustrate this, consider a contrast between two individuals who exhibit identical actions and have the same coarse-grained mental profile but form a marked contrast with respect to the finer-grained and higher-order considerations.

Brutal Bart

Brutal Bart goes into his former workplace (where he was recently fired), shoots his old boss, takes the petty cash fund, and runs. Bart believes he has a right to the money since he'd worked there for a full year without a raise. He desired to shoot his boss and take the money and believed he could get away with it. He has certitude that his boss forfeited his life when he fired him and no reservations about what he has done.

Reluctant Ralph

Ralph goes into his former workplace (where he was recently fired), shoots his old boss, takes the petty cash fund, and runs. Ralph believes he has a right to the money since he'd worked there for a full year without a raise. He desired to shoot his boss and take the money and believed he could get away with it. However, Ralph is just barely convinced he has a "right" to the money since he sees that his boss had a legitimate grievance with him. In fact, when he thinks about it, he believes his desire to do this is one he should not have and in fact desires not to have this desire. After he has done it, he deeply regrets it, believing it to have been a wicked act and desiring that he could undo his wrong.

This contrast represents the possibility of undetectable mental bases of moral character which provide reason to doubt our ability to make the kinds of judgments necessary to certain defenses. One popular defense is the soul-making defense which appeals to goods of character, and argues that these goods are valuable but only available or considerably more probable on the condition that certain evils exist. One primary objection to this is that if God had soul-making as a goal then the evils people are exposed to make it *less* likely that they develop, for example, courage. Certain evils diminish a person's self rather than developing it. Yet the success of this objection turns on our ability to detect particular kinds of mental states for which we often lack evidence.

A third skeptical problem with conceived defenses is *the prediction problem*. We do not know the future states of a person or how a person will develop over time. Many of the great world religions maintain that there is life after death. If there is, we know very little about how a particular person will respond and develop in this state.[9] But even apart from the possibility of life after death, we

---

[9] For an intriguing possibility see Lewis (2001a).

know little about how a person will change over time. Some defenses, such as the soul-making defense, posit that some evils occur because they are required or probabilistically relevant to valuable traits of character. One objection to this defense is that people do not respond in character-building ways to some evils. But the full defense is permitted to appeal to future states, and we lack significant knowledge about the relevant future states.

A fourth skeptical problem is *the playbook problem*. When watching a football game, we sometimes rightly complain that the wrong play was called. On third and three a strong running team decided to call for a long pass. We complain that they should have called a toss sweep because we know the playbook well enough to know what the relevant options are. But when it comes to figuring out what a perfect being should do instead of what actually occurs, we lack knowledge of which options are metaphysically possible given certain goals. Some object to the free will defense that if God wanted a world with free creatures then he could have done so with significantly less pain and suffering. But this assumes that we know that the relevant options are indeed in the divine playbook. But a divine playbook is a book of complete worlds. It is the book on all the metaphysically possible total states of affairs. It does not follow that a complex state of affairs is metaphysically possible because each of its component states of affairs is metaphysically possible. It may be that any world similar to ours in positive value contains a world with similar or worse evils. Because we don't know the book of worlds, we aren't in a position to fully determine the adequacy of the free will defense.

A fifth skeptical problem that afflicts our ability to determine the success of the conceived defenses is *the deception problem*. Many objections in the problem of evil argue that there is no person-centered reason for permitting evil. A person-centered reason is a reason for permitting an evil that appeals to the good of a person. The person may be the sufferer, the perpetrator, or the onlooker. Many of these objections argue that the evil is unnecessary for some good or not probabilistically relevant for some good. If God wanted Jones to trust in him, he could have achieved this goal in a much less painful manner. But this assumes that Jones would have responded in a desirable way given much less pain. We like to think this is true for us and others, but what justification do we have for this? People often forget past failures and take a rosy-eyed view of human nature. If self-deception is genuine, then it afflicts our ability to properly assess what the evidence indicates with respect to whether there's a God-justifying reason for permitting evil.

The sixth skeptical problem is *the Goldilocks' problem*. We don't know what kind of suffering is just right for the purposes of various goods. We know that sometimes pain is necessary for a good. You cannot run a marathon unless you are willing to suffer. How much suffering is just right for running a marathon? It depends on how much you desire to run a marathon and how much suffering you're willing to endure. Objections to theism from evil often argue that an evil is too horrible for various person-centered goods. A perfect being could have secured those goods with less suffering. But apart from the playbook problem, we face the problem of determining the probabilities of success for each relevant option—goal combination. Suppose God wanted significantly free creatures with true virtue. What's the best way of achieving this goal? The best way is the one for which there's no better way. And to know that there's no better way is to know all the relevant ways and the probabilities of success for each way. But we don't have this knowledge.[10] Because we lack this knowledge, we are not in a position to determine whether the porridge is too hot or too cold.

The last skeptical problem I will mention is *the estimation problem*. Several objections to theism proceed like this. God could have prevented the worst n% of evils, but this evil is among the worst; consequently, there's no God. The claim that a particular evil is among the worst n% of evils can be understood as the worst n% of *actual* evils or the worst n% of *possible* evils. For the objection to go through it is required to be the worst n% of *possible* evils; that an evil is the worst of actual evil is a trivial relational property. One must claim that the worst actual evils are really bad. One way of doing this is that it's in the n% of worst possible evils. But do we know what are among the worst possible evils? Was Hurricane Katrina among the worst possible hurricanes? Arguably, no. Do we know what the worst possible hurricane is? Perhaps, we can imagine one that is much, much worse, but our imagination is significantly constrained by laws of nature.[11] It's epistemically possible that a perfect being has prevented the worst n% of possible horrors.

2.2 Two Examples

Let us look at two defenses to see how the above skeptical problems arise in context. My discussion of these two defenses closely follows William Alston's discussion of skeptical problems afflicting our assessment of these defenses.

2.2.1 *Eleonore Stump's Natural Evil Defense*

Eleonore Stump suggests that the purpose of natural evil may be to fix our wills heavenward. Stump writes,

> Natural evil—the pain of disease, the intermittent and unpredictable destruction of natural disasters, the decay of old age, and the imminence of death—takes away

---

[10] This knowledge doesn't require that we know each and every way. Rather it requires that we know all the relevant ways and know that this way (the purported objector's way) is better.

[11] The energy in hurricanes comes from the heat in the ocean water. When imagining the worst possible hurricane we must canvas all the relevant possibilities; possibilities in which the ocean's temperatures are much much warmer including perhaps worlds in which the boiling point of water is above 100 degrees C.

a person's satisfaction with himself. It tends to humble him, show him his frailty, make him reflect on the transience of temporal goods, and turn his affections toward other-worldly things, away from the things of this world. No amount of moral or natural evil ... can *guarantee* that a man will seek God's help. If it could, the willing it produced would not be free. But evil of this sort is the best hope, ... and maybe the only effective means, for bringing men to such a state.[12]

One can object to Stump's suggestion along multiple dimensions: natural evils are among the worst possible evils, people do not and will not respond effectively to these evils, there are options available to a perfect being that would have been more successful, people do not need these kind of evils to fix our wills heavenward, and this amount of suffering is too much. Each of these objections is undermined by our lack of knowledge. We often do not know how people respond inwardly to instances of natural evil, do not know the future development of persons, do not know what other means are available to a perfect being, and do not know whether our attempts to judge the relative successful of the different options are reliable. In short, we cannot determine whether Stump's suggestion is adequate because it depends on details we are not in a position to assess. Thus, some natural evils are inscrutable in sense 2; there are natural evils that we cannot determine whether Stump's natural evil defense is adequate.[13]

2.2.2 Marilyn Adams's Martyrdom Defense

Marilyn McCord Adams suggests that martyrdom "is an expression of God's righteous love toward the onlooker, the persecutor, and even the martyr himself."[14] Focusing on the benefits of martyrdom to the martyr Adams remarks,

> The threat of martyrdom is a time of testing and judgment. It makes urgent the previously abstract dilemma of whether he loves God more than the temporal goods that are being extracted as a price ... The martyr will have had to face a deeper truth about himself and his relations to God and temporal goods than ever he could in fair weather ... The time of trial is also an opportunity for building a relationship of trust between the martyr and that to which he testified. Whether because we are fallen or by the nature of the case, trusting relationships have to be built up by a history of interactions. If the martyr's loyalty to God is tested, but

---

[12] Stump (1985: 409).

[13] The claim that a defense is adequate runs together two issues. First, whether the defense is adequate to the facts on the ground. Second, whether the defense is morally adequate. This distinction opens up the possibility that a defense can be morally adequate–if the facts are like the defense requires then the defense does offer a morally adequate reason for divine permission–without being factually accurate. My response pushes skepticism about the relevant facts on the ground.

[14] Adams (1986: 257). This discussion is heavily influenced by Alston (1991).

after a struggle he holds onto his allegiance to God and God delivers him (in his own time and way) the relationship is strengthened and deepened.[15]

Adams suggests that other suffering has redemptive potential by extrapolation from martyrdom. Suffering from natural evil, for example, may be an opportunity for the sufferer to face a hard truth about himself: does he love comfort and ease more than he loves God? Moreover, Adams's defense extends to goods to the onlooker. Adams explains,

> For onlookers, the event of martyrdom may function as a prophetic story, the more powerful for being brought to life. The martyr who perseveres to the end presents an inspiring example. Onlookers are invited to see in the martyr the person they ought to be and to be brought to a deeper level of commitment. Alternatively, onlookers may see themselves in the persecutor and be moved to repentance. If the onlooker has ears to hear the martyr's testimony, he may receive God's redemption through it.[16]

Additionally, Adams suggests that martyrdom may be redemptive for the persecutor. She explains,

> First of all, the martyr's sacrifice can be used as an instrument of divine judgment, because it draws the persecutor an external picture of what he is really like—the more innocent the victim, the clearer the focus. . . In attempting to bring reconciliation out of judgment, God may find no more promising vehicle than martyrdom for dealing with the hard-hearted.[17]

The adequacy of each of these suggestions depends on the details of the facts on the ground that we don't know. We don't know a person's inward or future response and the full range of options together with their probabilities.

William Alston extends Adams's remarks on the possible redemptive consequences of martyrdom to the case of Sue. This case concerns the brutal rape and death of a young girl at the hand of her mother's boyfriend. Alston claims that there may be significant goods to the onlookers of Sue's suffering. He explains that even if we cannot see these kinds of benefits, we remain ignorant of the inward responses of people and how these responses may affect future outcomes. Furthermore, Alston contends that we are in a poor position to judge whether God had more effective means to evoke an optimal response among free creatures, many of which may be particularly stubborn. Apart from this knowledge, we are not in a position to make a firm judgment about whether Sue's suffering is gratuitous.[18]

---

[15] Adams (1986: 259).   [16] Adams (1986: 257).   [17] Adams (1986: 258).

[18] Alston (1991: 52). Paul Draper has argued against a similar proposal on the grounds that the connection between suffering and sanctification is merely causal and an omnipotent being has the power to bring sanctification about directly. First, it may not be possible to bring the same individual to sanctification without enduring suffering. Second, the sanctification may not be as valuable without the suffering.

2.3 Conceived Defenses and Skepticism about Value

I have gone on at length to stress that there are multiple reasons for thinking that the conceived defenses face significant skeptical problems. In attempting to answer the specific theodical question of whether there are reasons that justify a perfect being in permitting horrendous evils, we lack relevant data about a person's inward and future response, face complexity far greater than we can handle, suffer the difficulty of determining which conceptual possibilities are genuinely metaphysically possible, face ignorance of the full range of metaphysical possibilities and ignorance about the probabilities of success for genuine options, face concerns about self-deception, and lack the ability to determine the worst possible evils.[19]

These skeptical problems, however, do not claim that we should be skeptical about natural judgments about value. The deception problem, for instance, is an epistemic problem about our ability to reach accurate judgments about ourselves. The Cartesian problem is an epistemic problem about the paucity of information we have concerning the higher-level attitudes of an individual and their future states. This is all compatible with our ordinary, natural judgments about what kinds of things are valuable, and to that extent, it is compatible with thinking that a perfect being will bring about certain kinds of states of affairs and prevent others. If that is correct then there is a solid basis for inverse probability arguments for theism. I expand on this theme below.

3. VALUE CONSIDERATIONS AND THE EXPLANATORY POWER OF THEISM

My aim in this section is to argue that (Inscrutability 2) is consistent with positive evidence for the existence of God. For the purposes of this argument I assume that we understand evidence in terms of probability. One proposition, e, is evidence for another proposition, p, just in case $Pr(p|e) > Pr(p)$. This assumption is not without some motivation; new evidence for p gives us more reason to believe p, which suggests that p is more probable given the new evidence. Furthermore, I assume that the confirmation of a theory is a relational manner depending on the theory's existing competitors. The main advantage of this relational approach of confirmation is that it allows us to ignore the difficulties posed by unconceived theories, difficulties that occur when one requires that confirmation depend on the relation of a theory to

---

[19] Part of this list comes from Alston (1991: 59–60).

its negation. I will thus work with the relative odds form of Bayes's theorem which states

$$\frac{Pr\left(H_1 \mid e\right)}{Pr\left(H_2 \mid e\right)} = \frac{Pr\left(H_1\right)}{Pr\left(H_2\right)} \times \frac{Pr\left(e \mid H_1\right)}{Pr\left(e \mid H_2\right)}$$

I take naturalism to be the main competitor to theism. For the sake of argument, I assume that $\dfrac{Pr\left(theism\right)}{Pr\left(naturalism\right)} \approx 1$, which means that theism (henceforth T) and naturalism (henceforth N) have roughly the same prior. Thus, I shall be concerned to argue that (Inscrutability 2) is consistent with there being some evidence, e, such that $Pr\left(e \mid T\right) > Pr\left(e \mid N\right)$. This judgment requires showing that there's some proposition we have more reason to expect is true given theism than given naturalism. If this judgment is correct then, together with the above assumptions, it follows by the relative odds form of Bayes's theorem that e gives us more reason to think that theism is true than that naturalism is true.

For the sake of this argument, let us take the relevant evidential proposition to be *H: humanly free creatures exist.* Human beings are free creatures of limited knowledge, power, and goodness. To argue that we have more reason to expect H if theism is true than naturalism, I will argue that H realizes some value that a perfect being can reasonably be thought to be concerned to bring about whereas H doesn't have any value for naturalism and naturalism doesn't lead us to expect H. What value might that be? According to Swinburne, the existence of humanly free creatures realizes the values of consciousness and freedom. Consciousness is itself valuable, and the ability to freely act in light of one's beliefs is also valuable.[20] Because a perfect being will bring about the best act if there is one, and will satisfice otherwise, we can expect that a perfect being will seek to realize valuable states of affairs. However, there are many different, incompatible, yet valuable states of affairs. Thus, unless we have some reason of dividing up the space of possibilities in a favorable way it doubtful that one can simply move from the value of H to the judgment that theism predicts H.

Swinburne argues that there is a principled way of dividing up the relevant possibilities.[21] He starts by partitioning substances into inanimate and animate substances. Among the animate substances, he distinguishes between creatures of habit and free creatures, and then among the free beings, there are divine (or perfect) free beings and non-divine (or imperfect) free creatures. These four classes of beings realize values to different degrees. A perfect free being possesses supreme value, whereas the value of an inanimate substance is less than the value of an animate substance. Furthermore, because conscious

---

[20] Swinburne (2004: 118).   [21] Swinburne (2004: 118).

free creatures are more valuable than creatures of habit, we can reconstruct a
scale of value on which the

> V(divine beings) > V(non-divine free creatures) > animate creatures of
> habit) > V(inanimate substances).

This value ranking is supported by natural judgments about the relative values
of consciousness and free choice. If those judgments are accurate then we have
a sound basis for thinking that a divine being has more reason to bring about
animate creatures than merely bringing about inanimate creatures, and more
reason to bring about humanly free creatures than merely a world containing
inanimate substances and creatures of habit. Thus, there's an argument from
theism to a world filled with a plurality of value. A perfect being will bring
about valuable states of affairs to the extent it is consistent with his character.
Thus, $\Pr\left(H|T\right)$ is not very low.

What about the value of $\Pr\left(H|N\right)$? Naturalism doesn't predict the existence
of humanly free creatures.[22] Why? There is nothing about the content of the
naturalist hypothesis that predicts H. Value considerations pertaining to H
play no role whatsoever in naturalism's ability to account for H. According to
naturalism, H is the result of blind processes working over millions of years.
It's very surprising that H would be true given naturalism. Thus the value of
$\Pr\left(H|N\right)$ is very low, much lower than the value of $\Pr\left(H|T\right)$. Consequently, it
follows from the relative odds forms of Bayes's theorem together with our ini-
tial assumptions that $\Pr\left(T|H\right) > \Pr\left(N|H\right)$. We, therefore, have some evidence
for classical theism that is consistent with (Inscrutability 2).[23]

I have argued thus far that *if* our natural value judgments are accurate then
there is good reason to think that the relevant probabilities needed for an
inverse probability argument exist. These skeptical reasons don't undermine
the defeasible claims that consciousness and freedom have value. As such, it
doesn't undermine the claim that a perfect being has a reason to bring about
conscious beings and free beings. However, it does put some pressure on our
ability to assign a very high value to $\Pr\left(H|T\right)$. Given that we cannot see all pos-
sible ends with God's decision to actualize H we are not in a position to claim
that $\Pr\left(H|T\right) \approx 1$. Yet the argument that H is evidence for theism doesn't
require this. It only requires that we are in a position to argue that the relevant
ratio— $\dfrac{\Pr\left(H|T\right)}{\Pr\left(H|N\right)}$ —favors theism. I've argued that this is the case. Given the
immense value of humanly free creatures there is a natural presumption that

---

[22] I set aside the problem of old evidence. We can reason about the explanatory power of a
theory with respect to known facts. Einstein's theory is made probable by the precession of the
perihelion of Mercury even though that fact was already known.

[23] One important caveat about the argument to this point is that I have given no reason for
thinking that theism is more probable on all the evidence than naturalism.

a perfect being can be expected to bring about humanly free creatures. To be sure, whether a perfect being brings about humanly free creatures depends on a very delicate and complicated judgment about overall value. While we may not have firm judgments on just how likely it is that God brings about human persons, it is not unreasonable to think that the existence of human persons is more likely on theism than on naturalism. A skeptical theism which endorses (Inscrutability 2) is not committed to any general value skepticism and as such it is well positioned to argue that there are still considerations with favor theism over naturalism.

Kenny Boyce and Philip Swenson have both objected that my argument at this point is undermined by the same considerations I gave to undermine the evidential force of inscrutable evils.[24] If H is evidence for theism then we must reject the following inscrutability thesis: we have surveyed all the reasons we are aware of pertaining to God actualizing H and we are unable to determine whether they are adequate. If this thesis is true then H isn't evidence for theism. Two points mitigate this challenge. First, the argument that H is evidence for theism assumes that we can make a comparative judgment to the effect that there is more reason for H on theism than on naturalism. As such we do not need a very strong argument for H from theism; rather we only need the comparative claim that theism provides more support for H than naturalism. Second, while there are legitimate skeptical concerns about our ability to justifiably judge that there are gratuitous evils, there are not legitimate skeptical concerns about our ability to justifiably judge that consciousness and freedom have immense value. As such, a perfect being has a reason to bring about H. The question then is one about how much reason a perfect being has. But we needn't wade into these turbulent waters; for given the first point, the primary issue is whether there is *enough* reason to support the comparative claim that there is more support for H from theism than from naturalism.

4. EPISTEMIC PROBABILITY AND BEAUDOIN'S OBJECTION

I've argued that skepticism theism can be defended by arguing for (Inscrutability 2) on the basis of skepticism about details of the conceived defenses. Furthermore, I've argued that this does not undermine some inverse probability arguments for theism. I now consider a recent objection by John Beaudoin. I will argue that my approach sidesteps the issues that Beaudoin raises.

---

[24] Personal conversation.

Beaudoin argues that the combination of skeptical theism and van Inwagen's conception of epistemic probability undermines inverse probability arguments for theism.[25] On van Inwagen's conception of epistemic probability, judgments about the epistemic probability of a proposition require that one can make judgments about the real, objective chance that p is true.[26] In some cases, we are able to make these kinds of judgments—the real, objective chance that a die will land on an even number greater than three. But in other cases, we are not in a position to determine objective chances. Suppose, for example, I have drawn a number from 1 to 100. Refer to that number as n. I then put n black balls in an urn and 100-n white balls in the same urn. What is the probability that a black ball is selected from the urn?[27] Van Inwagen contends that this question lacks an answer.[28] Given the information one has to go on, one cannot make a reasonable judgment about the objective chance that a black ball is chosen. It could be 5, 35, or 90 percent; any answer is just as good as another.

Van Inwagen then applies this account of epistemic probability to the claim the existence of inscrutable evils makes it probable that there are gratuitous evils. Van Inwagen argues that this probabilistic judgment depends on our ability to judge how likely inscrutable evils are on theism. He claims that we are not in a position to estimate the objective chance that a world containing inscrutable evil is a theistic world because we are not in a position to judge the proportion of theistic worlds containing inscrutable evils relative to all the theistic worlds. The reasons here are similar to the ones we considered in Section 2. We don't know crucial matters of detail involved in estimate this proportion.

Beaudoin argues that a consequence of adopting this move is that it undermines the crucial kinds of claims involved in an inverse probability argument for theism. In particular, it would imply that we cannot judge that $\Pr(H|T) > \Pr(H|N)$. Beaudoin reasons that anything the theist appeals to as a good that God may bring about, that good might also realize a disastrous consequence that lies beyond our comprehension in which case God will not bring about that good.[29] Beaudoin is right that we are not in a position to assign $\Pr(H|T)$ a value close to 1. But this does not imply that we cannot judge that there's more reason to think that theism predicts H than naturalism predicts H. For all we know, there are unconceived felicitous consequences to realizing H that lie beyond our powers of discovery. Our evidential situation with unconceived matters is perfectly symmetrical. Thus, the unconceived values wash out. As I've argued the reasons we possess support the claim that there's more reason to expect H given theism than naturalism, and skepticism about the conceived defenses do not undermine that. The upshot of this response is that Beaudoin is wrong to think that it's a consequence of van

---

[25] Beaudoin (1998: 413).   [26] See van Inwagen (1998: chapter 5).
[27] See van Inwagen (1998: 74) for this example.   [28] van Inwagen (1998: 74).
[29] Beaudoin (1998: 413).

Inwagen's conception of probability undermines our justification for thinking that $\Pr(H|T) > \Pr(H|N)$.

5. CONCLUSION

Beaudoin argued that skeptical theists face a dilemma: either evil is evidence against God's existence or considerations of value do not provide evidence for God's existence.[30] I've argued that this is a false dilemma. One need not advance skepticism about value to support skeptical theism. Skeptical theism can be defended by (Inscrutability 2). This has the advantage of leaving intact positive arguments for God's existence from considerations of value. In the end, evidentialism is compatible with skeptical theism.

---

[30] Beaudoin (1998).

Selected Bibliography

Abraham, William J. (2006). *Crossing the Threshold of Divine Revelation* (Grand Rapids: Eerdmans).

Adams, Ernest (1998). *A Primer of Probability Logic* (Stanford: CSLI Publications).

Adams, Marilyn M. (1986). "Redemptive Suffering: A Christian Solution to the Problem of Evil." In *Rationality, Religious Belief, and Moral Commitment* (eds. Robert Audi and William J. Wainwright) (Ithaca: Cornell University Press).

——and Adams, Robert M. (ed.) (1990). *The Problem of Evil* (Oxford: Oxford University Press).

Adams, Robert M. (1985). "Plantinga on the Problem of Evil." In *Alvin Plantinga* (eds. James E. Tomberlin and Peter van Inwagen) (Dordrecht-Holland: D. Reidel Publishing Co), 225–55.

Almeida, Michael and Oppy, Graham (2003). "Sceptical Theism and Evidential Arguments from Evil." *Australasian Journal of Philosophy* 81: 496–516.

Alston, William P. (1991). *Perceiving God: The Epistemology of Religious Experience* (Ithaca: Cornell University Press).

——(1996a). "Some (Temporarily) Final Thoughts on Evidential Arguments from Evil." In *The Evidential Argument from Evil* (ed. Daniel Howard-Snyder) (Bloomington, IN: Indiana University Press), 311–32.

——(1996b). "The Inductive Argument from Evil and the Human Cognitive Condition." In *The Evidential Argument from Evil* (ed. Daniel Howard-Snyder) (Bloomington, IN: Indiana University Press), 97–125.

Anderson, David James (2012). "Skeptical Theism and Value Judgments." *International Journal for Philosophy of Religion* 72(1): 27–39.

Aquinas, Thomas (1954). *De Veritati* (trans. Robert Schmidt) (Chicago: Henry Regnery Co).

Baier, Annette (1995). "Trust and Anti-Trust." In *Moral Prejudices: Essays on Ethics* (Cambridge: Harvard University Press), 95–129.

Barr, James (2006). "Is God a Liar? (Genesis 2-3)—and Related Matters." *Journal of Theological Studies* 57: 1–22.

Barrett, Justin L. (2004). "*Why Would Anyone Believe in God?*" (Lanham: AltaMira Press).

Basham, Lee (2002). "Why God Lied to Me: Salvationist Theism and Justice." *Journal of Religious Ethics* 30: 231–49.

Beaudoin, John (1998). "Evil, the Human Cognitive Condition, and Natural Theology." *Religious Studies* 34: 403–18.

—— (2003). *Catechism of the Catholic Church*, 2nd edn. (New York: Doubleday).

—— (2005). "Skepticism and the Skeptical Theist." *Faith and Philosophy* 22: 42–56.

Bergmann, Michael (2001). "Skeptical Theism and Rowe's New Evidential Argument from Evil." *Noûs* 35: 278–96.

—— (2005). "Defeaters and Higher-Level Requirements." *The Philosophical Quarterly* 55: 419–36.

—— (2006). *Justification without Awareness: A Defense of Epistemic Externalism* (Oxford: Oxford University Press).

—— (2009). "Skeptical Theism and the Problem of Evil." In *The Oxford Handbook to Philosophical Theology* (eds. Thomas Flint and Michael Rea) (New York: Oxford University Press), 374–99.

—— (2012). "Commonsense Skeptical Theism." In *Science, Religion, and Metaphysics: New Essays on the Philosophy of Alvin Plantinga* (eds. Kelly Clark and Michael Rea) (Oxford University Press), 9–30.

—— and Rea, Michael (2005). "In Defence of Sceptical Theism: A Reply to Almeida and Oppy." *Australasian Journal of Philosophy* 83(2): 241–51.

Bok, Sissela (1998). *Lying: Moral Choice in Public and Private Life* (New York: Vintage Books).

Bovens, Luc and Ferreira, José Luis (2010). "Monty Hall drives a wedge between Judy Benjamin and the Sleeping Beauty: a reply to Bovens." *Analysis* 70(3): 473–81.

Boyer, Pascal (2001). *Religion Explained: The Evolutionary Origins of Religious Thought* (New York: Basic Books).

Bradley, Richard (2005). "Radical Probabilism and Bayesian Conditioning." *Philosophy of Science* 72(2): 342–64.

Butler, Joseph (1833). *The Analogy of Religion* (Oxford: Oxford University Press).

Calvin, John (2007). *Calvin's Bible Commentaries: Jeremiah and Lamentations, Part III*, (trans. John King) (Charleston, SC: Forgotten Books).

Caputo, John D. (2010). "Only as Hauntology Is Religion without Religion Possible: A Response to Hart." In *Cross and Khôra: Deconstruction and Christianity in the Work of John D. Caputo* (eds. Marko Zlomislić and Neal DeRoo) (Eugene, OR: Pickwick Publications), 109–17.

Cargile, James (2000). "Skepticism and Possibilities." *Philosophy and Phenomenological Research* 61(1): 157–71.

Carnap, Rudolf (1962). *Logical Foundations of Probability*, 2nd edn. (Chicago: University of Chicago Press).

Chisholm, Robert B. Jr. (1998). "Does God Deceive?" *Bibliotheca Sacra* 155: 11–28.

Christensen, David (2007). "Epistemology of Disagreement: The Good News." *Philosophical Review* 116: 187–218.

Clark, Kelly James and Rea, Michael (2012). *Reason, Metaphysics, and Mind: New Essays on the Philosophy of Alvin Plantinga* (Oxford University Press).

Climacus, John (1982). *The Ladder of Divine Ascent (Classics of Western Spirituality)* (trans. Colm Luibheid and Norman Russell) (Mahwah, NJ: Paulist Press).

Clines, D.J.A. and Gunn, D. M. (1978). "'You Tried to Persuade Me' and 'Violence! Outrage!' in Jeremiah XX 7–8." *Vetus Testamentum* 28: 20–7.

Cohen, Stewart (2010). "Bootstrapping, Defeasible Reasoning, and *A Priori* Justification." *Philosophical Perspectives* 24: 141–59.

Conee, Earl and Feldman, Richard (2008). "Evidence." In *Epistemology: New Essays* (ed. Quentin Smith) (Oxford: Oxford University Press), 83–104.

Coope, Christopher Miles (2001). "Good-Bye to the Problem of Evil, Hello to the Problem of Veracity." *Religious Studies* 37: 373–96.

Crisp, Thomas (2011). "An Evolutionary Objection to the Argument from Evil." In *Evidence and Religious Belief* (eds. Kelly James Clark and Raymond Van Arragon) (Oxford: Oxford University Press).

Cullison, Andrew (2011). "A Defence of the No-minimum Response to the Problem of Evil." *Religious Studies* 47(1): 121–3.

Darwin, Charles (1958). *The Autobiography of Charles Darwin, 1809-1882* (ed. Nora Barlow) (W. W. Norton & Co).

Descartes, René (1960). *Discourse on Method and Meditations* (trans. Laurence J. Leafleur) (New York: Macmillan).

Dougherty, Trent G. (2008). "Epistemological Considerations Considering Skeptical Theism." *Faith and Philosophy* 25: 172–6.

—— (2011a). "Further Epistemological Considerations Concerning Skeptical Theism." *Faith and Philosophy* 28(3): 332–40.

—— (2011b). "Recent Work on the Problem of Evil." *Analysis* 71(3): 560–73.

—— (2012). "Reconsidering the Parent Analogy: Further Work for Skeptical Theists." *International Journal for Philosophy of Religion* 72(1): 17–25.

—— (2013). "Dealing with Disagreement from the First-Person Perspective: A Probabilist Proposal." In *Disagreement and Skepticism* (ed. Diego E. Machuca) (New York: Routledge), 218–38.

—— (2014) Dougherty, Trent, "Skeptical Theism," *The Stanford Encyclopedia of Philosophy* (Spring 2014 edn.), Edward N. Zalta (ed.), <http://plato.stanford.edu/archives/spr2014/entries/skeptical-theism/>.

—— and McBrayer, Justin P. (2014). *Skeptical Theism: New Essays* (New York: Oxford University Press).

Douven, Igor and Romeijn, Jan-Willem (2011). "A New Resolution of the Judy Benjamin Problem." *Mind* 120(479): 637–70.

Draper, Paul (1989). "Pain and Pleasure: An Evidential Problem for Theists." *Noûs* 23: 331–50. Reprinted in (1996), *The Evidential Argument from Evil* (ed. Daniel Howard-Snyder) (Bloomington, IN: Indiana University Press), 12–29.

—— (1996). "The Skeptical Theist." In *The Evidential Argument from Evil* (ed. Daniel Howard-Snyder) (Bloomington, IN: Indiana University Press), 175–92.

—— (2001). "Critical study of *Providence and the Problem of Evil*, Richard Swinburne (Oxford University Press, 1998)." *Noûs* 35: 456–74.

—— (2004). "More Pain and Pleasure: A Reply to Otte." In *Christian Faith and the Problem of Evil* (ed. Peter van Inwagen) (Grand Rapids, MI: Eerdmans Publishing Co), 41–54.

—— (2009). "The Problem of Evil." In *The Oxford Handbook to Philosophical Theology* (eds. Thomas P. Flint and Michael Rea) (Oxford: Oxford University Press), 332–51.

—— (2011). "Review of Eleonore Stump, *Wandering in Darkness: Narratives and the Problem of Suffering* (Oxford University Press, 2010)." Notre Dame Philosophical Reviews. <http://ndpr.nd.edu/news/24772-wandering-in-darkness-narrative-and-the-problem-of-suffering/>.

—— (2012). "Darwin's Argument from Evil." In *Scientific Approaches to the Philosophy of Religion* (ed. Yujin Nagasawa) (Palgrave Macmillan), 49–70.

—— (2013). "The Limitations of Pure Skeptical Theism." *Res Philosophica* 90: 97–111.

—— (2014a). "Confirmation and the Truth about CORNEA." In Skeptical Theism: New Essays (eds. Trent G. Dougherty and Justin P. McBrayer) (New York: Oxford University Press).

—— (2014b). "Meet the New Skeptical Theism, Same as the Old Skeptical Theism." In Skeptical Theism: New Essays (eds. Trent G. Dougherty and Justin P. McBrayer) (New York: Oxford University Press).

—— (2013). "The Limitations of Pure Skeptical Theism." *Res Philosophica* 90(1): 97–111.

—— and Dougherty, Trent (2013). "Explanation and the Problem of Evil." In *A Companion to the Problem of Evil* (eds. Daniel Howard-Snyder and Justin P. McBrayer). (Wiley-Blackwell), 71–87.

Evagrius Ponticus (1972). *The Praktikos and Chapters of Prayer* (trans. John Eudes Bamberger) (Kalamazoo, MI: Cistercian Publications).

Feldman, Richard (2005). "Respecting the Evidence." *Philosophical Perspectives* 19: 95–119.

—— (2006). "Reasonable Religious Disagreements." In *Philosophers without Gods: Meditations on Atheism and the Secular Life* (ed. Louise M. Antony) (New York: Oxford University Press), 194–214.

Fischer, John Martin, Kane, Robert, Pereboom, Derk, and Vargas, Manuel (2007). *Four Views on Free Will* (Malden, MA: Blackwell Publishing).

Foot, Philippa (1967). "The Problem of Abortion and the Doctrine of Double Effect." *Oxford Review* 5: 5–15.

French, R.W. (1982). "Reading the Bible: The Story of Adam and Eve." *College Literature* 9: 22–9.

Fumerton, Richard (2006). "Epistemic Internalism, Philosophical Assurance, and the Skeptical Predicament." In *Knowledge and Reality: Essays in Honor of Alvin Plantinga* (eds. Thomas M. Crisp, Matthew Davidson, and David Vander Laan) (Dordrecht: Kluwer), 179–91.

Gale, Richard M. (1996). "Some Difficulties in Theistic Treatments of Evil." In *The Evidential Argument from Evil* (ed. Daniel Howard-Snyder) (Bloomington, IN: Indiana University Press), 206–18.

Giblin, Charles H. (1980). "Suggestion, Negative Response, and Positive Action in St. John's Portrayal of Jesus." *New Testament Studies* 26: 197–211.

Greco, John (1999). "Agent Reliabilism." *Philosophical Perspectives* 13: 273–96.

—— (2000). *Putting Skeptics in their Place: The Nature of Skeptical Arguments and their Role in Philosophical Inquiry* (Cambridge: Cambridge University Press).

Gregory of Nazianzus (2002). *On God and Christ: The Five Theological Orations and Two Letters to Cledonius* (trans. Frederick Williams and Lionel Wickham) (Crestwood, NY: St Vladimir's Seminary Press).

Guleserian, Theodore (2001). "Can God Be Trusted?" *Philosophical Studies* 106: 293–303.

Haack, Susan (1978). *Philosophy of Logics* (Cambridge: Cambridge University Press).

Hájek, Alan (2003). "What Conditional Probability Could Not Be." *Synthese* 137: 273–323.

Haldane, Elizabeth and Ross, G. R. T. (1967). *The Philosophical Works of Descartes Volume II* (Cambridge: Cambridge University Press).

Harrison, Verna E.F. (1995). "The Relationship Between Apophatic and Kataphatic Theology." *Pro Ecclesia* 4: 318–32.

Hasker, William (2004). *Providence, Evil, and the Openness of God* (New York: Routledge).

—— (2010). "All Too Skeptical Theism." *International Journal for Philosophy of Religion* 68: 15–29.

Helm, Paul (2002). "The Perfect Trustworthiness of God." In *The Trustworthiness of God: Perspectives on the Nature of Scripture* (eds. Paul Helm and Carl R. Trueman) (Grand Rapids: Eerdmans), 237–52.

Hick, John (1974). *Evil and the God of Love* (London: Fontana).

—— (1978). *Evil and the God of Love*, rev. edn. (New York: Harper and Row).

—— (1981). "An Irenaean Theodicy." In *Encountering Evil: Live Options in Theodicy* (ed. Stephen T. Davis) pp. 39–68. (Atlanta: John Knox Press), 237–52.

Holley, David M. (2010). *Meaning and Mystery: What it Means to Believe in God* (Wiley-Blackwell).

—— (2011). "How Can a Believer Doubt that God Exists?" *The Philosophical Quarterly* 61: 746–61.

Home, Henry (2005). *Essays on the Principles of Morality and Religion* (Indianapolis: Liberty Fund).

Howard-Snyder, Daniel (1992). "Seeing through CORNEA*." *International Journal for Philosophy of Religion* 32: 25–49.

—— (1996a). "The Argument from Inscrutable Evil." In *The Evidential Argument from Evil* (ed. Daniel Howard-Snyder), (Bloomington, IN: Indiana University Press), 286–310.

—— (1996b). *The Evidential Argument from Evil* (Bloomington, IN: Indiana University Press).

—— (2009). "Epistemic Humility, Arguments from Evil, and Moral Skepticism." In *Oxford Studies in Philosophy of Religion Volume 2* (ed. Jonathan Kvanvig) (Oxford: Oxford University Press), 17–57.

—— and Bergmann, Michael (2004). "Evil does not Make Atheism more Reasonable than Theism." In *Contemporary Debates in Philosophy of Religion* (eds. Michael Peterson and Raymond VanArragon), 13–25.

Howard-Snyder, Frances (1994). "The Heart of Consequentialism." *Philosophical Studies* 76: 107–29.

Howson, Colin and Urbach, Peter (2006). *Scientific Reasoning: The Bayesian Approach*, 3rd edn. 9La Salle, Illinois: Open Court).

Hudson, Hud (2014). "The Father of Lies?" In *Oxford Studies in Philosophy of Religion Volume 5* (ed. Jonathan Kvanvig) (Oxford: Oxford University Press), 117–32.

Huemer, Michael (2001). *Skepticism and the Veil of Perception* (Lanham: Rowman & Littlefield Publishers, Inc.).

—— (2007). "Compassionate Phenomenal Conservatism." *Philosophy & Phenomenological Research* 74: 30–55.

Hume, David (1947). *Dialogues Concerning Natural Religion* (ed. Norman Kemp Smith) (New York and Indianapolis: Bobbs-Merril).

—— (1993). *Dialogues Concerning Natural Religion* (ed. J. C. A. Gaskin) (Oxford: Oxford University Press).

Jordan, Jeff (2006). "Does Skeptical Theism Lead to Moral Skepticism?" *Philosophy and Phenomenological Research* 72: 403–16.

—— (2009). "Evil and van Inwagen." *Faith and Philosophy* 20(2): 236–39.

—— (2011). "Is the No-minimum Claim True? Reply to Cullison." *Religious Studies* 47(1): 125–7.

Kalaitzides, Pantelis (2009). "Challenges of Renewal and Reformation Facing the Orthodox Church." *The Ecumenical Review* 61: 136–64.

Kelly, Thomas R. (1992). *A Testament of Devotion* (San Francisco: Harper).

—— (2005). "The Epistemic Significance of Disagreement." In *Oxford Studies in Epistemology*, vol. 1 (eds. Tamar Szabo Gendler and John Hawthorne) (Oxford: Oxford University Press).

Keynes, John Maynard (1921). *A Treatise on Probability* (New York: Dover Publications).

Kierkegaard, Soren (1983). *Fear and Trembling and Repetition* (trans. Howard V. Hong and Edna H. Hong) (Princeton, NJ: Princeton University Press).

Lackey, Jennifer (2008). *Learning from Words: Testimony as a Source of Knowledge* (Oxford: Oxford University Press).

Lenman, James (2000). "Consequentialism and Cluelessness." *Philosophy and Public Affairs* 29: 342–70.

Levine, Michael P. (2000). "Contemporary Christian Analytic Philosophy of Religion: Biblical Fundamentalism, Terrible Solutions to a Horrible Problem, and Hearing God." *International Journal for Philosophy of Religion* 48: 89–119.

Lewis, C. S. (2001a). *The Great Divorce* (New York: HarperOne).

—— (2001b). *The Problem of Pain* (New York: HarperCollins).

Lewis, David (1993). "Evil for Freedom's Sake?" *Philosophical Papers* 22: 149–72.

Littlewood, A. R. (ed.) (1995). *Originality in Byzantine Literature, Art and Music: A Collection of Essays* (Oxford: Oxbow Books).

Logan, William Bryant (2012). *Air* (W.W. Norton & Company).

Louth, Andrew (1996). Maximus the Confessor (London: Routledge).

—— (2002). *St John Damascene: Tradition and Originality in Byzantine Theology* (Oxford: Oxford University Press).

Lukits, Stefan (2014). "The principle of maximum entropy and a problem in probability kinematics." *Synthese* 191(7): 1409–31.

MacGregor, Kirk R. (2012). "The Existence and Irrelevance of Gratuitous Evil." *Philosophia Christi* 14(1): 165–80.

Maclean, Norman (1992). *Young Men and Fire* (Chicago: Chicago University Press).

Maher, Patrick (2007). "Explication Defended." *Studia Logica* 86(2): 331–41.

Maitzen, Stephen (2007). "Skeptical Theism and God's Commands." *Sophia* 46(3): 235–43.

—— (2009a). "Skeptical Theism and Moral Obligation." *International Journal for Philosophy of Religion* 65(2): 93–103.

—— (2009b). "Ordinary Morality Implies Atheism." *European Journal for Philosophy of Religion* 1: 107–26.

—— (2010a). "On Gellman's Attempted Rescue." *European Journal for Philosophy of Religion* 2: 193–8

—— (2010b). "Does God Destroy Our Duty of Compassion?" *Free Inquiry* 30: 52–3.

—— (2014). "Agnosticism, Skeptical Theism, and Moral Obligation." In Skeptical Theism: New Essays (eds. Trent G. Dougherty and Justin P. McBrayer) (New York: Oxford University Press).

Martin, Hubert M. Jr. (1987). "To Trust (The) God: An Inquiry into Greek and Hebrew Religious Thought." *The Classical Journal* 83: 1–10.

Martin, Michael (1978). "Is Evil Evidence Against the Existence of God?" *Mind* 87(347): 429–32.

Mason, Elinor (2004). "Consequentialism and the Principle of Indifference." *Utilitas* 16: 316–21.

Matheson, Jonathan D. (2009). "Conciliatory Views of Disagreement and Higher-Order Evidence." *Episteme: A Journal of Social Philosophy* 6(3): 269–79.

—— (2011). "Epistemological Considerations Concerning Skeptical Theism: A Response to Dougherty." *Faith and Philosophy* 28(3): 323–31.

Maximus Confessor (1985). *Maximus Confessor: Selected Writings (Classics of Western Spirituality)* (trans. George C. Berthold) (New York: Paulist Press).

McBrayer, Justin P. (2009). "CORNEA and Inductive Evidence." *Faith and Philosophy* 26: 77–86.

—— (2010a). "Skeptical Theism." In *Internet Encyclopedia of Philosophy* (ed. James Fieser). Stable URL: http://www.iep.utm.edu/skept-th/.

—— (2010b). "Skeptical Theism." *Philosophy Compass* 5(7): 611–23.

—— (2012). "Are Skeptical Theists Really Skeptics?: Sometimes Yes and Sometimes No." *International Journal for Philosophy of Religion* 72(1): 3–16.

Meyendorff, John (1979). *Byzantine Theology: Historical Trends and Doctrinal Themes*, 2nd edn. (New York: Fordham University Press).

Moberly, R.W. L. (1988). "Did the Serpent Get It Right?" *Journal of Theological Studies* 39: 1–27.

—— (2008). "Did the Interpreters Get It Right? Genesis 2–3 Reconsidered." *Journal of Theological Studies* 59: 22–40.

Moore, G. E. (1959). *Philosophical Papers* (London: Allen and Unwin).

Moser, Paul K. (2008). *The Elusive God: Reorienting Religious Epistemology* (Cambridge University Press).

—— (2010). *The Evidence for God: Religious Knowledge Reexamined* (Cambridge University Press).

—— (2013). *The Severity of God: Religion and Philosophy Reconceived* (Cambridge: Cambridge University Press).

Neil, Bronwen and Allen, Pauline (ed. and trans.) (2003). *The Life of Maximus the Confessor: Recension 3* (Sydney: St Pauls Publications).

Nichols, Aidan (1993). *Byzantine Gospel: Maximus the Confessor in Modern Scholarship* (Edinburgh: T & T Clark).

St. Nikodemos of the Holy Mountain and St. Makarios of Corinth (1979). *The Philokalia: The Complete Text*, vol. 1 (eds. and trans. G. E. H. Palmer, Philip Sherrard, and Kallistos Ware) (London: Faber and Faber).

—— (1981). *The Philokalia: The Complete Text*, vol. 2 (eds. and trans. G. E. H. Palmer, Philip Sherrard, and Kallistos Ware) (London: Faber and Faber).

—— (1984). *The Philokalia: The Complete Text*, vol. 3 (eds. and trans. G. E. H. Palmer, Philip Sherrard, and Kallistos Ware) (London: Faber and Faber).

Origen (1998). *Homilies on Jeremiah, Homily on 1 Kings 28* (trans. John Clark Smith) (Washington, DC: Catholic University of America Press).

Otte, Richard (2004). "Probability and Draper's Evidential Argument from Evil." In *Christian Faith and the Problem of Evil* (ed. Peter van Inwagen) (Grand Rapids, MI: Eerdmans Publishing Co), 26–40.

Paley, William (1879). *A View of the Evidences of Christianity* (New York: Robert Carter & Brothers).

Pascal, Blaise (1995). *Pensées*, rev. edn. (trans. A. J. Krailsheimer) (New York: Penguin).

Pereboom, Derk (2005). "Free Will, Evil, and Divine Providence." In *God and the Ethics of Belief* (eds. Andrew Dole and Andrew Chignell) (New York: Cambridge University Press), 77–98.

Perrine, Timothy and Wykstra, Stephen J. (2014). "Skeptical Theism, Abductive Atheology, and Theory Versioning." In *Skeptical Theism: New Essays* (eds. Trent G. Dougherty and Justin P. McBrayer) (New York: Oxford University Press).

Piper, Mark (2007). "Skeptical Theism and the Problem of Moral *Aporia*." *International Journal for Philosophy of Religion* 62: 65–79.

—— (2008). "Why Theists Cannot Accept Skeptical Theism." *Sophia* 47: 129–48.

Plantinga, Alvin (1974). *The Nature of Necessity* (Oxford: Clarendon Press).

—— (1977). *God, Freedom, and Evil* (Grand Rapids: Eerdmans Publishing Co).

—— (1990). *The Twin Pillars of Christian Scholarship* (Grand Rapids, MI: Calvin College and Seminary).

—— (1995). "Pluralism: A Defense of Religious Exclusivism." In *The Rationality of Belief and the Plurality of Faith: Essays in Honor of William P. Alston* (ed. Thomas D. Senor). (Ithaca, NY: Cornell University Press), 191–215.

—— (1996). "Epistemic Probability and Evil." In *The Evidential Argument from Evil* (ed. Daniel Howard-Snyder) (Bloomington, IN: Indiana University Press), 69–96.

—— (1998). "The Free Will Defense." In *The Analytic Theist: An Alvin Plantinga Reader* (ed. James F. Sennett), (Grand Rapids: Eerdmans Publishing Co), 22–49.

—— (1999). "On Heresy, Mind, and Truth." *Faith and Philosophy* 16: 182–93.

—— (2000). *Warranted Christian Belief* (New York: Oxford University Press).

—— and Tooley, Michael (2008). *Knowledge of God* (Blackwell Publishing).

Poston, Ted and Dougherty, Trent (2008). "Hell, Vagueness, and Justice." *Faith and Philosophy* 25(3): 322–8.

Pruss, Alex (2012). "Conditional probabilities." *Analysis* 72: 488–91.

Pryor, James (2000). "The Skeptic and the Dogmatist." *Noûs*, 34: 517–49.

Ramsey, Boniface (1985). "Two Traditions on Lying and Deception in the Ancient Church." *The Thomist* 49: 504–33.

Rancourt, Benjamin T. (2013). "Egoism or the Problem of Evil: A Dilemma for Sceptical Theism." *Religious Studies* 49(3): 313–25.

Rea, Michael C. (2009). "Narrative, Liturgy, and the Hiddenness of God." In *Metaphysics and God: Essays in Honor of Eleonore Stump* (ed. Kevin Timpe) (New York: Routledge), 76–96.

—— (2014). "Skeptical Theism and the 'Too Much Skepticism' Objection." In *The Blackwell Companion to the Problem of Evil* (eds. Justin P. McBrayer and Daniel Howard-Snyder) (Blackwell Publishing), 482–506.

Rees, Martin (2012). *From Here to Infinity: A Vision for the Future of Science* (New York: W. W. Norton).

Rowe, William (1979). "The Problem of Evil and Some Varieties of Atheism." *American Philosophical Quarterly* 16: 335–41.

—— (1988). "Evil and Theodicy." *Philosophical Topics* 16: 119–32.

—— (1991). "Ruminations about Evil." *Philosophical Perspectives* 5: 69–88.

—— (1996). "The Evidential Argument from Evil: A Second Look." In *The Evidential Argument from Evil* (ed. Daniel Howard-Snyder) (Bloomington, IN: Indiana University Press).

—— (2004). "Is Evil Evidence against Belief in God?" In *Contemporary Debates in Philosophy of Religion* (eds. Michael L. Peterson and Raymond J. Van Arragon) (Blackwell Publishers), 3–13.

—— (2006). "Friendly Atheism, Skeptical Theism, and the Problem of Evil." *International Journal for Philosophy of Religion* 59.

Russell, Bruce (1996). "Defenseless." In *The Evidential Argument from Evil* (ed. Daniel Howard-Snyder) (Bloomington, IN: Indiana University Press), 193–206.

—— and Wykstra, Stephen (1988). "The 'Inductive' Argument from Evil: A Dialogue." *Philosophical Topics*16: 133–60.

Schellenberg, John L. (2002). "What the Hiddenness of God Reveals: A Collaborative Discussion." In *Divine Hiddenness: New Essays* (eds. Daniel Howard-Snyder and Paul Moser) (New York: Cambridge University Press), 33–61.

—— (2007). *The Wisdom to Doubt: A Justification of Religious Skepticism* (Ithaca, NY: Cornell University Press).

—— (2009). *The Will to Imagine: A Justification of Skeptical Religion* (Ithaca, NY: Cornell University Press).

—— (2010). "The Hiddenness Problem and the Problem of Evil." *Faith and Philosophy*27(1): 45–60.

—— (2013). *Evolutionary Religion* (Oxford: Oxford University Press).

—— (2014). "Skeptical Theism and Skeptical Atheism." In *Skeptical Theism: New Essays* (eds. Trent G. Dougherty and Justin P. McBrayer) (New York: Oxford University Press).

Schnall, Ira (2007). "Sceptical Theism and Moral Scepticism." *Religious Studies* 43: 49–69.

Segal, Aaron (2011). "Sceptical Theism and Divine Truths." *Religious Studies* 47(1): 85–95.

Sehon, Scott (2010). "The Problem of Evil: Skeptical Theism Leads to Moral Paralysis." *International Journal for Philosophy of Religion* 67: 67–80.

Seigal, Joshua (2010). "Skeptical Theism, Moral Skepticism, and Divine Deception." *International Journal for Philosophy* 15: 251–74.

Senor, Thomas D. (ed.) (1995). *Rationality of Belief and the Plurality of Faith* (Ithaca, NY: Cornell University Press).

—— (1996). "The Prima/Ultima Facie Justification Distinction in Epistemology." *Philosophy and Phenomenological Research* 56: 551–66.

Stalnaker, Robert (1981). "A Theory of Conditionals." In *Ifs* (eds. W. L. Harper, R. Stalnaker and G. Pearce), pp 41–56. (Dordrecht-Holland: D. Reidel Publishing Co).

Stump, Eleonore (1985). "The Problem of Evil." *Faith and Philosophy* 2: 392–423.

—— (1990). "Providence and the Problem of Evil." In *Christian Philosophy* (ed. Thomas P. Flint). (Notre Dame, IN: University of Notre Dame Press), 51–91.

—— (2010). *Wandering in Darkness* (New York: Oxford University Press).

Swinburne, Richard (1998). *Providence and the Problem of Evil* (Oxford: Oxford University Press).

—— (2001). *Epistemic Justification* (Oxford: Oxford University Press).

—— (2004). *The Existence of God*, 2nd edn. (Oxford: Oxford University Press).

Tolhurst, William (1998). "Seemings." *American Philosophical Quarterly* 35: 293–302.

Tooley, Michael (1991). "The Argument from Evil." *Philosophical Perspectives* 5: 89–134.

—— (2009). "The Problem of Evil." *Stanford Encyclopedia of Philosophy*. Stable URL: http://plato.stanford.edu/entries/evil/.

—— (2012). "Inductive Logic and the Probability that God Exists: Farewell to Skeptical Theism." In *Probability in the Philosophy of Religion* (eds. Jake Chandler and Victoria S. Harrison) (Oxford University Press).

Toy, Crawford H. (1891). "Analysis of Genesis II., III." *Journal of Biblical Literature* 10: 1–19.

Trakakis, Nick and Nagasawa, Yujin (2004). "Skeptical Theism and Moral Skepticism." *Ars Disputandi* 4.

Tremlin, Todd (2006). *Minds and Gods: The Cognitive Foundations of Religion* (Oxford: Oxford University Press).

Trigg, Joseph (1988). "Divine Deception and the Truthfulness of Scripture." In *Origen of Alexandria: His World and His Legacy* (eds. Charles Kannengiesser and William L. Petersen) (Notre Dame, IN: University of Notre Dame Press), 147–64.

Tucker, Chris (2010). "Why Open-Minded People Should Endorse Dogmatism." *Philosophical Perspectives* 24: 529–45.

—— (2011). "Phenomenal Conservatism and Evidentialism in Religious Epistemology." In *Evidence and Religious Belief* (eds. Raymond Van Arragon and Kelly James Clark). (Oxford University Press), 52–73.

—— (2014) "Why Skeptical Theism Isn't Skeptical Enough." In *Skeptical Theism: New Essays* (eds. Trent G. Dougherty and Justin P. McBrayer) (New York: Oxford University Press).

van Fraassen, Bas C. (1989). *Laws and Symmetry* (Oxford: Clarendon Press).

van Inwagen, Peter (1988). "The Magnitude, Duration, and Distribution of Evil." *Philosophical Topics* 16: 161–87.

—— (1991). "The Problem of Evil, the Problem of Air, and the Problem of Silence." *Philosophical Perspectives* 5: 135–65.

—— (1995). "The Place of Chance in a World Sustained by God." In *God, Knowledge and Mystery: Essays in Philosophical Theology* (ed. Peter van Inwagen) (Ithaca, NY and London: Cornell University Press), 42–65.

—— (1998). *The Possibility of Resurrection and Other Essays in Christian Apologetics* (Westview).

—— (2006). *The Problem of Evil* (Oxford: Oxford University Press).

—— (2009). "The Hiddenness of God." In *Arguing about Religion* (ed. Kevin Timpe) (New York: Routledge), 369–81.

Ward, Benedicta (trans.) (1984). *The Sayings of the Desert Fathers: The Alphabetical Collection*, rev. edn. (London: Mowbray).

Ware, Bishop Kallistos (2000). *The Inner Kingdom, vol. 1: The Collected Works* (Crestwood, NY: St Vladimir's Seminary Press).

Westphal, Merold (1999). "Taking Plantinga Seriously: Advice to Christian Philosophers." *Faith and Philosophy* 16: 173–81.

—— (2001). *Overcoming Onto-theology: Toward a Postmodern Christian Faith* (New York: Fordham University Press).

White, Roger (2006). "Problems for Dogmatism." *Philosophical Studies* 131: 525–57.

Wielenberg, Erik (2010). "Skeptical Theism and Divine Lies." *Religious Studies* 46(4): 509–23.

Wiles, Maurice (1989). "Eunomius: Hair-splitting Dialectician or Defender of the Accessibility of Salvation?" In *The Making of Orthodoxy: Essays in Honour of Henry Chadwick* (ed. Rowan Williams) (Cambridge: Cambridge University Press), 157–72.

Wilks, Ian (2009). "Skeptical Theism and Empirical Unfalsifiability." *Faith and Philosophy* 26: 64–76.

—— (2013). "The Global Skepticism Objection to Skeptical Theism." In *The Blackwell Companion to the Problem of Evil* (ed. Justin P. McBrayer and Daniel Howard-Snyder) (Blackwell Publishing).

Willard, Dallas (1990). *The Spirit of the Disciplines* (New York: HarperOne).

—— (1998). *The Divine Conspiracy* (New York: HarperOne).

Witherington III, Ben (1995). *John's Wisdom: A Commentary on the Fourth Gospel* (Louisville: Westminster John Knox Press).

Wykstra, Stephen J. (1984). "The Humean Obstacle to Evidential Arguments from Suffering: On Avoiding the Evils of 'Appearance.'" *International Journal for the Philosophy of Religion* 16(2): 73–93.

—— (1990a). "The Humean Obstacle to Evidential Arguments from Suffering: On Avoiding the Evils of 'Appearance.'" In *The Problem of Evil* (eds. Marilyn McCord Adams and Robert Merrihew Adams) (Oxford: Oxford University Press), 138–60.

—— (1990b). "Reasons, Redemption, and Realism: The Axiological Roots of Rationality in Science and Religion." In *Christian Theism and the Problems of Philosophy* (ed. Michael Beaty). (Notre Dame, IN: University of Notre Dame Press), 118–61.

—— (1996a). "Have Worldviews Shaped Science? A Reply to Brooke." In *Facets of Faith and Science* (ed. Jitse Vander Meer) (University Press of America).

—— (1996b). "Rowe's Noseeum Arguments from Evil." In *The Evidential Problem of Evil* (ed. Daniel Howard-Snyder) (Bloomington, IN: Indiana University Press), 126–50.

—— (2002). "'Not Done in Corner': How to be a Sensible Evidentialist about Jesus." *Philosophical Books* 43(2): 81–135.

—— (2007). "CORNEA, Carnap, and Current Closure Befuddlement." *Faith and Philosophy* 24: 87–98.

—— (2008). "Suffering, Evidence, and Analogy: Noseeum Arguments Versus Skeptical Gambits." In *Philosophy Through Science Fiction* (eds. Ryan Nichols, Fred Miller and Nicholas Smith) (New York and London: Routledge).

—— (2011). "Facing MECCA: Ultimism, Religious Skepticism, and Schellenberg's 'Meta-Evidential Condition Constraining Assent.'" *Philo* 14(1): 85–100.

—— (2012). "Does Skeptical Theism Force Moral Skepticism? Hesitations over Bergmann's Defense." In *Reason, Metaphysics, and Mind: New Essays on the Philosophy of Alvin Plantinga* (eds. Kelly James Clark and Michael Rea). (Oxford: Oxford University Press), 30–7.

—— and Perrine, Timothy (2008). "Review of J. L. Schellenberg's *The Wisdom to Doubt*." (Notre Dame Philosophical Review).

—— and Perrine, Timothy (2012). "The Foundations of Skeptical Theism: CORNEA, CORE, and Conditional Probabilities." *Faith and Philosophy* 29(4): 375–99.

Zagzebski, Linda (2014). "Trust." In Kevin Timpe and Craig A. Boyd, *Virtues and their Vices* (Oxford: Oxford University Press), 269–83.

Index

Printed and bound by CPI Group (UK) Ltd, Croydon, CR0 4YY